THE STRUGGLE FOR POWER
IN MEDIEVAL ITALY

This book, recognized widely within Italy as the major postwar synthesis of medieval Italian history since its publication as a textbook in 1979, now appears for the first time in an English translation. It covers the whole political and social development of Italy from the late Roman Empire to the early Renaissance, weaving brilliantly the complete web of successive political structures in the Italian peninsula across a thousand years of history.

The roots of the Italian 'city states' that created the Renaissance are traced back to the Lombard kingdom of Italy, which Charlemagne conquered, and to the chaotic tenth and eleventh centuries, in which almost all government foundered. Tabacco's masterly and lucid exposition of what was essentially a process of gaining, holding on to or losing political power ranks with the most sophisticated analyses of the middle ages published in any language.

Cambridge Medieval Textbooks

This is a new series of specially commissioned textbooks for teachers and students, designed to complement the monograph series 'Cambridge Studies in Medieval Life and Thought' by providing introductions to a range of topics in medieval history. The series will combine both chronological and thematic approaches, and will deal equally with British and European topics. All volumes in the series will be published in hard covers and in paperback.

Already published

Germany in the High Middle Ages *c.* 1050–1200
HORST FUHRMANN
Translated by Timothy Reuter

The Hundred Years War: England and France at War *c.* 1300–*c.* 1450
CHRISTOPHER ALLMAND

Standards of Living in the Later Middle Ages:
Social Change in England *c.* 1200–1520
CHRISTOPHER DYER

Magic in the Middle Ages
RICHARD KIECKHEFER

The Struggle for Power in Medieval Italy:
Structures of Political Rule
GIOVANNI TABACCO
Translated by Rosalind Brown Jensen

Other titles are in preparation

THE STRUGGLE FOR POWER IN MEDIEVAL ITALY
Structures of political rule

GIOVANNI TABACCO

Professor of Medieval History
University of Turin

Translated by Rosalind Brown Jensen

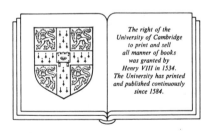

The right of the
University of Cambridge
to print and sell
all manner of books
was granted by
Henry VIII in 1534.
The University has printed
and published continuously
since 1584.

CAMBRIDGE UNIVERSITY PRESS

Cambridge
New York   Port Chester
Melbourne   Sydney

Published by the Press Syndicate of the University of Cambridge
The Pitt Building, Trumpington Street, Cambridge CB2 1RP
40 West 20th Street, New York, NY 10011, USA
10 Stamford Road, Oakleigh, Melbourne 3166, Australia

First published 1989

Printed in Great Britain
by the University Press, Cambridge

British Library cataloguing in publication data

Tabacco, Giovanni
    The struggle for power in medieval Italy: structures
    of political rule. – (Cambridge medieval textbooks)
    1. Italy. Political events, history
    I. Title II. Egemonie sociali e struttere del potere
    nel medioevo Italiano. *English*
    945

Library of Congress cataloguing in publication data

Tabacco, Giovanni.
    [Egemonie sociali e struttere del potere nel Medioevo italiano.
English]
    The struggle for power in medieval Italy: structures of political
rule/Giovanni Tabacco: translated by Rosalind Brown Jensen.
        p.   cm. – (Cambridge medieval textbooks)
    Translation of: Egemonie sociali e struttere del potere nel Medioevo italiano.
    Bibliography.
    Includes index.
    ISBN 0-521-33469-1. – ISBN 0-521-33680-5 (pbk.)
    1. Italy – Politics and government – 476-1268.   I. Title.
II. Series.
DG503.T2913   1989
945–dc20   89-9771 CIP

ISBN 0 521 33469 1 hard covers
ISBN 0 521 33680 5 paperback

UP

CONTENTS

INTRODUCTION

In reissuing this text prepared in 1973 for Einaudi's *Storia d'Italia*, it seemed suitable to preface it with an explicit discussion of the role of medieval Italy in the formation of the European world, as well as with a summary of the path which historical research has followed to arrive at the present ways of analysing and interpreting our distant past. We will also discuss how a global history can be conceived of which does not neglect the relative autonomy of its component structures; this history may be defined through a particular structure, which is selected as fundamental, in accordance with the viewpoint chosen to set these separate structures within a coherent perspective. In this instance the chosen viewpoint is the socio-political one. 'Socio-political' history is here understood as the conscious acquisition by groups or hegemonic classes, and by a political power-structure which gradually becomes institutionalized, of clearly-expressed forms of dominance and of the related general task of co-ordinating political control.

1 For over two centuries there has been a certain intolerance towards a vision of the past which reduces the wealth of human experience to the societies that focus on the Classical Mediterranean world and to the subsequent development of Europe; this is a response to the desire to discover cultural horizons different from those within which Europe has produced us. It is a response to the attraction of remote unexplored regions, and at the same time to the need to evaluate ourselves critically by setting in proportion the world of our own problems. But the commitment to explore in other directions has not in the least shaken the historically-established centrality of European

development, which has gradually drawn in all other cultures and forced them finally to seek in our past the origins of their own troubled present condition.

Our past has divided spontaneously into the concepts of ancient and modern as it acquired awareness of its own development, and between these concepts, in turn, is interposed the idea of a thousand-year-long crisis which ended in a 'gloriously' innovating Renaissance. This tripartite model, too, has suffered from two centuries of intolerance, which arose when certain areas of late-medieval civilization were perceived to coincide with the first development of the national experiences which we consider as modern. It is increasingly difficult to define the transition from medieval to modern, which varies according to where one places the emphasis among the socio-economic, political and cultural structures which underwent deep changes in western Europe from the thirteenth century onwards. Despite this, the tripartite model is destined to withstand any attempt to demolish it. No historiographical optimism about the 'continuity' between the Classical and the modern world can wipe out the reality of the great migrations, which threw into confusion the peoples who for centuries or millennia had been organized in stable societies around the Mediterranean. These migrations, having long undermined the structure of the Roman Empire, deprived the Roman inland sea, the Mediterranean, of its role as a meeting point and force for synthesis between different cultures focused on the hegemony of the city, inside a unitary political and economic formation. The migrations created an enterprising Latin–Germanic West which was destined to experience seigneurial anarchy and the particularism of local autonomous socio-political experiments, until its fruitful restructuring in the late medieval and modern periods. Indeed the formation and fate of the Roman Empire must regain their true position within the perspective of a thousand-year-long tension between the world of territorially organized populations and the vast world of tribal and semi-nomadic peoples, a perspective which the Romans themselves merely glimpsed. This tension became more acute all around the Mediterranean area, and was represented by myriad clashes and renewed agreements,[1] up to and after the events which did most to bring the Germanic peoples into the Roman West and settle them in their definitive territories in symbiosis with Latin culture. The Middle Ages coincides with this symbiotic process of territorial settlement which gradually spread to the other peoples of central and

---

[1] See E. Demougeot, *La Formation de l'Europe et les invasions barbares*, 1: *Des origines germaniques à l'avènement de Dioclétien* (Paris, 1969); L. Harmand, *L'Occident romain* (Paris, 1970).

eastern Europe, with the consequent further destabilization of all social structures, of whatever ethnic and cultural origins, in a continual series of restless and contradictory institutional developments, until the innovations appeared which heralded the rationalized dynamism of the modern world.

What place did Italy have in these events? The West drew its earliest origin from the expansion of Roman Italy, but in the late Classical period its focus was the cultural and social aristocracy of the great Gallo-Roman landowners and the episcopate which was drawn from their number.[2] Later it developed around the expansive force of the Franks, of their military aristocracy and the ecclesiastical institutions that worked in partnership with them. This grafted the ideology of universalism of the episcopal and monastic church on to the warrior traditions of the Franks and the restless ambitions of its aristocracy, who were gradually stabilized and strengthened by acquiring landed power in the Gallo-Roman tradition,[3] and this was the force which enabled the Merovingian dynasty from the sixth century onwards to sketch the outlines of expansion in Europe, and which enabled the Carolingians to bring it about two centuries later.[4] Italy, formerly in a central position in the Mediterranean and the seat of a Roman pontificate which, under imperial protection, claimed primacy over the Christian churches, found itself after the Germanic immigration on the boundary between the area which was still controlled by the Empire surviving at Byzantium and that which gravitated towards the Franks. It became the terrain for a confrontation between two political systems, polarized in opposite directions but (both aided by the episcopal network) competing in the administration of their common civil inheritance, which originated in the Roman Hellenistic world. They were competitors and rivals in administering that inheritance: at Byzantium within the robust patterns of a rigid bureaucratic centralism, and in Gaul according to the far more flexible and approximate models of a royal power which was both upheld and limited by the cultural preponderance of the episcopate and the military preponderance of the aristocracy. The Ostrogothic domination in Italy in the late fifth and early sixth centuries existed in

[2] M. Heinzelmann, *Bischofsherrschaft in Gallien. Zur Kontinuität römischer Führungsgeschichten vom IV. bis zum VII. Jahrhundert* (Munich, 1976).

[3] H. Grahn-Hoek, *Die fränkische Oberschicht im VI. Jahrhundert* (Sigmaringen, 1976).

[4] G. Tabacco, 'I processi di formazione dell'Europa carolingia', in *Nascita dell'Europa ed Europa carolingia: un'equazione da verificare* (XXVII Settimana di studio del Centro italiano di studi sull'alto medioevo, Spoleto, 1981), vol. I, p. 17–43.

an equilibrium between the Greek Empire of the East (whose supremacy Theodoric the Great formally recognized) and the Germanic dynasties of central and western Europe (with whom he wove a network of political and matrimonial agreements). Yet it failed to check the Frankish expansion in southern Gaul, and fell when the Eastern Empire regained control of the central Mediterranean. The subsequent Lombard immigration troubled both Franks and Byzantium, but for decades the Lombards acknowledged Frankish supremacy and never succeeded in avoiding Frankish interference,[5] while they never destroyed the Byzantine presence in large zones of the peninsula. Thus from the end of the fifth to the middle of the eighth century the fate of Italy remained uncertain, and its role between the Mediterranean and the area of Germanic expansion became ambiguous. The Lombard presence from the Alps to the Tyrrhenian Sea did indeed prevent Byzantium from using Rome and Ravenna to spread its diplomatic activity outward from Italy and thus bringing the Latin-Germanic West back under its own cultural, religious and political hegemony. At the same time, though, it also prevented the Merovingians from transforming their own superiority among the Germanic peoples of the continent into a system that opened more freely on to the central Mediterranean, in a more direct continuation of Roman power.

The two centuries in which the Lombard kingdom consolidated itself around its capital, Pavia, were thus sufficient to prevent the confrontation between Franks and Byzantium taking on a direct military character, and through the slow fusion of Latin and Germanic structures the period gave northern Italy (together with its extension into Tuscany) a socio-political configuration which was not unlike that of the symbiosis between Frankish and Gallo-Roman, although remaining distinct from it. This tradition was preserved even after the Carolingian conquest of the kingdom, so that Pavia remained capital of an autonomous Italian kingdom within the empire established in the West at the end of the eighth century. None the less it was still a kingdom incorporated into the Europe which the Franks had constructed, subject to Carolingian legislation and slowly permeated by customary usages concerning clientèles, and based on vassalage and the benefice. From then on these customs characterized central and western Europe for the whole medieval period, and from the tenth century onwards they were interwoven with the disintegration of public order and the development

---

[5] G. Tabacco, 'L'inserimento dei Longobardi nel quadro delle dominazioni germaniche dell'Occidente', in *Longobardi e Lombardia: aspetti di civiltà longobarda* (VI Congresso internazionale di studi sull'alto medioevo, Spoleto, 1980), vol. I, p. 225–46.

of local seigneurial powers with a base which was either landed and military or urban and ecclesiastical. This was taking place while the growth of population and settlements and the progress of agricultural techniques and commerce (which everywhere provoked the communal movement in the eleventh to twelfth centuries within the fabric of seigneurial structures, particularly within the cities and more vigorously in the cities of the kingdom of Italy) altered the appearance of the West, which had been almost exclusively rural, economically depressed and ecclesiastical in culture, and gave the Lombard and Tuscan world a completely new importance and a leading role in the reorganization of society and the laicization of culture. In this sense the Po plain and Tuscany were truly an integral part of the enterprising European West, and participated in an intense circulation of men, customs and institutions with the regions beyond the Alps. But the kingdom of Italy did not have only this function, one of a geographic extension of the European movement with its own particular outstanding civic development.

In effect, the Carolingian kingdom of Italy had also been the bridge between the Frankish domination of the continent and those areas of Italy with a Byzantine tradition, which had been partly conquered by the Carolingians and assigned to the Roman church under overall Frankish political control. Thus it had represented that opening on to the central Mediterranean which the Merovingians had failed to obtain. Rome and Ravenna, by means of the Italic kingdom and Frankish protection, had entered into the sphere of the Carolingian Empire, but conserved their own cultural tradition, which was grafted on to that which had formed from the partnership between Franks and the transalpine episcopate. Most important was the role that Rome had won for itself as the focal point for a unitary vision of the Frankish Empire and, more generally, of the whole Christian West, which had already been extended in preceding centuries to the Celts of Ireland and the Angles and Saxons who had arrived in Britain, through the organization of the episcopal and monastic church. It is true that when the Carolingian Empire faded away and political dissolution penetrated all the kingdoms which had composed it, affecting even the ordering of the churches, the religious reaction of reformers against the disintegration of these institutions came not from Rome but rather from the periphery of the ecclesiastical world. Yet this reaction found in Rome the symbol of a unitary restoration and, having won over the Church of Rome in the eleventh century, made it the tool to construct a papal monarchy over the Western churches, a monarchy which in the later Middle Ages made the Catholic order increasingly rigid. This was the monarchy, of universal inspiration, with which all the social and political forces of

Western Christianity had to reckon, and which conditioned Italy in
particular.

From this point of view, from the end of the Carolingian period Italy
took on its own fundamental role in a European perspective, equal to
that of the Franks. It was the seat of a Roman church operating in the
centralizing spirit which had already been nourished in the church itself
by the imperial tradition of the late Classical and Byzantine periods,
which was then further encouraged at a more coherent level of action
by the alliance with the Franks and by its incorporation into the new
Carolingian Empire, and which was finally translated by the reforming
movement of the eleventh century into a conscious project to construct
a universal monarchy. Certainly the papal action carried with it forces
springing from all of Western Christianity, but up to the thirteenth
century it was sustained by a specifically Roman organism, with men in
the main drawn from the peninsula, in a political and cultural climate
inseparable from the position of the peninsula in the centre of the
Mediterranean, with the immediate spur of Muslim aggression and of
the problem of coexistence with the Byzantines. It was this Roman and
Italian situation which, for century after century, constantly complicated
the activity of the dominant forces of Europe, from the Carolingians to
the German kings who became emperors, to the crusaders of France and
Germany and the Capetian monarchy, committing them to action in
southern Italy and in the East. These offensive and defensive plans were
by no means marginal to the history of the West, since they called for
large movements of men, influenced the development of the military
and mercantile aristocracies, and provoked cultural confrontations
which had profound significance for innovation.

The role of Rome in the European link with the Mediterranean
conferred importance on the south of Italy. The Mezzogiorno certainly
participated in the various phases of European history in a manner which
was marginal at most, following its own different rhythm, sometimes
even in an opposing direction.[6] It was territorially fragmented ahead of
its time, as early as the Carolingian period, it received feudo-vassalic
institutions only as late as the Norman period and as part of a colonial
settlement, and it anticipated the Europe-wide reconstruction of a state
apparatus when elsewhere city communes flourished and were

[6] See the contributions of J. M. Martin, H. Taviani, G. Noyé and H. Bresc to
the 'Colloque international organisé par le Centre national de la recherche
scientifique et de l'Ecole Française de Rome' (October 1978), *Structures
féodales et féodalisme dans l'Occident méditerranéen (Xe-XIIIe siècles)* (Rome,
1980).

enterprising enough to encroach commercially even on the premature kingdom of the south. Yet it was this area, the Mezzogiorno and the Tyrrhenian islands, which offered itself to all the great forces in expansion of Europe and of the western and eastern Mediterranean, as a theatre for the most decisive contests. So was it more a passive object than an actor in history? In part this was indeed so. The populations of the south not uncommonly saw their liveliest experiences of autonomy destroyed. But the capital cities which developed there played an important role in elaborating models of government, formulating political programmes of great breadth, and in doctrinal and juridical reflections on the ordering of power and society.

Italy's history in the Middle Ages is thus far from unitary. By that we do not mean territorial fragmentation, or the heterogeneous nature of forces whose interaction produced a great variety of local situations; we mean rather the different overall orientation of north and south, between which the Roman papacy in its turn had its own European role. None the less this profound diversity between regions which, according to the particular structures of their social hegemonies, focused on the more animated European world or the colonial one of the Mediterranean did not prevent constant communication between the two geographical areas of Italy, or the intensification of that contact as the capacity of every society to radiate its influence increased after the year 1000. This growing intensity of relations in every sphere, without, however, the extinction of the cultural diversity between north and south, led to the creation of an overall area of Italian culture, characterized in its socio-political aspect precisely by the living-out of such a dichotomy. This was the culture that led to a humanism recognized in Europe as typically Italian.

A Middle Ages as rich in experiences and implications as that of Italy, yet so easily recognizable in the interweaving of its multiple lines and playing such a profound role in the fabric of European history, could not but arouse the interest of historians from very different countries, once the study of the Middle Ages took on the dimensions of a European endeavour and aimed systematically to seek the origins of the modern world, as happened in the eighteenth to nineteenth centuries. Among the learned everywhere Italian sources became an object of study, with the intention of discovering clear evidence for historical directions which were crucial to the subsequent development of every nation.

2   Above all, historians sought evidence on the notable contribution of Italy to the free urban civilization of Europe. The sources which by their nature are best suited to suggest a first outline of the Italian Middle

Ages, that is, the narrative sources, were in fact mostly chronicles of
individual cities.[7] In the humanist period and the Renaissance these
sources had already been drawn on by the more or less official historians
of the regional states of central and northern Italy, states largely built
around cities which had been extremely active in the communal period
and which had then become focal points for rebuilding territories with
a wide political scope. So it is obvious that the Italian Middle Ages
appeared to European culture in both the Enlightenment and the
Romantic period to have a purely urban flavour, inside the boundaries
of the Italic kingdom of the communal period. And, since the attention
given to the communal antecedents of an Italy which was universally
admired for the flowering of its arts and letters in the Renaissance was
accompanied by an equally traditional examination of the ancient ruin
of the political apparatus which had maintained Classical civilization in
the Roman Empire, the overall pattern of the Italian Middle Ages could
not be in doubt: an irruption of barbarians leading to crisis, the recovery
of institutions with the prodigious growth of autonomous cities, leading
to a more stable organization formed of regional states. In any case, this
model had already been outlined in the bold comprehensive narrative of
the mid-fifteenth century, the *Historia ab inclinatione Romani imperii* of
Biondo Flavio of Forlì.[8] The scholarly Biondo Flavio, by now working
outside any universalist interpretation rooted in theology and looking
beyond individual local perspectives, gathered together a thousand years
of Western history around an Italy which decayed after the ruin of
Rome and flowered again in its cities. This same model was strengthened
a century later by Carlo Sigonio of Modena in his *Historiae de regno
Italiae* from the sixth to the thirteenth centuries, a work that arose
alongside his commitment to studying the history of Bologna, which
was in the more usual urban perspective.[9]

   Biondo and Sigonio did not limit themselves to compilations from
the most accessible of preceding chroniclers, for their antiquarian tastes
and critical sensitivity led them into archival study of some breadth, to
compare differing information drawn not only from narrative sources
but also from legislation and more general regulations, chancery records

[7] O. Capitani, 'Motivi e momenti di storiografia medioevale italiana', in
Nuove questioni di storia medioevale (Milan, 1969), pp. 770ff., 791ff.

[8] R. Furbini, 'Biondo Flavio', in *Dizionario biografico degli Italiani*, vol. 10
(Rome 1968), p. 543.

[9] G. Fasoli, 'Appunti sulla "Historia Bononiensis" ed altre opere di Carlo
Sigonio', *Atti della Accademia delle Scienze dell'Istituto di Bologna, Classe de
scienze morali, Rendiconti*, 61 (1972–3) p. 69ff, reprinted in G. Fasoli, *Scritti di
storia medievale* (Bologna, 1974), p. 683ff.

and letters. Yet the final co-ordination of their data to depict the creation
of the Italian world followed the method of the annalists, suggested both
by the chronicles which were at the base of their historical exposition
and by the example of the great Classical historians. The transformations
of institutions and of the forms of social coexistence, with all their
implications at the level of civil and human communication, were
essentially deduced from the conscious actions of military, political and
ecclesiastical powers, and from those events and people who were
prominent in the chronicles because they had visibly affected the
experience of their contemporaries and had seized their imagination.
The invasions appeared as great military conquests, and even the
transformation of much of Italy into a land of flourishing city
communes was initially deduced, in the account of Sigonio, from the
high-level political programmes which he supposed had been worked
out after the German conquest of the Italic kingdom in the tenth
century. Otto I, now King of Italy and Emperor, following his great
project of re-ordering the kingdom, was thought to have conferred on
the cities the privilege of self-government according to their own norms
and customs, with their own jurisdiction and independent public
revenues, although under the royal supremacy. From this was thought
to have derived the institution of consuls in each city, with the duty to
swear obedience to the bishop or to the representative of the king.[10] In
the course of time, Sigonio explained, as the Milanese grew in prosperity
and ambition for liberty and other cities followed their example, the
kingdom's military force, occupied in the struggle with the church of
Rome, was despised and the supreme jurisdiction of the ruler ignored,
so that disputes of the cities among themselves or with others were
resolved by combat and their autonomy was translated into political and
territorial expansion.[11]

Thus Sigonio did not only examine individual pieces of information
but also sought to penetrate the interplay of political forces which
appeared from the chronicles to be decisive, by suggesting connections
and formulating hypotheses which seemed plausible to him, used as he
was to a world dominated by efficient church and state apparatuses. In
particular the will of the conquerors and the firmest rulers and the
clashes between the highest powers functioned in his account as the *deus
ex machina* to which he could attribute the resolution of the most
important historical problems in the transformation of society, going

[10] *Caroli Sigonii Mutinensis Opera Omnia*, vol. 2 (Milan, 1732), coll. 441ff, 448
('Ex quibus omnibus intelligi potest, universam ab hoc tempore Italiam
renovatam atque aliam prope in omni institutorum genere esse factam').
[11] *Ibid.*, vol. 2, coll. 615, 618ff.

beyond explicit evidence and proceeding by conjecture. One example, as we have seen, was that of the regime of the cities; another was the system of seigneurial autonomies, of which Sigonio noted in his own time considerable survivals within the state organism and which traditionally took the legal form of fiefs and vassalage. The interpretative links which he suggested led him to go back to the Lombard period, to the restructuring of the kingdom that took place around the end of the sixth century after the decade of ducal anarchy described in the account of Paul the Deacon.[12] King Authari, in the account of this famous monk, restored security to society by agreeing with the dukes over the provision of the royal power with an economic base adequate for its operation. But in Sigonio one finds more than this; he says that Authari left the dukes effective control over the cities, keeping for the kingdom only the rights of eminent domain, and that he respected the hereditary succession of the dukes in their duchies as long as they remained loyal.[13] With the conquest of Charlemagne, the Frankish system of loyalties and autonomies was supposedly grafted on to that of the Lombards, and the pattern finally attained completion with the German conquest, in a perfect hierarchy of fiefs and vassals, set alongside the freedoms conceded to the cities of the kingdom. The seigneurial hierarchy of the countryside then made feudally subordinate to the cities a large number of the castles which the king had given them in fief.[14] In this fashion, according to Sigonio's conception, medieval Italy acquired its feudal and urban coherence, arising from successive conquests and royal initiatives, and the initiative then moved to the new political protagonists working with their plans and expedients in the urban centres and in the territorial spheres that radiated outwards from the cities.

This overall interpretation was in harmony with the political sentiments and historical vision of Machiavelli and Guicciardini, the great narrators of more or less recent Florentine and Italian history, which were based on the historical reconstruction of innumerable political projects and expedients. In the sixteenth and seventeenth centuries this overview was juxtaposed with ecclesiastical learning in a European perspective, called forth by the great polemics between Protestant and Catholic. The *Annales ecclesiastici* of Cesare Baronio and his continuator Odorico Rinaldi gave a major place to Italy, and the dense harvest of information offered by the Vatican archives was exploited for a narrative rigorously concentrated on the Roman church. The *Annales* focused on

[12] *Pauli Historia Langobardorum*, ed. G. Waitz (Hanover, 1878), *MGH Scriptores rerum Germanicorum*, I.III, c. 16 p. 123.

[13] *Sigonii Opera Omnia*, vol. 2, coll. 33ff.

[14] *Ibid.*, vol. 2, coll. 231ff, 441ff, 618ff.

the papal power and its many adversaries so that again, in the annalistic tradition, the decisions of official power and the greatest armed conflicts were given a privileged importance; more seriously, the apologetic aim of the *Annales* to uphold the unfailing perennial significance of the papacy, although it permitted the alternation of grandeur and decadence in its narrative, left no room for a real interest in profound institutional changes. But in the course of the seventeenth century the scholarly celebration of Catholicism was transformed into a systematic research into the history of all prominent local churches and religious communities, with extensive archival investigation, without favouring the Church of Rome, and with decisive progress in the use of philology and diplomatics as techniques for testing the age and authenticity of the sources. In this manner an image of the whole Middle Ages was taking shape which expressed its great animation through episcopal power and the monastic and canonical movement. France was the epicentre of this modern development of learning, which took its place in a more general expansion of studies on the culture of every period, from the Classical to the modern world, and it found its most vigorous expression in the commitment of the Benedictine group of the Maurists, above all in the industry of Jean Mabillon (1632–1707), an explorer of monastic archives and diplomatist. The French scholars, however, hastened to search for manuscripts and documents in the libraries and archives of Italy, for varied learned purposes (one thinks of Mabillon's *Museum Italicum*), and by their example they also drew in Italian learning, particularly among churchmen,[15] for example the erudition of a monk such as Benedetto Bacchini, teacher at Modena of Ludovico Antonio Muratori, at the end of the seventeenth century.[16] In Muratori himself the living annalistic tradition of Sigonio and the French-influenced ecclesiastical culture met, together with the tradition of historical–juridical controversy which was particularly characteristic of German culture,[17] to give a new face to the Italian Middle Ages in all its complexity.

The traditional annalistic models were inadequate for the progress made by ecclesiastical learning, since (as one can see in the *Annales ordinis sancti Benedicti* of Mabillon and the *Histoire ecclésiastique* of Abbot Fleury) they forced into a chronologically structured narrative a wealth of detail which passed beyond the usual narrative of events from one year to the

[15] B. Neveu, 'Muratori et l'historiographie gallicane', in *Atti del Convegno internazionale di studi muratoriani*, vol. 2, *L. A. Muratori storiografo* (Florence, 1975), p. 244ff.

[16] S. Bertelli, *Erudizione e storia in Ludovico Antonio Muratori* (Naples, 1960), pp. 16ff., 36ff.   [17] *Ibid.*, pp. 165ff., 225ff.

next and which encompassed problems of institutions, customs and culture which persisted over long periods, evolving in their own deep and slow rhythm. Fleury, for example, in order to follow his own model, had to divide the discussion of ecclesiastical problems in the eleventh century, and even details about the cultural sphere and the literary production of major religious figures such as Peter Damian, among different events in different years, placing them under individual years alongside information of a completely different nature. To help the reader he therefore added brief introductions to some volumes of his weighty work, extremely summary 'discourses' on a whole period or on a vast problem such as that of the religious orders. The discomfort of the narrator when faced with such an ancient historiographic structure had often been evident in the past: Sigonio, for example, felt the need to provide a brief synthesis of communal institutions in 1106, at the death of Emperor Henry IV.[18] One may observe here that the annalistic pattern itself, suggested by the excessive importance which the chronicles gave to the most conspicuous events, indicated in its turn the sort of historical explanation which derived institutional and social change from precise political and ecclesiastical decisions and from great military conflicts. But now that ecclesiastical learning, as a result of archival exploration spread through so much of Europe and animated by a unitary plan with an aim which was apologetic and ideological to varying degrees, had so much to say for each year, with such great problems of co-ordination year by year, it became clear that a different structure was needed for exposition, one which would be capable of organizing information according to the categories of the ecclesiastical system themselves. So the problem of exposition came to coincide with the problem of understanding the past in the complexity of its structural developments.

But there was another learned pattern ready to meet these demands, a pattern no less ancient than that of the annals in its Greco-Roman and humanist origins. This was the antiquarian erudite tradition, traditionally committed not to the explanation of historical movements but rather to the collection and classification of the 'reliquiae antiqui temporis', the evidence concerning different aspects of a single particular historical period.[19] This was a systematic rather than chronological ordering of data, which did not in itself recognize any organized system but simply expressed the need to see and describe the past with some order in its multiple juxtaposed aspects. In the case of ecclesiastical learning,

[18] *Sigonii Opera Omnia*, vol. 2, coll. 615–18.

[19] See A. Momigliano, *Contributo alla storia degli studi classici* (Rome, 1955), p. 69ff.

however, when scholars chose the descriptive rather than the narrative method, and the object of study was seen in the perspective of a unitary ideology, the systematic character of the study appeared; it was apparent not only in a descriptive presentation, in the classificatory sense, but also through the internal structure of the medieval ecclesiastical world itself, which was conceived as a totality whose separate forms appeared as partial expressions of a coherent whole. Thus, in the history of historical writing, attention should be paid to the results attained in works such as the *Vetus et nova ecclesiae disciplina* of the theologian and jurist Louis de Thomassin, a contemporary of Mabillon. In this work the presentation by historical periods of the hierarchical structures of clergy and monks, of the operation of their communities, of the temporal enrichment of the churches and their expansion into the arenas of law and politics, was placed within a descriptive scheme which is rigorously antiquarian; at the same time, as each argument is presented in successive horizontal slices of history, the work illustrates an impressive edifice in its triumphant organic growth and its gigantic retreats and decline. Hence Muratori made extensive use of this work in his *Antiquitates Italicae medii aevi* when he wanted to recall fortunate and unfortunate periods, development and regression in the ecclesiastical power of the Italian Middle Ages.

It was in fact in the *Antiquitates* rather than in the *Annali d'Italia* that Muratori produced at several points a work of true history.[20] His *Annali*, which was purely aimed at a philological discussion of the sources in order to specify the succession of separate facts in the customary design of great events, left no room for the analysis of the social and institutional fabric; instead, it found its proper position at several points in his antiquarian dissertations. Here he discussed numerous themes of medieval society; the correspondences he drew between the most disparate arguments from one dissertation to the next were certainly still odd, but in many cases they showed a new capacity for understanding, especially in the study of institutions, compared with preceding Italian studies and even the particular French schools from which he took his bearings. This capacity came from his own commitment to learning, which extended to the monumental publication in the *Rerum Italicarum scriptores* of all the available narrative sources for medieval Italy and the parallel edition of all the documentary evidence (royal and episcopal diplomas, court cases, private notarial charters) which he included in the *Antiquitates* and used to discuss the forms of power and life proper to the

[20] G. Tabacco, 'Muratori medievista', *Rivista storica italiana*, 85 (1973), pp. 200–16.

Middle Ages in Italy. This great body of information forced his mind, which was already well-trained by a very varied apprenticeship in subtle philological and juridical investigations directed by his personal literary ambition or by the interest of his prince at Modena, to overcome certain traditional interpretative models. Here one must point out that what counts, from the point of view of historiography, is not simply that Muratori took part in a widespread re-evaluation of the Lombards or of the barbarians as a whole, or that he discussed many aspects of the Italian Middle Ages in a certain anti-papal spirit; it is, rather, that his zeal in gathering and comparing sources led him to profound revisions in the type of explanation which had been usual up to then. This type of explanation was the one which was usual in the annalistic model, which traditionally had the role of indicating reasons for historic movements, whereas in the antiquarian model it seemed that the descriptive method was far from demanding explanations. But, as we have seen, the systematic expansion of ecclesiastical antiquarianism had led scholars to clarify the changes within structures from one period to the next, without necessarily having recourse to the *deus ex machina* of the sudden major decisions which were the subject of the annalistic style. The systematic study which Muratori also decided on for his dissertations on military and civil institutions, for which he had gathered a rich and often contradictory mass of material, and which thus called for detailed discussion to make sense of it, enabled him to understand in some measure the deep movement of institutions whose spontaneity had escaped Sigonio, the historian to whom Muratori still turned when outlining the major changes in the kingdom of Italy.

These major changes were in the direction of feudalism and the communal movement, and Muratori reduced them to a slow evolution of customs which had emerged outside any broad political programme, as the result of seigneurial pressures and urban forces working gradually and imperceptibly within a royal public order which they were slowly breaking apart, until the kingdom and its subdivisions were totally transformed into a territory with an intensely active political life; the whole development was a great political adventure, dissolved into a multitude of rival autonomies according to changeable relations of force, which slowly translated on to the institutional and juridical level the social hegemony achieved by the most enterprising groups. Within this tumultuous activity of heterogeneous bodies and collectivities Muratori was able to identify separate phases and patterns, distinguished by unstable juridical institutions but endowed from one period to the next with identifiable features. He distinguished the precarious benefice of the vassal from the inherited fief into which it evolved, the fief with a purely economic content from the lordship exercised under the name of a feudal right, and that in its turn from the dominion and jurisdictions claimed by seigneurial dynasties and ecclesiastical bodies over their purely allodial property. He also distinguished the powers of rural seigneurs from the autonomies of collectivities centred on fortifications, acquired in imitation of the urban collectivities, and the civic *res publica* that emerged before the communal period, and which still operated under episcopal direction as a decentralized organ of the kingdom, from the *res publica* of the communes which was clearly self-governing and oriented towards an autonomous state structure. These distinctions are mostly fortunate ones, made possible by close critical discussion and by means of the comparison between the formulae of documents, both when examined on their own and when placed in the historical framework summarily suggested by chronicles and legislation. Muratori could here make use of the attitudes he had formed in the service of the Este family and in controversy with the Pope, to claim in the prince's favour rights with a long historical descent. But in the *Antiquitates Italicae* he did not use juridical distinctions like a lawyer, for the sake of controversy, nor were they translated into dry classifications; they became a tool for understanding a political environment anomalous with respect to ancient or more modern periods. With this tool he could penetrate the peculiar mentality of the central Middle Ages, when power was the object of contractual exchanges, fragmented and reconsolidated in a continual interplay of agreements and usurpations, in conceptual contradiction with the persistent or re-emerging awareness of the *res publica* as the framework of a state with the dimensions of a kingdom, of a dynastic or ecclesiastical principate, or of a city dominating its own territory. All this (and here Muratori could use the antiquarian learning of Thomassin) was concomitant with the growth of an ecclesiastical system which, in that abnormal social and political coexistence, developed its own abnormal ambitions, degenerating into a type of power usurping the wealth and rights pertaining to society and civil governments.

In this way the reconstruction of a major historical event turned into a more or less covert polemic against the degeneration of institutions as a whole and ecclesiastical ones in particular; the latter a degeneration which appeared doubly reprehensible to Muratori since it prejudiced the correct exercise of public power and religious authority. Within this perspective are placed a positive evaluation of the Lombards, who are as yet immune from the political dissolution of later centuries, and the anti-papalism which is transparent in so many places in Muratori's writing. In truth, this was also the limitation of his historical work, since he did not try to understand the meaning of this degenerative process, which was not merely an aberration in human behaviour that preceded and prepared for better times, the times in which Muratori lived (and even these were not without some hateful remnant of that old anomaly). But whatever judgement Muratori passed on the Middle Ages, the important point is the identification of the great anomaly, the singling out of a very particular political situation, whose first signs can be seen in circumstances characterized by royal weakness but which had found its surprising result in a gradual process common to the kingdom, over the course of centuries. Muratori perceived the centrality of this political problem since, in referring specifically to civic liberties, he declared it both 'obscure' and 'of great, indeed the greatest, importance for the history of Italy, and therefore not to be neglected', despite the 'shadows' by which it was surrounded.[21] In Muratori's writing the Italy of the cities, whose restless political operation and amazing cultural rise had been handed down by the medieval chronicles and the annalistic studies of humanists and scholars, retained its external appearance but emerged from a general transformation of institutions, the depth of which was marked by the very 'obscurity' he had pointed to. The 'shadows' to which he referred, he said, were certainly identical with the 'poverty' of the documentation, but his unappeased desire for a more thorough documentation sprang from the complexity and spontaneity of a process which could not be traced back to individual dramatic events.

When one adds to this that the *Antiquitates Italicae* spread well beyond the theme of political and ecclesiastical administration, to embrace peculiarities and curiosities of all kinds relating to social stratification and economic activity, language and personal names, rites and customs, literary and material culture, the agrarian landscape and topography of the Middle Ages, one can understand the stimulus Muratori's work gave in the direction of a history of Italy which would be culturally comprehensive (although mostly centred on sources from Lombardy, Emilia and Tuscany),[22] and diametrically opposed to the formal and limited history of the annalistic method. This was so even though the stimulus, oriented without much organization in many different directions, was highly fragmented and managed to produce effective results above all at the level of the history of institutions; here the argument was based on legal thinking and on a cautious polemic inspired by the question of jurisdictions, which tended to unify the discussions still further.

---

[21] L. A. Muratori, *Antiquitates Italicae medii aevi*, vol. 4 (Milan, 1741), col. 4.

[22] G. Fasoli, 'Vitalità delle "Antiquitates"', in *L. A. Muratori storiografo*, p. 36.

As a contrast to a history of Italy which had expanded in its contents but was still conceived essentially as an investigation of the Italic kingdom and its transformation into a plurality of autonomous urban developments, there stands the *Istoria civile del regno di Napoli* by a great contemporary of Muratori, Pietro Giannone.[23] This work, by giving events in the southern kingdom their own importance, is sufficient to underline the obvious dichotomy in the Italian Middle Ages, in its chronicles and the resulting historical writing from the humanist period onwards. It too is presented, like some of the antiquarian scholarship but indeed in a more explicit fashion, as a history of institutions, sharply different from the annalistic narrative and with the strong support of a juridical culture. But the force with which Giannone felt the problem of ecclesiastical encroachment, although it enabled him to build a vigorous history of southern legislation, its civil operation and its degradation without the slackness of the annalists or antiquarian digressions, freed him too much from learned scruples and from a commitment to dispassionate understanding, so that his work was not widely influential in the development of a more demanding historiography.

3 Giannone's work was not ignored by the first scholar to attempt a general history of Italy freed from scholarly models, the Piedmontese Carlo Denina, with the volumes of his *Rivoluzioni d'Italia* (Turin 1769–70);[24] but in his general construction Denina was not inspired by Giannone. He brought together the annalist and antiquarian models of Muratori, which centred on problems of the Italic kingdom, to produce an account similar to the histories of civilization whose exemplar was provided by the philosophers of the European Enlightenment, above all Voltaire. His account, however, had fewer polemical intentions and less ambition to re-evoke the past; instead, it had a rigorous respect for scholarly teachings. This respect did not prevent Denina from declaring openly the novelty of his own work in comparison with the Italian tradition – indeed he did not hesitate to judge as 'burdensome and tedious' the *Annali* of Muratori 'because of the need to pass from one feature to another, from Milan to Naples, from Florence to Venice, in different matters',[25] nor to declare with respect to the *Antiquitates* that

---

[23] G. Ricuperati, *L'esperienza civile e religiosa di Pietro Giannone* (Milan-Naples, 1970), pp. 143–229.

[24] G. Ricuperati, 'Ludovico Antonio Muratori e il Piemonte', in *Atti del Convegno internazionale di studi muratoriani*, vol. 3, *La fortuna del Muratori* (Florence, 1975), pp. 81ff. See *Illuministi italiani*, vol. 3, *Riformatori lombardi, piemontesi e toscani*, ed. F. Venturi (Milan and Naples, 1958), pp. 707ff; G. Marocco, 'La storiografia piemontese di Carlo Denina', *Bollettino storico-bibliografico subalpino*, 76 (1978), pp. 290ff.

[25] C. Denina, *Delle rivoluzioni d'Italia*, vol. 1, 3rd ed. (Venice, 1792), p. v.

'Muratori in these dissertations collected into a single bundle things belonging to many centuries, whereas we must deal in each place only with those things which regard the period of history which we are dealing with at the time.'[26] The resulting account was still rich in facts, but without the bond of rigid chronological succession year after year. It was an account of events put together according to the internal connections of each period, so that exposition could more easily alternate with a rapid presentation of the great problems, such as the origin of the Lombards, the nature of their political governments, their religious changes and similar questions, or of information, for the late Middle Ages, about commerce, agriculture, the silk and wool guilds, luxuries, and the rise of liberal arts and learning. Still, it is true that the information on medieval patterns of life remained set apart, so that Denina's *Rivoluzioni* basically deals with political events and the institutional changes of an Italy seen above all as the centre and north, as Muratori too had seen it.

In these same years Condillac at Parma was rewriting his extremely full *Cours d'études*, which presents a 'philosophical' history of the Middle Ages, with the by now usual alternation, always difficult to balance, between narration of facts and reflections which are often inserted as digressions.[27] Here Italy appears in the exuberant history of the papacy and in the disordered development of the city-republics, as well as in the associated movement towards the culture of the Renaissance[28] – exactly, that is, in the ways which were already characteristic of the historiography which had developed into the erudition of Muratori (and now into Denina's *Rivoluzioni*), and with judgements not very different from those expressed in Voltaire's *Essai sur les mœurs*, although the latter had judged with more explicit favour the mercantile and urban development of Italy which set up a more direct relation between the free cities and the new cultures.[29] Thus erudite history and philosophical history were converging, in Italy and Europe, to present the same interpretation of the Italian Middle Ages, with the same orientation towards political and institutional aspects, against an uncertain background of the history of civilization. The old annalistic model, elaborated in the fifteenth and sixteenth centuries, was enriched with information with a wider social range, with a new sensitivity to the

---

[26] *Ibid.*, vol. 2 (3rd ed., Venice, 1793), p. 320.

[27] See L. Guerci, *Condillac storico* (Milan-Naples, 1978), pp. 85, 110ff, 153ff, 253ff.

[28] *Ibid.*, pp. 284ff, 312ff.

[29] L. Gatto, *Medioevo voltairiano* (Rome, 1973) pp. 168ff; L. Guerci, *Condillac storico*, pp. 321ff.

spontaneous nature of certain developments; but the new convergence maintained intact at the moment of general exposition the centrality of the problems that had already emerged within the annalistic model. Indeed, the historiography of the Romantic period, although it modified or overturned certain evaluations, still functioned within this now consolidated tradition.

The problem of the medieval civilization of Italy became ever more decisively the problem of civic liberties. We should recall in particular the Genevan Sismondi and his *Histoire des républiques italiennes du moyen âge* (Zürich 1807–18), which in its procedure was actually strongly annalistic but which had a declared ethical and political inspiration, particularly in the introduction and in the 'considerations' which were occasionally interpolated. Sismondi made an abridged version of this work in 1832, the *Histoire de la renaissance de la liberté en Italie, de ses progrès, de sa décadence et de sa chute*, which is like a great ideological manifesto, sustained by the historical picture which previous scholarship had constructed and which Sismondi himself reduced to greater coherence. But more important in the development of historiography was the commitment of the Germans as a closely-bound group to the study of Italian liberties. The 'obscurity' in the formation of the communes which Muratori had pointed out had to be dispelled. This historical process, with the culture that emerged within it, could no longer be derived chiefly from acts of royal power, initiatives of princes, or conscious political plans, but rather from a process of evolution from which political decisions drew inspiration and into which they were incorporated. And so Friedrich Karl von Savigny, in studying the presence of Roman law in the Middle Ages (his great work was published at Heidelberg in 1815–31), thought it necessary to link this presence with what he supposed to be a persistent evolution of municipal bodies with a Roman tradition in the medieval cities of Italy, bodies destined to receive greater vitality from the definitive fusion of the Germanic element with the urban collectivity.[30] In this way Romantic historicism took to its logical conclusion Muratori's intuition of the gradual formation of the urban communal experience, even as far as the absurdity of denying ruptures even in the period of the Lombard arrival and the organization of the conquest. But a reaction quickly arose in the heart of Romanticism itself, since this evaluation of the Roman tradition removed all creative significance from the gradual formation of new institutions, and ran the risk of assuming that customs were survivals

[30] See the criticism of von Savigny by H. Leo, *Entwicklung der Verfassung der lombardischen Städte* (Hamburg, 1824), pp. 39, 91 note 1.

that had lain inert for centuries. Heinrich Leo, who passionately appreciated the ruthless Lombard and Tuscan world and – despite being Protestant – the world of papal power, contested Savigny's thesis, beginning with his dissertation of 1820 on 'the ordering of the free Lombard cities in the Middle Ages', which was rewritten in 1824. Leo underlined the harsh conditions which the Lombards created for the Latins, and the growth of the bishops' temporal power, strengthened by immunities given by the king, from the Frankish period onwards. From this point he followed the formation of civic autonomies under episcopal jurisdiction up to the appearance of the communal regime with its aristocratic hegemonies and its social tensions, a vast communal movement involving the whole of Tuscany which made Florence the highest expression of the Italian genius, which was offered to Europe in its transition towards the modern world.[31]

Some years later Leo took up his model again in a lengthy 'history of the Italian states from the fall of the Roman Empire'. Starting with the various soils and climates of the Italian regions, it focused on the different destiny and structuring of the Italian kingdom compared with the South and the islands, its political dissolution and the simultaneous development of seigneurial and communal autonomies within a framework of empire and papacy which was little more than nominal. He sketched this picture with acuteness and coherence, and always with an eye turned to fundamental changes, until at a certain point he failed to hold together the threads of a development which divided clearly into many separate processes of state formation. The highly-coloured account of events region by region then got the better of general historical reflection, even in him. An exception is provided by digressions on arts and letters in the Medici period, which Leo interpreted above all as expressions of the 'abundant force of the Florentines', which was finally oriented in a fruitful fashion 'instead of the continual political disturbances in which it had earlier vented itself'.[32]

Leo's work, as with his earlier dissertation, was soon translated in Italy, and with that of Savigny exercised a deep influence there. The German hegemony over the methods used by the most rigorously scientific medieval scholarship in Italy dates from that time. This was also the period when François Guizot enjoyed most esteem: his histories of European, and chiefly French, civilization were truly exemplary in replacing a narrative of events by an ordered and clear exposition of

[31] H. Leo, *Entwicklung*, pp. 83ff, 90ff, 198ff.

[32] E. Leo, *Storia degli stati italiani* (Italian translation, Florence, 1840), vol. 1, pp. 750, 782.

social, institutional and cultural evolution, in harmony with the demands of a broad humanist scope already stressed by Enlightenment historiography but lacking the corrosive eighteenth-century polemical digressions. Certainly Guizot, and French historiography in general in these politically and socially impassioned decades, left fruitful traces on the whole span of Italian culture, including of course medieval studies. But German science made a profound impression through the attention that learned Germany constantly turned on the Lombard and Tuscan world from the time of Savigny and Leo, taking the traditionally Italian perspective of the turbulent cities which were destined to give Europe the Renaissance. It is true that these were the same years in which the great debate on the conditions that the Lombards created for the Latins flared up.[33] We need look no further than the vast and extremely erudite labours of the Neapolitan Carlo Troya, who expanded the discussion from the Lombards to the whole of ancient Germanism, coming to terms, on a personal level as well, with the 'most famous Grimm'.[34] But the problem of the Lombards in Italy, subordinated as it was to the problems of the limits of continuity between Roman and medieval institutions, took on importance in relation to the traditional problem of communal culture. Leo had explicitly declared as much at the end of his dissertation. It is clearly apparent in Troya, when, after denying the presence of two ethnically-organized collective bodies in the individual cities of the kingdom after the edict of Rothari, he declares that only the priesthood, as preserver of Classical culture, provided the link between Roman and medieval,[35] a continuity which he shrewdly affirmed to be 'wholly intellectual' and destined to be vigorously fertile from the twelfth century onwards.[36] The Turinese Cesare Balbo was equally concerned to draw closer to the new German learning,[37] and in his summary of Italian history simply added to the customary line of interpretation his laments for the almost constant foreign domination of the peninsula; if, despite everything, he wanted to rescue something from the history which led from the Lombard and Frankish dominion to that of the Germans, it was the period of the 'little republics', which enjoyed a 'freedom which was still servile' but on the whole some

[33] G. Falco, 'La questione longobardo e la moderna storiografia italiana', *Atti del I Congresso internazionale di studi longobardi* (Spoleto, 1952), pp. 153–66.
[34] C. Troya, *Storia d'Italia del medio evo*, vol. 4.2 (Naples, 1853), p. xix.
[35] *Ibid.*, vol. 1.4 (Naples, 1843), appendix, p. 52.
[36] *Ibid.*, vol. 4.1 (Naples, 1852), p. xlv.
[37] See E. Passerin d'Entrèves, 'Cesare Balbo', in *Dizionario biografico degli Italiani*, vol. 5 (Rome, 1963), p. 398.

autonomy as well.[38] The liberal-Catholic school, to which Troya, Balbo and so many others belonged,[39] limited itself to perfecting the model focused on the cities only at those points where Italian history raised itself to European levels thanks to the Roman papacy, and particularly where the struggle against the empire, from Gregory VII to the end of the Staufer period, seemed to suggest a providential orienting of civic liberties around the papal supremacy. In this presentation Italy's Middle Ages took on a significance which was not simply episodic, thanks to the same forces which (except for the opposing ideological orientation) had dominated the historical vision of so many scholars and philosophers of the eighteenth century.

Meanwhile German science applied its methods to the problems of medieval Lombardy as well. It produced ever more rigorous philological editions of sources, based on systematic research and classification of the codices and charters that supplied evidence for each source, and compared exhaustively the sources relating to each particular event, institution or problem. This was carried out without concessions to current opinion or interpretations hallowed by time or by eminent authorship; the limits of these opinions and interpretations were set out as a preliminary to each new enquiry, with an orderly indication of their origins, inter-relationships and fortunes, while their cultural conditioning and weaknesses when confronted with the sources were condemned; after this critical history of each great question, a solution scientifically based on the sources alone could be reached, at least in principle. In this complex labour of demolition and reconstruction, whenever the historian's interest went beyond ascertaining single facts or events it was drawn towards the analysis of juridical patterns. This was the direction suggested in Germany by the broad interests of the school of legal history, already famous through the work of its founders, the Romanist Savigny and the Germanist Karl Friedrich Eichhorn. *Recht und Verfassung*, law and constitution, were understood as a network of norms emerging from the consciousness of a people and from the culture of its interpreters, i.e. the legists and legislators, and of a parallel network of powers and functions operating with different ranges of action, from the family and the village up to the largest-scale religious and political institutions. Each of these networks was conceived in such a manner as to produce together a system of norms and institutions within which men lived, conditioned by them and at the same time conditioning in

---

[38] C. Balbo, *Della storia d'Italia dalle origini fino ai nostri tempi. Sommario*, ed. G. Talamo (Milan, 1963), p. 177.

[39] B. Croce, *Storia della storiografia italiana nel secolo decimonono*, vol. I (Bari, 1930), especially pp. 140ff.

turn the evolution of the system. Thus legal analysis revealed its effectiveness, as it already had in the ecclesiastical learning of the eighteenth century and in the researches of men such as Leibniz and Muratori; it suggested a broader presentation of the political and social arrangements than that given by political narrative, without any risk of abandoning itself to the taste for a highly-coloured and more or less imaginary re-evocation of civilization. The most notable results of this effectiveness were gathered together in the *Deutsche Verfassungsgeschichte* of Georg Waitz, the famous work on Germanic, Frankish and German institutions whose first volumes appeared in 1844 (on the pre-medieval Germanic world) and 1847 (on the Merovingian Franks). Together with the beginning of this imposing *Verfassungsgeschichte* there appeared in 1846 Moritz von Bethmann-Hollweg's study of the origins of the liberties of the Lombard cities and in 1847 the two volumes of Karl Hegel on the history of urban institutions in Italy from the Roman period to the twelfth century. Thus in the field of interest of German scholars the pre-medieval and medieval *Verfassung* of the Germanic peoples and countries corresponded perfectly with the pre-medieval and medieval *Städtverfassung* (civic order) of Italy.

Bethmann-Hollweg followed step by step the 'revolutions'[40] of the first six medieval centuries in Italy in order to derive from them the new development of the social classes in the cities under the hegemony of the bishops, up to the violent clashes between groups of citizens attested by the chronicles; he attributed the creation of the consulate, as the first communal institution, to the surmounting of these clashes by means of a sworn peace. In this fashion he went beyond the vision of Muratori and, more recently, of Leo, who had indeed set the birth of communal institutions within an evolutionary process but who had supposed that it came about through the mediation of some pre-existing collective body of citizens (not necessarily Roman in origin). On this issue, Bethmann-Hollweg opposed himself to what he called an abuse of historical method, through which constitutional development was seen only as a transformation, and not also the production of new forms by the new needs and conditions of life.[41] Karl Hegel in his turn was substantially in agreement with the perspectives of Troya and Bethmann-Hollweg but based himself on a fuller and more subtle exegesis of Lombard and Frankish documents, and those from later Lombardy and Tuscany. He reduced the ethnic problem, of the Lombard period onwards, to a problem of the movement of legal and

---

[40] M. A. von Bethmann-Hollweg, *Ursprung der lombardischen Städtefreiheit* (Bonn, 1846), p. 6.   [41] *Ibid.*, p. 147.

social strata, and saw the variety of communal formations, decisively set in contrast to the preceding episcopal regime, as springing from the variety in this dynamic process.[42] In a productive comparison, he extended his enquiry to the whole of Classical and Byzantine Italy, and also included a final comparison with the civic autonomies of France and Germany, in every case citing peculiarities deriving from different social and civil contexts.

At this point the desire to set the problem of urban Italy in an even broader perspective, without reducing it to a process that would diminish its originality, was finally to suggest a less one-sided historical view of the Italian Middle Ages. The ethnic problem of the Lombard period, however it was resolved, revealed ever more clearly its autonomous historical value, as a problem about the meeting and symbiosis between different cultures. Gradually the rural world acquired its own importance as the basis of economic power for the military and ecclesiastical aristocracy, as the environment for the life of the great part of the population, and as the theatre for a post-Carolingian process of fortification (*incastellamento*) which was destined to shake up the whole organization of the kingdom. This wider historical perspective was at the same time developed by the broad interests of German legal history, which formed an example to Europe, as it realized the programme of the historical school of law and Savigny and Eichhorn. While Waitz was building up his *Deutsche Verfassungsgeschichte*, which was based on the public order of the early Middle Ages, Ferdinand Walter began publication in 1852 of his *Deutsche Rechtsgeschichte*,[43] which included a synthesis of the *Verfassungsgeschichte* and then developed a systematic historical treatment of private, trial and criminal law, in which he gave particular attention to the medieval, especially early medieval, phases of evolution of the individual legal institutions. This transformed the 'German legal antiquities', collections of information in the seventeenth-century tradition which had been revived in the Romantic period by the 'most famous Grimm', into the history of a legal system.[44] Walter was attempting to incorporate this legal system into an entire civilization, romantically conceived as the total expression of the Germanic genius, and was therefore committed to avoiding the analysis of legal structures on their own; instead, they were to be made the most conscious and rigorous manifestation of an evolving politico-social and civic totality.

---

[42] K. Hegel, *Geschichte der Städtverfassung von Italien*, vol. 2 (Leipzig, 1847), pp. 85ff.

[43] The second edition, 'sehr verbesserte und vermehrte', was published in Bonn in 1857 (see vol. 1, p. viii for a reference to the preceding edition).

[44] This is the expression of Troya, *Storia d'Italia*, vol. 4.2, p. xix, cited above. I refer here to J. Grimm, *Deutsche Rechtsalterthümer* (Göttingen, 1828).

A vision, an experimental attitude, of this kind were strongly present at this time in the German culture of the Hapsburg Empire as well, and so were reflected in the teaching at Padua University (before the Veneto's annexation by the Kingdom of Italy). Antonio Pertile's teaching at Padua, from 1857 onwards,[45] began the construction of a lengthy *Storia del diritto italiano*. It was largely modelled on the *Rechtsgeschichte* of Walter, both in its basic division between developments in public, private, criminal and procedural law and in its gathering into successive phases the history of the public power as the expression of political and social forces, while the history of other legal developments was distributed according to systematic distinctions made between different institutions.

The history of law, then, was not to be only a specialist history. On the contrary, one may say that for Pertile, and for those who followed his footsteps, cultivating the new historical–juridical discipline, so-called 'history' *tout court* was still conceived of as a narration of events and great deeds, while it was the history of law that lent itself to analysis of what we would now call the deep 'structures' of a people's development. 'Civil history itself' wrote Pertile, 'receives a far from negligible aid from our science. Indeed it may be said that our science provides the basis for and complement to it by investigating the inner life, the household gods, so to speak, and the social conditions of the peoples whose external deeds are described by civil history.'[46] And to clarify further this shift of the focus of historiography from traditional 'civil history' to legal history, Pertile added 'and these deeds themselves often find in them [that is, in legal–historical researches] their ultimate explanation'.

One may compare the work of scholars such as these (as with the studies of Francesco Shupfer on social orders and landed property among the Lombards and in the pre-communal society of Lombardy, or those of Giuseppe Salvioli on the special jurisdictions and immunities of the churches) with the contemporary activity of outstanding historians with a philological and literary background, such as Pasquale Villari.[47] Villari followed the tradition of Sismondi and the vehement intelligence

---

[45] This is clear from A. Pertile, *Storia del diritto italiano dalla caduta dell'impero romano alla codificazione*, vol. 1 (Padua, 1873), p. x. Publication of the work began in 1872 with the third volume, dealing with personal and family law.

[46] A. Pertile, *Storia del diritto italiano*, vol. 1, p. 7.

[47] The study by E. Artifoni is useful in revising the historiographical model offered by Crocian teaching, in relation to the philological historians whom Croce accused of base positivism; E. Artifoni, 'Il giovane Salvemini: un momento di una formazione medievistica', *Nuova Rivista Storica*, 68 (1984), pp. 367–80.

of Edgar Quinet. The latter's *Révolutions d'Italie* (published in 1848–52) had renewed the celebration of the cultural resurgence of the Italian cities, and combined it with the evocation of a 'class war' between nobles and bourgeois, between *popolo grasso* and *popolo minuto*, following the indications of the chroniclers (of Florence in particular) and the contemporary political and social experiences of Quinet himself. As a result he also paid attention to the fiscal policy of the ruling classes in Florence, and stressed the 'terror' of the 'bourgeois aristocracy' at the memory of the popular revolution of the Ciompi.[48] In his turn Villari, from the 1860s onwards, presented the Italian communal experience as a continual struggle of the 'renewed Latin race' against the heirs of the Germanic peoples, and exalted Florentine liberty with respect to earlier freedoms; at the same time, in accord with the new positivist and socially aware climate, he engaged in research on commerce and the major guilds (taking the *Antiquitates* of Muratori as his starting point), and linked them with thoughts on the struggle of political parties and on institutional evolution.[49] Thus he showed a specific wish to include in the study of the cities of the communal period the examination of conditions which went beyond those 'external deeds' to which Pertile wanted to confine the narratives of 'civil history'. But in this spontaneous meeting between historiographies of literary and of juridical inspiration, one cannot help but see that the former remained strongly anchored to the political urban model, while the latter spread into a global and specific study of all the forms of public and private life, in all the social and territorial environments of the Italian Middle Ages, wherever these forms took on some stability and legal rigour, even if only through customary usage.

Thus legal analysis still seemed the best road open, as it had been at least from the time of Muratori, to broaden the historical horizon with a rigourous awareness of the whole development of civic life, without reducing it to analyses that would favour moments of exceptional importance and would hide the more humble but more diffuse and tenacious expressions of life. But precisely in this juridical extension of historical interests there re-emerged with new clarity the impossibility, already obvious in the old antiquarianism, of dominating the past through a single coherent vision.

4   The possibility of such a coherent mastery of the past had been the illusion of Romantic culture, which had imagined a natural convergence,

---

[48] See E. Quinet, *Le Rivoluzioni d'Italia*, ed. C. Muscetta (Bari, 1935), pp. 40, 182.

[49] P. Villari, *I primi due secoli della storia di Firenze* (Florence, 1905), pp. 4, 24, 295ff., where earlier essays, from the preceding forty years, are reprinted.

in the name of the 'genius' of the people, of all forms of life towards a spiritual centre, unifying each great national tradition. It was this illusion, above all, that had inspired the programme of the historical school of law in Germany. But now, with the systematic expansion of historical–legal studies, it turned out to be impossible to bring the most varied expressions of a people into the same rhythm. History could not be reduced to a system. The individual institutions of private law, precisely those which permitted the intimate penetration of the social fabric, revealed rhythms of evolution which were slower than those of the political institutions, and heterogeneous even among themselves. Hence, in the German work of Walter as in that of Pertile, their history had to be set out in parallel autonomous pictures, following a process of classification which continued down to the handbooks of today. Nino Tamassia, in his commemoration of Pertile in 1895,[50] described him as he followed from one region and one time to another each individual network of norms, formed around the status of individuals and the family, the forms of property and inheritance, contractual obligations and penal law; he saw each network disappearing in one place to reappear elsewhere, sometimes distorted, in a confused turmoil of customs, reaction, resistance and deviations,[51] until it acquired a rigid form in modern codices. The more the history of law refined its distinctions between the different legal manifestations of a particular relationship, and gradually indicated in them the meeting between mental habits, cultural traditions and the needs of daily life, the more it risked being turned into a great catalogue of formulae.

It was proposed, then, to study more concrete activities, the experiences of life which had prompted the formulae in different contexts and the real changes in those same experiences, beneath the diversity of the formulae themselves, which are intellectually and spiritually significant but tend to break up attempts at an inclusive history. Social needs, and the economic activity born to satisfy them, were to be rediscovered; they had already attracted the attention of scholars from the end of the eighteenth century, and through the nineteenth century they became increasingly present in historical research in connection with contemporary political and social upheavals, the industrial revolution and class tensions. This presence had become clear both in historical narrative of literary inspiration, as we have noted above with Villari, and in legal historiography, particularly in the

[50] N. Tamassia, *Scritti di storia giuridica* (Padua, 1964), pp. 685ff.
[51] For the development in those decades of the theme of the family, see for example G. Tabacco, 'Il tema della famiglia e del suo funzionamento nella società medievale', *Quaderni storici*, 33 (1976), pp. 895ff.

historical school of law; from the latter there derived in the mid-nineteenth century in Germany the historical school of national economy, a tendency autonomous of its historical and juridical context.[52] In 1879, the first national economic history in the context of this school was the *Deutsche Wirtschaftgeschichte* of Karl Theodor von Inama-Sternegg. It discusses above all the structure and administration of the great landed patrimonies, the economic base for most of the Middle Ages both of royal and ecclesiastical power and of the dominant aristocracy, and the principal framework for the life of the rural multitudes. In these same decades, concomitant with the developments of the historical school of national economy, the historical materialism of Marx and Engels was spreading and becoming more precise, helping to give relationships of economic production a central importance in globally-oriented historical writing. In this complex cultural picture, at the end of the nineteenth and beginning of the twentieth centuries, one must place the German and Italian scholars who, in their aim to find a unifying structure in Italian development, placed the emphasis on the economic system and its transformations.

This was the aim of Ludo Moritz Hartmann in the 1890s when he began his fundamental work, the *Geschichte Italiens im Mittelalter*,[53] a work exemplary in its philological rigour and sensitivity to the complex interplay of historic forces. Beginning in the same years, Hartmann contributed a series of studies, *Zur Wirtschaftsgeschichte Italiens im frühen Mittelalter*, which he collected and published under this title in 1904: these were contributions to the economic history of the first centuries of the Latin, Germanic and Byzantine Middle Ages in Italy. It was a scientific undertaking permeated with the intellectual rigour which he derived from his exacting liberal culture, but at the same time it was in harmony with the most recent tendencies of German political thought. In fact Hartmann supported the Austrian–German social-democratic movement and was the most prestigious of the founders of the first journal of economic and social history.[54] No less than Inama-Sternegg, Hartmann was convinced that agrarian and seigneurial structures were central to the Middle Ages. And he was sensitive to the themes of human settlement, human geography and demography which had extensively penetrated the 'Kulturgeschichte', the 'history of civilization' of the

[52] See G. von Below, *Die deutsche Geschichtschreibung von den Befreiungskriegen bis zu unsern Tagen* (Munich-Berlin, 1924), pp. 171ff.

[53] It was interrupted in 1915 at 1018.

[54] See H. Aubin, 'Zum 50. Band der Vierteljahrschrift für Sozial- und Wirtschaftsgeschichte', *Vierteljahrschrift für Sozial- und Wirtschaftsgeschichte*, 50 (1963), pp. 8ff, 12ff.

eighteenth century and Romanticism, which at the end of the nineteenth century was expanding in particular into the study of material culture (what today we would call economic structures and infrastructures). The *Geschichte Italiens* opens with precisely these themes. But Hartmann was a student of Theodor Mommsen, the great historian of Classical Rome and its institutions, and he was convinced that any true historian should be at least half a jurist.[55] Therefore it seemed obvious to him to set the institutions of the political framework at the heart of his *Geschichte*. This was, after all, exactly what enabled historians of law, when they laid out as a first step the successive phases of public law, to avoid that fragmentation into classifications which unfortunately seemed inevitable when dealing with the institutions of private law. So the *Geschichte Italiens*, although born from a fervent economic and social interest, ended up becoming largely a political and institutional history. Indeed, when Hartmann had passed the Lombard period and the first arrival of the Franks in Italy, he proceeded several times in his narrative to favour major political events (up to the beginning of the eleventh century, where the work ended), even though he was aware of the capillary crisis of political power in a society that was in the course of profound transformation.

In a climate such as that of Germany, what happened to medieval Italian studies in what was later identified as the economic and juridical school? In Salvemini's study of a socially turbulent moment in Florentine communal life, or in Gioacchino Volpe's discussion of the general problem of urban and rural communes, attention to social contrasts (already lively in Villari) was emphasized; through frequent contacts and partnership with historians of law and German scholars, especially Hartmann, knowledge of agrarian pacts and artisans' guilds, formal conditions and real diversity among the peasants, market rights and tolls, was deepened. But in the studies of Gino Luzzatto, where the acquisition of juridical competence was most coherently used, together with an interest in the great collective facts of production and commerce, a tendency towards an intensely economic vision of the Italian Middle Ages appeared, with the avowed renunciation of an all-inclusive history (which none the less remained desirable).[56] This became more explicit in Luzzatto's work after 1910, which moved ever more markedly in the direction of economic history, particularly commercial history, in contrast to his early scholarly activity at the

[55] E. Stein, 'Zur Erinnerung an L. M. Hartmann', *Vierteljahrschrift für Sozial- und Wirtschaftsgeschichte*, 18 (1925), p. 315.

[56] See G. Luzzatto, *Dai servi della gleba agli albori del capitalismo*, with an introduction by M. Berengo (Bari, 1966), p. xliv.

beginning of the century at a time of enthusiasm for political–social history. While Luzzatto was realizing this programme of consciously specialized history, a complex reaction took shape against the social–economic interpretation, which had tried to understand the significant aspects of the Italian Middle Ages through the successive phases of the agrarian and seigneurial economy and urban mercantile dominance.

Already in the first years of the century Volpe had hesitated between this latter interpretation[57] and the programmatic affirmation of a general interdependence between all the constituent processes, first of disintegration and then of coalescence, of the Italian Middle Ages.[58] In the work of synthesis on the European Middle Ages which he began in 1917,[59] removing a narrative of events in no way reduced the difficulty of expressing the interdependence of the structures without favouring any one among them. Volpe's own insistence on the novelty of the processes of recoalescence, the 'creative spontaneity',[60] with respect to the Roman and German traditions which had entered into crisis at their encounter with each other, was also ineffective. The need not only to juxtapose the problems but also to explain their connections led him to indicate the arrival and the passing of the 'natural economy', a production limited to the immediate needs of consumption, as central issues. But the aim of writing a history which was human and concrete, rather than specifically and one-sidedly economic, brought back to centre stage the failures and successes of political co-ordination, the so-called 'feudal State' and civic and dynastic institutions, together with all

[57] G. Volpe, *Medio evo italiano*, 2nd ed. (Florence, 1961), p. 91: 'A deep transformation in the landed economy and in the agricultural classes, though hidden, lies behind this whole renaissance of the Italian people, which then culminated in the major cities, where it is more visible than anywhere else; an economic and juridical transformation which is above all the work of the peasants themselves' (in the essay on 'Questioni fondamentali sull'origine e svolgimento dei comuni italiani', of 1904).

[58] G. Volpe, *Medio evo italiano*, p. 89 (in the essay cited above: 'After the year 1000 there begins instead the opposite process of concentration, reconstruction, definition, separation, in demography, in the borders between peoples, in social groupings, in the powers of the state, in the law, in lay and clerical life, in short, in the whole culture'); p. 289 (in the essay on 'Sistema della costituzione economica e sociale italiana nell'età dei communi': 'The individual elements, and the institutions and laws, are the result of many different systems of forces…and, however weak in their actions, they are sufficient to undermine the suggestion that all forms of culture in an era are derived from that era's economic resources').

[59] See G. Volpe, *Il medio evo* (reprinted Florence, 1958), p. xi.

[60] *Ibid.*, p. 203.

the complications relating to the churches. But were these latter only complications of a power that was essentially political? Did Catholicism only juxtapose one institution and another, in a world which could be reduced on one side to an economic base and on the other to political experimentation?

Here the 'vitalism' of Volpe's vision,[61] his celebration of the ever-innovatory movement of history (a celebration tempered by sensitivity to political actions as conscious expressions of that dynamism and as forces destined to discipline it) found its limit. Yet he forced himself to include within this creative spontaneity the 'revolutionary myths of that religious age'[62] as well, and seemed to envisage the goal of the whole prodigious adventure of the Middle Ages in the West as the 'Italian intellectual empire',[63] linking in his imagination its 'task', the 'spiritual' unification of Europe, with that of Classical Rome in the Mediterranean.[64] To superimpose such a 'task' on the stormy Italian Middle Ages was perhaps a surrender *in extremis*, in the face of the example of Italy, by the vitalist interpretation to the centuries-old tendencies of European culture. This surrender itself opened the problem of the limitations of Volpe's interpretation. In more than one respect these limitations were also those of the economic explanation in general, within an institutional and social presentation of the Italian Middle Ages, limitations which at the beginning of the century had forced some of the most politically committed scholars of Germany and Italy (such as Salvemini, Hartmann and Luzzatto) to express reservations about the weight of cultural and moral forces in history in general and in Italian history in particular; on consideration, these are exactly the type of forces which were at the root of their own zeal as men and as scholars.

Any reservations about the ethical, political and ideological motivations of human behaviour declined between the two world wars. In Italy this decline appeared in the rhetorical language used by official power, which boldly displayed those motivations, but also within the elites who opposed for reasons of culture and morality the narrowness of the official 'heroic' vitalism. At this time tendencies appeared in Italian medieval studies which were to result in Giorgio Falco's *Santa romana repubblica* (1942).[65] Linking itself with the historicist idealism of Benedetto Croce,[66] this work interpreted the Middle Ages as the basis

---

[61] See I. Cervelli, *Gioacchino Volpe* (Naples, 1977), pp. 49, 139.

[62] G. Volpe, *Il medio evo*, p. 203.

[63] *Ibid.*, p. 535.   [64] *Ibid.*, p. 541.

[65] See G. Severino, 'Giorgio Falco: un medievista nella crisi dell'idealismo storiografico', *La Cultura*, 12.2 (1974), p. 186.

[66] See Croce, *Storia della storiografia italiana*, vol. 2, p. 261, on the 'ever greater perfection of ethical–political, or religious, history'.

of a Europe founded in its civil life and institutions on the Church of
Rome, which was in its turn firmly rooted in Italian culture. The same
tendencies also led to the essays of Raffaello Morghen, dating mainly
from the 1940s and collected in his *Medioevo cristiano* (1951). While not
neglecting the institutional aspect of ecclesiastical and imperial universalism in the Roman tradition, Morghen saw the more purely
Christian experience, both orthodox and heterodox, as the 'fundamental
and essential inspiration and creative force of all medieval civilization',[67]
and followed the historiographical line traced by Ernesto Bonaiuti in
emphasizing the effectiveness of the eschatological myth.[68] The positions
reached by Falco and Morghen were in harmony with the expansion of
European 'Kulturgeschichte' (as history of the constituent forms of a
civilization) from the sphere of economic production and material
infrastructure, which had been the centre of social interest at the end of
the last century, into the sphere of psychological and mental conditions
inherent in any human community and of spiritual movements, or
'Geistgeschichte'. For the role given to the religious Middle Ages in the
construction of Western civilization, we need only refer to the neo-
Protestantism which inspired the studies of Ernst Troeltsch on the social
doctrines of churches and Christian groups, and the modernist neo-
Catholicism of Ernesto Bonaiuti's *Storia del cristianesimo* (vol. 2, 1943),
while for the decisive progress in knowledge of the links between heretic
movements and the creative experiments of the religious orders in the
late Middle Ages we may refer to the research of Herbert Grundmann
on the twelfth and thirteenth centuries. In 'Geistgeschichte' the assertion
of relative functional autonomy for the world of beliefs and culture,
with respect to any other social structure, tended to extend into rejection
of the economic explanation for overall developments; it replaced the
economic explanation with one founded on spiritual experiences and
cultural acquisitions, open to creative innovation and to transmission
from one social organization to another, capable of conferring civil
significance on this same organization through a particular framework
of institutions. Ecclesiastical institutions would thus have constituted the
fundamental form of organization in the Middle Ages, permeating
political power and the structure of societies. Religious dynamism,
generating ecclesiastical institutions but not always faithfully represented
in them, would then be the measure of the functional character of those
institutions and their limits within medieval civilization.

    5   Legal reflections, economic analysis and greater cultural depth

---

[67] R. Morghen, *Medioevo cristiano* (Bari, 1951), p. 6.
[68] *Ibid.*, p. 362.

were gradually used with the aim of reaching below the surface of a confusing series of events, in order to grasp a broad encounter between structured forces; in their turn, these forces can be unified to exemplify, in the arena of Italy, a phase in the formation and development of the European West. This unification can also incorporate moments when the disintegration of institutional frameworks paradoxically coincided with economic recovery, or the triumph of civic initiative with the development of ecclesiastical conformism. But if the medieval cosmos is open to any definition at all, the problem ought instead to be resolved by observing the real situation, shot through with experiments in contradictory directions, and a society that failed to co-ordinate itself except within a roughly-outlined system; this system, always fluid and open, is that of permanently unstable structures in perennial conflict. One might object that this could in fact be a definition of the tormented modern world, particularly in its most recent and enterprising phases. So we will say that the Middle Ages is the inchoate, endemically violent expression of a co-existence between highly malleable forces, which interact among themselves but cannot be organized into a system or understood through a summary description. We need a method of presenting the Middle Ages that would gradually approach it through one of its dimensions, drawing the other aspects into that one but without attempting to make an impossible reduction to some 'whole', whose supposed unity cannot be described. This method is certainly a valid approach for any historical period, but must necessarily be applied above all where a unique multi-directional and voluntaristic dynamism such as this has developed, a dynamism which attained a clear self-awareness in the modern world.

An anticipation of this later process can be pointed out by following the internal dynamics of medieval Christianity, which dramatically acquired self-awareness at the ecclesiological level, in that tireless religious reflection which Raoul Manselli interprets in terms of eschatology,[69] a voluntary projection of the self towards a goal indefinitely far away, and which Ovidio Capitani has felicitously described as 'awareness of the system'.[70] It must be borne in mind,

[69] Of particular significance in this respect is R. Manselli, *La 'Lectura super Apocalipsim' di Pietro di Giovanni Olivi. Ricerche sull'escatologismo medioevale* (Rome, 1955).

[70] O. Capitani, 'Impressioni sullo stato della storia della Chiesa medioevale in Italia', *Convegno dell'Associazione dei medioevalisti italiani (Roma 1975)* (Bologna, 1976), pp. 59ff, reprinted in *Forme di potere e struttura sociale in Italia nel medioevo*, ed. G. Rossetti (Bologna, 1977), with the title 'Storia ecclesiastica come storia della "coscienza di sistema"', pp. 46ff. See O. Capitani, 'Crisi

however, that the ethos of the Middle Ages was something quite different from this religious desire. The system whose awareness was expressed through ecclesiastical institutions, eschatological doctrines and great spiritual upheavals, coincides only in part with the cosmos of the Middle Ages, which included the strong autonomous tendencies of economic changes, political affirmation, intellectual curiosity and aesthetic sensitivity, dimensions which cannot be reduced to an ethical–religious tension in the community, and which have their own internal logic. To be sure, all these dimensions were in different ways conditioned by the presence of the ecclesiastical system but at the same time they all interfered in that system with their own reasons for existence, so much so that the ecclesiastical system became more complex and moved towards wealth, power, hedonistic and intellectual indulgence, purposes extraneous and opposed to its Christian core. In each of these dimensions the Middle Ages revealed its own particular voluntaristic tensions, the initiatives of classes and groups which were in various ways and to various extents outside or rebelling against the official 'system', and which were all destined one day to express their extraneous character or rebellion with complete self-awareness.

In the last thirty years, it is true, Cinzio Violante has continually struggled for a completely comprehensive history,[71] explicitly appealing to the globalizing ambitions of Volpe and the historiographical revival encouraged in France by the foundation of the *Annales* (1929; the journal of Marc Bloch and Lucien Febvre, culturally related to Henri Berr's *Révue de synthèse historique*, which was already in existence at the beginning of the century[72]); he has sought to combine these historiographical bases with a proposed interpretation of the Middle Ages which is globally Catholic. But this struggle has settled into an invitation to explore the Italian Middle Ages in the multiplicity of its aspects, with the seriousness of methods derived from European experience. So too, in a wider cultural framework, the great debate of the *Annales* appears today ever more open to every form of intellectual curiosity about the past, and ever more committed to a bold encounter with the methodologies of all the 'human sciences'. Obviously such an openness, heralded in various ways for more than two centuries, cannot help but include in the study of every individual aspect of the past the

---

epistemologica e crisi di identità: appunti sulla ateoricità di una medievistica', in *A Gustavo Vinay* (Spoleto, 1977), p. 446 note 51 (*Studi medievali*, ser. III, 18.2 (1977), p. 1,012 note 51).

[71] See O. Capitani, 'Crisi epistemologica', pp. 439ff.

[72] M. Cedronio, F. Diaz, C. Russo, *Storiografia francese di ieri e di oggi*, with an introduction by M. Del Treppo (Naples, 1977), pp. ixff, 15ff.

reference to its multiple connections, but (and this is the point which demands greater clarity) it must not confuse the developments that gradually intertwine in the Middle Ages, in the illusion that it possesses the ideological key to open the secrets of the 'whole'.

In this respect it is significant that not long ago Pierre Toubert (the author of a recent systematic study of Lazio from the ninth to the twelfth centuries with a declared aim of an inclusive history, realized through an extremely rigorous analysis of the most disparate structures of the region and their reciprocal influences[73]) felt the need to reflect further, with Jacques Le Goff, on the possibility of an 'histoire totale du moyen âge'. He had identified this possibility in the free choice of an historical phenomenon which functioned in a given area of the European Middle Ages in such a broad and profound connection with the others that it assumes the role of a 'phénomène globalisant'.[74] In the case of Lazio, for the central centuries of the Middle Ages, the phenomenon chosen by Toubert was the *incastellamento*; this is not, one should note, a structure that can be conceived as an essential constituent in the development of human society, but rather an empirical fact of such exceptional dimensions that it visibly involves the most diverse structural developments and signals their interdependence. The thought may occur that, at its extreme limit, such a conception of global history can also lead to the rehabilitation of the events characteristic of the old annalistic accounts, since it might be possible to identify an event of great importance which, when attentively analysed, would permit one to see the most diverse structures of a society operating around it as it took place. In the same way one might also be able to restore the description of a single well-documented personality, insofar as his experience shows culture and mentality concretely at work, the material conditions of life, and the whole historically-determined world. This world would at the same time have to be examined in other studies juxtaposed and connected among themselves, still with that flexible criterion of globality which allows one to set a particular development in the foreground as the specific object. In fact Toubert, in building up his exemplary work on Lazio, undertook a series of studies parallel to that on *incastellamento*, each with its own relative autonomy and different

[73] P. Toubert, *Les Structures du Latium médiéval. Le Latium méridional et la Sabine du IXe siècle à la fin du XIIe siècle*, 2 vols. (Rome, 1973). See the review by G. Tabacco in *Studi medievali*, ser. III, 15 (1974), pp. 901–18.

[74] J. Le Goff, P. Toubert, 'Une Histoire totale du moyen âge est-elle possible?', *Actes du 100e Congrès national des Sociétés savantes (Paris 1975), Section de philologie et d'histoire jusqu'à 1610, 1: Tendances, perspectives et méthodes de l'histoire médiévale* (Paris, 1977), p. 37.

temporal rhythms, studies which obviously can be carried out by different scholars at different times.[75]

In short, after so much disdain for research of too definite a nature, the historian is recovering his entire freedom in the name of a global history interpreted in this way, as long as his chosen object of study has an appropriate intrinsic wealth of cultural correlations. The ambitious extension of the field of enquiry, desired and in various ways attempted for centuries in order to comprehend totally the development of the human condition, has revealed in man a plurality which cannot be summarized in a unifying structure, but rather one which can be considered dialectically from different angles in its complex diversity. Certainly the emergence of hegemonic social classes and of institutionalized powers, chosen as the object of the present study, offers a felicitous point of observation for an overall vision, if it is not adopted as an exclusive point of view but accepted with all its particular details, rich in the correlations from among which the kernel must be extracted. A greater problem is the choice of geographical framework. Italy is a region historically highly differentiated between north and south, precisely on the socio-political level. The focus of historiographical interest has always been northern Italy, which participated directly in the travails of power in mainland Europe; but the south, constantly in equilibrium between Europe and the East, has finally in the last century attracted greater attention from European historiography, through the influence of the involvement of the Germanic world and the kingdom of France in the events of the medieval Mediterranean. The first major works published in the first decade of this century followed the prevailing interest in political narration and institutional analysis; Jules Gay on Byzantine domination in the Italian Mezzogiorno, Ferdinand Chalandon and Erich Caspar on the Norman domination and the foundation of the Kingdom of Sicily, Edouard Jordan on the origins of the Angevin domination. It has now become possible to present the Italian Middle Ages in contrapuntal form between north and south. We will play on this contrapuntal theme to make one history of Italy out of the two histories which in the Middle Ages attracted to themselves the most vigorous European forces and today attract the interest of the most vigorous historical writing.

[75] See J. Le Goff, P. Toubert, 'Une Histoire totale', p. 41.

I

ITALY IN THE DECLINE OF THE EMPIRE

At the opening of the imperial period Italy was emerging, within the context of the Roman ascendancy, with its own clear political individuality even though composed of a multitude of peoples. When considered as corresponding to the present mainland peninsula, Italy was the sole region of the Empire in which the whole free population, rather than certain individuals or particular collective bodies, enjoyed Roman citizenship and escaped organization into provinces. Italy was the aggregate of those peoples who, as heirs and continuators of the *populus Romanus*, formally held dominion over the world that focused on the Mediterranean. In reality, at the political level this dominion was summarized in the participation in the active political life of the Empire of two social orders prominent among the *cives Romani* for their wealth and explicit official recognition, the senatorial and the equestrian orders. The analysis of these orders, their ties with the military power of the prince and with the bureaucracy that worked in the shadow of that power, is a prerequisite for understanding the strong social and political significance of the imperial power-structure, and thus for understanding the significance on Italian soil of the powerful Roman–Italic system within that construct and in furtherance of it. This was the system that, when institutionally and culturally complemented by a Catholic framework and sustained by a new Germanic military apparatus, persisted under the early 'barbarian' regimes with undiminished effectiveness.

The senatorial order was not just a hegemonic social class. It was defined through an organ still politically central in the first three centuries of the Empire, the Senate of Rome, access to which was normally through a traditional *cursus honorum*, a career of magistracies of Republican origin and of Roman civic character, from the quaestorship to the consulate. The Senate itself, under imperial control, made elections to these magistracies, principally elevating from among the members of families distinguished by a very high tax assessment the sons of the senators themselves. This was not a matter of individual abuse; it was due to the obligation laid on sons of senators, with few exceptions, to present themselves as candidates at the elections, and the regular custom that they should be successful.[1] Recruitment to the Senate thus happened by a system midway between co-optation and inheritance, a system further complicated by the frequent injections of *homines novi* through personal decisions of the emperor. The Senate thus composed expressed the continuity of a narrow aristocracy, initially almost completely Italian (there were 600 members of the Augustan Senate at the beginning of the Imperial period, in comparison with several million *cives Romani*[2] and tens of millions of subjects in the whole imperial territory), an aristocracy sustained by a strong economic base of landed property, which was gradually supplemented by new elements chosen by the emperor and was sometimes reduced by the ruler's persecutions.

This aristocracy, which by the nature of its immense wealth supplied a considerable portion of the rural population with a social framework,

---

[1] It is usual, on the basis of certain sources, to distinguish as far back as the early Empire between the *ordo senatorius* and the *Senatus*, since the *laticlavium*, the broad purple stripe that marked the tunic worn by senators, was also allowed to the sons of senators (and those whom the emperor ranked as such) even before they entered the magistracy or the Senate (O'Brien Moore, 'Senatus', in Pauly-Wissowa, *Real-Encyclopädie der classichen Altertumswissenschaft*, supplement VI (Stuttgart, 1935) col. 761; F. De Martino, *Storia della costituzione romana*, vol. 4.1 (Naples, 1962), p. 462–4). But it is also known that the sons of senators, before they took part in the Senate, were considered as knights (A. Stein, *Der römische Ritterstand* (Munich, 1927), p. 189, O'Brien Moore, 'Senatus', and De Martino, *Storia della costituzione romana*, p. 473), and therefore members of the *ordo* that is alleged to have been officially distinct from the senatorial one. Thus the idea of an *ordo senatorius* broader than the Senate was not always very clear and in any case included only the Senate and those who were destined for it.

[2] S. Mazzarino, *L'Impero romano*, vol. 2 of G. Giannello and S. Mazzarino, *Trattato di storia romana*, 2nd ed. (Rome, 1963), p. 35 note 1.

at the same time represented in its complex intellectual formation a type of elite culture which characterized the unity of the Empire. In addition it was present in many political and administrative contexts according to well-determined customs, reflecting the ad hoc origins of the imperial constitution. From the aristocracy were drawn the proconsuls which the Senate itself, not without some interference from the emperor, placed in charge of a dozen 'senatorial' provinces with powers of civil administration and jurisdiction: Sicily, sometimes Corsica and Sardinia, and other regions of the Empire, mostly those completely pacified. From the same aristocracy were drawn the *legati Augusti*, representatives of the ruler in the military and civil government of other provinces with a chiefly military character, the 'imperial' rather than senatorial provinces whose number was increasing in the first and second centuries.[3] Only a few imperial provinces were entrusted by the emperor to governors not of the senatorial class, such as the powerful prefect of Egypt, and the prefects and procurators of culturally backward provinces, such as those in northern Italy, of the Maritime Alps, the Cottian Alps, Rhaetia and Noricum; however some of these provinces, first entrusted to procurators, were later also put under the control of legates of the senatorial class, as was the case with Noricum from the end of the second century.[4] One may add to this that not only the legates in charge of military provinces but also the *praefectus urbi* placed by the emperor in charge of policing the city of Rome, and all the *legati legionis* (representatives of the ruler in command of individual legions, with the exception of the legions stationed in Egypt and later also in Mesopotamia, which were entrusted to prefects from outside the Senate), belonged to the senatorial class during the early Empire and until after the middle of the third century. And the emperor himself, in the first two centuries, was normally of senatorial extraction.

And so while the Senate, as the official organ of government, came to find itself in a position of serious weakness when faced with the military strength of the ruler and the broad range of his political action, the power of the ruler in its turn could not find expression without extensive recourse to the members of the Senate, whose composition was not the result of pure imperial will, as the large number of senators of senatorial

---

[3] W. Eck, *Senatoren von Vespasian bis Hadrian* (Munich, 1970).

[4] G. Winkler, *Die Reichsbeamten von Noricum und ihr Personal bis zum Ende der römischen Herrschaft* (Vienna, 1969), p. 75. More generally, see H. G. Pflaum, *Les Procurateurs équestres sous le Haut-Empire Romain* (Paris, 1950), and, by the same author, the reconstruction of the individual careers of knights up to Gallienus in three volumes with an appendix of tables, *Les Carrières procuratoriennes équestres sous le Haut-Empire Romain* (Paris, 1960–1).

origin makes clear.[5] This restriction on the supreme political action was
sharply felt by the emperors, who, although they remained convinced
of the irreplaceable central role of the Senate in the Roman state
tradition, gradually constructed their own central and peripheral
bureaucracy, for the most part drawing its middle and upper grades
from the equestrian order, a social class which also sprang from the civic
structure of Rome but was never given voice in an autonomous political
organ.

The knightly stratum had arisen from the need for a military
organization of the Roman people on the basis of tax-assessment, and
had subsequently marked itself out as a social order separate from the
senatorial aristocracy by an economic base that was only partly formed
by landed property, supported by the commercial and financial
speculations that were formally forbidden to senators. But at the
beginning of the Empire the equestrian order too was now mainly a
landed aristocracy, although it lacked an hereditary character since entry
was solely by the decision of the prince, even though the prince's
attention in the choice of candidates qualified by assessed wealth, free
birth and approved morals was turned above all to the sons of knights.[6]
So it was chiefly recruited from among the eminent families of the
Italian cities (*municipia*), and therefore from the heart of those local
aristocracies on whom depended the autonomous administration of the
cities and which through their Roman citizenship were at the same time
members of the people which was officially responsible for the Empire.
The recruitment of the equestrian order, precisely since it was founded
on the free choice of the ruler rather than on the Republican traditions
of the Roman magistracies, made the order a more socially representative
class than was the Senate, a class able to adapt more rapidly to the
evolution of relations between Italy and the provinces of the Empire.
But even so it was still a very limited order (of some thousands of
privileged persons) in comparison with the free population of Italy and
the provinces, an order that was hierarchically superimposed, alongside
the Senate, over the immense variety of social groups and peoples that
made up the Empire.

From the equestrian order the emperor drew the prefects and
procurators to whom he entrusted the provinces not governed by

[5] This was still the case in the third century. G. Barbieri, *L'albo senatorio da
Settimio Severo a Carino (193–285)* (Rome, 1952), pp. 474–518, 529–32.

[6] Stein, *Der römische Ritterstand*, pp. 72–5, 175–86. For an updating on the
problems concerning the class of knights, see L. Ruggini, 'Esperienze
economiche e sociali nel mondo romano', in *Nuove questioni di storia antica*
(Milan, 1968), pp. 725–34.

proconsuls of the Senate or by *legati Augusti*, the procurators whom he sent to senatorial and imperial provinces with fiscal duties, the prefect in charge of provisioning Rome, the office-holders of the prince's court, and the larger part of the army's officials in each grade up to the praetorian prefects who commanded the personal guard of the emperor. Eventually the equestrian order appeared socially almost identical to that part of the administrative and military apparatus of the Empire which formed the bureaucracy and the personal power-base of the emperor, and which expressed the orientation of imperial power in the most severely monarchical direction, concomitant with the declining authority of the Senate.

This decline of the Senate was in reality above all a great process of transformation of the stratum which was still the highest in imperial society, the stratum which was to experience remarkable metamorphoses even after the end of the Empire and which in its landed base and seigneurial development was to form the model for the aristocracies which dominated the European Middle Ages. When the Emperor Gallienus (253–68) excluded senators from the command of legions in favour of the equestrian class, so making the military condition of all the provinces comparable with that of Egypt and Mesopotamia,[7] the ruin of the Senate appeared imminent. Then when at the end of the third century Diocletian eliminated the division between senatorial and imperial provinces and extended provincial government to the whole of Italy, placing all areas under two distinct hierarchies of civil and military officials, it seemed that perfection had been attained in the hierarchical bureaucratic construct culminating in the emperor, which had until then been limited by senatorial authority, and in the civil and political levelling of the subjects which had been heralded in 212 by the extension of Roman citizenship to almost the whole population of the Empire. Yet it was then that the two supreme classes, traditionally juxtaposed, revealed their social potential. The equestrian order, precisely in the period in which it attained its greatest political extension, entered a period of crisis as a class distinct from the senatorial aristocracy. In the course of the fourth century it was fading away; but this was as a result of its absorption into the senatorial tradition, to which it brought fresh vigour.[8]

To understand this event, rich in consequences over later centuries,

---

[7] R. Grosse, *Römische Militärgeschichte von Gallienus bis zum Beginn der byzantischen Themenverfassung* (Berlin, 1920), pp. 3–11.

[8] See C. Lécrivain, *Le Sénat romain depuis Dioclétien à Rome et à Constantinople* (Paris, 1888), pp. 50, 57; Stein, *Der römische Ritterstand*, pp. 455ff, 464ff; O'Brien Moore, 'Senatus', col. 796.

we should consider the continuing social prestige of the senatorial order, which in comparison with the equestrian order appeared from the Republican era onwards as a nobility whose stability was guaranteed by its identification with an autonomous organ, which had its seat in Rome and which was a symbol of the whole Roman tradition. Certainly, throughout the whole early Empire knights and sons of knights were already being admitted to the senatorial order by the emperor's specific decision.[9] This was undoubtedly the result of the imperial interest in supplementing the Senate by adding loyal elements; at the same time, though, it corresponded to the aspirations of those who distinguished themselves in the service of the emperor and derived from the conviction of the emperor himself that what was necessary to the Empire was a Senate in which the 'equestrian' tradition of loyalty to a personal and military power of monarchical significance would be grafted on to an autonomous aristocratic structure, a permanent organization of interests which had been summoned to represent 'civil' society.

Thus we can understand how Constantine, at the foundation of Constantinople in 330, also founded a second Senate. By this time the bureaucratic apparatus had attained such density and organic unity that it allowed the monarch to restore, without risk, to an hereditary aristocratic class which was divided between the two Senates of Rome and Byzantium, its traditional task of co-ordinating the privileges of a stable landed wealth and high culture with the functioning of the imperial government. It came about that civil government of the provinces and the high grades of central administration were increasingly assigned to the senatorial class.[10] In the course of the fourth century the latter was rigidly divided into three ranks, called by titles that had already appeared in the early Empire, the *viri clarissimi*, the *viri spectabiles* and the *viri illustres* (in increasing order of importance), ranks which corresponded to the three categories (with identical names) into which the whole upper hierarchy of public officials was dividing with increasing clarity. But this correspondence of titles had a complex significance.

The ever more systematic linking of the high ranks of government and administration with the three classes of the Senate in fact signifies

---

[9] Stein, *Der römische Ritterstand*, pp. 213–362; Barbieri, *L'albo senatorio*, pp. 533–42.

[10] See the senatorial careers of the fourth century in A. Chastagnol, *La Préfecture urbaine à Rome sous le Bas-Empire* (Paris, 1960), pp. 391–449. More generally, on the constitution of the Empire in the fifth century see De Martino, *Storia della costituzione romana*, vol. 5 (Naples 1967).

above all that the emperor surrendered his aim to set up a bureaucratic class more directly tied to himself, in opposition to the senatorial aristocracy. But by that decision itself a prevalently bureaucratic hierarchy, controlled by the imperial will, was introduced into the Senate. This was technically possible since it was provided that the status of *clarissimus* received at birth by sons of senators should not only open the Senate to them (always through some magistracy with an old Republican name, though now without any real content) but should also be a valid title for entering on a high bureaucratic career. Vice versa, the status of *clarissimus* connected with certain ranks of the upper bureaucracy would confer the right on one who was not already a senator to enter into the Senate and remain there permanently. As for the higher rank of the *spectabiles* and the highest one of the *illustres*, these normally presupposed the status of *clarissimus* (in whatever way it had been acquired) and they could be obtained, with the usual exception of particular imperial concessions, through the highest responsibilities of government and office-holding. Such procedures made superfluous the traditional intervention of the prince to promote to the senatorial order individual knights who had particularly distinguished themselves in imperial service, and they guaranteed, for whomever reached certain high public responsibilities, entry into that senatorial aristocracy which had always been the target of the social rise of the great. The expansion of the senatorial order in the upper imperial bureaucracy (at any given moment the number of members of the Senate of Constantinople was not less than 2,000, and the same was probably true by now of the Senate of Rome) converged with the ambitions of the equestrian order, at its upper levels, to enter into a nobility which was marked out by its hereditary organization into a solemn assembly.[11] Thus the senatorial aristocracy of the late Empire can be said to be the result of the confluence around, and in apposition to, the monarchical power, of the two most vigorous political and social traditions of the early Empire.

The traditions that we have just discussed corresponded in the early imperial period with the hegemony of Italy over the peoples of the Empire. But through the centuries this hegemony was decreasing, through the attenuation and eventual suppression of tax exemptions, judicial autonomy and military privileges for Italy, with the growing introduction of provincial elements into the equestrian order and the Senate itself, with the extension of Roman citizenship to almost all the free men of the Empire, and finally with the application to Italy, in the

---

[11] For the dynamics of the Senate in the late Empire, see A. H. M. Jones, *The Later Roman Empire* (Oxford, 1964), vol. 2, pp. 523–62.

civil administration, of a division into provinces just like that of the non-Italian regions.[12] In the fourth century, and up until the beginning of the fifth, a *vicarius Italiae* had his seat at Milan, with authority over between four and seven civil governors of the provinces making up northern Italy and Rhaetia (between the Alps and the Danube). In a parallel fashion, even after the fall of the Empire a *vicarius urbis* resided at Rome, and subordinate to him were a dozen governors of the peninsular and insular provinces of Italy (the so-called suburbicarian provinces) who had the task of supplying the city, while northern Italy was burdened by the military *annona*, the contribution in kind for the armies accompanying the emperor. The two vicars were in their turn subordinate to the praetorian prefect of Italy, who was also in charge of several provinces to the east of the Italian vicariate and on the north coast of Africa. He was one of the four praetorian prefects who had been responsible for supervising the civil administration of the four quarters into which the Empire had been divided, since the time of Diocletian and Constantine; at that time the praetorian cohorts which once guarded the prince had shrunk and then disappeared, and the role of praetorian prefect had definitively lost its original military character, developing instead to their extreme certain duties of a judicial and financial nature.

None the less, in Italy there remained the most conspicuous exception to the normal order of the Empire, linked both with the significance of Rome and with the new settlement reached by the senatorial aristocracy in the West with respect to the monarch. Abandoned by the emperors and their court, Rome in the late Empire consolidated its own particular administrative regime. It was not part of any province, even though it was the seat of the *vicarius urbis* to whom many Italian provinces were subordinate. It was not subject directly or indirectly to the praetorian prefect of Italy. It continued to come under the particular authority of the *praefectus urbis*, the high official of senatorial rank in charge of all the services of the populous city (which had some hundreds of thousands of inhabitants) and of its ports at the mouth of the Tiber, who was therefore the highest official and responsible for both the Roman police and the administration of civil justice in the city. Indeed the criminal and civil jurisdiction of the urban prefect extended well beyond the walls of

---

[12] L. Cantarelli, 'La diocesi italiana da Diocleziano alla fine dell'Impero occidentale', *Studi e documenti di storia e diritto*, 22–4 (1901–3); R. Thomsen, *The Italic Regions from Augustus to the Lombard Invasion* (Copenhagen, 1947), pp. 311–16; Chastagnol, *La Préfecture urbaine*, pp. 26–42; L. Ruggini, *Economia e società nell' 'Italia annonaria'* (Milan, 1961), pp. 1–4; De Martino, *Storia della costituzione romana*, vol. 5, pp. 281–4.

Rome, for a radius of a hundred miles, thus notably restricting the jurisdiction of the praetorian prefect of Italy and his subordinate officials, not to mention the urban prefect's appellate jurisdiction, which often extended further than the district of a hundred miles and involved all the provinces dependent on the vicar resident in Rome.[13]

Certainly the prefect of Rome was named by the emperor, a fact which in one respect was the more serious in that he was not only the normal judge of the senators but presided over the Senate and supervised its recruitment. This recruitment, although it took place above all on the criteria of heredity or high bureaucratic position which have already been discussed, did not exclude the introduction of members who were not members of the clarissimate, by virtue of individual imperial decisions (which from the time of Constantine were preceded by a proposal presented by the Senate to the monarch). But the imperial nomination of the urban prefect, this powerful personage who, from his seat in the city, conditioned the life of the Empire's aristocracy, was rarely made without the agreement of the senatorial order. He was usually a senator who had arrived in the Senate through the hereditary status of *clarissimus* and was often a member of a great family of the city, even if he had recently been promoted by imperial favour through a career of governorships or in the central bureaucracy until he reached the peak of such a career with the prefecture of Rome itself. So he represented most visibly the necessary bond between the monarchical power and the aristocracy organized in the Senate of Rome, and through certain of his attributes, radiating out from Rome to more or less extensive areas of Italy, he attested to the continuing tie between the idea of the Empire and the hegemonic role of the city which had founded it.

GERMANIC EXPANSION WITHIN THE ITALIAN POLITICAL
SYSTEM OF THE FIFTH CENTURY

After its gradual levelling to the status of the other provinces, Italy from the fifth century onwards was once more destined to take on an autonomous political appearance with respect to the other parts of the world once unified by Rome, as a result of the disintegration of the West provoked by the Germanic peoples. This form of autonomy was entirely different from that of centuries before, since it was founded no longer on the privilege and dominion exercised by the upper classes of Italy in the whole Mediterranean basin but rather on the convergence of

[13] Chastagnol, *La Préfecture urbaine*, pp. 84–136.

and competition between a particular Germanic element and the senatorial aristocracy most closely tied to Rome.

In fact it so happened that in the fourth and fifth centuries the disappearance of the old formal dualism between the hegemonic classes of senators and knights was accompanied by the formation of a much more serious rivalry within the Roman state framework, between the military fortunes of the Germanic leaders and groups and the authority and political control still held by senators and bureaucrats. The emperor, with his officially despotic power consecrated by rites and ideologies of Oriental origin, found himself at the head of a profoundly heterogeneous apparatus in which, together with certain compromises at the highest level, there appeared entirely new antipathies reflecting tensions and contradictions different from those traditional to the complex society of the Empire.

Ethnic and cultural antagonism was grafted on to the separation between the careers of military and civil officials, which had been unknown at the time of the growing fortunes of the equestrian order. The Constantinian restoration of the senatorial order to the upper bureaucratic hierarchy was in fact accompanied by the expansion of the Germanic element in the army, both among the *limitanei*, restricted to the border provinces, and among the *comitatenses*, the important new tactical forces created within the Empire which were at more immediate imperial disposition.[14] This resulted from a recruitment which increasingly took place not only among the barbarian groups welcomed or introduced – sometimes with the aim of repopulation[15] – on the Roman side of the frontiers, but above all among the populations settled beyond the Rhine and Danube, peoples either bordering on the Empire and bound to it by a treaty or wholly free and extraneous to the Empire.[16] In reality the general rules of recruitment into the army provided that soldiers should be procured, in parallel with the exaction of other taxes, from large and small landed proprietors, the latter being grouped so that the obligation to supply one or more recruits fell jointly on a consortium of people. Thus the burden fell on the peasant

---

[14] D. Van Berchem, *L'Armée de Dioclétien et la réforme constantinenne* (Paris, 1952), pp. 108–18; E. Gabba, 'Considerazioni sugli ordinamenti militari del tardo impero', in *Ordinamenti militari in Occidente nell'alto medioevo* (Spoleto, 1968), vol. I, pp. 77–80.

[15] L. Ruggini, 'Uomini senza terra e terra senza uomini nell' Italia antica', *Quaderni di sociologia rurale*, 3.2–3 (1963), pp. 20–41; Demougeot, *La Formation de l'Europe et les invasions barbares*, vol. I, pp. 539–50.

[16] J. Vogt, *Constantin der Grosse und sein Jahrhundert*, 2nd ed. (Munich, 1960), pp. 234ff.

population, above all on the dependent *coloni*, and in time the service imposed on the soldiers stretched to twenty years, with an associated tendency, particularly among the *limitanei*, for it to become an hereditary obligation. But instead of men the great landowner or the consortium could offer a sum of money which would allow the official responsible for recruitment to procure soldiers elsewhere, and this was the path which favoured the growing recourse to Germanic elements, who were more readily disposed to enlist.[17]

Since the Germanic soldiers, in comparison with those supplied by landed proprietors as a tax obligation, also displayed good military qualities, and the Roman army also accepted Germans already accustomed to command in their own tribes, the presence of this element in the imperial army took on an importance which was not simply numerical.[18] In the course of the fourth century the proportion of military officials of barbarian origin, compared with those from the upper classes of the Empire or veterans promoted from among the rural recruits, continued to increase. They even rose to the highest grades; they became ever more numerous among the *duces*, to whom was assigned above all the military command of regions near the borders, and they also became supreme commanders, *magistri peditum* and *magistri equitum*, subordinate only to the emperor. From the second half of the fourth century, thanks to the incorporation of high military grades into the hierarchy of offices, the *duces* acquired the dignity of *clarissimi* and then of *spectabiles*, and the *magistri militum* that of *illustres*, so Germans also entered into the Senate. Reactions varied. The great senatorial families on the whole did not disdain to extend to these Germans, powerful in the imperial court and through the economic resources that followed as a result, the alliances, including marriages, with which they customarily reinforced each other. The assimilation of Germans with senatorial rank into the aristocracy of the Empire might therefore appear complete. But their origin was not forgotten, because it put them in a special relationship with respect to all the Germanic groups not assimilated by the Empire, who were present in conspicuous numbers in the armed forces, and with whole populations which were alternately allies and enemies of the Empire.

This happened everywhere – in the West, the East, and also in Italy.

---

[17] S. Mazzarino, *Aspetti sociali del IV secolo* (Rome, 1951), pp. 271–344; Gabba, *Considerazioni*, pp. 85–90.

[18] Liebenam, 'Exercitus', in Pauly-Wissowa, *Real-Encyclopädie der classischen Altertumswissenschaft*, supplement VI.2 (Stuttgart, 1909), coll. 1626–9; Grosse, *Römische Militärgeschichte*, p. 257; E. Stein, *Histoire du Bas-Empire*, French edition ed. J. R. Palanque, vol. I (Bruges, 1959), p. 124.

In the 380s, at the time of Theodosius the Great, Emperor in the East, when several emperors disputed control of the West, eminent military men of Germanic stock worked by their side, at the head of armies mainly constituted of Germanic soldiers. In a political framework with a tradition – particularly dramatically demonstrated for most of the third century – of decisive intervention by military forces in the crises of the central power, the preponderance of the Germanic element (now well-established in large sectors of the army) was to alter profoundly the interplay of social forces which influenced the actions of the monarch, even though that interplay still tended to follow the broad path offered by the senatorial tradition, bringing a powerful Germanic stratum into convergence with that same path. One of the Roman commanders of Germanic stock who had aided Theodosius the longest, the Frank Arbogast, was appointed *magister peditum praesentalis* (that is, head of the army in the imperial presence) in Gaul at the side of Theodosius' young colleague Valentinian II Emperor of the West, and proceeded to fill not only the high military ranks but even the civil bureaucracy with Franks. In 392, faced with Valentinian's reaction, he caused the emperor's death and had the army proclaim as emperor a court functionary, Eugenius, former professor of rhetoric at Rome, who had risen to high office under Valentinan precisely through the support of his Frankish friends. Eugenius then came to Italy and gained the support of the large and influential sector of the Romano-Italic aristocracy which was still faithful to paganism; he accepted their request to re-establish the altar of Victory in the Senate, restored to non-Christian senators goods confiscated from the old temples, and named as prefect of Rome a typical representative of this powerful group, Nicomachus Flavianus the Younger, son of the praetorian prefect of Italy and son-in-law of Symmachus the great orator.[19]

Nothing is more significant than this convergence between representatives of the pure aristocratic Roman culture and tradition and a Frankish military commander surrounded, in the army and the imperial court, by men of his own race. A similar convergence and similar tensions were repeated, in a different form, in the period of Stilicho. He was the son of a Vandal who had served the Empire in the command of Germanic militias and he pursued a Roman military career to its highest

---

[19] A. Piganiol, *L'Empereur Constantin* (Paris, 1932), pp. 261–8; Stein, *Histoire du Bas-Empire*, vol. i, pp. 210–18; Chastagnol, *La Préfecture urbaine*, pp. 163ff; ibid., *Les Fastes de la préfecture de Rome au Bas-Empire* (Paris, 1962), pp. 239–44; H. Bloch, 'La rinascita pagana in Occidente alla fine del secolo iv', in *Il conflitto tra paganesimo e cristianesimo nel secolo IV*, ed. A. Momigliano (Turin, 1968), pp. 201–24.

rank, collaborating with Theodosius in the latter's last years at both the military and political levels. His marriage with a niece of Theodosius represented the surmounting at the highest social level of all ethnic prejudice. At the emperor's death in 395, Stilicho found himself protecting the succession of Theodosius' second son, the young Honorius, to imperial power in the West; in fact he was the lord of the Western Empire, exercising his dictatorship over the imperial court resident at Milan and then at Ravenna on the basis of the military power that he possessed as *magister utriusque militiae*.

To sustain and justify itself this military dictatorship needed to collaborate with the Senate of Rome. At a moment in which the imperial power was weakened through its passage to a boy, a Vandal sustained by the greatest military prestige, and by an army now in great part Germanic, inherited the substance of the monarchical power of Constantine and Theodosius, the supreme military and political responsibility, and the concomitant necessity to establish a bond with the prominent forces of 'civil' society. Faced by an aristocracy ever more divided by religious conflict, the problem was one of choice. Theodosius himself had hesitated in Italy between the aristocracy which was strongly represented by the Catholic episcopate (led by St Ambrosius)[20] and that which was faithful to the ancient rites; he appointed as praetorian prefect Nicomachus Flavianus the Elder, father of Eugenius, prefect of Rome. Eugenius too hesitated in Italy, before choosing the party of the Nicomachi. The religious tolerance exercised by Stilicho for some years is to be explained likewise, pressured as he was by the intransigent Catholics of Milan and concerned not to alienate certain members of the Roman aristocracy; Nicomachus Flavianus the Younger returned in 399 to the prefecture of Rome, and up to 405 had successors who were no less favourable to the ancient rites.[21]

If even this deference towards the Senate and the many merits of his military activity against the barbarian invasions did not save Stilicho, this was because he, a Vandal, also attempted a policy of conciliation with Alaric's Visigoths, in a tradition of openness towards the Germanic population and organic use of their military force which went back in particular to Theodosius. At that time entire barbarian populations, accepted within the borders, had begun to be allowed to keep their own political–military structure and autonomy, so that they were tied to the Empire only with a pact (hence the name *foederati* they were given)

[20] J. Gaudemet, *L'Eglise dans l'empire romain* (Paris, 1958), p. 337.
[21] S. Mazzarino, *Stilicone. La crisi imperiale dopo Teodosio* (Rome, 1942), pp. 231–49; E. Demougeot, *De l'unité à la division de l'empire romain* (Paris, 1951); Chastagnol, *La Préfecture urbaine*, p. 445.

analogous to that which had already bound for some time the peoples settled along the Rhine and Danube borders. Stilicho's policy was to become all the more hated in Italy since at precisely that time a violent anti-Germanic reaction had prevailed in the East, with the massacres of the year 400 and the elimination of barbarians from the government and army. These events had a decisive effect on the destiny of the Byzantine state framework, since in the East, even when the barbarians were again recruited into the army, the state did not return to the Theodosian system; it did not permit, except in the crisis of the end of the fifth century, the presence of autonomous armed peoples in the Empire, and it did not allow the occupation of high military ranks by too many officials of German stock.[22]

In Italy the anti-Germanic reaction[23] could not develop in such a radical fashion. In 408 militias of Roman nationality, incited by a high functionary of Honorius' court who thus translated the hostility felt by the civil bureaucracy of Roman origin towards the top military hierarchy,[24] rebelled; many friends of Stilicho died; Honorius passed to the anti-Germanic party; and Stilicho himself was killed. But in the West the military situation was now entirely different from that of the East. Less than two years before Stilicho's death a great migration of Vandals, Alans and Sueves had crossed the Rhine. They flooded into Gaul just at the moment when in Italy more than 100,000 Goths under Radagaisus, who had penetrated across the Danube and the Alps, had been suppressed and when the Visigoths of Alaric, for decades in motion within the Roman Empire alternately as federates and as a destructive force, were pressing on Italy from the Illyrian border in the east and were negotiating with Stilicho. The murder of Stilicho, with the resulting crisis in the army and uncertainty in the imperial court, left the way open for Alaric's sack of Rome in 410. Thus the first decade of the fifth century sealed the different fates of the two parts of the Empire. The convergence on the West of the barbarian peoples provoked a definitive disruption of the unitary state framework of the regions of Latin culture, when the political apparatus was already internally torn by tensions between Germanic and Roman elements in the army and court, and by the divisions of the senatorial aristocracy of Italy between fidelity to the old cults and adhesion to official Christianity.

[22] G. Ostrogorsky, *Geschichte des byzantinischen Staates*, 2nd ed. (Munich, 1952), p. 45; Stein, *Histoire du Bas-Empire*, vol. 1, pp. 237ff.

[23] L. Ruggini, '"De morte persecutorum" e polemica antibarbarica nella storiografia pagana e cristiana', *Rivista di storia e letteratura religiosa*, 4 (1968), pp. 433–47.

[24] V. A. Sirago, *Galla Placidia e la trasformazione politica dell' Occidente* (Louvain, 1961), pp. 43–72.

Among the regions of the West only Italy, which was in direct contact with the restored imperial apparatus of Byzantium, still seemed open to an anti-Germanic fate. None the less, in the very days of Alaric's advance on Rome, a significant episode heralded a Germanic and military solution of the Italian political problem, a solution that was still both Germanic and senatorial. Alaric induced the Senate to create a new emperor in opposition to Honorius, and the Senate chose the urban prefect Priscus Attalus, an orator and poet of Greco-Oriental origin.[25] When Alaric himself then deposed him, Attalus none the less remained close to him, and later in Gaul he composed an epithalamium for the marriage, celebrated with Roman pomp, between Athaulf, successor of Alaric as leader of the Visigoths, and Galla Placidia, sister of Honorius, captured by the Visigoths in Italy; there in Gaul, at the side of the Romanizer Athaulf, Attalus briefly became emperor again. This double episode in Rome and Gaul is thus a symbol of the convergence between the military and tribal systems of the Germanic peoples and the aristocratic Roman tradition of Italy and Gaul, in the persistent aim to keep alive through the imperial name a political community between the Latin peoples on either side of the Alps.

The history of Galla Placidia was of a complexity in part different from that of Attalus' adventure among the Visigoths, and was broader and richer. It too unwound at first between Italy and Gaul (and in the Iberian peninsula), but later between Ravenna and Byzantium, and ended with the long regency exercised by Galla Placidia in Ravenna for her son the Emperor Valentinian III. At Ravenna, when Valentinian was installed there by a Byzantine army in opposition to John (a high bureaucrat elevated to the Empire by the Roman Senate in 423, in the tradition of Attalus),[26] Galla Placidia represented above all the hegemony of the Eastern Empire; this was an experiment in dynastic autocracy, supported by alliance with an external and anti-Germanic state apparatus, in a direction that would eventually have as its outcome Justinian's conquest of Italy and as a long epilogue the Byzantine presence in many parts of the peninsula for centuries. But in the later part of Galla Placidia's regency and during the rule of Valentinian III the convergence of Roman and barbarian forces was again displayed, following the alternative political direction which was to lead to the regime of Odoacer and the Ostrogothic kingdom of Italy. Between 430 and 454 the convergence was the work above all of Aetius, a military commander of Roman stock and formerly a supporter of John, the emperor desired by the Senate, but it was always set within a complex

[25] Chastagnol, *Les Fastes*, pp. 266–8.
[26] Sirago, *Galla Placidia*, pp. 244–54.

relationship of alliances and containment with respect to the Huns and Germans, according to the schemes of action already tested by Theodosius and Stilicho. Nor did the convergence dissolve into a pure contest of Roman and barbarian military strength. Among the protagonists in the political activity the senatorial presence was always very clearly apparent, whether around Aetius, *magister utriusque militiae*, where Nicomachus Flavianus the Younger once again appeared as praetorian prefect, or around the Emperor Valentinian, particularly in the person of the influential Petronius Maximus who in these years became prefect of Rome and then praetorian prefect of Italy.[27] Divided between different political orientations, the wealthy senatorial aristocracy was profoundly torn between the desire to guarantee their own greatness by the social and economic privileges which gave them force and cohesion, and the need to ensure the operation of, and a broader base for, the imperial apparatus. Under Valentinian, prominent members of the aristocracy promoted legislation which sought to abolish fiscal abuses and to open to the lower bureaucracy the prospect of easier advancement to those higher offices which carried senatorial rank.

After the successive violent deaths of Aetius and Valentinian, in 455 Rome underwent a sack by the Vandals, now firmly settled at Carthage, and saw the islands of Sardinia and Corsica fall into their hands. The peninsula, menaced from the Mediterranean, sought to maintain ties with Gaul and the Germanic peoples settled there. For two decades, in a dizzying series of accords and conflict, the most contradictory relations were woven between the Gallo-Roman aristocracy, the Roman Senate, the Roman military commanders, the emperors at Ravenna and the Germanic peoples who were federates of the Empire in Gaul (Visigoths, Burgundians, Franks), complicated by Byzantine and Vandal interference. At the centre of this highly fluid military and political tangle there stood for sixteen years a Sueve, Ricimer, *magister utriusque militiae* at the side of the emperors of Gallo-Roman, Romano-Italic and Greek origin that he accepted, created and removed at Rome and Ravenna. After Ricimer died in 472 and the last struggles for the throne of Ravenna between Romano-Germanic and Romano-Byzantine forces died away in 476, there was no attempt to create further emperors in Italy. Following the example which Ricimer had already provided for almost two years in his long predominance, a Germanic commander of the Palatine militias, Odoacer, son of a Scirian prince and formerly a colleague of Ricimer, exercised a military dictatorship in Italy for

[27] Stein, *Histoire du Bas-Empire*, vol. 1, pp. 337–42; Chastagnol, *Les Fastes*, pp. 244, 281–6.

thirteen years. He recognized no emperor other than that of the East, and was supported by the military units that hailed him king of the Germanic peoples of Italy and by the collaboration of the Senate of Rome and the bureaucracy of Ravenna.

Compared with the preceding decades these were years of peace for the peninsula – a peace founded on renunciation of any remaining imperial ambitions in favour of links with the stormy affairs of the Roman and Germanic peoples of Gaul, and in particular on an acceptance of the Alps as the natural frontier with the Visigoths of southern Gaul. Meanwhile in the Mediterranean the Vandals, although retaining Sardinia and Corsica, restored to the government of Ravenna control of Sicily, which had been occupied for some years; in the East Dalmatia was reinstated as a dependency of Ravenna after a recent separation; and north of the Alps there was an attempt to maintain control of the countries sloping down towards the Danube. In this Roman area, reduced not only with respect to the much greater extent of the vanished Western Empire but even with respect to the territory controlled by the prefecture of Italy before the Vandal expansion in Africa and the islands, all the central and peripheral institutions of the civil administration of the Empire remained alive, from the praetorian prefect and the prefect of Rome to the ministers in charge of the chancery, finances, and fiscal patrimony, to the upper bureaucracy and governors of all the traditional Italian provinces, and all the lower bureaucracy. And these institutions remained in the hands of functionaries of Roman stock, following the example of the military dictatorships which since the time of Stilicho had so often ruled Italy.[28] The ad hoc regime of Odoacer, disposed to accept the formal supremacy of Byzantium over a confluence of Germanic militias and Romano-Italic bureaucracy, seemed to reconcile all opposition and to respect all the external and internal pressures on Italy: from Visigoths and Vandals to the Eastern Empire, from the bureaucratic and senatorial tradition to the social needs of the military nuclei present in the peninsula, from the

[28] L. M. Hartmann, *Geschichte Italiens im Mittelalter*, vol. 1, 2nd ed. (Gotha, 1923), chapter 1; G. Romano, A. Solmi, *Le dominazioni barbariche in Italia (395–880)* (Milan, 1940), pp. 118–40; L. Schmidt, *Geschichte der deutschen Stämme bis zum Ausgang der Völkerwanderung. Die Ostgermanen* (reprint of 2nd ed., Munich, 1941), pp. 317–36. For Sicily see F. Giunta, *Genserico e la Sicilia* (Palermo, 1958), pp. 45–73. For Sardinia, see P. Meloni, *L'amministrazione della Sardegna da Augusto all' invasione vandalica* (Rome, 1958), pp. 175–9. For the old interpretations of the deposition of Romulus Augustulus, see A. Momigliano, 'La caduta senza rumore di un impero nel 476 d. C.', *Rivista storica italiana*, 85 (1973), pp. 5ff.

organization of the Catholic churches, gravitating in the West towards the Church of Rome, to the Arian Christianity spread among the Germanic peoples. The fact that for more than a decade such an equilibrium was maintained without any imperial presence at Ravenna and without any constitutional definition of the dictator's political and territorial power reveals very clearly the effective forces that had by now exercised hegemony over Italian society for a century, forces and institutions that seemed to calm down and become more moderate in the very moment in which they renounced the struggle for choice and control of an emperor at Ravenna.

SENATORIAL AND GERMANIC HEGEMONY OVER ITALIAN SOCIETY

A clear sign of this meeting of forces was the influence that the senator Basilius, 'sublimis et eminentissimus vir', who was at the same time both praetorian prefect of Italy and official representative of the 'præc-ellentissimus rex' Odoacer, exercised over the election of Pope Felix III, who was the son of a Roman priest of the great senatorial family to which Pope Gregory the Great later belonged.[29] In the course of the fifth century the vestigial loyalty to the ancient religion of Rome had faded away even among the most tenacious senatorial groups, and the urban aristocracy now turned increasing attention to the vigorous ecclesiastical organization which had grown up in the city under imperial protection and which through the merit of Peter and the dignity of Rome (as a constitution of Valentinian III, published to strengthen the disciplinary authority of Pope Leo the Great over the episcopate of Gaul, expressed it in 445), aimed to gather the Western churches around the primacy of jurisdiction of the 'apostolic see'.[30] A parallel aristocratic orientation had been apparent north of the Alps from the fifth century, when the episcopal organization of Gaul had become almost a monopoly of the Gallo-Roman senatorial class. Episcopal rank now entailed many demands in addition to its original pastoral and ritual core: demands for literary and judicial culture, ability to command, capacity to consult with the military and civil powers. It thus appeared the natural conclusion of a coveted *cursus honorum*, whether ecclesiastical

[29] E. Caspar, *Geschichte des Papsttums*, vol. 2 (Tübingen, 1933), pp. 24–6; G. B. Piciotti, 'Sulle relazioni fra re Odoacre e il senato e la chiesa di Roma', *Rivista storica italiana*, ser. v, 4 (1939), pp. 363–86; O. Bertolini, *Roma di fronte a Bisanzio e ai Longobardi*, vol. 9 of *Storia di Roma* (Bologna, 1941), pp. 23–32.
[30] For the significance of Leo the Great's pontificate see Caspar, *Geschichte des Papsttums*, vol. 1 (Tübingen, 1930), pp. 423–564.

or lay, for anyone educated in the arts of rhetoric and law and with experience of high-level diplomacy, in the tradition of the Roman aristocracy.[31]

When one reflects on the progressive subordination of urban and rural populations to an ecclesiastical framework, the multiplication of buildings destined for a fundamentally uniform religious worship, the diffusion and imposition of sacramental and liturgical models which universally articulated the rhythm of time and individual and communal life in harmony with an ever more systematic complex of doctrines,[32] one can understand the significance, for the regulation of all social classes, of the absorption of the highest ecclesiastical dignitaries into the same class that was already identified with the highest ranks of the bureaucratic hierarchy. It was a class now almost defenceless, in Italy as much as in Gaul, but one which was cloaked in such sacred and secular prestige, and permeated by a culture at once so privileged and so easily extensible – through a thousand ecclesiastical adaptations – to the lowest classes, that the military forces avoided opposition to it and sought a political compromise. This happened even where whole Germanic peoples, particularly the Visigoths, had settled in a body within the Roman borders and, dissolving the *foedus* with the Empire, asserted themselves as the race militarily dominant over old imperial territories and their populations; it happened where the senatorial aristocracy, now separated from Rome and the Senate which had up until then co-ordinated them juridically, continued none the less to organize the Roman population under both the civil and ecclesiastical aspects. This was all the more pronounced in Italy, where the formal tie of the great aristocracy with the Senate persisted, and where no Germanic people had settled with its own leaders and social order.

The militias that acclaimed Odoacer as king belonged ethnically to several Germanic peoples and had, up to then, no other unity than the fact that they made up the largest part of the Roman army in Italy. It is true that this acclamation marked their desire to marshal themselves around Odoacer, who would no longer be simply a Roman commander but their own Germanic leader, analogous to the kings who ruled elsewhere over peoples federated with the Empire. But this was not enough to give these few thousand Heruls, Scirians and other Germans of whom Odoacer became king the unity of tribal social order which constituted the strength of individual Germanic peoples. They obtained from Odoacer the allowance (we do not know for what proportion of Italy) of one third of the lands of Roman proprietors, in imitation of

---

[31] K. F. Stroheker, *Der senatorische Adel im spätantiken Gallien* (Tübingen, 1948), pp. 71–5, 92–6, 100–4.   [32] Gaudemet, *L'Eglise*, pp. 515–710.

what had taken place among certain federate groups north of the Alps but presumably with a greater dispersive effect on the small numbers of Odoacer's heterogeneous militias.[33] Certainly such a *hospitalitas* on Roman lands, a Germanic participation in land ownership through the division of the houses, lands, tenants and livestock of each Roman proprietor, instead of a simple quartering in houses with the enjoyment of a military *annona*, oriented the Germanic element towards integration in the Romano-Italic social structure, even though on the other hand the creation of a Germanic royal power, dissociated in Italy from the idea of a territorial kingship independent of the Empire (Odoacer was *rex gentium*, not *rex Italiae*), stressed the separation which was already suggested by ethnic difference, military role and the profession of Christianity according to the precepts of the Arian churches.

The distribution of lands to the Germans was thus the price paid by the Roman proprietors to allow the operation of Odoacer's military regime, a regime which was not at all subversive on either the social or the political and administrative levels. It is possible, anyway, that this distribution fell more heavily on the middle-sized landowners than on the great landed aristocracy, protected by its dominance of high bureaucratic offices. Odoacer practised a most prudent respect towards them and towards their senatorial organization, as is apparent not only in the preservation of the traditional apparatus, the recourse to its members in dealings with Byzantium and the recognition of the importance of the praetorian prefect and Senate in the affairs of the Church of Rome, but also from the concession of privileges, and in particular from archaeological and epigraphical evidence from the Colosseum. In fact the last updating of the inscriptions on the first two tiers of this amphitheatre dates back to the time of Odoacer. These tiers were reserved for senators and their families, and there the names of the *viri illustres*, the *viri spectabiles* and *viri clarissimi* are placed according to their rank, which mostly coincided with their age since the *clarissimi* were mainly the young sons of the *illustres*.[34] Questions of title and precedence had an important place in the somewhat crystallized aristocracy of the late Empire. The commitment to guarantee them their ancient privilege in the amphitheatre was no small sign of the strict formal respect that the Germanic leader and his collaborators showed towards these powerful men.

[33] Piciotti, *Relazioni*, pp. 379ff.; Schmidt, *Geschichte der deutschen Stämme*, pp. 326–8.
[34] A. Chastagnol, *Le Sénat romain sous le règne d'Odoacre. Recherches sur l'épigraphie du Colisée au Ve siècle* (Bonn, 1966).

This was not the power of an impersonal political organ. In the Senate, for some decades now only the *illustres* had voted; nor did all the *illustres* live at Rome and thus have the chance to participate in the Senate's activity. Odoacer and his military successors accorded to the Senate and the senatorial families of Rome a respect and esteem due to the social class into which had flowed all the wealth which had made the senatorial and equestrian orders eminent in Italy throughout the early Empire, sustaining its culture and its attitudes to the civil and ecclesiastical government. It is indeed true that the political and administrative structure of the Roman Empire was always founded on the cities, that the provision of efficient urban services and the adornment of the city with baths, gymnasia and theatres, with temples and the monumental basilicas destined for judicial sessions and commerce, summed up the best of the *civilitas* expressed by the prosperous classes of Italy and the provinces. It is also true that local, regional and imperial trade and associated financial operations were at the root of many fortunes in the urban centres,[35] and that from artisan activity there sprang spontaneously a very rich range of professional associations through which some other fortunes were formed.[36] Yet the dominant object of commerce was agricultural produce, and wealth, however acquired, was transformed largely into investment in land, while the disposable capital of great merchants and shipowners was primarily in land as well.[37] All this had conspired for centuries, within the fabric of economic life and in customary usage, to create the concept that dominion over land and peasants was the foundation of any stable family prosperity and the most coveted means of social ascent. This could be accomplished through the way in which the most prosperous class of proprietors, furnished with rural property and living in the cities, constituted the municipal aristocracy, the class that supplied members of the civic curia and the magistrates elected by the curia. It could be accomplished through the imperial recruitment of *homines novi*, destined for the equestrian order (as long as that order flourished) and for the high state bureaucracy, from that same aristocracy of the cities, and through the subsequent introduction of the most outstanding knights or sons of

[35] M. Rostovzev, *Storia economica e sociale dell'Impero romano* (Florence, 1953), pp. 151–228; Harmand, *L'Occident romain*, pp. 291–353.

[36] L. Ruggini, 'Le associazioni professionali nel mondo romano-bizantino', in *Artigianato e tecnica nella società dell'alto medioevo occidentale* (Spoleto, 1971), pp. 78–134.

[37] M. Rostovzev, *Storia economica e sociale*, pp. 232–47; Ruggini, 'Le associazioni', p. 155 note 189.

knights and the highest non-senatorial bureaucrats in the senatorial order, which was the ultimate goal of individual and family interests and ambitions.

This movement, so intimately associated in its upper levels with the development experienced by the state apparatus over five centuries of the imperial power-structure, was at the same time complicated by a strong network of kinship and solidarity at the highest level, which led to enormous expansion of the great landed family estates. Meanwhile the state taxation system, whose weight increased through the growing density of bureaucracy and above all through military exactions which were ever more pressing in the face of the broad and intensified external pressure of the barbarians, brought on a crisis among the curial class, the urban aristocracies of landowners which had traditionally acted as mediators between the greatest extremes of social and economic status.[38] In the time of Odoacer the decadence of the cities had perhaps not yet become as obvious as it was north of the Alps. But the great estates (*latifundia*) had been expanding for centuries in Italy too, at first in the peninsula and the islands and then more slowly but just as inexorably in the Po plain;[39] and they emerged to confront Odoacer not only as massive economic presences, even when they were not territorially compact, but as organizations of multitudes of *coloni*, whether slave or free, and as evidence of a crushing social hegemony over the whole rural population and even over the class of minor landowners which still persisted in the cities. The forms in which the hegemony of the *latifundia* owners was expressed in Italy are not well known. In the East, legislation reveals that the patronage exercised by the powerful over public bodies – all of which constantly needed private protection in the face of pressure from the Roman judicial and political apparatus – was developing into the *patrocinium vicorum*, that is, into the defence exercised by the great landed lords (often also bureaucrats or military commanders) over a clientèle of free rural villages against the imperial tax system.[40] The supremacy of the *latifundia* owners would have been developing in Italy as well, if not in these forms then through analogous or equivalent forms of protection and pressure, but complicated by another force which was now also linked with the aristocratic structures

---

[38] J. Gagé, *Les Classes sociales dans l'empire romain* (Paris, 1964), part III; *cf.* E. Gabba, 'Considerazioni sulla società dell' impero romano', *Rivista di filologia e di istruzione classica*, ser. III, 94 (1966), pp. 306–16.

[39] L. Ruggini, 'Vicende rurali dell'Italia antica dall'età tetrarchica ai longobardi', *Rivista storica italiana*, 76 (1964), pp. 266–81.

[40] L. Harmand, *Un Aspect social et politique du monde romain. Le patronat sur les collectivités publiques des origines au Bas-Empire* (Paris, 1957), pp. 421–9, 448–61.

of society and was growing everywhere at the economic and social levels. This was the power of the episcopal churches, beginning with that of Rome, which were now present in the front line of the great landed proprietors and were equipped with high prestige and the capacity of exercising guardianship over public collectivities.[41]

The invasion of the Ostrogoths and other Germans, between 489 and 493, which ended Odoacer's regime was thus incorporated into a political and social context which from the time of Stilicho had been prepared for coexistence between a Germanic military power and a senatorial economic power, converging in the state apparatus, and which had reached with Odoacer a substantially peaceful equilibrium between the two ruling systems.

OSTROGOTHIC DOMINATION AND REINTEGRATION INTO THE EMPIRE

It was perhaps not impossible to dominate a region once belonging to the Empire without taking into account the *latifundia* owners of the Roman tradition, but on one sole condition: their elimination. Something like this was attempted in the Vandal kingdom set up in Africa towards the middle of the fifth century. In the region of Carthage, where the Vandals settled most densely, land was systematically confiscated and the Roman proprietors expelled, the *potentes* set to flight and the Catholic churches despoiled.[42] But not all the territory was reduced to the same condition, and the Roman population was too firmly set within the social framework created by the Catholic clergy for conflict between Vandal Arianism and the African churches to be avoided; with the despoliation of ecclesiastical goods this turned into religious persecution, and became a permanent weakness of the kingdom. The Catholic framework now functioned as the powerful connective tissue of a society which, although internally divided by serious economic imbalances, rejected any intervention which might be harmful to its cultural unity.

The African kingdom of the Vandals, after a long unrest which also saw the restoration of some positions of power to Romans, was destroyed in a few months between 533 and 534 under the military assault of the Eastern Empire, shortly before the same Byzantine forces began the invasion of the Ostrogothic kingdom of Italy. The Ostrogoths

---

[41] Gaudemet, *L'Eglise*, pp. 288–315, 350–6.

[42] C. Courtois, *Les Vandales et l'Afrique* (Paris, 1955), pp. 275–89; Stein, *Histoire du Bas-Empire*, vol. 1, pp. 325–8, 579; L. Musset, *Les Invasions. Les vagues germaniques* (Paris, 1965), pp. 105–8, 252–5, 288.

had attempted a different means of survival in a Roman country, that
suggested by Odoacer, but their fate was the same as that of the Vandals.
The leader who brought them from the middle Danube into Italy,
Theoderic the Great, had had changeable and contradictory relations
with Byzantium; at various times he had even been officially recognized
with the status of *magister militum*, with corresponding military
responsibilities in the Danube regions of the Empire, and his people had
in any case been for some time federates of the Empire.[43] In Italy
Theoderic's rule took on the same dual appearance as Odoacer's, but
both the Germanic and Roman elements of his power are more clearly
visible.

   In fact he was king of his people even before coming into Italy, king
of the first people of Germanic stock who settled in the peninsula more
or less as a body and with any prospect of stability. This element
emphasized the parallel with other Germanic kings federated with the
Empire and settled within it, which Odoacer had already sought to
make effective by assuming the royal title. But at the same time it is
noteworthy that, after the definitive suppression of Odoacer at Ravenna,
Theoderic had himself proclaimed king by the whole victorious army,
in which the Ostrogoths were prevalent but not alone: in this respect he
linked himself to Odoacer's regime, which, although born through
improvisation, had none the less by its degree of stability created some
important precedents. On the other hand, Theoderic had arrived in Italy
with imperial approval and with a Roman military rank (that of *magister
militum*) which, although conferred on him in the East in different
circumstances, had traditionally been associated in Italy through the fifth
century with responsibilities for control and intervention in all political
life. After some years of repeated requests, Theoderic obtained from
Constantinople an explicit recognition of these responsibilities, for
which Odoacer had waited a decade in vain. This was recognition for
formal acts carried out by Theoderic, according to the concept of a
general delegation of imperial powers within the geographical area
corresponding to the praetorian prefecture of Italy, and at the same time
a recognition of his royal rank in Italy; this rank, conceived by
Byzantium within the limits of a particular link with the Germanic
element, remained substantially distinct from the acknowledged
supreme functions of Theoderic, which he assumed as successor of

[43] Hartmann, *Geschichte Italiens im Mittelalter*, vol. 1, chapter 1; Schmidt,
   Geschichte der deutschen Stämme, pp. 272–93; W. Ensslin, *Theoderich der Grosse*
   (Munich, 1947), pp. 42–61; Stein, *Histoire du Bas-Empire*, vol. 2 (Paris, 1949),
   pp. 10–20.

Odoacer, over all the peoples of the Italian territory.[44] Therefore the sacral language used in Roman tradition for the imperial palace and certain central offices at Ravenna did not extend to the possessions or person of the king. He is called several times *Flavius Theodericus rex*, using a *gens* name given him when he was still in the East, and this title sums up the ambiguity of his power, which rested on Germanic military force and was expressed at a Roman level, in rivalry with the Eastern imperial might but without being confused with the sacral character and superior dignity of the emperor.

When the official power of Theoderic, in association with the broad radius of his political action among the Germanic kingdoms north of the Alps, extended beyond the praetorian prefecture of Italy into Provence, he established as the highest level of the financial and judicial administration of this not very large area a praetorian prefect of the Gauls at Arles, distinct from the praetorian prefect of Italy who was resident at Theoderic's side at Ravenna. So even beyond the Alps, within the limits allowed by military occupation, he applied the concept of a Roman imperial restoration, though without conceding the effective supreme power which the arms of his Goths conferred on him. But behind the appearance of an interplay of pure forms and titles Theoderic was expressing a precise reality. His dominion avoided any subversive act; it was expressed, at the centre and on the periphery, as the continuation of an ancient order, with a perspective radically different from that pursued by the first Vandal kings of Africa. The conservation of titles and patterns from the Roman tradition shows spontaneous acceptance of a world which he desired to dominate and to reinvigorate, because it was the same world of which Theoderic and his people had for a long time found themselves a part in the East, and was the obvious means open to him to be accepted by that world in his turn. If the aristocracy and episcopate of Italy (in many cases from the war years onwards) found no difficulty in abandoning Odoacer and collaborating with his adversary, it was because Theoderic, as much an Arian German as the conquered king, represented better than Odoacer the explicit desire for a closer encounter between the military power and the prominent sectors of Romano-Italic society.

At Ravenna the *comites* and *magistri* of the supreme civil administration, the *viri illustres* working surrounded by all the employees of

---

[44] Schmidt, *Geschichte der deutschen Stämme*, pp. 360–91; Stein, *Histoire du Bas-Empire*, vol. 2, pp. 116–24; W. Ensslin, 'Beweise der Romverbundenheit in Theoderichs des Grossen Aussen- und Innenpolitik', in *I Goti in Occidente* (Spoleto, 1956), pp. 509–36.

the *officia* which assisted them, not only continued to function but were very often, in the thirty years' rule of Theoderic and his immediate successors, chosen from members of the most noted families of the bureaucratic and senatorial tradition. This was the case with Cassiodorus the rhetorician, son of a minister of finance of Odoacer, and with Boethius the philosopher, who belonged to a branch of what was in the late Empire the greatest of the *gentes* of Rome, the Anicii; it was also the case with individuals less famous for their culture but equally powerful socially, such as the senator Flavius Faustus, who had been given the rank of consul in 490 by Odoacer but was already in 492 *magister officiorum* of Theoderic and his envoy to Constantinople to plead to the emperor the cause of his new master. And if the king happened to moderate the influence of the great families by also promoting to offices with senatorial rank lower functionaries, of origins perhaps not humble but less dangerous, this conformed to the purest imperial tradition, the ruler's desire to enter as a dynamic element into the play of ambitions of the greater and lesser aristocracy, the former already linked with the Roman Senate, the latter still rooted in a purely provincial environment but awaiting promotion through the favour of the court. This interplay is itself further evidence of the vitality, in the long years of peace that Theoderic's reign signified for Italy, of that intermediate class of proprietors which for more than a century had been subjected to the heavy trial of fiscal burdens and the privileges of the wealthy.[45]

The link with the interests and culture of the class of prosperous proprietors extended spontaneously to the upper Catholic clergy, particularly to the very wealthy church of Milan and its educated clergy. Thus the metropolitan bishop Laurentius was ready to support the new barbarian leader and expose himself during the war years to the reprisals of Odoacer, and with Epiphanius, bishop of *Ticinum* (Pavia), he strongly influenced the king, dissuading him from the desire to punish the prominent Romano-Italic individuals who had remained longest with the defeated ruler. Around Laurentius there formed a renowned circle of grammarians and rhetoricians, among whom considerable influence was acquired by Ennodius, a Gallo-Roman noble under the protection of Faustus, senator and minister of the king, who had first entered the clergy at Pavia alongside Epiphanius. The rhetorician Ennodius, a complacent and artificial versifier of both sacred subjects and bold secular themes, was the author of a celebrated panegyric of Theoderic and was twice sent to Constantinople at particularly delicate moments

[45] Bertolini, *Roma*, pp. 76–80; Stein, *Histoire du Bas-Empire*, vol. 2, pp. 124–30; M. A. Wes, *Das Ende des Kaisertums im Westen des Römischen Reiches* ('s Gravenhage, 1967), pp. 85–7.

at the order of the pope, at a time when Theoderic had good relations with the Roman church; meanwhile, pursuing his ecclesiastical career, he had become Bishop of Pavia. A protégé of Laurentius and student of Ennodius was the poet Arator, whose father was praised by Cassiodorus for his fluency and erudition. Arator went on from Milan to Ravenna to follow a bureaucratic career, and after the king's death, he became chief minister of his successor Athalaric, but the end of the Ostrogothic kingdom impelled him to a religious *conversio* and he ended his active career in Rome as sub-deacon of Pope Virgilius, where he composed a poem on the apostles Peter and Paul to the greater glory of the Primate of Rome.[46]

What extraordinary careers! They reflect the robustness of those courtly and literary cultural models which for centuries had conferred esteem on the ostentatious enjoyment of social predominance, a dominion which nobles and clerics exercised with delicacy, tenacity and elegance, through ranks of public and private agents radiating from the *officia* and the *domus* of the cities to the most remote houses of the *coloni*. Within this powerful network of aristocratic customs, friendships, clientèles, and favours which involved the ecclesiastical apparatus, we should also place the most celebrated building activity of Theoderic's time: the churches raised in Milan by the metropolitan Laurentius, the baths and palaces which the king ordered at Verona and Pavia, the royal palace of Ravenna with the palatine Arian church of the Saviour (today Sant'Apollinare Nuovo), and the king's own mausoleum. In the year 500 Theoderic was at Rome for several months. He honoured the church of St Peter (as devotedly as if he were Catholic, notes a chronicler), was welcomed in the hall of the Senate, spoke to the people, directed the restoration of the imperial palace and the city walls, provided for free annual distributions of grain, and raised to the praetorian prefecture of Italy a member of the powerful Roman family of the Decii. This stay at Rome consecrated the king's elevation to the centre of an ancient social system whose myths and complexities he accepted without reservation, including the connections that the religious revolution had set up between the stratification of society and the new ordering of communities.

The persistence of the Roman social system in its economic bases and aristocratic outlines through all the vicissitudes of the political regimes of the fifth and early sixth centuries was conditioned in reality by the triumphant expansion of the ecclesiastical order. Hence the elevation of

[46] M. Manitius, *Geschichte der lateinischen Literatur des Mittelalters*, vol. I (reprinted Munich, 1959), pp. 162–6. For Ennodius see E. Sestan, *Stato e nazione nel'alto medioevo* (Naples, 1952), pp. 216–21.

the king, even though an Arian, to guardian of the episcopal Catholic churches as well, beginning with the Church of Rome, which was contested between the political cliques of the Senate and the factions of the Roman clergy. These were the years in which renewed controversies on the nature of Christ, refined translations on to the intellectual level offered by the careful cultural formation of the episcopate of widespread hopes in universal salvation and of a passionate unity in the expectation of the Second Coming, also involved the prestige of the Church of Rome, which founded the affirmation of Roman primacy on the need for community and unity. This was the source of the intransigence of the party in Rome which was led by Pope Symmachus and the senator Flavius Faustus (the protector of Ennodius) in defending the formulae to which Pope Leo the Great had committed himself half a century earlier. But since such formulae on the two natures of Christ, proposed at the time of the violent debates and subtle compromises of the Council convoked at Chalcedon in 451 by the emperor of the East,[47] had not been enough to pacify the multiform and doctrinally seasoned Greek episcopate, and new suggestions for compromise had been formulated at Byzantium, the intransigence of some Roman clergy placed in dangerous disagreement the two forces on which Catholic universalism now rested, the sacralized power of the Eastern Empire and the authority of the Church of Rome. Hence the opposition to Pope Symmachus in certain Roman circles led by the more flexible Laurentius, the Pope vigorously supported by the leader of the Senate Flavius Festus. Theoderic found himself invested with responsibility for putting an end to the schism; he ordered the reunion of a synod of Italian bishops in Rome and for years wavered between the two contenders and between the parties that fought each other in the Senate and the city with asperity, sometimes with extreme violence, disrupting the whole Italian episcopate. The schism finally died away with definitive support from the king for the cause of Symmachus.[48] And when, after the death of Symmachus, the Roman church carried out a tenacious action to influence the imperial court and obtain a reconciliation, Theoderic created no obstacles even though the emperor entered into direct relations with the Roman Senate itself.

One may note that the formulations of the Roman See, of the Council

[47] Caspar, *Geschichte des Papsttums*, vol. 1, pp. 516–18; G. Bardy, 'Le "Brigandage d'Ephèse" et le concile de Chalcédoine', in A. Fliche, V. Martin, *Histoire de l'église* (Paris, 1948), vol. 4, pp. 234–6.

[48] G. B. Piciotti, 'Osservazioni su alcuni punti della politica religiosa di Teoderico', in *I Goti in Occidente*, pp. 173–226; Wes, *Das Ende des Kaisertums*, pp. 99–110.

of Chalcedon, and of the Byzantine court, rivals in their theological zeal, were all part of the centuries-long Catholic offensive against the Arian interpretation of the nature of Christ, and Arianism itself was the most effective element of cohesion in the people through whom Theoderic militarily dominated Italy. Thus the correctness of Theoderic's behaviour during the tension between Rome and Byzantium (in years in which there were also serious episodes of conflict between Byzantium and Ravenna) is a clear sign of the composite nature of his rule. The necessary insistence on the Romano-Italic, and therefore also Catholic, role of Theoderic's regime should not lead us to interpret the Ostrogothic domination as simply the instrument of a society extraneous to the Gothic people, either at the centre or at the periphery.

In the *consistorium* of Ravenna, the ruler's council which continued the imperial tradition of the *sacrum consistorium*, the high bureaucrats of Roman stock prevailed in number but the Gothic *comites*, holding high military functions, also constituted an influential minority. Outside the centre, alongside the *iudices provinciarium* (the civil governors of the Roman population nominated by the king at the suggestion of the praetorian prefect), the Gothic *comites* exercised military powers and judged the Germanic population. This too corresponded to a Roman tradition by which the military element was withdrawn from ordinary civil jurisdiction. But now the division between military and civil reflected with new rigour, as had never happened in Italy even under Odoacer, a contrast which was ethnic in character. The Goths, as with every barbarian people faithful to its own juridical tradition and merely federated with the Empire, were not Roman citizens, and the army, from which any Roman element was rigidly excluded, ceased even formally to be the Roman army. Notable consequences must have been obvious even at the highest level, since the *primates* of the Gothic people (an aristocracy perhaps partly hereditary), even when they attained high military responsibilities, entered the *consistorium*, and were honoured with the title of *viri illustres*, no longer acquired senatorial rank as had the *viri illustres* of Germanic origin in the late Empire. This was so even for the Gothic *comes* whom Theoderic sent to Rome to watch over the city and the Senate, a body more powerful than the prefect of Rome, who still represented the voice of the senatorial aristocracy even though nominated by the king but now rarely expressed an active rap-prochement between the power of the king and the authority of the Senate.[49] In this way the opportunity was lost for social integration

---

[49] N. Tamassia, 'Alcune osservazioni intorno al "comes Gothorum" nelle sue attinenze colla costituzione romana e lo stabilimento dei barbari in Italia',

between the leading men of each people. Such an integration, however, was in any case already undermined by the separation of the two Christian churches, Arian and Catholic, a separation which was clearer than it had previously been and which was in a certain sense attenuated, for some time after the reign of Stilicho, by the persistence in the Roman senatorial class of groups faithful to ancient cults, or indifferent to religion.

Even the agents which Theoderic used to keep in touch with the officials of the provinces and to watch over them were divided into two different categories; in his relations with the civil governors he often used, with various titles, the usual *agentes in rebus* subordinate to the *magister officiorum*, according to the imperial tradition, while the *saiones* were Goths and soldiers, directly bound to the person of the king and used by him for the most diverse tasks, obviously including his relations with military commanders. But what counted most was the distribution of the Gothic people in Italy. This took place through the same system used by Odoacer in assigning to the Germanic soldiers a third of the proprietors' land, and created a considerable settlement, principally in northern Italy and along the northern and central Apennines as far as Samnium. This population was notably more dense, as well as more homogeneous, than that formed by the families that Odoacer had settled on Roman property, amounting to at least 100,000 people.[50] Certainly they were in the midst of a Romano-Italic population of several million, but to understand the social significance of such a settlement it is necessary to consider it in relation not to the entire Roman population (mostly *coloni* of the immense fiscal, ecclesiastical or senatorial *latifundia*, or cultivators of the estates of the lesser Romano-Italic aristocracy and of all the barbarian lands, or small artisans in the cities), but rather in relation to the class of proprietors among which they found themselves. Even so they were a minority with respect to these latter, without doubt, but an armed minority subordinate to their own *comites* of Gothic nationality and tied to the king by ethnic tradition and religious confession.

(1884), reprinted in *ibid.*, *Scritti di storia giuridica*, vol. 1, pp. 361–94; Ensslin, *Theoderich*, pp. 193–202; Stein, *Histoire du Bas-Empire*, vol. 2, p. 124; G. Vismara, 'Romani e Goti di fronte al diritto nel regno longobardo', in *I Goti in Occidente*, pp. 418–37, 493ff; Schmidt, *Geschichte der deutschen Stämme*, p. 370.

[50] Schmidt, *Geschichte der deutschen Stämme*, p. 293; K. Hannestad, 'Les Forces militaires d'après la guerre gothique de Procope', *Classica et medievalia*, 21 (1960), pp. 155–68; V. Bierbrauer, 'Zur ostgotischen Geschichte in Italien', *Studi medievali*, ser. III, 14 (1973), p. 10.

Whatever Theoderic's political designs may have been, his variegated experience of life in the East and in Italy and the heterogeneous reality of the two peoples subordinate to him, with their lay and sacerdotal aristocracies, created a new political regime. It was a regime whose path had undoubtedly been prepared by a century of complex Italian history, and yet which was new in Italy because of the clarity with which the two apparatuses converging in the person of the king were visible; they are still distinguished according to the pattern of distinct military and civil responsibilities, of Germanic and Roman traditional roles, but are now based on the juxtaposition of two societies organized as if unrelated to each other. The political equilibrium which has usually been attributed to a decision by Theoderic was in reality suggested by a far deeper equilibrium between opposing and coexisting social orders. It was not the improvised policy of a ruler, but his recognition of the real conditions of the country, that permitted an effective dualism of political power for more than thirty years (a long period of stability when one considers the eternally recurring disturbances of the fifth century). This is clear when we compare Italy with the experience, often very similar, of the Visigoths in the kingdom which for many decades was centred on Toulouse, for that kingdom found itself in a critical situation precisely at the time of Theoderic through the combination of internal tensions and Frankish expansion, and was able to transfer its forces to the Iberian peninsula, where it resumed the intermittently dualistic tradition of fifth-century Toulouse.[51] It fell to the Ostrogoths in Italy to support the kingdom during the crisis of its political transfer, and Theoderic, as guardian of the young Visigothic king, had no trouble in entering into a tradition of government parallel to that set up by him in Italy. When one considers the vigour and capacity for evolution of the kingdom which finally found its focus at Toledo, at the centre of the Iberian peninsula, Theoderic's political construction cannot be judged as intrinsically too fragile and necessarily destined to perish, even though this construct, in the context of the forces then at work in the Mediterranean, did fail to survive for long after the death of the king.

In fact Italy had already, for some time, been in effect contested between two opposing expanding forces. From the north, the west and Africa it was menaced by the movement of the Germanic territorial lordships, the Franks, Alamans and Burgundians, Visigoths and Vandals – lordships often without constitutional form but endowed with a crude conquering dynamism which was restrained only by their mutual

---

[51] Schmidt, *Geschichte der deutschen Stämme*, pp. 462–528; D. Claude, *Adel, Kirche und Königtum im Westgotenreich* (Sigmaringen, 1971), pp. 36–54.

rivalries. But on the other hand Italy, still constitutionally converging on Rome and open to influence from the Catholic Empire of Constantinople, could not be ignored by those in the East who appealed to the Roman tradition and orthodox universalism – that is either to the ancient political significance of the city or to the religious authority, in the raging theological conflicts between the eastern patriarchs, of the eminent patriarch of Latin Christianity. The strength of the Eastern Empire, restored militarily on the basis of an unprejudiced recruitment of mercenaries within a strong Roman framework, was sustained at the level of social and religious integration by an arrogant display of Catholic orthodoxy, of which theological disputes were only the most heated expression. The kingdom of Theoderic, which for some years seemed to exercise a hegemony over most of the Germanic territorial lordships in the West through a web of kinship, protection and compromises, and which was nevertheless included within the horizon of the Roman Empire, faithfully reflected this ambivalence in its own structure. But it was precisely this feature which made it possible that the inevitable tremors of the Ostrogothic kingdom's internal life, the tremors which cannot be suppressed in the life of any political organism, might easily combine with an external situation made suddenly fluid and dangerous by a coincidence of events. Hence the political seriousness of the cruel errors of the great king in the last years of his life, when, after the religious rapprochement between Byzantium and Rome had taken place with the mutual recognition of the Council of Chalcedon, his suspicions were aroused by the persecution of Arians in the East and the declaration of obedience to the Eastern Empire made by certain members of the Roman senatorial aristocracy, which provoked the condemnation to death of the philosopher Boethius and the leading senator Symmachus, and the imprisonment of Pope John I.

After Theoderic's death in 526 the problems of orientation of the highest Gothic political levels in Italy, with their pro-Roman emphases and anti-Roman distrust, surrounded by the alarmed or uncertain expectancy of the senatorial class, Catholic clergy and Gothic army, coincided with the rise to the Byzantine throne of a prince, Justinian, who had broad plans for the restoration of the Empire, and with the rapid downfall of the Vandals in Africa. The Ostrogoths in their turn were caught up in a terrible conflict with the Empire. There followed twenty years of war in Italy, an interminable war of manoeuvres which spared no region, with the additional intervention of Burgundians, Franks and Alamans and vast destruction, famines and plagues which produced a very high mortality among the population.

The duration and intensity of the military operations – Milan was destroyed, Rome suffered four sieges and was captured and recaptured many times by one or other party – demonstrate, in comparison with the rapid and definitive collapse of the Vandal kingdom, the ability of the Ostrogoths compromised by Theoderic's complex political experiment to reorganize themselves even after failures and defeats. Certainly the chiefs who led the Goths in the ventures of that fearsome war showed themselves ready enough to rescue the Gothic presence in Italy by means of broad renunciations, drastic reductions of territory, and proposals of submission to the Empire and its representatives in Italy even in the form of an army without any political autonomy. But that was in the nature of these populations of federates which had learnt, in their long tradition of dealing with the Empire, the art of political compromise and flexible behaviour when faced with the prospect of their own social affirmation. For the Goths wanted to survive as an armed population of landowners; that is quite apparent from all the negotiations of those twenty years and proves how much they were now rooted in the possession of land (even if somewhat reluctant to pay the associated taxes[52]) and in the role assigned to them by Theoderic within the praetorian prefecture of Italy. Byzantine intransigence, fed by the optimism of military commanders and the pressures of Roman senators in exile at Constantinople,[53] prevented compromises and led to a more radical solution, which the forces of the Empire later showed themselves to be unable to maintain. The end of all Ostrogothic domination opened the way to the Lombard invasion, a solution just as radical for much of Italy but in exactly the opposite sense to the Justinianic one.

The Ostrogoths did not lack a bold political imagination at certain dramatic moments, when they considered unexpected solutions, made sudden appeals to a past which seemed buried and had recourse to forces that had been passive for centuries in Italy. In 540 King Witigis and his Goths, under siege at Ravenna, offered to proclaim Belisarius, conqueror of the Vandals and for many years supreme commander of the Byzantine forces in Italy, emperor in the West, as ruler of the Italians and Goths.[54] The narrative of Procopius, the great Greek historian of the Gothic war, stresses the episode and sets it in a context of mistrust between the powerful Belisarius, some of the Byzantine commanders in Italy, and the court in Constantinople. The proposal of the Goths came rather late, to say the least, but in itself it cannot have seemed absurd.

[52] Ensslin, *Theoderich*, pp. 203ff.
[53] Bertolini, *Roma*, pp. 167–70; Stein, *Histoire du Bas-Empire*, vol. 2, pp. 366ff, 595.
[54] Stein, *Histoire du Bas-Empire*, vol. 2, p. 367; Wes, *Das Ende des Kaisertums*, pp. 182–94.

Everything must still have seemed possible in Italy. The shift to the Byzantine cause of the senators most compromised by the Ostrogothic government had been slow. Witigis had with him until 538 Cassiodorus, the praetorian prefect of Italy, the rhetorician and minister who until that date remained imperturbably beside his kings, even in the darkest years, to preach harmony between Goths and Romans, and to expound the Theoderician experiment as a wise use of the different characteristics of the two peoples and of their aristocracies.

Later, confronted with the now general hostility of the senatorial aristocracy and the Catholic episcopate and with the flight of powerful individuals to Constantinople (Cassiodorus too arrived there, and the metropolitan of Milan had already lived there for years), King Totila seemed to attempt a reversal of social attitudes. He showed respect for the peasants of the abandoned or confiscated *latifundia* and exhorted them to work without fear, paying to the kingdom the rents once due to their landlords as well as the taxes already owed.[55] This was not a proposal for social revolution, but the episode illustrated the seriousness of the confusion in which the war placed the system of social relationships created and consolidated over the centuries, which the Ostrogoths of Theoderic had accepted and protected. Totila sometimes made rather liberal use, in southern Italy, of the recruitment of such peasants, and even of slaves fleeing from the *latifundia*, whom he freed; Procopius, however, points out that they found themselves facing the armed peasants of an enterprising *latifundia*-owner Tullianus, ally of the Byzantines. The rural population, which the original Roman expansion in Italy and the development of the aristocratic urban regime of the Empire had gradually reduced to a multitude of *coloni*, inert at the social level and incapable of political resistance, seemed to become once again, as in the recruitment of the imperial period, the object of military exploitation as well. It is true that Totila and Tullianus now had urgent need of faithful and convinced supporters, since in the harshness of the murderous conflict the political apparatus that protected the social system had collapsed. But the clash between these peasants was lost to sight among the military operations of the Byzantine mercenaries and the lesser and great Gothic landowners.

The definitive collapse of the Gothic domination did not signify the radical elimination of the Goths. Those who escaped the war became mercenaries for Byzantium or remained on their lands, among the proprietors, as is shown by the documents attesting economic

---

[55] Hartmann, *Geschichte Italiens im Mittelalter*, vol. 1, chapter 7; Stein, *Histoire du Bas-Empire*, vol. 2, pp. 568–76; Ruggini, *Economia e società*, pp. 337ff.

transactions in later periods. Some attained notable office in the Byzantine administration, as *tribuni* and *comites, duces* and *magistri militum*, or they were designated in private documents as *viri illustres* or *viri magnifici* or *spectabiles feminae*, terms which now did not have the specific meanings of the late Empire.[56] In Rome itself two churches remained Arian until the end of the sixth century. Not even their particular religious confession impeded the substantial integration of the Goths into the Italic–Byzantine class of proprietors.

Meanwhile after the last king, Teias, died in battle and the resistance from other Germanic forces united to the Goths in Italy faded away, the emperor in 554 established a new territorial order for the peninsula, with a distinction in almost every province between the *iudex*, entrusted with civil government, and the *dux*, responsible for the armed protection of the territory. Particularly striking is the arrangement that the choice of civil governors, who were subordinate to the praetorian prefect of Italy, be entrusted to the bishops and notables of the province; the obvious aim was to institutionalize the link between the power of the emperor and the traditional framework of Romano-Italic society. But since the war had overturned the economic bases of their social dominance, meticulous measures prescribed the reinstatement of the *latifundia*-owners in the land and other property which they had possessed up to the time of the 'most evil' Totila (including the peasants and slaves whom Totila had freed), and the annulment of the contracts which had been drawn up in the time of Totila to the advantage of supporters of the 'tyrant's' cause.[57] And as if to underline again the immediacy of the bond between the great landlords and the imperial court, it was provided that the 'gloriosissimi ac magnifici senatores' should be allowed for any reason to 'navigare' to the presence of the emperor (a voyage to Constantinople which was certainly impossible for anyone of only middling wealth), and that the Italian senators now resident at Constantinople should suffer no obstacle in travelling to Italy whenever they wanted, over matters concerning their lands. As for the damages suffered by the Catholic churches during the war, they were indemnified by large assignations of goods confiscated from the Arian churches, churches which were anyway now mostly destined for the Catholic cult.

[56] L. Schmidt, 'Die letzten Ostgoten', *Abhandlungen der Preussischen Akademie der Wissenschaften, Phil.-hist. Klasse* (1943), no. 10 pp. 3–15.

[57] C. Diehl, *Etudes sur l'administration byzantine dans l'exarchat de Ravenne (568–751)* (Paris, 1888), pp. 82–92, 133–140; L. M. Hartmann, *Untersuchungen zur Geschichte der byzantinischen Verwaltung in Italien* (Leipzig, 1889), pp. 35–46; *ibid., Geschichte Italiens im Mittelalter*, vol. 1, chapter 8; Stein, *Histoire du Bas-Empire*, vol. 2, pp. 612–22.

The imperial restoration thus appeared principally as the restoration of a social system which was no longer focused (as it had been in Italy for more than half a millennium and as had been vigorously maintained up to the time of the 'most evil' Totila, with all the Catholic complications of the last century) around Rome or around Rome and Ravenna, as supreme and complementary seats of military and political powers, of bureaucratic organs, of an ancient assembly and a new religious authority. Rather, it was now focused on the court of Constantinople, which precisely at the time of Justinian revealed its firm energy in leading the Roman church back to the role of faithful collaborator in the ecclesiastical government of Catholicism, and which at Ravenna, even after the end of military operations, had as its supreme representative in Italy the Byzantine commander of the armed forces of the peninsula.

2

THE LOMBARD RUPTURE IN THE HISTORY OF ITALY

·

THE SOCIAL AND POLITICAL STRUCTURES OF BYZANTINE ITALY CONFRONTED BY THE LOMBARD INVASION

The Italy that Justinian reorganized around Ravenna after the definitive defeat of the Goths was more limited in its territory than the kingdom of Theoderic. Already, during the Gothic war, the praetorian prefecture of Arles had disappeared, with the incorporation of Provence into the dominion of the Franks. Sicily, which at the time of Odoacer and Theoderic, and then again under Justinian by his express declaration, was considered a special possession of the prince, had an administration separate from that based on Ravenna; the civil governor, named praetor by Justinian in an explicit reference to the ancient Roman model, had his seat at Syracuse according to the regional tradition of government, and was subordinate not to the praetorian prefect of Italy but to the upper officials of the sacred palace at Constantinople. The latter were also directly responsible for hearing appeals from the sentence of the duke, who was in charge of the military defence of the region, even though on the level of military action properly speaking Sicily could still, then and for some time afterwards, be placed under the supreme command of the Byzantine armed forces in Italy.[1] Nor did the Byzantines make

---

[1] W. Ensslin, 'Zur Verwaltung Siziliens vom Ende des weströmischen Reiches bis zum Beginn der Themenverfassung', *Atti dell'VIII Congresso Internazionale di studi bizanti*, vol. 1 (Rome, 1953), pp. 355–64; S. Borsari, 'L'amministrazione del tema di Sicilia', *Rivista storica italiana*, 66 (1954), pp. 134–8.

Sardinia and Corsica subordinate to Ravenna after the disappearance of the Vandals; the islands were still dependent on Carthage, seat of an administration which extended over all western Byzantine Africa.[2] As for Dalmatia, traditionally placed under the praetorian prefect of Italy, it is not clear whether it still maintained some dependence on Ravenna.[3] So Ravenna was, as far as we can be certain, head of the Italian peninsula alone, within the limits marked out by the sea and the Alps, up to and including Istria. But this residual territorial complex lasted as an integral whole for only fifteen years after its pacification. In 569 the Lombards, arriving like the Ostrogoths from the middle Danube, were already at Milan.[4]

The Lombards too had entered into a close relationship in the Danube basin with the Eastern Empire and had drawn up treaties with them, supplying amongst other things some thousands of men to the Byzantines in the last phase of the Gothic war. But the behaviour of these bands, relates Procopius, was so uncontrolled and violent that the commander of the Byzantine army in Italy, who at that time was Narses, released them with rich gifts in order to free himself of them. The Lombard presence at the borders of the Empire was a recent fact, compared with the centuries-long experience of Romans that the Goths possessed, and above all it was concomitant with the disappearance from those regions of many forms of life and culture characteristic of the Roman world, as the result of the serious disorders that were already occurring in the fifth century.[5] Nor had Alboin, the king who led the Lombards into Italy, spent ten years at Constantinople, as Theoderic had done in his youth. The migration into Italy, prompted by pressure on the Lombards from the Altaic people of the Avars along the Danube, had no formal structure, and was not impeded by any official relationship of peace or war with the Empire and with the imperial forces of Italy. It was a people, or rather an agglomeration of barbarian populations, with a numerical majority of Lombards who held the military leadership, and as a whole it was perhaps not superior in numbers to the

---

[2] P. Goubert, *Byzance avant l'Islam* (Paris, 1965), vol. 2, pp. 195–7.

[3] A. Guillou, *Régionalisme et indépendance dans l'empire byzantin au VIIe siècle. L'exemple de l'Exarchat et de la Pentapole d'Italie* (Rome, 1969), p. 97 note 95.

[4] See O. Bertolini, 'La data dell'ingresso dei Longobardi in Italia', (1920), reprinted in *Bertolini, Scritti scelti di storia medievale* (Livorno, 1968), vol. 1, pp. 21–61; C. G. Mor, 'La marcia di re Alboino', in *Problemi della civiltà e dell'economia longobardo* (Milan, 1964), pp. 179–97.

[5] J. Werner, 'Die Langobarden in Pannonien', *Abhandlungen der Bayerischen Akademie der Wissenschaften, Phil.-hist. Klasse 55A* (1962), p. 121.

peoples brought into Italy by Theoderic.[6] It was a people on the march towards new lands, in search of booty and pastures and sedentary populations to exploit in a settled fashion, but it lacked a definite and agreed plan of territorial conquest, as is shown by the fact that not long after the occupation of Milan, while Ravenna and most of the Italian cities were still firmly in Byzantine hands, some bands pressed onwards over the western Alps into Gaul. These latter incursions provoked a firm reaction from the Franks, who not only drove the Lombards back from the Rhone basin but also excluded them from the Italian valleys of Aosta and Susa, which became permanently integrated into the Frankish kingdom of Burgundy.[7]

One may add that other Lombard bands, without taking too much heed of what was happening in Northern Italy, penetrated deeply into the peninsula along the Apennines, arriving after a few years at Bruttium, which is present-day Calabria. In short, the territorial confusion was such that, at the centre of the peninsula and the Apennines, the Byzantines at Perugia and the Lombards at Spoleto, only a few dozen kilometres apart, were in permanent confrontation, in order to prevent each other from obtaining a secure link between the zones that each controlled. Due to this opposition the Byzantines found it difficult to move between Rome and Ravenna, which remained firmly in their hands for more than a century and a half, and for the Lombards it was certainly no easier to communicate between Apennine Tuscany and the regions of Spoleto and Benevento, all of which were zones of the definitive settlement of the Lombards and centres of their political force until the collapse of the kingdom (and, in the case of Benevento, for another three centuries after that). The shape of the two opposing social orders remained for many years as uncertain as the territorial situation was confused. The Lombards reached such a point that they remained for ten years without a king, from 574 to 584; the military commanders, or *duces* (as they were called in imitation of Rome and Byzantium), controlled the various territories with full autonomy. These territories themselves, scattered across the peninsula with varying density, both confronted and were surrounded by territories in which Byzantine rule had in its turn become territorially fragmented.

---

[6] Romano and Solmi, *Le dominazioni barbariche*, p. 270; E. Sestan, 'La composizione etnica della società in rapporto allo svolgimento della civiltà in Italia nel secolo VII', in *Caratteri del secolo VII in Occidente* (Spoleto, 1958), vol. 2, pp. 656–60.

[7] Hartmann, *Geschichte Italiens im Mittelalter*, vol. 2.1 (Leipzig, 1900), chapter 3; Romano and Solmi, *Le dominazioni barbariche*, pp. 271–6.

Think of Justinian's imperial design, of the solemn declaration with which in 554 he extended to Italy the laws he promulgated in the East and the new corpus of legislative and jurisprudential texts of the Roman period, in order to give the juridical tradition greater coherence – in other words, the declaration that the Roman *res publica* was now one sole body, and so the law in force, in West and East, should also be one. Measure the discrepancy between such a vigorous desire for unification and the new reality, a few years after the death of the emperor, of an Italy dismembered into heterogeneous and fluid areas, in conflict or only communicating among themselves with difficulty. No other region of the world which had been Roman knew in those centuries such a political and territorial confusion. The situation reached this point because, while the Lombards undertook the conquest with insufficient consistency, the Byzantines for their part for a long time deluded themselves that the fragmentary Lombard occupation was only provisional, and that (while waiting for the affairs of the Balkans and Asia to permit a firmer military commitment in the West) it should be resisted primarily from organized strips of the Italian territory which communicated with Byzantium by sea, where the imperial fleet held uncontested sway for a century from the end of the Vandal and Ostrogothic kingdoms up to the expansion of the Arabs in the Mediterranean.[8]

Nor, as far as Byzantium was concerned, was it only a matter of the violent reduction and break-up of the territories it controlled. The demands of war, of a war a hundred times suspended and resumed in every part of Italy, imposed on the Byzantine lands the absolute prevalence of military authority over the civil powers. This was evident both in the central administration of Ravenna, where the praetorian prefect had since the end of the sixth century been reduced to almost purely financial functions and was strictly subordinated to the exarch (supreme head of the armed forces in Italy, with supreme responsibility in the civil administration as well), and in a parallel fashion in the provinces – or rather, one should say, in the new military districts which were forming as autonomous blocks, corresponding to the areas under pressure by the Lombards from several sides. These comprised the Ligurian coast and, up to the first years of the seventh century, part of the Tuscan coast; the littoral of the Veneto, soon reduced to the lagoon area, and Istria; the region which was directly governed from Ravenna and which was later called the exarchate in the proper sense of the term, stretching to the Adige in the north, beyond Bologna in the west, and

---

[8] E. Eickhoff, *Seekrieg und Seepolitik zwischen Islam und Abendland* (Berlin, 1966), pp. 9–13.

to the Apennines in the south-west; the Pentapolis, bordering on the exarchate and stretching along the coast from Rimini to Ancona with its associated hinterland; the land corridor, permanently threatened, which with its centre in Perugia placed the Pentapolis in communication with the area centring on Rome; the Roman duchy, as the large belt of territory along the Tyrrhenian coast from Civitavecchia to the gulf of Gaeta was later called; the territory of Naples, between the gulfs of Gaeta and Salerno; present-day central-southern Apulia (then *Calabria*) and a large part of modern Calabria (then *Bruttium*).[9]

This unification of local powers in the hands of the Byzantine military commanders was a solution of the political and administrative problem which was radically different from the programme set out by Justinian; the latter had stressed the distinction of civil from military functions and the choice of provincial judges within the provinces themselves, with the aim of correcting certain tendencies, which had been manifest even in the best years of Theoderic, to place the civil administration under the vigilance of the military leaders, the Gothic *comites*. The Byzantine government now seemed, far from correcting these tendencies, actually to reverse both Justinian's programme in Italy and the whole late imperial tradition, to which Odoacer and Theoderic had remained substantially faithful. The separation between military and civil careers was gradually fading away with the progressive disappearance of the civil bureaucracy itself, at least in its highest ranks. The praetorian prefect of Italy, his powers already diminished, disappeared in the course of the seventh century. The same fate befell the civil governors of the provinces, all the more since the old provinces were disappearing in the face of the division into districts which was imposed by the requirements of military defence. The *magistri militum* or *duces* of the new circumscriptions were military leaders named, at first, by the exarch, and the very name of *iudex*, once used to distinguish civil jurisdiction, was eventually applied also to dukes and the subordinate military officials, the *tribuni*.

In Byzantine Italy, therefore, an omnipresent politico-military apparatus seemed to take shape, intended to compensate by the rigidity of a single hierarchy of power for the discontinuity of the territory and the resulting difficulties of a unitary government. In reality the transformation of the political constitution was accompanied by and interwoven with a profound social transformation, which gave that new constitution quite a different significance from the one foreseen.

The contraction of the Byzantine territory and its fragmentation for

[9] Diehl, *Etudes sur l'administration byzantine*, pp. 42–78; Goubert, *Byzance avant l'Islam*, vol. 2, pp. 39–48.

an indefinite period into constantly threatened blocks threw into disorder both the original Roman political structure and the class of *potentes* who represented the strongest support and the proud reflection of that structure. The disorder provoked by the Gothic war, although serious, would have been overcome through the gradual restoration of landed estates and the re-binding of the many links between the Romano-Italic aristocracy and the court of Constantinople and its subordinate centres of power in Italy (the Byzantine government of Ravenna, the Senate and the Church of Rome). But now, instead, the ancient structure of the great aristocracy was permanently shattered. Already the reduction of the Western Empire to Italy had forced the aristocracy, in the course of the fifth century, to give its economic forces a new scope, since it had been deprived of a landed presence in many areas outside the peninsula. At the beginning of that century Valerius Pinianus and his wife Valeria Melania, both of powerful senatorial stock, still possessed countless landed properties, *villae*, in Italy, Sicily, proconsular Africa (the province ruled from Carthage), Numidia, Mauretania and the Iberian peninsula.[10] Now, however, something even more radical than the reduction in landowning of the fifth century was taking place. The aristocracy that had been imperial lost its property in all the parts of Italy permanently occupied by the Lombards, and it also lost the ability to communicate easily between the regions remaining to Byzantium, that is, to provide an efficient direction and defence of its residual economic base. Thus it had necessarily to shrink to provincial dimensions.

In this sense the Lombard invasion, even in areas where the Lombards did not penetrate, did indeed represent a definite point of rupture in the history of Italy such as Gaul, for example, did not experience. Visigoths and Burgundians did not destroy the Gallo-Roman senatorial class, as happened with the Romano-Italic aristocracy in the Lombard kingdom, nor did they enclose the senatorial class within encircled provincial islands, such as formed in Byzantine Italy. The advance of the Franks into the Seine valley at the end of the fifth century, and the subsequent annihilation of the last autonomous political formation of the Roman dominion in Gaul, certainly produced a crisis among the Roman senatorial class north of the Loire, but the further military expansion of the Franks into formerly Visigothic and Burgundian Gaul was mitigated by the flourishing survival of 'senators' (as they continued to call themselves) of Gallo-Roman origin. Through the latter, the Frankish kingdom already in the course of the sixth century displayed the

[10] D. Gorce, *Vie de sainte Mélanie* (Paris, 1962).

fundamental process of integration between the senatorial families and the military tradition of the Germanic aristocracy.[11] Within the remains of the Byzantine dominion in Italy there was indeed also some integration between classes of heterogeneous origins, notably at the social and political level, but the character of the dominant classes that emerged from this integration was the result of new conditions of life in the separate regions of Italy; it was not due to a clear convergence between social hegemonies which had been long present in the structure of two peoples meeting on the same soil. We shall consider the process as it took place in some of these regions, the most important parts of the shrunken imperial system of Italy.

The Byzantine presence in the peninsula in the seventh century was founded principally on the two territorial blocks of the exarchate of Ravenna, with the neighbouring Pentapolis, and the duchy of Rome; the two communicated not by the ancient Via Flaminia, interrupted and occupied for a long stretch by the Lombards of the duchy of Spoleto, but rather by a more westerly road which ran along the Tiber and was fortified in several places, with Perugia, midway, as its stronghold and focal point. In the Ravennate and in the Roman territory, guarded with particular firmness, one can therefore grasp better than elsewhere the transformation of the society dominated by the Greeks.

Ravenna, some hundreds of metres from the sea in the middle of a network of watercourses and canals on the southern edge of what was then the vast delta of the Po, operated by means of several harbours as the principal port of the Adriatic, maintaining close relations with the Eastern and Greek world. The permanent presence of Greek elements in the city, a presence encouraged for centuries (and not only in Ravenna) by trade and the movement of men,[12] was already growing rapidly at the outset of Byzantine rule, until Greeks were responsible, in the records of economic transactions which have survived from the early eighth century, for as many entries as the total of both Latins and the last surviving Goths.[13] The growth resulted above all from the influx of mercenaries of the Byzantine army and functionaries sent from Constantinople, but, as appears from the nature of the documents that record this increase, there was a tendency in both groups to settle

---

[11] Stroheker, *Der senatorische Adel*, pp. 84–136; F. Irsigler, *Untersuchungen zur Geschichte des frühfränkischen Adels* (Bonn, 1969), pp. 82–8, 142–55, 254; E. Zöllner, *Geschichte der Franken bis zur Mitte des sechsten Jahrhunderts* (Munich, 1970), pp. 118–20.

[12] L. Ruggini, 'Ebrei e Orientali nell' Italia settentrionale fra il IV e il VI secolo d. C.', *Studia et documenta historiæ et juris*, 25 (1959) pp. 250–77.

[13] Guillou, *Régionalisme et indépendance* p. 95; see also pp. 78ff.

permanently in the Ravennate, to participate in an active fashion in the economic life of the region and to become landowners. They became great or small property-owners, mingling with the Latins and gradually assimilated by them linguistically, although even so their distinct origin was reflected in the development of a Greek clergy and Greek monasticism, which was less easily assimilated. At the same time it happened that elements indigenous to the region entered the Byzantine bureaucracy of the exarchate and the Pentapolis, among the 'judges' with military and civil authority and among the chancellors, assessors, notaries and scribes who assisted them. Indeed the influx that took place was all the more abundant because it was combined with the new recruitment of the imperial army within Italy.

This was now an army intended less for broad manoeuvres of war than for the simple territorial defence, zone by zone, of what remained in Byzantine hands in Italy. And, since the military commitments of the Empire in the East prevented it from sending to the West forces adequate for such a defence, the recruitment of the militias, in the Ravennate as in every other Byzantine part of Italy, took place mostly on the spot, so that eventually the whole class of proprietors, whatever their origin, was brought into the military framework. Thus the military burden once more lay directly on landed property. But this was not, as in the Imperial Roman era, in the form of contributions of manpower (largely *coloni* torn away from their work in the fields) presented by landowners, or even in the form of a substitute money payment, but rather an obligation of direct personal service from the landowners. If the *coloni*, as is documented for Istria, were summoned in certain circumstances to a city to organize territorial defence, this took place under the command of their individual masters, who formed the basic framework of the army. Military service was in fact rendered within the region and according to a hierarchy of responsibilities which corresponded more or less to the hierarchy of wealth and social prestige, while prestige in its turn was modified by the rank attained in the military hierarchy. At a certain level this rank became at the same time, through the expansion of military government into the sphere of civil administration, a hierarchy of jurisdictional functions, that of the tribunes and dukes, who were all subordinate to the exarch.[14]

The political and military apparatus installed in the separate Byzantine regions thus managed to embody a social settlement which was gradually taking definite shape, in various ways in the different regions,

[14] Hartmann, *Untersuchungen zur Geschichte der byzantinischen Verwaltung in Italien*, pp. 52–73, *Geschichte Italiens im Mittelalter* (Leipzig, 1903), vols. 2.1, chapter 5, 2.2, chapter 2; Guillou, *Régionalisme et indépendance*, pp. 149–63,

as a reordering of the propertied class. To turn to the best-known regional situation, we do not know what were the fortunes, in the formation of the Ravennate army (the *exercitus Ravennae*, the *militia* of the various districts of the exarchate divided into *numeri* headed by the city), of the great Latin families of *latifundia* owners which are documented in the Ravennate at the beginnings of the Byzantine domination.[15] We may assume that they were absorbed into the landed and bureaucratic aristocracy of Latin and Oriental origin which was closely centred on the military and ecclesiastical institutions of the city. But this would mean that they disappeared into a class different from that which had established itself in a Romano-Italic perspective, different not only because the Ravennate aristocracy officially appeared to be as one with the new Byzantine military system, but because the new political system was gradually revealing itself to be an excellent means by which purely local social structures could assert themselves under imperial protection. The municipal curias, which in the Roman era had organized the civic aristocracy in a sort of autonomous local senate, had been decadent for centuries, and were now everywhere fading away; their social role was replaced in practice by the presence of families conspicuous in the politico-military government of the region, and by the solidarity which was spontaneously created among the *optimates* in the government. The burden of fiscal responsibilities, which had crushed the old curias confronted by the harshness and abuses of the imperial administration of the provinces, certainly still weighed heavily on the property-owners of the region, because perhaps nothing functioned in the Byzantine period with greater perfection than the assessment of contributors and the exaction of their contributions. But it was no longer a matter of exploitation of the local landed class by political bodies extraneous to their interests. The contributors, mainly *coloni* and those holding concessions of other people's land, were protected by the landowners, who were indeed responsible to the government for the contributions but who were themselves present in the government of the region, present as an armed militia capable of challenging the exarch and the supreme imperial government.

Aside from the issue of fiscal exactions the military crises connected with religious and ecclesiastical questions are also instructive in this context. In 693, on the occasion of clashes between the Empire and the Roman church over some disciplinary measures resolved on by a Constantinopolitan synod, the militias of the exarchate and the

[15] See the discussion by E. Patlagean in *Studi medievali*, ser. III, 2 (1970), pp. 263, 266.

Pentapolis (apparently without the intervention of the exarch) rebelled
and moved on Rome, where they threatened the Lateran palace in order
to release Pope Sergius from the pressure of the imperial envoy, and
obtained the expulsion from Rome of the latter. One may note that this
was a move against the peremptory action of the emperor in the area of
ecclesiastical discipline, which until then had been different in Italy from
in the East. The motive was not, then, an unconditional devotion
towards the Roman church, which indeed was strongly resented, before
and after the Ravennate expedition to Rome, by the population of
Ravenna, who supported the autonomy of their own metropolitan.
Regional feeling was thus strong, and there was a decided desire, in the
population as a whole and in its subdivisions, to resist external forces and
to support their own convictions with effective means, even within the
region. During the conflicts which were provoked in Italy in the 730s by
Emperor Leo III's hostility to the cult of sacred images, the Pentapolis
rose in rebellion and the exarchate divided into factions. In the
disturbances that followed the exarch was killed. Then, when an
expedition from the East arrived to punish the Ravennate rebels, the
population reunited, defeated in battle the Greek army (according to the
account a century later of the priest Agnellus of Ravenna, significant
evidence in any case for a flourishing local tradition), caught up with the
soldiers on the ships where they had fled, and massacred them.

Regional sentiment in the exarchate was all the more vigorous since
it was not only fed by the solidarity between the *optimates* in the military
and political government, but also sustained by the dense network of
economic and ecclesiastical interests which had developed around the
metropolitan bishop. He summed up in his person the myth of the city
and its independence, with the splendour of the churches and their rites.
There was no possible comparison between the landed patrimony of the
Ravenna Church, additionally enriched by the goods that formerly
endowed the Arian churches protected by Theoderic, and the patrimony
of any other organization or family in the region. And although the
economic power of the archbishop reached far beyond the boundaries of
the exarchate (he owned landed properties from Istria to Sicily and could
use his own mercantile fleet to link them[16]), the greater part of his goods,
and the best-controlled, was certainly concentrated in the various districts
of the exarchate and the Pentapolis. It was an immense fortune, largely
managed through *emphyteuses*, long-term contracts lasting up to three
generations (or even in perpetuity) which were issued not to the
cultivators themselves but to the *milites*, the *tribuni*, even the exarch –

[16] Guillou, *Régionalisme et indépendance*, pp. 181–6.

that is, the military class which coincided with the class of landowners. With an economic base and social ties such as these, and with the responsibility that Byzantine legislation gave to the whole imperial episcopate to supervise actively the public administration, the archbishop of Ravenna gathered into his hands the predominant temporal power of the region. It was a power formally distinct from the official public order but linked with individual members of that same order, and complemented by the network of ecclesiastical subordination through which all the bishops and monasteries of the exarchate recognized the pastoral and priestly authority of the metropolitan. Hence there developed that ecclesiastical ambition which brought the emperor in 666 to recognize the Ravennate church as autocephalous, with disciplinary independence from the bishop of the Church of Rome. An ecclesiastical privilege (obviously contested by Rome), but a privilege with great political significance, since it hallowed with religious authority a regional hegemony that would not tolerate any rivalry other than the inevitable one of the exarch of Italy resident at Ravenna.[17]

This gradual co-ordination of a whole society around a dominant prelate was paralleled by developments in the Roman duchy. The *patrimonium sancti Petri* in fact came to signify, in the last phase of the Byzantine domination in Rome, a patrimonial and fundamentally political power with a regional character, the exact counterpart of the metropolitan of Ravenna, its rival on the ecclesiastical level. Finally it developed into a dominion which was also officially political, a public power sanctioned in the agreements between the papacy and the Franks when, in the middle of the eighth century, the Byzantine domination in central Italy entered its final crisis.

The original notion of the 'patrimony of St Peter' had in reality a different and broader application. At the time of Pope Gregory the Great (590–604) it referred to an enormous number of *latifundia* stretching from southern Gaul, in the political sphere of the Franks, to the Balkan peninsula and the coasts of Africa, and in particular in all the Italian regions controlled by Byzantium, both in the islands and in the areas subject to the exarch of Italy. These were aggregations of landed properties called *massae* and *condumae*, and they were grouped in their turn, in each politically distinct region, into one or more *patrimonia*, entrusted to the control of a *rector* who as subdeacon or simple cleric was incorporated into the bureaucratic hierarchy. As was the case with the procurators in charge of groups of imperial *latifundia* and the public

---

[17] S. Mochi Onory, *Vescovi e città (secoli IV–VI)* (Bologna, 1933), pp. 300–12; G. Vismara, *Episcopalis audientia* (Milan, 1937), pp. 133–57; A. Simonini, *Autocefalia ed esarcato in Italia* (Ravenna, 1969), pp. 75–96.

officials of the central and peripheral bureaucracy of the Empire, the *rector* was assisted by his own *officium*, a well-developed nucleus of minor functionaries and scribes. For its economic management the *rector* usually also had under his control a band of *conductores*, each of whom held a *massa* or *conduma* of moderate size on a short-term contract, and was answerable to the *rector* for the rents in money and kind that were due to the Roman church from the *coloni* who were subordinate to him. This structure is known particularly well in the case of Sicily, where the Roman church possessed enormous landed wealth, administratively grouped into the two 'patrimonies' of Syracuse and Palermo.[18] The *rector* and the *officium* which assisted him were at the same time used by the pope to obtain political and ecclesiastical information from the region where the *patrimonium* lay, and to maintain direct relations with the public officials, episcopal churches and monastic foundations of that region. Only when one pays attention to the structure, size and geographical distribution of this enormous economic and administrative support-structure for the religious authority of the Roman church, is it possible to understand how from the end of the sixth to the beginning of the eighth century the Church of Rome maintained its capacity for ecclesiastical action and social and political influence in the area of the West under Byzantine rule, in contrast to its extremely feeble activity in the Romano-Germanic kingdoms of the West,[19] and how in the mid-eighth century it could direct itself towards a vast plan of politico-territorial domination in the centre of Italy.

The unfolding of these multiple attitudes of the Roman church to the organization of power, which was displayed at the most disparate levels of collective life and which in the management of the 'patrimonies' had found the regional reference points and necessary source of income for co-ordinated and concrete development, was in fact concentrated in the group of areas on which up to then the Byzantine dominion in Italy had been founded, the great strip (narrowing in the central Apennines) which reached from the middle of the Tyrrhenian coast to the Po delta. This concentration was prompted by a double series of events which occurred in conjunction with each other in the first half of the eighth century: the Lombard advance on Ravenna and Rome, and the catastrophic crisis suffered by the papal 'patrimonies' of Sicily and

---

[18] Hartmann, *Geschichte Italiens im Mittelalter*, vol. 2.1, pp. 138–48; Bertolini, *Roma*, pp. 263–8; Ruggini, *Economia e società*, pp. 238–61.

[19] T. Schieffer, 'La chiesa nazionale di osservanza romana', in *Le chiese nei regni dell' Europa occidentale e i loro rapporti con Roma sino all' 800* (Spoleto, 1960), pp. 75–9, 310.

southern Italy as the result of measures taken by the imperial government against the rebellious papacy during the Iconoclast struggle.[20] The Church of Rome, which in the upheaval provoked in Italy by the controversy over the cult of images had already been operating in a diplomatic role with respect to the Lombards, replacing and representing the absent imperial power, saw itself virtually stripped of those 'patrimonies' which oriented it towards the south. It sought, therefore, to compensate for this (particularly in the time of Pope Zacharias, 741–52) by extending and improving the administration of the *patrimonia*, already numerous and notable, which it possessed in the Roman duchy.[21] From this massive landed base which focused on Rome, it was easy for the papacy to construct a politico-territorial dominion which formally supported the Byzantine duchy of Rome and in reality replaced it. This solid regional framework appeared in its turn, in the defensive requirements of the whole Byzantine area menaced by the Lombards and in the plans and activity that emerged from Rome under the successors of Pope Zacharias, as the basis for a much wider political responsibility of the Roman See. This responsibility was eventually boldly translated into an attempt to construct an anti-Lombard territorial association through negotiation with the Franks, and to replace the Byzantine presence both in the exarchate of Ravenna and in the Roman duchy, even if perhaps it was still conceived up to the end of the eighth century as being within the theoretical boundaries of the Empire which had its capital in Constantinople.[22]

These Roman plans sometimes lacked clear outlines and in practice took on the dimensions of a papal expansion, in the form of a restoration of the *res publica Romanorum* in Italy, over a great part of the Apennine Italy occupied by the Lombards, far beyond the confines within which Byzantine rule had sustained itself in peninsular Italy after the Lombard invasion. But even just in the rough limits of a substitution of the popes for the Byzantine dominion these plans encountered serious difficulties

[20] Caspar, *Geschichte des Papsttums*, vol. 2, pp. 665–8, 738–40.
[21] Bertolini, *Roma*, pp. 484–91, 509–13; 'La ricomparsa della sede episcopale di "Tres Tabernae" nella seconda metà del secolo VIII e l'istituzione delle "domuscultae"' (1952), reprinted in *Scritti scelti*, vol. 2, pp. 695–701.
[22] Bertolini, 'Le prime manifestazioni concrete del potere temporale dei papi nell'esarcato di Ravenna (756–757)', reprinted in *Scritti scelti*, vol. 2, pp. 569–612, 'Il problema delle origini del potere temporale dei papi nei suoi presupposti teoretici iniziali' (1948), reprinted in *Scritti scelti*, vol. 2, pp. 487–547, 'Sergio archivescovo di Ravenna (744–769)' (1950), reprinted in *Scritti scelti*, vol. 2, pp. 551–91; Simonini, *Autocefalia ed esarcato*, pp. 133–66.

in their realization, then and for centuries afterwards. Above all, they ran up against the real strength of the Ravenna archbishop. The Ravennati, who were in agreement with the Roman See to check and drive back the Lombard advance into the exarchate and duchy of Rome through the intervention of the Franks, began to place their hope in the Lombards when they saw that the 'restitutions' which the Franks forced from the Lombards were consigned not to the official authorities of the Empire, nor to both the great ecclesiastical sees which in each region had co-ordinated a large part of the local forces, but to the Roman church alone, which was now determined to realize its great Italian project of a politico-territorial power-base. It is true that in the war between the two Germanic kingdoms the Franks were repeatedly victorious, until the kingdom so hated by the Roman See collapsed in 774, and thus officially the Franco-Roman view prevailed in the formerly Byzantine area. But the position of the archbishop of Ravenna was too solid, depending not on the dramatic clash of armies or the subtle game of diplomacy, but rather on the tenacious fabric of economic and social relationships. And so the papal triumph was transformed into a transient series of compromises which preserved intact the hegemony of the archbishop over the exarchate, beneath the barely tolerated supremacy of Rome and the more or less firm protection of the Franks. This hegemony was certainly still qualified, but no longer by the activity of the exarch and by the link with Byzantine – rather by a greater or less intense papal interference in the choice of public officials and by the power of the Franks.

The 'patrimony of St Peter' thus settled into something very different both from the vast economic and administrative network of the past of the scattered *patrimonia* of the Roman church, and from the ambitious territorial construction that had emerged from the Frankish–papal agreements. It became the basis for a regional network which embraced the lower Tiber valley and the neighbouring zones, reaching south as far as Terracina and towards Gaeta, which was surrounded by papal landed properties. But Gaeta remained politically within the Byzantine duchy of Naples. It is interesting to note how at the beginning of Frankish rule in Italy, the oscillations of the political border between Terracina and Gaeta occurred not only in relation to the direct involvement (including military involvement) of the Roman See and to the military intervention of the Byzantine duke of Naples, the Lombard duke of Benevento (the duchy survived the kingdom of which it had been a part) and the king of the Franks, but also in relation to the interests and orientation of the local *militiae*. There was a point at which Terracina and Gaeta, clearly autonomous, joined with the duke of Benevento against the ambitions of Rome.[23] Papal ambitions remained vast in those years, but were undermined by the need for involvement in abrupt minor local clashes in order to ensure at the least the consolidation of the Roman duchy in the hands of the papacy. But it was precisely here, in the duchy, that it was truly possible to establish a solid political power, since the regional hegemony of the Roman Church had long since been founded, not on a theoretical diplomatic construct but on a fabric of interests analogous to that which sustained the archbishop of Ravenna in the exarchate.

In fact the old system of *conductores* had not hindered the broad diffusion in certain papal *patrimonia*, namely in those of the Roman duchy itself, of long-term contracts in emphyteusis, prompted by the attraction that the enormous landed dominance of the Roman church exerted on the regional aristocracy. Like that of the exarchate, this aristocracy had been born from the convergence of Byzantine and ecclesiastical bureaucracies, of Roman and Eastern elements; clerics and monks in particular were of Eastern origin, often having taken refuge at Rome as the theological struggles between East and West became harsher, and in the Byzantine period even a large number of the popes were Eastern. It was a convergence of landowners of various origins, set in the social framework of a *militia*, the *exercitus Romanus*, which was no less enterprising than that of Ravenna. Indeed this convergence had developed in such a way as to call for a reordering of the economic administration, through which Pope Zacharias began to create centres of direct management, the *domuscultae*. These in their turn, as centres of agrarian life less exposed to abuses like those possible for the *conductores*, constituted particular strong-points of the papal presence in the midst of leases in emphyteusis and the property of the aristocracy. The latter had clearly also, from the seventh century, absorbed the remaining senatorial class resident in Rome (for example the kin-group to which Pope Gregory the Great belonged), that is, the descendants of those among the imperial aristocracy domiciled at Rome who, after fleeing the city repeatedly besieged by Byzantines and Goths, had not remained at Constantinople or on one of their own distant *latifundia*.

As the constitutional organ of the city, the Senate of Rome was to suffer, in the eighth century, a fate not very different from that of the municipal curias. In chronicles and documents over half a millennium one sometimes comes across reference to a Roman Senate, until in the mid-twelfth century a Senate of Rome, organized as an institution, reborn in

[23] M. Merores, *Gaeta im frühen Mittelalter* (Gotha, 1911), pp. 3–7; E. Caspar, *Das Papsttum unter fränkischer Herrschaft* (1935, reprinted Darmstadt, 1965) pp. 46–8; V. von Falkenhausen, *Untersuchungen über die byzantinische Herrschaft in Süditalien vom 9. bis ins 11. Jahrhundert* (Wiesbaden, 1967), p. 11.

a very different form from that of the old Senate.[24] But the so-called Senate of the many intervening centuries was none other than the new urban aristocracy, linked to the pope and operating as a regional aristocracy. Perhaps there is no clearer sign than this of the transformation which had taken place, in the parts of Italy which appealed to the continuity of Roman tradition, among the great social and political systems which formerly made up the Empire. As for the public order of the Byzantine tradition, of which the apex in this region had been the duke of Rome, it was to be absorbed without difficulty by the Roman church into the sphere of its own activity. The central bureaucracy of the papacy was modelled on the example of the imperial court of Byzantium, while the ties between the ecclesiastical apparatus and the regional aristocracy limited possible resistance by functionaries loyal to the idea of an imperial administration, all the more so since a public administration (at least in the city) had already been for some time an integral part of papal responsibilities, particularly in the areas of poor relief and food supplies.[25]

If such was the fate of the regions which, due to the presence of powers of general or universal importance (the powers of the exarch of Italy and of the pope of Rome), seemed the most unwilling to close and reinforce themselves within their own specific boundaries, it is that much easier to understand the more or less autonomous character of local life acquired in the eighth century by the duchy of Naples, the many small cities of the Istrian peninsula, and the area of the Venetian lagoons – a group of islands which had become a duchy active not only in defence of its own commercial interests against the rival Comacchio but also in the political affairs of the northern Adriatic as a whole during the crisis of the exarchate.[26] In these various zones there was no

---

[24] A. Frugoni, 'Sulla "renovatio senatus" del 1143 e l' "ordo equestris"', *Bullettino dell'Istituto storico italiano per il Medioevo*, 62 (1950), pp. 159–74; O. Bertolini, 'Appunti per la storia del senato di Roma durante il periodo bizantino', (1951), reprinted in *Scritti scelti*, vol. 1, pp. 229–62.

[25] L. Duchesne, *I primi tempi dello stato pontificio* (Turin, 1967), pp. 45–50; O. Bertolini, 'Per la storia delle diaconie romane nell' alto medioevo sino alla fine del secolo VIII', (1947), reprinted in *Scritti scelti*, vol. 1, pp. 309–456.

[26] H. Kretschmayr, *Geschichte von Venedig*, vol. 1 (Gotha, 1905, reprinted Aalen, 1964), pp. 29–54; G. de Vergottini, *Lineamenti storici della costituzione politica dell' Istria durante il medio evo* (Rome, 1924), pp. 30–8; V. Cavallari, 'La costituzione tribunizia istriana', *Rivista storica del diritto italiano*, 23 (1950), pp. 37–68; C. G. Mor, 'Aspetti della vita costituzionale veneziana fino alla fine del x secolo', in *Le origini di Venezia* (Florence, 1964), pp. 123–40; Falkenhausen, *Untersuchungen*, pp. 9–12.

ecclesiastical power capable of stably co-ordinating around itself the ambitions and interests of collectivities and leading individuals. The metropolitan of Grado (which had become the seat of the Aquileian patriarch for the Byzantine territories of the northern Adriatic after the metropolitan's flight from Aquileia at the Lombard advance in the sixth century) certainly had much property and influence in Istria, but its rivalry with the competing patriarchal seat, also called Aquileia, installed in the heart of Friuli for the population of the Lombard hinterland, and the consequent precariousness of its political position and the impossibility of a vast patrimonial expansion, prevented any development comparable with that of Ravenna or Rome. Therefore the social and political organization in these regions, founded as elsewhere on the *militia* of landowners and the functions of the *tribuni* or *iudices*, continued to have at its peak a high Byzantine official, the *magister militum* in Istria (who disappeared at the end of the eighth century with the conquest by the Franks), and the *dux* in the lagoons, a duke who in the course of the same century, under cover of a nomination that was officially imperial, became like the tribunes an expression of the local aristocracy and showed a tendency to make the office hereditary. The process in the duchy of Naples was analogous: indeed, in the 760s, the duke and bishop of the city belonged to the same family.

At Naples, however, there was a complication, in the form of the city's military subordination to the *strategos* of Sicily. This had been established at the end of the seventh or beginning of the eighth century, when the Arabs had already invaded the exarchate of Carthage and the island and the Byzantine lands of southern Italy were incorporated into a new military circumscription, the theme of Sicily. The *strategos* was a sort of military governor who, as he gradually subordinated to his own office all activities of a public nature and then directly assumed the supreme civil functions as well, can be considered as parallel to the figure of the exarch (set up earlier at Ravenna and Carthage), or to that of the Byzantine dukes in several parts of Italy. In fact this administrative evolution – which in the Byzantine West and particularly in the exarchate of Italy was prompted at a very early date, between the sixth and seventh centuries, by the need for a firmer military structure in the more exposed outer provinces – took place more generally in the Empire from the seventh century onwards, with the progressive rearrangement of provinces into themes entrusted to *strategoi*, who recruited the army largely among the inhabitants of the province.[27]

[27] For the question of origins see A. N. Stratos, *Byzantium in the Seventh Century* (Amsterdam, 1968), vol. I, pp. 265–81.

Since these circumscriptions were the result of purely military requirements, it could appear advisable to link districts which had formerly been separate. This was the case with the connection established between Sicily, the duchy of Naples and a duchy of Calabria which included the remains of the Byzantine dominion in the Salento peninsula (Otranto and Gallipoli) and in Bruttium; thanks to the title given to the duchy which included it, it was at this time that Bruttium finally lost its ancient name and took on that of Calabria, which it retained.[28] Thus Byzantine southern Italy came to focus on Syracuse rather than on Ravenna, at a time when the final crisis of the Italian exarchate was imminent thanks to the intensification of Lombard pressure and the delineation of autonomous regional developments in the Ravennate and the Roman duchy.

When the duke of Naples and the cities subject to him, in agreement with the Lombards of Benevento, sought to check and restrict the papal domination radiating from Rome, they encountered support from the *strategos* of Sicily, to whom they were subordinate; on this occasion the *strategos* himself was at Gaeta. But Naples was too far from Syracuse, and too sensitive to central Italy's orientation towards autonomy, for its subordination to the *strategos* to have an impact on the public order of the duchy. The case of Calabria, and naturally Sicily, was different: the control of these regions from Syracuse was much easier. Here a singular fact concerning Byzantine Italy deserves emphasis: no historical source for Sicily and Calabria suggests that the power of the *strategos* was conditioned by local power-relationships. Nor, besides, does it appear that Sicily and southern Italy took part in the insurrection of the Byzantine provinces in Italy during the Iconoclast struggle; indeed, in reaction to the papal rebellion, the imperial court was able to place Sicily and Calabria under the patriarch of Constantinople without local opposition. Several factors may help us to explain this passivity: the absence of a 'Sicilian army' with a structure like that of the *militiae* of Ravenna and Rome and other districts of the exarchate of Italy, because until the recent creation of the theme Sicily had lacked a dominant military order with which the landed class could involve and identify itself; the pre-eminence of the Greek element among the populations of Sicily and Calabria, with the consequent tendency of the two regions to respect all their ties with Byzantium; the first attacks of the Arabs on Sicily, at the end of the seventh century and in the first half of the eighth, with the resulting attention turned on external problems that were able

---

[28] Ensslin, *Zur Verwaltung*, pp. 363ff; Borsari, *L'amministrazione*, pp. 138–51; Falkenhausen, *Untersuchungen*, pp. 3–12.

to distract the population from any possible disagreement with the government of the island.[29]

Thus Sicily alone among the regions which we now call Italian remained intensely tied to Byzantium, a temporary outpost of the Empire in the centre of the Mediterranean. During the crisis of the Italian exarchate Sardinia, once the exarchate of Carthage to which it belonged had been overwhelmed by the Arab advance, suffered its first Muslim invasions, which then continued for three centuries. Meanwhile Corsica had been occupied by the Lombards, who were replaced at the fall of their kingdom by the Franks. The Ligurian coastline was already Lombard from the first half of the seventh century.

THE LOMBARD SETTLEMENT AND THE MILITARY MONOPOLY OF POWER

By an entirely different path from that followed by the populations officially subject to the Byzantine exarchate of Ravenna, Lombard Italy too attained in the eighth century the construction of a social system in which the class of landowners was identified with a military and political class. The *exercitus Senensis*, recorded alongside the clergy in a private charter of 730 drawn up by the gastald Warnefrid of Siena,[30] was a Lombard equivalent of the *exercitus Ravennae* or the *exercitus Romanus* which functioned in those same years in the territories subject to Byzantium. The Sienese *exercitales* were simultaneously the landowners and the free armed men of the Lombard military district which had succeeded, within broader boundaries, the administrative territory that had formed in the Classical period around the Roman colony of Siena.

They were no less rooted in local life than were the *milites* of the Byzantine cities, nor did they lack enterprise despite the heavy hand with which King Liutprand ruled his Lombards at that time, after his ascent to the thone of Pavia in 712. Fifteen years before the charter of 730, in which 'magnificus Warnefrid' solemnly announced the foundation of the church and monastery of S. Eugenio built with his own private money, that same Warnefrid, already gastald of Siena and in this instance functioning as such (that is, as ruler of the Sienese military

---

[29] S. Borsari, *Il monachesimo bizantino nella Sicilia e nell'Italia meridionale prenormanne* (Naples, 1963), pp. 7–38; A. Guillou, 'Grecs d'Italie du Sud et de Sicile au moyen-âge: les moines', *Mélanges d'archéologie et d'histoire*, 75 (1963), pp. 81–3; M. I. Finley, *A History of Sicily. Ancient Sicily to the Arab Conquest* (New York, 1968), pp. 183–8.

[30] L. Schiaparelli, *Codice diplomatico longobardo*, vol. 1 (Rome, 1929–33), p. 165: 'exercitum Senensium civitatis'.

district in the name of the king), had had occasion to express, through a certain high-handed action, not the directives of the Pavian royal court but rather a purely local ambition of the Sienese population, its clergy and its army. This ambition was that the Sienese diocese, which had retained the limits of the ancient territory of the Roman colony, should everywhere reach as far as the boundaries of the gastaldate, incorporating a dozen pieval districts (the vast rural parishes of the time) dependent on the bishop of Arezzo. The disagreement between the episcopal churches of Arezzo and Siena over these boundaries was not a recent matter, but the organized commitment of the *exercitales* of the Sienese diocese to support, not without violence, their bishop's desire for expansion was of recent origin. King Liutprand intervened. He sent to Arezzo a 'majordomo' of his, who pronounced judgement in favour of the Aretine church. This was not enough to persuade the Sienese. Then he sent a *missus* to make a broader inquiry, to ascertain among the clerics and laity of the disputed parishes which bishop had exercised diocesan authority in the past in each place. While awaiting the *missus*, Warnefrid tried to intimidate some clerics from whom he expected evidence unfavourable to Siena. As a cleric of Montepulciano (in the territory contested between the two dioceses and subject to the military command of Siena) testified to the *missus*, '[Warnefrid said] "Look, the *missus* appointed for the inquiry is about to arrive, and you, if you are questioned, what will you say?" I answered, "Take care that he does not question me, because if I am questioned I will speak the truth." He answered me, "You must keep silent before the king's *missus*!"'[31]

That cleric was not the only one to bear witness in favour of Arezzo. Evidence to this effect was also given by those *exercitales* who were militarily subject to Siena but rooted in the religious traditions of the disputed pieval districts. The 'army' of the Lombard king was thus settled throughout the kingdom; it was a class that appeared everywhere, in the cities and in the small rural centres. The adherence to parishes and diocese was not only a religious matter, but represented the incorporation of the *exercitales* into a social framework, their membership of that same class of landowners from which bishops and local priests were mostly recruited.

Indeed the bishops, and in a parallel fashion the royal gastalds, came from the aristocracy of the richest landowning classes. The monastery of S. Eugenio of Siena was not only founded by the gastald Warnefrid, but endowed very richly with the property he had acquired through inheritance or purchase close to Siena and in the valley of the Merse,

---

[31] Schiaparelli, *Codice*, p. 74; see also pp. 48–51.

which was also within the Sienese diocese: agglomerations of landed property (the *curtes* into which the property was organized), olive groves, herds of livestock, various tools and and also clothing and precious ornaments. One can understand how such an individual, through his family tradition so clearly a full member of the aristocracy of the Sienese territory, should have been so sensitive to the claims of the local episcopal church, placing its ambitions above the office given him by the king. A somewhat later will, dictated in 754 at the time of King Aistulf by Bishop Walprand of Lucca, reveals, albeit in general terms, that the family patrimony of Walprand was no less considerable than that of Warnefrid and even extended into Corsica.[32] One may note that the will was drawn up at the moment when the bishop was leaving for the wars, since it includes the remark 'By order of King Aistulf I am bound for the army to depart with him.' We do not know what particular practical purpose was served by the bishop's presence in the military expedition, but certainly it signified close political collaboration between a member of the upper Lombard aristocracy who had attained high ecclesiastical responsibilities and the person of the king.

So in the eighth century the hierarchy of public and ecclesiastical offices corresponded, as much in the Lombard kingdom as in the Byzantine exarchate of Italy, to the various levels of a social and economic hierarchy which both officially appeared and really was an armed class, sustained by predominantly landed property through which it was more or less completely integrated into the individual regional or local context. But through what process had it arrived at a structure so similar, at least in appearance, to the system in operation in the Byzantine territories?

The armed bands which invaded Italy in the sixth century under the leadership of King Alboin displayed a military order which still largely corresponded to the tribal organization of the people. The units of the armies were internally divided according to the kinship groups to which the warriors belonged, that is, into *farae*, as recorded by Paul the Deacon, the Lombard monk who at the end of the eighth century, after the end of the kingdom, narrated the history of his people by drawing on earlier sources. Paul himself explains that the term *fara* indicated a *generatio vel linea*, and so a nucleus which referred back to a common ancestry.[33] The

---

[32] Schiaparelli, *Codice*, p. 335.

[33] *Pauli Historia Langobardorum* (Hanover, 1878, reprinted 1930. *MGH, Scriptores rerum Germanicarum in usum scholarum*) I. II, c. 9 p. 91. This is also confirmed by Byzantine sources (see A. Pertusi, 'Ordinamenti militari, guerre in Occidente e teorie di guerra dei Bizantini', in *Ordinamenti militari*, vol. 2, p. 680), and is valid whatever the original significance of the term (G. P.

settlement of the people in the various regions of Italy came about through the gradual halting of expeditionary units and the distribution of the *farae* between each territory, as many place-names still demonstrate. Even later, in particular movements from one part of the kingdom to another, the migration of the Lombards took place not individually but through kin-groups, at least up to the time of Rothari, who referred to them, using the old term *fara*, in the edict promulgated in 643 with which Lombard legislation began. The leaders of the separate units, the dukes, settled in fortified centres, mostly in old walled Roman cities but sometimes also in other sites (for example at S. Giulio d'Orta rather than at Novara), and became territorial leaders. Since each group of *farae* which made up an occupying force involved complex internal relationships, dependent not only on territorial location but also on kinship ties and a common tradition of war and conquest, each duchy revealed the tendencies to autonomy which led, as has been seen above, to the interregnum from 574 to 584. According to Paul the Deacon, more than thirty dukes without a common leader dominated as many territories, and these may often have corresponded approximately (where the Lombard occupation was least disturbed by the survival of Byzantine territories) to the old Roman municipal circumscriptions whose centres, the fortified cities, had become ducal seats.[34] The need for a common defence against external dangers forced the restoration of the royal power, and from that moment the evolution of the Lombard people and of its relations with the Roman population was strongly influenced by the court of Pavia's orientation towards a monarchical regime tending to the Roman in character.

This influence is still not enough in itself to explain the evolution of the Lombards, which took place above all as the result of their increasing stability in their new settlements and their prolonged co-existence with the Roman populations. In the confusion of the earliest period, especially in the decade of ducal anarchy, the search for booty led to the destruction of almost all the greater and lesser landed aristocracy;[35] the landlords took shelter in the nearest Byzantine lands or perished in the

Bognetti, 'L'influsso delle istituzioni militari romane sulle istituzioni longobarde del secolo vi e la natura della "fara"' (1953), reprinted in *L'età longobarda*, vol. 3 (Milan 1967), pp. 12–27.

[34] F. Schneider, *Die Reichsverwaltung in Toscana* (Rome, 1914), pp. 32–42; C. G. Mor, 'Lo stato longobardo nel vii secolo', in *Caratteri del secolo VII*, vol. 1, pp. 272–9, with the discussion on pp. 328, 333; C. Brühl, *Fodrum, gistum, servitium regis* (Cologne-Graz, 1968), vol. 1, pp. 335–61.

[35] For some possible exceptions see G. Fasoli, 'Aspetti di vita economica e sociale nell' Italia del secolo vii', in *Caratteri del secolo VII*, vol. 1, p. 112; Sestan, *La composizione etnica*, pp. 667ff.

massacres. There was a profound upheaval of all social relationships. The great Roman proprietors, of senatorial rank or provincial tradition, disappeared. What happened to the complex management of their patrimonies? The metropolitan bishop of Milan and all the Milanese upper clergy fled to Genoa as early as 569 and stayed there for many decades under Byzantine protection. The patriarch of Aquileia fled to Grado with his clergy. Siena remained without a bishop until the time of Rothari, and, when the ecclesiastical see was restored, it was for precisely this reason that the first disputes over boundaries arose with the church of Arezzo, which had not suffered any interruption and indeed had acted as temporary deputy several times for the vacant Sienese see. Although these are the best-known cases they were certainly not isolated, and they represent extreme situations in a confusion which struck all the episcopal churches of the region occupied by the Lombards, who were recently and only crudely converted from their traditional cults to Arian Christianity; almost all the ecclesiastical estates suffered encroachments, according to Paul the Deacon.

On the other hand the same Paul informs us that when the dukes restored the royal power after the decade of anarchy (574–84) they ceded to King Authari half of their goods, and that the Bavarian Catholic Theudelinda, wife of Authari and then of his successor Agilulf, secured from her second husband the donation of much property to the churches to remedy the unhappy condition of the bishops. And it is well-documented that in the eighth century kings and dukes made ample gifts to the churches, to their own friends and to their *gasindi*, men tied to them by a special personal fidelity. All this presupposes an enormous quantity of public land, consisting for the most part of lands that had already been public earlier, whether belonging to the emperor or to civic and perhaps rural collectivities,[36] and of the great properties of the Roman aristocracy and the churches. Thus it presupposes a continuity in the concept of the great landed estate, despite all the possible disruptions of the topographical structure of the preceding estates and all the weakening of the forms of economic administration which had guaranteed the social hegemony of an earlier time. The great estate sustained military and political power at its highest levels, and was confused with the land owned personally by the king and the dukes, since it was hereditary in the same way as their power, a power which passed only with difficulty from one family to another without the extinction of a lineage or violence.

With respect to the more or less considerable Lombard estates not

---

[36] G. I. Cassandro, *Storia delle terre comuni e degli usi civici nell'Italia meridionale* (Bari, 1943), pp. 75, 93–100.

directly connected with the formation of royal or ducal dynasties or
with the restoration of the church, nothing is recorded about their
origin. Undoubtedly the closeness of each single family's relations with
the court of Pavia or the ducal courts had a notable bearing on their
development. This is clearly evident in the eighth century, and emerges
as an important factor for understanding the structure of certain family
estates, which could be scattered over several regions of the kingdom.
Indeed, through royal donations landed wealth was increased even in
zones distant from those where the economic force of a great family was
concentrated, as has been seen above in the case of the Luccan bishop
whose lands extended to Corsica. But what was the initial nucleus of
such expansion? It is probable that in certain cases (which there is no
reason to consider as typical) the nucleus derived from the first divisions
of land among the Lombards in Italy, as the result of military
responsibilities of some importance which had been borne by particular
warriors connected with the dukes or the king in the course of the
conquests and first phases of settlement, whether or not their families
had been distinguished by a tradition of nobility or social pre-eminence
in Pannonia (the Danubian region where they were settled before
coming to Italy).[37] Other families prominent in the eighth century were
perhaps descended from simple *arimanni*, the ancient Lombard name
which survived for centuries in Italy and designates the ordinary soldiers.
But here there appears the broader problem of the initial establishment
of the *arimanni* as a class of landowners.

From Paul the Deacon it appears that in the first period of their
presence in Italy, up to the restoration of the kingdom with Authari, the
Lombards lived on a systematic requisition of one third of the fruits of
the earth, as well as on plunder. Then they themselves were transformed
into landowners. But, it must be asked, did the *arimanni* insert
themselves among the ranks of small Roman landowners, principally
making use, like their military leaders, of lands drawn from the
public and ecclesiastical patrimonies and from the destroyed Roman
aristocracy? Or was the upheaval of the first period of violence and
requisitions great enough to involve and wipe out the whole class of
Roman landowners? If we examine the legislation and notarial
documents of the eighth century, there is no doubt that the major part
of the landowners from the time of Liutprand to the end of the kingdom
in 774 were Lombards, free men who in matters of private law followed
the Lombard judicial tradition.[38] Perhaps it is not impossible that at the

---

[37] Werner, 'Die Langobarden in Pannonien', pp. 32, 46, 80, 117, 120.

[38] G. Tabacco, 'Dai possessori dell'età carolingia agli esercitali dell'età
longobarda', *Studi medievali*, ser. III, 10.1 (1969), pp. 221–68. See J. Jarnut,

end of the seventh century, when the conversion of the Lombards to Catholicism was almost complete, their co-existence in the same social class with the remnants of the class of Roman landowners should have led some Romans to accept the judicial tradition of the dominant people, perhaps through an initial infiltration of Roman elements into the army, as the personal names of the *exercitales* in the succeeding reign of Liutprand might suggest. But there is no sign that at that point there had already taken place any substantial legal and military assimilation of a free Roman population by the Lombards. Therefore the upheaval in the conditions of property-owning at the end of the sixth century was vaster and more radical than the annihilation of the Roman aristocracy would lead one to suppose. Probably it was not the same in all the Lombard regions of Italy, since the settlement of the new people was not equally dense everywhere. It was greatest in present-day Lombardy and much less, for example, in certain parts of the vast southern duchy of Benevento, which stretched from the borders of the Byzantine duchy of Rome and the Lombard duchy of Spoleto to the gulf of Taranto.[39] But in any case the Lombards reduced the Roman population to the margins of social power at every level, and identified it for the most part with the class of the *coloni*, which in preceding periods had already been numerically superior.

None the less the habits of work in the rural world of Italy were not in fact disrupted, since in the first phases of their history in Italy the *arimanni* did not join the cultivators but placed themselves above the latter, whether the cultivators had been small landowners or *coloni*.[40] Certainly the means employed to exploit the peasant population underwent some changes, both through the brutal crudeness – and the consequent simplification – of the dominion exercised by the new masters of the land, and through the collapse of the political and administrative scaffolding on which had been based a robust system of public taxation, which had burdened the peasants in addition to private exactions. But the Lombards certainly acquired a strong sense of

Prosopographische und sozialgeschichtliche Studien zum Langobardenreich in Italien (Bonn, 1972), pp. 403–27.

[39] F. Sabatini, *Riflessioni linguistici della dominazione longobarda nell'Italia mediana e meridionale* (Florence, 1963), pp. 41, 55, 121–9, and the observations of P. Toubert in *Le Moyen Age*, 75 (1969), pp. 125–7.

[40] Hartmann, *Geschichte Italiens im Mittelalter*, vol. 2.1, pp. 40–4; vol. 2.2, pp. 48–52; G. P. Bognetti, 'Storia, archeologia e diritto nel problema dei Longobardi', *Atti del I Congresso internazionale di studi longobardi* (Spoleto, 1952), pp. 92–5, 'La proprietà della terra nel passaggio dal mondo antico al medio evo occidentale', in *Dopo il primo convegno internazionale di diritto agrario* (Milan, 1958), pp. 124–38.

individual property, thus returning to the disrupted Roman tradition;
this sense gradually developed as each *fara*, spreading across the
settlement area, broke up into a plurality of families ever more loosely
tied among themselves. A sense of individual property was already clear
at the time of Rothari even within families, as is apparent from the
chapters in the edict on patrimonial succession. Only uncultivated and
wooded areas remained in common to the whole nucleus of settled
arimanni which had been a *fara*: the *silva arimannorum*, the *mons
arimannorum*, the *gualdus exercitalis*, reserved to the *exercitales* as pasture
from their horses and livestock and for any other form of exploitation;
traces of these areas remain in place-names and in the charters of the
eighth century onwards. It is possible that these wooded areas did not
always originate in the first distribution of lands among the Lombards
but in much later allocations made by kings or dukes to reinforce
economically the groups of *arimanni* most deeply engaged in military
defence – this may be the case with certain *gualdi* recorded in the
Carolingian period in the territory of Rieti, within the duchy of
Spoleto.[41] But these uncultivated common lands did not disturb the
familial or individual character of ownership of cultivated land or
movable goods, just as in the Classical period the idea of individual
property had not been disturbed by the presence of common land
belonging, through possession or through use, to urban or rural
collectivities. The possession of common lands by groups of *arimanni*,
and their exclusive enjoyment of it, instead helped to distinguish them
on the social level both from any remaining Roman landowners and
from the great Lombard landowners who had more or less vast
uncultivated areas within their own private estates.

   This social and economic distinction underlined in its turn a purely
political fact. The right to arms, proper to the Lombards, implied
participation not only in enterprises of war and the military defence of
the territory, but also in the control and political domination of the
Roman population. The latter were not all serfs; they were also, to a
considerable extent (even when one leaves aside the problem of a
Roman minority of landowners), cultivators who were personally free
even though economically dependent, free merchants and artisans in the
(certainly impoverished) cities, and clerics. In particular, the celebrated
inquiry ordered by Liutprand in the area disputed between the bishops
of Arezzo and Siena allows us to grasp the intensity of the control
exercised by the local political authorities over every movement of

---

[41] G. Tabacco, *I liberi del re nell'Italia carolingia e postcarolingia* (Spoleto, 1966),
pp. 113–38; see A. Haverkamp, *Herrschaftsformen der Frühstaufer in Reichsitalien*
(Stuttgart, 1970–1), vol. 1, pp. 297ff.

clerics outside the military district to which they belonged, even if it were only a journey to Arezzo to be consecrated by the bishop. One may note that there was no autonomous provision of a police or tribunals; justice corresponded to the operation of the territorial leaders and their closest collaborators, the *sculdasci*, *centenari* and *decani*, who were in charge of small divisions of the army and of a finely-spread vigilance over the land, and to the activities of all the *exercitales* settled in the territory, who were always ready for actions which we would today call policing and for public attendance at the judicial sessions presided over by greater or lesser leaders. The succession itself in the duchies and in the kingdom, and the promulgation of royal edicts, although in fact sanctioned principally by the presence and consent of the aristocracy, always implied an appeal to the broader consensus of 'all the most fortunate army', as one reads, for example, in the conclusion of Rothari's edict of 643. This was not a purely theoretical appeal: in the frequent struggles for the kingdom, the candidates for power competed for the support of the 'armies' or sections of 'armies' settled in the various districts.

In this sense the Lombard people, as a 'most fortunate army' settled in Italy, held the monopoly of political power, surrounding and collaborating with their leaders, together with the social hegemony and with an absolute prevalence in landed property.

THE RECONSTRUCTION OF THE SOCIAL APPARATUS WITH THE DEVELOPMENT OF THE LOMBARD MONARCHY

The social hegemony of the Lombards in Italy was in reality limited by the continuous operation of the Catholic churches, since the interruption in the succession of bishops was not a general occurrence.[42] The case of Siena should not make us forget that of Arezzo, where the bishop also acted as deputy in the Sienese territory. Nor did the flight of the upper clergy of Milan signify the disappearance of the whole Milanese ecclesiastical hierarchy; the minor clergy remained in the city and in the diocese, providing a religious and civil framework for the population. The reduction of the political system to a barbarian military structure reduced for the Roman population the civil significance of the royal and ducal order to a protection against the most excessive and violent acts,

[42] G. P. Bognetti, 'La continuità delle sedi episcopali e l'azione di Roma nel regno longobardo', in *Le Chiese nei regni dell' Europa occidentale*, pp. 415–54. See some corrections in G. Tabacco, 'Espedienti politici e persuasioni religiose nel medioevo di Gian Piero Bognetti', *Rivista di storia della Chiesa in Italia*, 24 (1970), pp. 504–23.

and as a result the role already adopted by the clergy from the Roman period onwards assumed greater importance, in the provision of a general orientation for the Catholic laity and the supervision of the forms of social co-existence.

Despite some decrease in wealth, the Catholic clergy had maintained a tie with the forms of Roman culture peculiar to earlier ages and to the remaining Byzantine lands, and they had therefore preserved their social position, as is apparent from their capacity for action even within the world of the Lombards. One cannot otherwise explain King Authari's prohibition of his subjects baptizing their children according to the Catholic rite. The Lombard population, in part still tied to non-Christian beliefs, had on the other hand, in the Arianism of the Germanic tradition, only a recent and imperfect ecclesiastical defence; Arian bishops and priests had no organization of concepts and of worship capable of resisting the activities of the rival clergy.[43] After Authari even the court of Pavia was open to Catholic influence, even with episodes in an opposite direction, which throughout the seventh century were linked with analogous crises in the aristocracy and the army. But meanwhile the reconstruction of a landed base for the church, encouraged by Theudelinda and by the donations of the military leaders and *arimanni* who were slowly being converted, restored intact to the Catholic episcopate its former dignity, favoured its progressively increasing recruitment among the Lombard aristocracy, and put an end to the dualism in the eyes of the Roman population between the power of the dominant people and the oppressed yet vigorous authority of the traditional Italian clergy. Yet again, exactly as had happened at the end of the Roman world, and as happened in direct continuation from the Roman Empire in the world dominated by the Franks and in the empire of Byzantium, the authoritarian forms of the ecclesiastical order entered into symbiosis with the social class that provided a political and economic structure for the population.

This symbiosis of the upper clergy was now no longer with a political class prominent for its intellectual awareness and literary formation, but with a military hierarchy – and this not with a co-ordination of *milites* constructed, as in the Byzantine lands in Italy, on pre-existing social and bureaucratic gradations and still reflecting a certain kind of culture, but rather with a simple aristocracy of warriors who were moved only by a certain degree of religious anxiety.

It is true that during the long labour of conversion there was some attempt to re-establish certain patterns of the ancient *civilitas*. There is evidence for this at Pavia at the end of the seventh century, when Bishop Damian, who was probably of Greek origin, set up sacred and secular buildings, churches and baths to clean souls and bodies, as his epitaph declares.[44] This occurred because from the time of Theudelinda, and under the kings of the Catholic dynasty who descended from her (a dynasty that alternated on the throne with vigorous Arian kings such as Rothari), the missionary activity of local nuclei of Catholic clergy in the Lombard regions was sustained and culturally strengthened by the influence of the churches under Byzantine political control in Italy, and by the presence of some of those Greek and Oriental clerics who were then so numerous in Rome, Ravenna and every part of Byzantine Italy. But those baths were no more than a starting point, only possible at a fortunate moment in the activity of Oriental clerics who were powerful in the capital of the Lombard kings. While Byzantium was withdrawing from central Italy, members of the Lombard aristocracy flocked to the Catholic episcopate of the eighth century. Meanwhile, through the work of the king and other powerful individuals, monastic foundations multiplied, and abbots and abbesses of royal stock or from other great Lombard families followed one another in the administration of the wealthy monastic houses.[45] All Catholic 'spirituality', within the ritual and ascetic models developed in antiquity, converged with the desire of the dominant race to establish itself and to command.

But together with these models the Lombard world was penetrated by a concept of political power different from the traditional one through which king and dukes expressed, in a simple form, an enterprising people's desire for conquest and warfare. This new concept conquered the court from the time of Agilulf (591–616) onward. For centuries Catholicism had been something more than an instrument of religious unrest and the pacification of souls. Its character as a social system was the result of a compromise between its tradition as a religious community and its authoritarian tendencies, which were derived from the great Roman power-structure: at the same time, the Catholic church was accustomed to operate under the protection of that same great political organization. Therefore its very presence, and its language drawn from

---

[44] G. P. Bognetti, 'S. Maria Foris Portas di Castelseprio e la storia religiosa dei longobardi' (1948), reprinted in Bognetti, *L'età longobarda*, vol. 2 (Milan 1966), pp. 514–18; see Tabacco, 'Espedienti politici', pp. 518ff.

[45] U. Pasqui, *Documenti per la storia della città di Arezzo nel medioevo*, vol. 4 (Arezzo, 1904), pp. 3ff; K. Voigt, *Die königlichen Eigenklöster im Langobardenreiche* (1909, reprinted Aalen, 1969) pp. 111–16; Schiaparelli, *Codice*, vol. 1, pp. 137ff; vol. 2 (Rome, 1933), pp. 73ff.

those ancient traditions, suggested the construction of disciplined hierarchies of power even to those who had lived within more transient forms of political co-operation. This was clear above all in sixth-century Gaul, when the bishopric with its senatorial Gallo-Roman tradition taught the Frankish king to think of himself as a 'new Constantine', a 'Christian' prince reigning at the apex of a state apparatus. There ensued from this the singular experiment of Chilperic I (556–75), who went beyond even the teaching of the bishops. That Frankish king, who felt himself invested with responsibilities worthy of a *basileus* of Constantinople, argued (not without acuity) against trinitarian theology, legislated on schools and reformed the alphabet. Above all – and this provoked rebellions among the Franks and dangerous hatred among 'abbots' and 'priests' – he did not permit exemptions from the army without adequate compensation, and directed the compilation of detailed registers where all the landowners, both Franks and Romans, appeared equal in their subordination to him, and were subjected to the exaction of public contributions in proportion to the extent of their landed property and the number of their slaves.[46]

There was no Chilperic at Pavia, and even in the world of the Franks the king abandoned certain ambitions which were too 'Roman'. But in the seventh century, on both sides of the Alps, the greatest territorial powers sought wherever possible to organize the territory according to a unitary plan, making use of agents expressly delegated to represent the person of the king, or of a duke of exceptional power and autonomy such as the dukes of Spoleto and Benevento. These agents were called counts, particularly in Gaul and in the various kingdoms of the Franks; although they had this name here and there in Lombard Italy, in Italy in general they were more often called gastalds. Probably first created by the administration of the royal fisc which was distributed in the various districts of the kingdom, they were ever more frequently employed as temporary officials (sometimes perhaps in the same centre alongside another gastald still in charge of the administration of fiscal property alone), to replace dukes, where wars or rebellions placed a duke in crisis.[47] Similarly, gastalds were created by the dukes of Spoleto and

[46] *Gregorii Episcopi Turonensis Historiarum Libri Decem* 1.11, c. 31; 1.v, c. 26, 28, 34, 44 (*MGH Scriptores rerum Merovingicarum*, vol. 1).

[47] R. Poupardin, *Les Institutions politiques et administratives des principautés lombardes de l'Italie méridionale* (Paris, 1907), pp. 30–4; C. G. Mor, 'I gastaldi con potere ducale nell'ordinamento pubblico longobardo', *Atti del I Congresso internazionale di studi longobardi*, pp. 409–15; G. P. Bognetti, 'Il gastaldato longobardo e i giudicati di Adaloaldo, Arioaldo e Pertarido nella lite fra Parma e Piacenza' (1940–1), reprinted in *L'età longobarda*, vol. 1, pp. 262–74;

Benevento in order to subdivide territorially their vast duchies. Spoleto was dominant up to the southern margins of the Pentapolis in the north and up to the boundaries of Samnium in the south, bordering for a long stretch in the east on the Adriatic, while the greater part of southern Italy was subject to Benevento.[48] The court of Pavia sought to exercise increasing control even over the dukes, in the regions in which they survived, but they represented a power too deeply rooted in the territory for the king, even a Liutprand (712–44), to succeed in appointing or removing them without violent conflict. In varying measure, the dukes represented the autonomy of a power in whose operation royal interventions had to compromise with the traditions of local *arimanni* and the dynastic tendencies of the ducal families.

Development of the royal power into a monarchy with a clear territorial base was thus limited by the survival of the duchies, and indeed, south of the line where the kingdom's territorial continuity was interrupted by the Byzantine districts of the Pentapolis, Perugia and Rome, these took shape as political formations oriented towards their own separate further development. The duchies were capable of imitating the royal court in defining lesser districts, in administration of the ducal fisc, in the creation of a small central bureaucracy and of a chancery which could give solemn form to the privileges conceded by the duke, drawing up diplomas according to a formulary worthy of the power of a prince. At Benevento, and in some measure also at Spoleto, royal authority received a recognition more often nominal than substantial. In this way the two great Lombard duchies inserted themselves among the Byzantine territories which were themselves tending towards autonomy, and accentuated the political fragmentation of the peninsula. But when considered in the dimensions which better correspond to its effective operation, that is, in the area which embraced the greater part of northern Italy and Tuscany (*Tuscia*), the Lombard kingdom exerted a considerable unifying pressure. The royal power elevated itself above the traditional people of the *arimanni* and its internal divisions, and expressed through legislation the spontaneous process that transformed the dominant people into a complex social class, which was defined and armed no longer according to the criterion of ethnic distinction but rather in accordance with the size of their property.

In fact King Aistulf, in an edict of 750, warned landowners not to neglect their own arms and divided them into several categories related

O. Bertolini, 'Ordinamenti militari e strutture sociali dei longobardi in Italia', in *Ordinamenti militari*, pp. 482–9.

[48] H. Müller, *Topographische und genealogische Untersuchungen zur Geschichte des Herzogtums Spoleto und der Sabina von 800 bis 1100* (Greifswald, 1930).

to their economic position, prescribing to the richest at least a cuirass, shield, lance and some horses, to those of the middle rank a shield, lance and horse, and to the *minores* a shield, bow and arrows. The edict is careful to indicate the wealth of landowners of the middle and upper levels, defining the former on the basis of property not less than forty *iugera* and the latter on the basis of at least seven tenancies cultivated by dependent peasant families, 'septem casas massarias'. The edict also provides for the case of one who possesses tenancies in multiples of seven, and prescribed that such a landowner should maintain a proportionate number of complete outfits, from cuirass to horses. And although attention is turned primarily on the owner of land, the merchants without landed property are not ignored: they too are divided into several categories, indicated with the generic terms *maiores et potentes*, *sequentes* and *minores*, with obligations to provide arms corresponding to the obligations of the landowners.[49]

As we have seen above, landed property was for the most part in the hands of Lombards, and it must be acknowledged that among the *negotiantes* in the cities the Lombard element was also present. But it should not be assumed that Lombards were also the most typical landless traders. Aistulf carried to its extreme consequences the spontaneous convergence of all *liberi homines* supplied with some economic income, whether Lombards or Romans, into the same social group, and incorporated them all officially into the Lombard military tradition, from the *maiores et potentes* down to the *minima persona* who was capable of arming himself in some way as an *exercitalis*. Certainly the greater part of the Roman population remained excluded, not because they were Roman, but because they formed the mass of the *coloni*, and a minority of Lombards were also excluded who had become impoverished in the century-long settlement in Italy. For the Lombards had learnt not only to base themselves on landed property but to compete among themselves economically; the transactions through which they did so were destined to modify and broaden the previous range of social positions, which had been determined only by responsibility assumed in the different ranks of the army, according to the military fame of the family and the personal skills of the individual.

The economic base originally acquired as a result of military responsibility influenced social positions and this in turn then affected the distribution of official power within the Lombard people, through the various unpredictable opportunities open to property owners; inheritance of a patrimony, the use of income from the land to increase

[49] Bertolini, *Ordinamenti militari*, pp. 497–503.

one's landed property through applying new skills, the introduction of more careful calculation in establishing profitable family ties, the search for fruitful friendships in the royal courts and with the dukes and gastalds. The private archive of one Alahis, a rich Lombard of the time of Liutprand, witnesses to these processes; he preserved there many generous diplomas in his favour from the king, and an even greater number of charters of private purchases and sales. The double source of changing fortunes in the seventh to eighth centuries was this: changing relationships with public officials and private land transactions. They were the cause of rise and also of decline, of *nobilitas* and *egestas*, as Paul the Deacon says with reference to his own family, which was caught up in the affairs of the Lombard kingdom at its very end.[50]

'Nobility' and poverty were incompatible in the animated social world of the late Lombard period. Precisely this convergence between the idea of a *nobilitas*, which still implied that the fame of powerful families was not established too recently, and the idea of landed power demonstrates that the network of kinship between the *optimates* and the interplay of links with the state functioned remarkably well in support of an identifiable and persistent Lombard aristocracy. Thus within the dimensions of the *regnum Langobardorum* a social apparatus was reconstructed which was in some respects analogous to that which had dominated the civil life of the peninsula in the last Imperial period and in the Theodorician age, in the form of a Romano-Italic aristocracy of senatorial rank or provincial tradition. It was analogous in its prevalently landed base, mostly concentrated in certain zones although not without a presence across vast regions of Italy, analogous in the underlying solidarity between the magnates despite the many episodic conflicts between fluid alliances of friends and kin, and finally analogous in its profound mutual interpenetration with both the public and ecclesiastical orders.

Even so, the new aristocracy of the Lombard kingdom differed in a fundamental fashion from those ancient social structures, because of the military tradition on which it was founded, through the links of the magnates with the ranks of *arimanni* who still constituted the tradition of an armed people despite their new form as a category of fairly modest landowners. From this standpoint the social and political system resembled the one that came into being, through a different process, in

[50] A. J. Njeussychin, *Die Entstehung der abhängigen Bauernschaft als Klasse der frühfeudalen Gesellschaft in Westeuropa* (in Russian, 1956; German translation, Berlin, 1961), pp. 392–423; G. Tabacco, 'La concessione fra potere e possesso nel regno franco e nel regno longobardo', in *I problemi dell' Occidente nel secolo VIII* (Spoleto, 1973).

the Byzantine territories of Italy. We may imagine, however, that the *primates* and the *milites*, born under the shadow of Byzantine authority and functioning within specific regional realities, still lived within a public order that, rooted as it was from Naples to Ravenna in an uninterrupted tradition of urban life, was less elementary than that formed by the *nobiles* and *exercitales* of the Lombard kingdom, despite the fact that the latter operated with a broader political horizon. Among the Lombards there is no sign that the public activity of the dukes, gastalds and *sculdasci* was anything more than military protection, complemented by judicial responsibility. Not even a uniform general system of public taxation survived. Obligations which had been imposed on proprietors since the Roman period did survive in order to keep in repair bridges and roads, but even this can only be deduced from directions issued by the Frankish kings in Italy a few years after the collapse of the Lombard kingdom. Such obligations answered precise military needs, of course, but we know nothing about how vigilantly the Lombard authorities imposed them in practice. As for the maintenance of public officials, beginning with the royal court itself, this was partly ensured by the right such persons had to be entertained by the greater and lesser landowners resident in the areas visited, but it rested above all on the property of the fisc. This consisted of the *curtes regiae* and *curtes ducales*, administered by appointed agents of the king or the dukes, but their administration must have been made difficult by the common interests of the *arimanni* and of the slaves resident on the fiscal lands since King Liutprand had to prohibit in 733, in an explicit and lengthy regulation, the purchase of royal land from *servi*, and had to menace those *actores* guilty of complicity or of insufficient vigilance.[51]

In pronouncing this ban Liutprand displayed his indignation over the injustice of the *arimanni*, whose personal property was guaranteed by royal legislation but who had no respect for the possessions of the king even though they were bound to him by an oath of fidelity. The regulation thus shows us that an idea of personal loyalty to the king and of the swearing of an oath had come to exist within the traditional relationship between the people of the *arimanni* and the power conferred on its military and political leader. There is no question of a fidelity that marks out specific units of the army or individual men, but even so it reveals the need the Lombard king felt to strengthen the bond created by joint military enterprises and by shared control of the mass of cultivators, through formal and solemn acts of devotion to the royal

[51] L. M. Hartmann, *Zur Wirtschaftsgeschichte Italiens im frühen Mittelalter* (Gotha, 1904) pp. 112–22; Brühl, *Fodrum*, pp. 357–92; Tabacco, 'Dai possessori', pp. 222–4, 234–46.

person. This appeal to personal fidelity recurs in the prologues of edicts promulgated by the kings, sometimes with specific reference to the fidelity owed them by their greatest subjects, the *optimates*, who from every part of Neustria and Austria (the two geographical areas into which Lombard northern Italy was customarily divided, western and eastern with respect to Pavia) and from Tuscany hastened to the great legislative deliberations, gathering around the 'most excellent king of the Catholics and most fortunate king of the Lombards'. Thus the old language of Rothari, his reference to the consensus of the *primates* and all the people of the most fortunate army, was complicated by a significant appeal to the new Catholic base of the kingdom and to the duty of faithful subordination, particularly by the powerful. The Lombards are still seen as a dominant people, tightly gathered around their leaders in exercising their common dominion, but the orientation towards a monarchical power, supported by a Catholic culture, and the evolution of the army into a complex social system with the hegemony of the great landed aristocracy, enrich the formulary used by the royal chancery and reveal the new problems of 'Lombard' society.

The danger to the existence of the Lombard domination was no longer represented by the centrifugal tendencies of the old tribal groupings which had united in very ephemeral forms for the conquest of the peninsula. Rather, it lay in the *optimates'* capacity for autonomous action when, on the basis of rich family lands which were capable of sustaining the burden of demand for abundant supplies, they pursued ducal power or other high offices in the kingdom, and enjoyed the consequent access to further wealth and the clear link with particular sections of the army which the armed landowners of the districts entrusted to them. In its turn, the royal power stressed the public character of the general subordination to the king of the *arimanni* and of officials and military leaders, reinforcing it with the bonds of personal devotion to the sole person who represented stability and political unity.

At the same time, in individual cases the recourse to personal fidelity was reinforced by a special legal concept, the gasindate: certain collaborators of the king, the *gasindi*, entered into a particular personal dependence, receiving privileged protection and rich gifts in return for loyal service. This is the institution of clientship, already recorded at the time of Rothari, an institution of which from then on, according to customs which the king respected, the dukes, and even powerful *homines privati*, also availed themselves.[52] Thus the gasindate was a weapon that

---

[52] P. S. Leicht, 'Gasindii e vassalli' (1927), reprinted in Leicht, *Scritti vari di storia del diritto italiano* (Milan, 1943), vol. 1, pp. 185–90.

could be used in two opposing directions. In the Lombard kingdom, however, it did not develop to such a point as to complicate very noticeably the equilibrium of coexisting forces. Before such developments came about, the kingdom was overwhelmed by the Franks, who experienced, and caused all Romano-Germanic Europe to experience, a similar institution, vassalage, in all its contradictory fruitfulness.

3

THE INCORPORATION OF ITALY INTO THE WORLD OF THE FRANKS

The expansion of the Franks in Europe in the course of the eighth century, an expansion which annexed a large part of Italy and ended the Catholic experiment of the Lombard monarchy, continues to amaze the historian who is aware of the ruinous condition of royal power and of the administrative structures of Gaul at the end of the seventh century. The royal dynasty of the Merovingians, sometimes divided into many branches, had ruled the Frankish world from the end of the fifth to the end of the eighth century and had become the symbol of political and sacral power in Gaul. It was then deprived of power by the great landed aristocracy, which had reabsorbed the rest of the Gallo-Roman senatorial class and the military sectors of the Frankish people, and in particular by the nobles who gathered around the Pippinids. This was the most powerful family of the Frankish kingdom of Austrasia, that is of the group of regions of the lower and middle Rhine valley (from the North Sea to the territory of the Alamans), an area where the Germanic tradition of the Frankish people had survived most vigorously with its peculiar strongly-marked military characteristics and which also preserved in large part the Germanic language. The Pippinids appropriated the office of Mayor of the Palace in the Merovingian court of Austrasia, founded their own dynastic presence on the hereditary nature of the office, extended their effective power over the whole Frankish world under the shadow of the Merovingians and finally, through election and popular acclamation, replaced the latter as the royal dynasty, to become the dynasty that we call Carolingian. Not only did the Franks draw tightly around this dynasty, but at the end of the eighth century the greater part of western Christianity found itself assembled into a single entity which in a celebrated Roman ceremony, through papal initiative, took the name of 'Roman Empire', thus definitively repudiating the universal claims of the Empire of Constantinople and claiming within Christianity a pre-eminent political role for the West united by the Franks. But how did the Pippinids succeed where the Merovingians failed? Not only did they succeed in disciplining the aristocracy and Frankish people, formerly divided into factions and rival groups of nobles, but they drove back the Muslim invasion, which had reached the Loire, they crossed the Rhine and subdued the Saxons, spread along the Danube as far as the duchy of Bavaria, and beyond the Alps overthrew the Lombard kingdom which, despite internal discord, seemed to have found a stable reference point in Pavia, a capital city such as the Frankish kingdoms did not have.

This took place through a series of challenges (to use the language of Toynbee[1]) to which the Franks, beginning with those of Austrasia, knew to give successive adequate responses. Between the seventh and eighth centuries the Franks of Austrasia had to defend themselves from the aggression of Saxons to the north and Alamans to the east, while the whole Frankish people was then threatened by Arab penetration deep into the area. The Pippinids found themselves at the heart of an aristocratic circle in Austrasia which was capable of accepting the multiple challenge, and of leading the Franks in the effective deeds of war which were felt to be urgently needed by the majority in Austrasia and in Gaul generally.[2] The successes that gradually followed, in these struggles undertaken by the Franks in order to survive as a dominant people, created a new military solidarity and a tradition of shared enterprises which extended and broadened at the time of Charlemagne into action across Europe. In this military and political expansion an important role was played by the ideological covering provided by the centuries-long assimilation of the Franks into the religious and ecclesiastical models that they had inherited from the Catholic late Roman Empire. These models on the one hand, by placing the whole population on the same level as the Franks, played a conservative role, guaranteeing the hierarchies that had formed in the whole social structure and promoting a common defence against

---

[1] A. Toynbee, *Le civiltà nella storia* (Turin 1950) p. 96ff.

[2] R. Spandel, *Der merovingische Adel und die Gebiete östlich des Rheins* (Freiburg im Breisgau, 1957), pp. 114ff.

external dangers; while on the other hand, by undertaking the ancient need to preach the Christian message to the peoples and reorganize them in communities disciplined by bishops, they displayed a vigorous capacity to break down the elementary forms of cultural and political autonomy of those Germanic and Slav peoples which had remained extraneous to the Christian world, in the vast spaces of northern-central and eastern Europe.[3]

These same models also operated in the Frankish intervention south of the Alps up to the disappearance of the Lombard kingdom in 774. It is true that the Lombards had by now taken on a strongly Catholic structure, but the persistent papal horror at the name of Lombard supplied the Frankish aggression in Italy, provoked by the entreaties of Rome, with a Catholic significance as a defence of the 'apostolic see'. The papacy felt threatened not so much in its religious autonomy, accustomed as it was to difficult disputes with the arrogant and theologically committed court of Constantinople, but in its character as a 'Roman' church which had always lived within the formal framework of a 'Roman' empire. It had lived within the empire uninterruptedly, since even Theoderic the Great had accepted, particularly with regard to the Senate and Church of Rome, the idea of the empire of which his kingdom was a part. The bishops of the Byzantine lands of Italy, around whom the Romano-Italic society which had fled from the Lombards was largely re-forming, were profoundly anchored to the tradition of the *res publica*, however weak imperial protection had become and however hateful the iconoclastic emperors appeared. The kings of Pavia represented a tradition foreign to the *res publica* and formally antithetical to it.

Concurrently with the social transformation of their people, the Lombard kings, as has been noted, were constructing a monarchy of a Catholic type, which also tended towards territorial coherence and therefore spread into the exarchate and the Roman duchy; this expansion was inevitable anyway, if the king aimed to have any co-ordinated and stable control from Pavia over the whole Lombard world as far as the gulf of Taranto, and to crush the interposed obstacles of the Byzantine lands of central Italy. A territorial and Catholic monarchy, then, was at issue; but the initial basis of royal authority still lay in its organization of Latin-Germanic continental Europe up to the Alpine people, who at the ideological level were transformed in the direction of Catholicism while always remaining within a reaffirmed continuity of

[3] See H. Löwe, 'Pirmin, Willibrord und Bonifatius. Ihre Bedeutung für die Missionsgeschichte ihrer Zeit', in *La conversione al cristianesimo nell'Europa dell'alto medioevo* (Spoleto, 1967), pp. 217–61.

tradition. And while this model was alive in the consciousness of the kings of Pavia, who still presented themselves always as natural leaders of a *gens* which coincided with the fortunes of an army, it was equally alive in the memory of the bishops, the *optimates* and the populations of the Byzantine lands of Italy, and terrified them; above all it terrified the apparatus of the Roman church, which was rooted in the idea of the Empire and had grown up in imitation of its institutions and within an exclusively Greco-Latin cultural sphere.

And so, on the one side, King Aistulf when he occupied the exarchate of Ravenna presented himself in the prologue to an edict of 750, as if to justify the *fait accompli*, in the compound figure of king of the Lombard people and lord of the Roman people who had been 'entrusted' to him by God. The edict solemnly recognized two distinct cultural models, which the king did not conceive of being able to unify except in his own person, and theoretically accepted that military expansion would not result in the incorporation of Romano-Byzantine society into the Lombard tradition of the kingdom. On the other side the Church of Rome, in the years that followed Aistulf's campaigns and saw the victories of the Franks in Italy, insistently presented itself as the holy church of the *res publica Romanorum*, a *res publica* conceived within an uninterrupted Roman tradition.[4] Was this, then, solely a contrast between two different concepts of ideas and titles? Evidently not, for the Roman horror at the name of Lombard reflected the determination of a social and ecclesiastical system to defend itself when faced with the danger represented by the upheavals a new political domination must bring with it. Pope Hadrian I, the most spirited promotor of Roman political autonomy (772–95), belonged to the high military aristocracy of Rome, a family furnished with a powerful landed base north of the city and already present in the middle of the century both in the office of duke of Rome and in the upper levels of the papal bureaucracy. But that defensive will was realized through strongly transmitted 'Roman' mental models, which were so intimately connected with the religious authority of the 'apostolic see' that they involved in Italian affairs the new royal dynasty of the Franks and raised it to the imperial Roman rank.

The papal plan was clearly expressed in the promises made in Rome by Charlemagne in spring 774, while the Lombard capital was still resisting the Frankish assault. Indeed, this plan aimed to limit the political presence of the Franks to the extreme north and north-west of Italy, and to incorporate into the Roman church's *res publica* the whole

[4] O. Bertolini, *Roma e i Longobardi* (Rome, 1972), pp. 64ff., 122ff.

Adriatic coast from Istria to Puglia, the Tyrrhenian littoral from the eastern end of Liguria to the boundary with the duchy of Naples and Byzantine Calabria, Corsica, and the whole inland area from Mantua and Parma to Lucania! So the Carolingians were entrusted with the organization of Latin-Germanic continental Europe up to the Alpine and pre-Alpine region and the outlets on to the Po plain, together with the old centre of the Lombard kingdom, centring on Pavia, where the denser settlement of the conquered people required direct military control by the Franks. The Byzantine fleet, from its bases in Sardinia, Sicily and Calabria, was left with the task of defending Western Christianity against Arab attack. The rest of Italy was to re-form around the church and the militias of Rome as an autonomous territorial entity, tied to the Franks by a military agreement and a religious bond and culturally united with the empire of Constantinople by the shared Roman tradition of the state. An absurd dream? Yet in 773, precisely when King Desiderius' military commitment against Charlemagne was greatest, the Lombards of Spoleto had abandoned the royal army and made their submission to the Roman church, electing as duke Hildebrand, who dated one of his diplomas of 774 not by the regnal years of Desiderius or Charlemagne but by the pontificate of Hadrian.[5] The subjection of a great part of Apennine and Adriatic Italy, from the lower Po to the Pescara river,[6] thus seemed a *fait accompli*, through the addition of the Lombard duchy of Spoleto to the Byzantine duchies of Perugia and the Pentapolis and the exarchate of Ravenna, with the possibility of expansion of the Tyrrhenian through the spreading influence of the duchy of Rome to the north and south.

Hadrian's project had a certain plausibility. In essence it proposed the convergence on Rome of all the regional tendencies towards autonomy, both Byzantine and Lombard, which had been apparent over the centuries of the struggle between the kings of Pavia and the Empire, and which were obstacles either to the expanding Lombard kingdom or to the European-wide construct that the Carolingians were realizing in the name and through the force of the Franks. But it was precisely the heterogeneous and centrifugal character of the forces which were to be united around the military and ecclesiastical aristocracy of Rome under the sign of St Peter which demanded simultaneously a flexibility in political forms and a strength in military organization both of which were foreign to the nature of the Roman church. The church functioned

[5] C. Brühl, 'Chronologie und Urkunden der Herzöge von Spoleto im 8. Jahrhundert', *Quellen und Forschungen aus italienischen Archiven und Biblio-theken*, 51 (1972), pp. 1–92.
[6] Müller, *Topographische und genealogische Untersuchungen*, p. 79.

through a bureaucracy which was as inflexible in its concepts of ecclesiastical and public institutions (one thinks of the resulting disputes in the exarchate of Ravenna) as it was powerless to create and dominate an army in Italy in the name of St Peter and under the authority of a high priest. In reality this Roman political project depended on the threatening power of the Franks, and this power, after the fall of Pavia and Charlemagne's assumption of the Lombard royal title, was great enough to attract the anxious attention of all those who in Ravenna and the Pentapolis, Tuscany or Spoleto, even at Benevento and in the Roman duchy itself, sought the protection or tolerance of the victor. After the death of Pope Hadrian his successor, Leo III, himself had to call on the power of the king, during disorders at Rome which struck at him in person. The king intervened as arbiter and lord of the city and it was then, in the year 800, that Charlemagne was crowned and acclaimed Roman emperor in the basilica of St Peter.

This was the Roman recognition of the supreme political power which Charlemagne held, through his many victories, over all Latin-Germanic Christianity, over the immense *regnum Francorum*, over the *regnum Langobardorum* and over the fleeting *res publica Romanorum* of Italy.[7] The aristocracy and clergy of Rome, who had resisted by every means the spectre of Lombard domination so that they could remain within the Roman tradition, now accepted a Germanic overlord, a military leader of Frankish origin from Austrasia. They joined with the Frankish and Lombard aristocracy and clergy in honouring as lord the victorious warrior, the 'new David' of Christianity as the Frankish court called him, but in order to free his image from the fearsome barbaric background from which he emerged, and to invest it with the sole fully legitimate temporal authority, they transformed Charlemagne through titles and symbols into a Roman emperor. In reality the papal political domination did not disappear. It became specific to the Roman duchy, now enlarged in the north by southern Lombard *Tuscia* and in the

---

[7] For a discussion of the political significance of the Empire, see G. Tabacco, *La relazione fra i concetti di potere temporale e di potere spirituale nella tradizione cristiana fino al secolo XIV* (Turin, 1950), pp. 105–28. For the Byzantine model of the Empire, see W. Ohnsorge, 'Byzanz und das Abendland im 9. und 10. Jahrhundert', *Saeculum*, 5.2 (1954), pp. 201ff; *Das Zweikaiserproblem im früheren Mittelalter. Die Bedeutung des byzantinischen Reiches für die Entwicklung der Staatsidee in Europa* (Hildesheim, 1947), pp. 15–31; 'Das Kaisertum der Eirene und die Kaiserkrönung Karls des Grossen', *Saeculum*, 14 (1963), pp. 221–47. On the convergence of several different ideas in the formal creation of the Empire, see P. Classen, 'Karl der Grosse, das Papsttum und Byzanz', in *Karl der Grosse*, 3rd ed. (Dusseldorf, 1967), vol. 1, pp. 537–608.

south, as noted, by Terracina, and was also exercised in the duchy of Perugia, in the Pentapolis with pretexts and interventions of varying strength, and in the exarchate in rivalry with the Ravennate archbishop. But everywhere it acted under Frankish protection and recognized Carolingian supremacy.[8]

This was the path by which the 'Roman' tradition of autonomy in certain Byzantine regions of Italy, interwoven with the religious authority of the papacy, came to clothe with official Roman dress the European dominion of the Franks, after directing the latter's bold expansion south of the Alps as a defence against the political dynamism shown by the Lombard kingdom in the eighth century. Beneath the new imperial name there remained the multiform reality of the peoples dominated by the Carolingians, which was made more complex wherever Carolingians extended their rule, north or south of the Alps, by the demands of a military domination which tended to be uniform and which was entrusted largely to Frankish elements imported into the subject areas. On the political and administrative level, this domination maintained the elementary forms of territorial protection and jurisdiction characteristic of the recent tradition of the Franks, and of every Germanic race which had settled within the Roman Empire.

And so, in the regions of Italy which had been an integral part of the Lombard kingdom – that is mostly northern Italy and Tuscany – Frankish domination could easily introduce itself as a continuation of the kingdom of Pavia. The kingdom retained its individuality and the name of Kingdom of Italy, even if the term *Italia*, like *Langobardia*, more often referred only to the part of the old *regnum Langobardorum* north of the Apennines.[9] It retained its legislation, in which the edicts of the Lombard kings kept their force and were continued juridically by the Carolingian capitularies promulgated or adopted by the kings of Italy.[10] And the capital was still Pavia, mostly with a Carolingian king different from those who reigned north of the Alps and who, when several Carolingian kings shared the Frankish political inheritance, was the only one to be decorated with the Roman imperial title, as the result of his ties with Rome and the protection he offered the papal see. The title symbolized the unity of the dynasty, even when there were several kings, and also

---

[8] Caspar, *Das Papsttum unter fränkischer Herrschaft*, pp. 49–69.

[9] P. S. Leicht, 'Dal "regnum Langobardorum" al "regnum Italiae"' (1930), reprinted in *Scritti vari*, vol. I, pp. 221–35; F. Crosara, 'Rex Langobardiae, rex Italiae', *Atti del II Congresso internazionale di studi sull'alto medioevo* (Spoleto, 1953), pp. 155–80; F. Manacorda, *Ricerche sugli inizii della dominazione dei Carolingi in Italia* (Rome, 1968), pp. 139–76.

[10] F. Calasso, *Medio evo del diritto* (Milan, 1954), pp. 115, 310.

the Carolingian control of Western Christianity, which focused theoretically and ecclesiastically on Rome. The kingdom also controlled the duchy of Spoleto, which had Frankish dukes after the death of Hildebrand, unlike the duchy of Benevento which, although it sometimes recognized Carolingian supremacy, followed its own Lombard path.

PUBLIC ORDER AND BONDS OF CLIENTSHIP IN CAROLINGIAN ITALY

The Frankish settlement in Italy had an entirely different character from the Lombard settlement or the preceding one of the Ostrogoths. There was no immigration by a people; instead there was an injection of small armed nuclei who were distributed more or less everywhere, but above all, it seems, in the cities and some zones of special strategic importance, to control the densest Lombard settlements or certain centres of river and road communication; they were present in particular in the heart of the old Lombard kingdom, from Milan to Pavia, in the territories of Piacenza and Parma, and around Verona and Lucca.[11] These nuclei were at the service of the counts, successors to the Lombard dukes or the royal gastalds in governing the districts into which the kingdom was still divided. The ducal title was preserved only by the governors of Spoleto and Friuli and intermittently by that of Istria, which was taken from the Byzantines after the fall of the Lombard kingdom; the count of Lucca also took this title in the ninth century, when his jurisdiction in Tuscany was expanding.[12] The title of duke alternated and united with the title of marquis, perhaps to signify the wider territorial responsibilities of governors in charge of border districts. Unlike the Lombard distinction between dukes and gastalds, with the former rooted in the separate traditions of the various Lombard settlements and with a dynastic tendency, and the latter removable officers solely dependent on the king, the counts and dukes or marquises of the Carolingian period were clearly instruments of the royal power, even though at the same time many showed a tendency to root themselves in their own landholdings in the area they governed, in a manner analogous to that of the gastalds formerly appointed by the Lombard kings in certain districts to

[11] See E. Hlawitschka, *Franken, Alemannen, Bayern und Burgunder in Oberitalien* (Freiburg im Breisgau, 1960), pp. 23–97; but the references to the groups of *arimanni* should be corrected by reference to Tabacco, *I liberi del re*, pp. 195–213.

[12] H. Keller, 'La marca di Tuscia fino all'anno mille', *Atti del V Congresso internazionale di studi sull'alto Medioevo* (Spoleto, 1973), pp. 117ff.

substitute for the duke. But how were the counts, and the warriers who accompanied them, recruited?

It is important here not to exaggerate the distinction between Franks and Lombards. In a capitulary of King Pippin of Italy, son of Charlemagne, dating from after 782 and before his father was emperor, Pippin calls himself 'most excellent king of the Lombard people' and appears surrounded by bishops, abbots, counts 'and other Franks and Lombards loyal to us, who are with us or staying in Italy', while in the course of the capitulary he refers explicitly to both Frankish counts and 'langubardiscos comites'.[13] Among the Lombards there was general acceptance of the Carolingians, after the failure of an attempt at revolt in 776 by the duke of Friuli with other Lombard leaders; subsequently many of the dukes were replaced by Frankish counts but not all were removed. The firmly loyal dukes were absorbed into the comital order which was extended from the *regnum Francorum* to the *regnum Langobardorum*. Only then, as the succession to individual Lombard counts fell vacant, was it the practice for the office to be filled by elements drawn from the Frankish aristocracy, even though exceptions are not lacking.[14] The political ruin of the Lombard kingdom thus did indeed finally signify, in the Carolingian period, the reduction of the Lombard aristocracy to the margins of political power. But this does not mean that the Frankish conquest represented a break comparable in any respect to that provoked two centuries earlier by the Lombard invasion. There was no destruction of the preceding social order or of any social class. Despite the numerous confiscations and the more or less gradual removal of powerful individuals from official responsibilities in military or political command, the Lombard aristocracy in large part remained almost unharmed in its landed base, and was extensively present in the ecclesiastical government. The powerful individuals who arrived from north of the Alps to take up the offices of count or marquis acquired a remarkably large landed base through royal donations and private exploitation of political power, through links with ecclesiastical institutions and through the calculated creation of kinship ties by the

---

[13] *MGH, Capitularia regum Francorum* (serie in-4°), vol. 1, pp. 191ff. See Manacorda, *Ricerche*, pp. 53–61.

[14] Hlawitschka, *Franken, Alemannen, Bayern und Burgunder in Oberitalien*, p. 58 note 21; D. A. Bullough, 'Leo, "qui apud Hlotharium magni loci habebatur", et le gouvernement du "regnum Italiae" à l'époque carolingienne', *Le Moyen Âge*, 67 (1961), pp. 237–45 (but see Hlawitschka, *Franken, Alemannen, Bayern und Burgunder in Oberitalien*, p. 220); J. Fischer, *Königtum, Adel und Kirche im Königreich Italien (774–875)* (Bonn, 1965), pp. 7–51.

Frankish elements, among themselves and with the richest Lombard families. As a result they formed for centuries the most important economic group in many areas of *Langobardia*. But this did not overturn the preceding social system; the newly powerful simply became integrated at a high level with the formerly dominant class.

Similarly the warriors who came from north of the Alps by royal command or in the train of the powerful, and who remained in Italy, became integrated with the class of lesser landowners, the *arimanni* or *exercitales*. They too were mostly of the Frankish legal tradition but sometimes (as was also the case with some of the more powerful) followed Alamannic, Bavarian or Burgundian law, when they came from regions in which Frankish domination had been imposed on other Germanic peoples, and where they had been absorbed into the Frankish army and into the service of the Carolingians or of persons bound to them. This is clear from the declarations of law of the Carolingian and post-Carolingian period, that is, the statements of which law one followed in court cases or in private acts that enabled the judge to pronounce sentence or the notary to draw up deeds in accordance with the legal tradition to which the individuals under judgement, or requiring a notarial deed, belonged. These declarations of law reveal the ethnically mixed character of the landowning class, both lesser and greater proprietors, and the absence for centuries of any juridical uniformity based on territory, such as had been implemented in the Mediterranean world through the extension of Roman citizenship to all free men, and which was progressively restored in the new political formations of the communal period in Italy and in Europe in general. From the ninth to eleventh centuries, a certain social mobility gradually modified the composition of the landowning class as it had established itself in the transition from the Lombard to the Carolingian period. Yet even on the eve of the communal period, when the custom of declaring personal law was about to disappear, in the central areas of *Langobardia* declarations of Lombard law in notarial charters were numerically greater than declarations of Roman law,[15] while Frankish and Lombard families divided among themselves the monopoly of the great landed property and political power.

None the less, there was an important innovation in the structures of Carolingian Italy with respect to the Lombard period. The Franks who, together with Alamans, Bavarians and Burgundians, penetrated the

---

[15] *Gli atti privati milanesi e comaschi nel secolo XI*, vol. 1, ed. G. Vittani, C. Manaresi (Milan, 1933), vols. 2 and 3, ed. C. Manaresi, C. Santoro (Milan, 1960–5).

Lombard economic–social system at various levels were an instrument of the Carolingian political dominion, thanks to the particular bond that joined them to the royal dynasty. The bond consisted first of all in the special and permanent service, military or political and military, which they supplied to the king or his representatives, and was in addition generally reinforced by the complex and solemn relationship of a client to the person of the king or to a powerful individual of transalpine origin who had come to Italy to collaborate with the king. This was the relationship of vassalage. It had spread widely in the world of the Franks, particularly around the Pippinids, during the eighth century, concurrently with the military enterprises and the solidarities created by war that raised the Pippinids to the royal and imperial thrones, and had been brought into Italy with the Frankish conquest; the institution was also applied to Lombards who were military clients of the Carolingians or of other powerful personages of the Italic kingdom, and it absorbed the Lombard institution of the gasindate.[16]

Earlier, in ending our discussion of the development of the Lombard monarchy, we compared Frankish vassalage with the Lombard gasindate, which was also a form of client relationship but did not undergo the developments experienced by the *vassaticum* among the Franks. Gasindate and vassalage were forms of commendation – that is, they signified the voluntary submission of a person (the one commended) to another (the lord) by virtue of an act that created the reciprocal obligation of assistance; the assistance was in the form of protection and economic aid from the lord, socially the stronger, to the vassal, socially weaker, and of obedience and service from the vassal to the lord. In the High Middle Ages commendations were frequently used, as can be demonstrated from the seventh century onwards for Gaul as well as Italy, to compensate for the insufficient protection afforded by the public power to the free population of modest wealth; above all there are records of individuals who commended themselves to ecclesiastical bodies, and formed a humble clientèle centring on the great landed patrimonies of episcopal and abbatial churches. In the eighth century vassalage and the gasindate were becoming distinct from these forms of commendation, through their increasing use in higher social relationships. The *vassi* in the most respected classes of the Frankish world gradually gained a special importance and particular diffusion as the *vassaticum* was applied to the military clientèles in an ever more exclusive and distinctive fashion; it was then that the act creating the

---

[16] P. S. Leicht, 'Il feudo in Italia nell' età carolingia', in *I problemi della civiltà carolingia* (Spoleto, 1954), pp. 71–93.

relationship of vassal took on the character of a complex ceremony, in which the *immixtio manuum* (the symbolic gesture with which the commender placed his joined hands within the hands of the lord) was complicated by an oath of military loyalty.[17] In this manner vassalage was elevated to a status above the usual relationship in other commendations, and in its turn the military clientèle, making use of the juridical form of vassal commendation with its rigorous bilateral obligations, hardened into a group working in the closest solidarity with their lord.

The metamorphosis of the professional warriors into a client group around a leader took place above all in the military enterprises led by the Pippinids, and guaranteed the latter the loyalty even of powerful families, first from Austrasia and later from every part of the world dominated by the Franks. Among the warriors who were most closely related to the Pippinids, wars and conquests created special loyalties, which could be expressed most clearly, and their persistence over time best guaranteed, in the juridical instrument of vassalage. These particular bonds emerged within the broader solidarity which, in many enterprises of the eighth century, drew the Frankish army closely around the victorious dynasty; the development of such bonds eventually transformed the very nature of the armies of the Carolingian period, on both sides of the Alps. Although indeed in the eighth and ninth centuries the royal order for military mobilization, in one or the other region of the Empire, was still officially directed at all free men with an economic basis sufficent to arm them, in fact within the Carolingian armies greater and greater importance was acquired by those free men who exercised a military profession as their vassal service, whether they were *vassi dominici* (vassals of the king) or *vassi* of counts, dukes, marquises, bishops, abbots or abbesses – that is, those who were men-at-arms bound by a personal loyalty to the holder of high political, administrative or ecclesiastical office.[18] As far as Italy is concerned this means that within the arimannic class, the class of armed landowners, professional warriors were distinguished by their military qualities and by their special relations with the holders of public or ecclesiastical power. The *exercitus*, which theoretically still represented in Italy the continuation of the old armed Lombard people, not only lost its ethnic foundation (as had already happened in the last Lombard period with the entry, though somewhat marginal, of Roman landowners among the *exercitales*, and

[17] F. L. Ganshof, 'L'origine des rapports féodo-vassaliques', in *I problemi della civiltà carolingia*, pp. 27–69.

[18] G. Tabacco, 'Il regno italico nei secoli IX–XI', in *Ordinamenti militari*, pp. 763–90.

which now became more emphatic with the introduction of warriors of transalpine origin), but accepted into its ranks select nuclei of armed men, the vassals, who were destined to take on a pre-eminent military role clearly distinct from that of the ordinary *arimanni*. This was all the more the case since the development of such clientèles, maintained by the king and by the aristocracy of public officials and church dignitaries, favoured the tendency to create corps of knights equipped with increasingly heavy defensive and offensive weapons.[19]

The transformation of the army of the people into a composite royal army, formed by the convergence of vassal clientèles and ranks of *arimanni*, could not be kept within a purely military context. It necessarily came to influence a society where the hierarchy of classes and powers was traditionally linked, at a certain level, with the different forms of war equipment, particularly forms of collective activity in territorial defence and attack, since the maintenance of vassals interfered with the patterns of landed possession. Although vassals did sometimes live in the house of their lord, more often they received from him land 'in benefice', that is, with usufruct for life, in return for the services they provided. In fact vassal service was eventually matched to the size of the benefice, just as the public service of the *arimanni* was roughly commensurate with the size of their economic base. However one should note that the vassal could also receive goods in full ownership and that normally he already belonged to a landowning family, sometimes indeed to a family with a powerful landed base, so that the benefice, held with a temporary title as repayment for service, was usually added to his own 'allods', the goods he had acquired through inheritance or through purchase and gift. The presence of lands held in benefice thus complicated the general outlines of both great and small landed properties, withdrawing from the lay or ecclesiastical lord of a vast patrimony the use of the lands which were conceded to vassals to complement their own economic strength. And as for the *vassi dominici*, they were distributed across the whole empire, particularly on lands of the fisc, which were present in all the districts of counts, dukes and marquises, and even on ecclesiastical lands, which were subject to the protection and interference of royal power.

Nevertheless one must avoid the error, still very widespread, of believing that in the Carolingian period society was completely entangled in the bonds of vassalage and benefices, or 'feudal' bonds, as it is more inaccurately put. The immense majority of the population was

---

[19] F. L. Ganshof, 'L'armée sous les Carolingiens', in *Ordinamenti militari*, pp. 122–6.

made up of cultivators of the land who in their work, whether they were free of servile, were largely subordinate to the greater and lesser lay or ecclesiastical aristocracy, in ways that normally bore no relation at all to the bond of vassalage. They were peasant families who, when they did not live on the owner's demesne (the land directly exploited by the lord, through agents who supervised servile cultivators), held a farm from the lord by customary concession or contract, with the obligation to pay rents in kind and money and to supply agricultural labour on the owner's demesne for some days of the week or some weeks each year.[20] When the holder of the concession was a free man, these prestations of labour were not a service owed through personal loyalty, but complemented the rent due to the owner of the land. If, as was sometimes the case, the holder of the concession was a serf of the lord, the prestations could appear also as a personal service, as well as an addition to the rent, but it was then an integral part of the service arising from the bond of necessary dependence, according to the traditions of Classical slavery, and not from a bilateral commitment created by the free will of the contracting parties.

At the peasant level the only analogy with vassalage occurred when the *liber homo* commended himself to a powerful person in order to receive protection and economic aid from him, as noted above, but here there was no oath of military loyalty. Although commendation was not rare it was nevertheless not at all a normal condition of dependence in the class of agricultural workers. The minor owners of allods, still quite numerous despite the social and economic pressures on them from the more powerful,[21] were normally free of any bond of personal dependence. They worked their own lands with the help of sons and possibly some slaves, and were dependent solely on the public power, as members of the free population, *liber et exercitalis populus*.[22] In Italy the people of the *arimanni* were obliged, to the extent their economic means allowed, to provide military prestations requested by the king, to maintain bridges and roads, public and ecclesiastical buildings, and to

---

[20] G. Luzzatto, 'I servi nelle grandi proprietà ecclesiastiche italiane dei secoli IX e X', (1909), reprinted in *Dai servi della gleba agli albori del capitalismo*, pp. 7–161; R. Boutruche, *Signori e feudalesimo*, vol. 1: *Ordinamento curtense e clientele vassallatiche* (Bologna, 1971), pp. 77–110. See Toubert, *Les Structures du Latium médiéval*, vol. 1, pp. 449ff.; V. Fumagalli, *Terra e società nell'Italia padana: i secoli IX e X* (Bologna, 1974), pp. 25ff.

[21] G. Duby, *L'economia rurale nell'Europa medievale*, 2nd ed. (Bari, 1970), vol. 1, pp. 84–90.

[22] Tabacco, *I liberi del re*, pp. 123–27; see especially pp. 96–112.

provide maintenance for public officials and prelates visiting a locality to exercise justice or carry out pastoral activity.

When the extent of vassalage and commendation as a whole is thus reduced to its real dimensions in Carolingian society, on both sides of the Alps, and the persistence of normal relations of a public nature between the royal power and the *liberi homines exercitales* is recognized, it none the less remains true that the relationship of vassalage assumed an importance in the Carolingian period which passed beyond the sphere of pure military activity and the tenurial complications that followed the concession of 'benefices' to warriors. This happened thanks to the tradition of both the Frankish and the Lombard kingdoms, in which military power broadened automatically to take on a political significance. The counts and dukes or marquises whom the Carolingian kings placed in charge of political–administrative districts, with policing and judicial functions, were military leaders, whom the king normally chose from among the warriors bound to him by vassalage or whom the king induced, if they were not already his vassals, to commend themselves to him and take a vassal's oath of loyalty. So they too were, or became, *vassi dominici*, even if the sources prefer to designate them by the title of *comes*, *dux*, *marchio*, the titles which indicated their public office. The subordination of the office-holder to the king was reinforced in this way by a tight personal submission. Without losing its public character, the office exercised the name of the king took on at the same time the form of a vassal service, rewarded with 'benefices' in fiscal lands, and with incomes connected with the exercise of jurisdiction, such as the right to hospitality (due to public officials wherever they went to exercise jurisdiction) and a share in fines and the proceeds of judgements. Indeed public office, as a means of social elevation and with the connected 'benefices' and income, finally itself appeared as a 'benefice', thus in a peculiar fashion confusing the service with its multiple rewards.

On this subject one may note that the *vassaticum* of the Carolingian period, although it was utilized by the king, did not, as is often believed, corrupt the relationship between the king and his representatives, but on the contrary formed an obstacle to the tendency towards the disintegration of political power, which was already quite evident among the Franks of the late seventh century in the disorders of the late Merovingian period. Nor did the application of the concept of 'benefice' to the functions of the count, duke or marquis change the king's traditional means of disposing of the office. Although it is true that the concession in benefice, as far as it corresponded to a solemnly affirmed vassal loyalty, implied the idea of stability, so that it usually lasted until the death of either vassal or lord, yet it is equally true that in earlier political traditions, such as those of the Franks from the end of the seventh century as well as those of the Lombards, it had already been the case that public office at the highest level was very rarely taken away from powerful personages who exercised it loyally. So it was not the absorption of major public offices and their occupants into the complex relationship of vassalage and benefices that caused royal commands to go astray. On the contrary, when, at the end of the ninth century, the Carolingian Empire had dissolved definitively into several kingdoms, and each kingdom (including that of Italy) in its turn proceeded more or less swiftly to its own internal dissolution, this took place despite the solemn bond of clientship between counts and marquises and the king, and not as a result of this bond.[23] As in the course of the Carolingian period the solidarity created in the Frankish people by the military enterprises of the eighth century gradually became weaker, and the Frankish aristocracy took root in estates scattered across the empire, so in the individual regions and provinces in which the Carolingian princes used them for military and political government, the bond of commendation was insufficient to check the tendency of public officials towards autonomy. The process that had halted in the eighth century recommenced, and eventually issued in the political anarchy of the pre-communal and communal periods.

This process of disintegration was undoubtedly aided by the spread of the vassal relationship, not because of the king's application of vassalage to his relations with his own officers but rather insofar as the great men of the kingdom imitated the king, and created their own clientèles of vassals as they constructed autonomous lordships. Here indeed the bond of clientship, from the Carolingian period onwards, had an effect on the transformations of political power. The diffusion of vassalage became part of the strengthening of ecclesiastical bodies and of the great military families, guaranteeing an autonomous defence for their wealth and actions, which was capable of developing into a special political organization of their territories. But in order to understand this evolution, we must consider the way in which ecclesiastical and lay power functioned, the connection between powerful individuals and the public order, and their economic base.

---

[23] H. Mitteis, *Lehnrecht und Staatsgewalt* (1933, republished Weimar, 1958), pp. 15–206; F. L. Ganshof, 'Das Lehnswesen im fränkischen Reich', in *Studien zum mittelalterlichen Lehenswesen* (Lindau-Konstanz, 1960), pp. 37–49; G. Tabacco, 'L'ordinamenti feudale del potere nel pensiero di Heinrich Mitteis', *Annali della fondazione italiana per la storia amministrativa*, 1 (1964), pp. 83–113.

THE COMPLICATIONS OF ECCLESIASTICAL POWER, AND THE
FIRST MOVEMENT TOWARDS SEIGNEURIAL POSSESSION OF
POLITICAL POWER

However simple the activity of public officials remained in the Carolingian period – reduced, as it had already been in Merovingian Gaul and Lombard Italy, to a military power essentially destined to suppress private violence – undoubtedly there was now a greater insistence on royal authority as a guarantee of an older type of culture, permeated by demands for universality. This was a culture of clerics and monks who were scholars and theologians, and they suggested to the ruler a concept of order far more complex than the mere physical coercion of whoever rebelled against Frankish arms and against the rights to possess men and goods. There was a spontaneous meeting between the growing need for cultural coherence (a need already manifest in the intense relations between episcopal and monastic schools throughout the West from the end of the seventh century[24]) and the tendencies towards uniformity which were inherent in the political domination of the Franks over the Latin-Germanic world. The ecclesiastical concept of a universal hierarchical order, in which the entire life of the masses took on the significance of a great drama and collective expiation in the face of death, became in its turn an instrument of uniform subjection to the power of the Carolingians, who were burdened by immense problems of military coercion and social discipline in Europe. A substantial portion of the capitularies, the legislation of the Carolingians, was therefore directed in favour of the process of the cultural unification of the church, the subordination of clerics and monks to conciliar canons and ascetic rules, and the unopposed moral dominion of priests and ascetics over the population. The zeal of the ruler, closely united with the court clerics and with the royal episcopate, turned towards determining the religious duties of the laity, making rules for the common life of the clergy and the individual poverty of monks, guaranteeing the operation of ecclesiastical structures through compulsory tithes and labour prestations, and promoting specific liturgical practices, the activity of schools, respect for the study of grammar, and the philologically-based emendation of sacred texts. The Carolingian Empire seemed, in certain respects, to take on the outlines of a great ecclesiastical power-structure, with a tendency to be unified by the increasing rigidity of all the rules of private behaviour and life in the community, of the written language and of liturgical chant, and of

[24] P. Riché, *Education et culture dans l'Occident barbare* (Paris, 1962), pp. 410–547.

sacred architecture; and this structure was complemented and protected by an apparatus of military leaders and professional warriors placed at its service and in its defence, ranging from the kings to the lowest of the vassals.[25]

On the other hand it is true that such a power-structure, with such a scholastic and theological basis, was influenced throughout by the very close symbiosis in which it operated, both with the military aristocracy from which the prelates were recruited and with the political–military institutions which protected the churches and religious communities. Those same kings who regulated the clergy and monastic life according to the authority of the canons, and enjoined the counts to collaborate with the bishops in government of the 'Christian' people, utilized the ecclesiastical order to supervise public officials and to ensure obedience from the people. They introduced loyal individuals into the goverment of bishoprics and abbeys, and had recourse to monastic foundations and church properties (although to a lesser degree than north of the Alps) to support the royal entourage during the travels of the court, to place as abbesses women of the royal family, and to provide an economic base for certain *vassi dominici*.[26] The growing intimacy and reciprocal influence between royal and ecclesiastical power thus favoured in Carolingian Italy, as it did north of the Alps, the development of an institution which had its roots in Merovingian Gaul, namely the concession to bishops and abbots of immunity from any intervention by public officials in the land that made up the landed patrimony of the episcopal churches and the great monasteries. This was not a simple exemption from particular burdens or contributions, such as the Lombard kings and even the Roman emperors had already conceded on occasion, but a radical prohibition banning all *iudiciaria potestas*, particularly the military and jurisdictional power of the court and his subordinate agents, from entering the lands of a given ecclesiastical body in order to demand fines or contributions, to hold judicial hearings, or

[25] H. Fichtenau, *L'impero carolingio*, 2nd ed. (Bari, 1972), pp. 230–95.

[26] Leicht, 'Il feudo in Italia nell' età carolingia', pp. 77–80, 89–92; O. Bertolini, 'I vescovi del "regnum Langobardorum" al tempo dei Carolingi', in *Vescovi e diocesi in Italia nel medioevo: secoli IX–XIII, Atti del II Convegno di storia della Chiesa in Italia*, (Padua, 1964) pp. 12–26; cf. H. Keller, 'Der Gerichtsort in oberitalienischen und toskanischen Städten', *Quellen und Forschungen aus italienischen Archiven und Bibliotheken*, 49 (1969), pp. 2–40, which is in its turn to be qualified on the basis of data supplied by H. Zelinski, *Studien zu den spoletinischen Privaturkunden des 8. Jahrhunderts und ihrer Überlieferung im Regestum Farfense* (Tübingen, 1972), p. 140; Brühl, *Fodrum*, vol. I, pp. 392–451.

to *distringere* for any purpose the peasants or other dependants of the body (that is, to exercise over them acts of force, whether or not connected with the normal public activity of policing and justice).

The motivation for such privileges lay in the *oppressiones* exercised by the public authority over the *coloni* of the churches, on whom it arbitrarily imposed tributes and prestations of labour on various pretexts. This presupposes an extensive disorder in the functioning of the kingdom, a widespread exploitation of power for the private interests of royal officials. The exploitation occurred at the expense of the whole peasant class and created conflicts between public officials and all landowners, whether they were small allod-holders (those *liberi homines* or *arimanni* in whose defence many capitularies condemned the abuses of counts and comital agents), or lay and ecclesiastical lords who were not linked through a particular friendship with the holders of public power in the provinces where their landed property lay.[27] The relations between the great ecclesiastical bodies and the great royal officials in charge of the provinces were therefore contradictory. The counts, whose military protection should have been exercised above all in favour of the churches, not uncommonly found themselves in conflict with bishops and abbots for reasons of personal and family power, so that gradually the prelates, one in imitation of the other, were led to seek royal concession of a diploma guaranteeing a special protection: the *mundeburdium*, which was exercised directly by the king and conferred perpetual immunity. And by such diplomas the king, who was head of the public order, deprived his own officials of authority in the ecclesiastical lands, encouraging there instead the seigneurial authority of bishops and abbots.

The fact that the royal diplomas of immunity, which excluded the public power from seigneurial lands, were not a Carolingian innovation but dated back in Gaul to the end of the sixth century, and that in the Merovingian period they are even attested in favour of lay *potentes*, demonstrates the continuity in the Frankish world of the tendency towards seigneural autonomy. But in the Carolingian period immunity spread in favour of most of the powerful churches, concurrently with the persistent expansion of ecclesiastical landownership through the continuous stream of royal and private donations; it took on new

---

[27] Njeussychin, *Die Entstehung der abhängigen Bauernschaft*, pp. 555–87; E. Müller-Martens, *Karl der Grosse, Ludwig der Fromme und die Freien. Wer waren die liberi homines der karolingischen Kapitularien?* (Berlin, 1963), pp. 66–142; G. Tabacco, 'Sulla protezione politica della libertà nell'alto medioevo', *Studi medievali*, ser. III, 5 (1964), pp. 723–39; *I liberi del re*, pp. 37–112; Fichtenau, *L'impero carolingio*, pp. 143–229.

dimensions which were to modify profoundly the structure of the Frankish Empire, and of the kingdoms which formed within it and emerged as independent after the death, in 888, of Charles the Fat (who was the last of the Carolingians to gather into his own hands, for a few years only, the entire inheritance of the empire of Charlemagne). The exclusion of the public power from immune lands led the prelates to develop a power over the residents of ecclesiastical lands that increasingly replaced that of the count, and eventually, in the post-Carolingian period, broke up the unity of the secular political–military circumscriptions. Originally immunity, on its own, did not remove from the count's jurisdiction the free population that was dependent on the holder of immunity. Strictly speaking, if the privilege, or customary usage, did not provide for special rules in the matter, the men who were economically dependent but not of servile condition remained subject to the comital tribunal for the actions that concerned them, even though the count's power could not reach them on the immune lands, and it was therefore the duty of the holder of immunity or of his agents to bring them before the public court for such actions. But the general spread of concessions of immunity among episcopal and abbatial churches merged with the custom by which, for some time already, seigneurial powers of constraint and justice had been extended from the servile class to include the free *coloni* who had lived for some generations on the lord's lands. That is, immunity was eventually interpreted as a guarantee, not only of the inviolability of the immune lands, but also of the autonomous organization of a power which was parallel to that of the public officials, and was directly protected by the king.[28]

The content of this particular seigneurial power, the *districtus* (that is, the right of coercion over all residents of immune land, for purposes of policing and of execution of sentences delivered by the tribunal of the holder of immunity) was so clearly analogous to the powers of command and justice which were proper to public authority that the *advocati*, the agents to whom bishops and abbots delegated such functions in ecclesiastical lands, are recorded on several occasions in the capitularies alongside the lesser public officials, the *centenarii* and *vicarii*

---

[28] M. Kroell, *L'immunité franque* (Paris, 1910), pp. 151–248; H. Brunner, C. L. von Schwerin, *Deutsche Rechtsgeschichte*, (1928, reprinted Darmstadt, 1958), vol. 2, pp. 382–404; F. L. Ganshof, 'L'Immunité dans la monarchie franque', in *Les Liens de vassalité et les immunités*, Recueil de la Société Jean Bodin 1, 2nd ed. (Brussels, 1958), pp. 171–216. For the extension into customary usage of seigneurial powers of coercion and justice in Carolingian Italy, the capitulary n. 93, c. 5 is important (*MGH Capitularia*, vol. 1, p. 196); for the date of the capitulary see Tabacco, *I liberi del re*, p. 103 note 339.

subordinate to the count, even though properly speaking the advocates were not public officials but seigneurial agents. Indeed the Carolingians were anxious that the advocates of the churches should be chosen from among persons suitable to exercise those functions of a public nature which had been transferred into ecclesiastical hands, and they prescribed that the choice be made by the prelate in agreement with the count and notables of the county. And so while on the one hand the king undermined the ordinary authority of the count, multiplying immunities to prevent the arbitrary behaviour of his own officials, on the other hand he distrusted the numerous holders of immunities, and subjected the choice of their agents to the supervision of the count and the landowning class. It was a complex attempt to maintain control over all holders of coercive power, by making use alternately of the official public order and the growing patrimonial power of the churches, as well as by appealing to the *exercitales*. But in this fashion the royal power emphasized and officially sanctioned – even though still only in the context of ecclesiastical ownership – the political significance that great landed property had already been assuming for some time, and transformed a fluid network of customs of seigneurial government over the peasant population into a rigid order. Through the immunities so widely conceded to the churches, and so broadly interpreted, it offered to the power of private individuals a model for political autonomy on the basis of landed property.

In this context the vassal clientèles of the seigneurs took on the role of a force for disintegration, which was very different from the purposes for which the Carolingians had accepted them. The capitularies prohibited private *trustes*, the armed nuclei organized by powerful individuals with the aim of local oppression or depradation,[29] but they did not interpret in this sense the armed service which was rendered by vassals of ecclesiastical and lay dignitaries. Rather, the latter was understood as a useful supplement to the service rendered by the vassals of the king, whether in protecting individual churches and public offices (that is, all the institutions by means of which the population was set within a social system), or as forces that could be used in the royal armies. But for every ecclesiastical body the vassals constituted above all a defence for their landed estates, already often protected by the royal *mundeburdium* and by immunity, and so they represented at the military level the autonomous organization of the church's seigneurial power. The personal and bilateral nature of the tie which bound vassals to a bishop or an abbot thus enabled the ecclesiastical lord to demonstrate by

[29] *MGH Capitularia*, vol. 1, p. 50, c. 14; p. 66, c. 15; vol. 2, p. 292, c. 3.

means of a small military force at his full and free disposition, that he exercised political dominion over a numerous population of serfs and freemen resident on ecclesiastical land, under the shadow of the king but in progressively increasing independence from the king's officials. One might add that, as remuneration, the vassal was normally endowed with a 'benefice' made up of some episcopal or abbatial holding: in fact he was placed as a benefice-holder within the ecclesiastical estate which it was his task to guard. The introduction of the armed clientèle into the landed lordship of the ecclesiastical body thus set the seal on the assimilation of coercive power and jurisdiction into landownership, and perfected the model of autonomy presented by the immune organizations.

As for the clientèles of counts, dukes and marquises, they did indeed strengthen the officials of the kingdom in the military and political control of the public districts. But they strengthened them through a personal tie, which was certainly not broken by the removal of a royal representative from his office, nor by his transfer from one circumscription to another at the king's direction. Nor did the count, duke or marquis live solely from 'benefices' and the income from his office. In the main he belonged to a family already powerful through its economic strength, and did not necessarily reward his vassals for their service by placing them on fiscal lands which he in his turn held as benefices from the king; rather he might place them on his own allods, on the patrimony inherited from his ancestors or acquired in full ownership by other means. And so here too, in exactly the same way as with the ecclesiastical lordships, the vassals could find themselves introduced into the heart of a landed power which was clearly distinct from the royal power, and which survived the death of the holder of royal office even when his heirs were no longer raised by the king to public responsibilities or taken into his own particular clientèle of vassals. Nor is there any reason to believe that the powerful family, when it lost such a specific formal bond with the kingdom, also abandoned the custom of maintaining armed vassals in its own service and of placing them within its own private estates. Such a family normally remained within the large circle of the powerful who were in particular contact with the imperial family, the circle from which the individual kings always drew the greater part of their own collaborators and representatives as appropriate.[30] Thus the favour which the Carolingians accorded to the formation of armed clientèles around the

[30] G. Tellenbach, *Studien und Vorarbeiten zur Geschichte des grossfränkischen und frühdeutschen Adels* (Freiburg im Breisgau, 1957), pp. 66–70, 329–34.

powerful individuals faithful to them turned into a development ever more closely connected to the familial traditions and landownership of the great landed lords. The latter, even though lacking the immunities enjoyed by bishops and abbots, enjoyed such customary usages of command and coercion over their own *coloni*, both free and servile, that they could easily exercise over the peasant population resident on their seigneurial lands the same powers of policing and justice which were accorded to the ecclesiastical institutions. The military control that the lord had over his own vassals further strengthened this power, with an efficiency and severity that were certainly greater than in the model of autonomy presented officially by the immune ecclesiastical lordships.

The almost complete absence of diplomas of immunity in favour of powerful laymen among those which survive cannot simply result from the fact that early medieval documents have been almost exclusively preserved by ecclesiastical archives, archives of bodies endowed with a stability over time such as lay families and secular institutions did not experience until the eleventh century; for, in fact, quite a few documents of other kinds, relating to lay individuals, have reached us through those same ecclesiastical archives. We must indeed conclude that the Carolingians rarely issued diplomas of immunity for the laity. But that must have come about because the seigneurial power of the great families, sustained by a tradition of military command in the royal armies, had much less need than the churches for explicit concessions of immunity; it was a power which aroused immediate respect in the kingdom's officials, who were in any case recruited from the same class. This respect developed through custom into a reluctance to make a forced entry into the lands of such lords, in order to carry out directly tasks of policing or justice. There is an indirect indication of this particular aspect of the private power of the laity in an Italian capitulary which forbids the collaborators of the count (the *iuniores comitum* and in particular the *fortiores vassi comitum*, the more important vassals of the count) to request from dependants of the churches and the 'rest of the population' agricultural labour services at the time of ploughing, sowing and harvesting, or any other forms of contribution. Instead it permits such requests to be made to the *potentiores vel ditiores*, to private individuals amply furnished with goods, since this latter contribution takes place spontaneously and through mutual affection, *mutua dilectione*, with the object of reciprocal assistance.[31] Thus, the small landowners and the peasants of the churches, who were placed together on the same level as deserving of particular royal solicitude, were contrasted with the

[31] *MGH Capitularia*, vol. 1, p. 197, c. 6.

lay notables, marked out as rich private individuals and agents of the count, who were in a position to grant each other mutual favours. It is obvious that the dispersion of ecclesiastical estates and the difficulties of the holders of churches in organizing effective military nuclei, even though they were authorized to surround themselves with vassals, would make it more difficult to defend the peasant population on ecclesiastical lands against the arbitrary exercise of public authority; it was much easier for powerful laymen to exercise control over the men and goods they owned, since they could more easily reach an understanding with the royal officials and with their vassals, in a sort of connivance or *mutua dilectio*. Hence the rarer recourse of the laity to royal diplomas of immunity, which the churches requested and had granted to them with ever-increasing generosity.

In order to arrive at a proper understanding of the complex and chaotic consequences of this development of both immune ecclesiastical bodies and private power, we must consider the structure of the great landed estates with respect to the forms of settlement of the rural population. Even where a substantial estate was not particularly scattered, and was contained largely within a specific geographical region or military or ecclesiastical circumscription, it was not at all compact, and through administrative necessity was divided into many *curtes*. The word *curtis*, designating a complex of landed property, had often in the Lombard period signified the area occupied by the house of any *liber homo*, with the other buildings and orchards immediately connected to it, but it then became the term used for the centres of the lord's administration, distributed across each great network of estates and each governed by a *villicus*, assisted in duties of a non-agricultural nature by *ministeriales* who were mostly of servile origin. Indeed, it now more often became the term used by notaries to indicate each complex of lands which was organized around such a centre. The *curtis* was usually composed of a *dominicum* (the directly administered lord's demesne from which the centre had arisen) and a *massaricium* (the cluster of *mansi* of farms entrusted to the care of free or servile families of peasants). The *curtes* of the same lord were not contiguous, and they were usually not compact but rather scattered among several villages.

In much of the Italic kingdom, as in much of the rest of Europe from ancient times onwards, the population actually lived not in isolated houses of *coloni*, but in villages where the tight ranks of dwelling-houses and orchards lay within a cultivated territory which was the sum total of the cereal fields, vines and meadows of the locality; this territory was grouped by peasant leases into several holdings, which were in their turn surrounded by pastures and woods, the uncultivated land in common use among all the families of the village. Each lord's *curtis*, considered as a whole with its *dominicum* and *massaricium*, usually did not cover exactly the territory either of a village or of several neighbouring villages, but rather penetrated into various parts of different villages, which were not always close to each other. The *curtis* was born solely from the need to unite administratively a number of pieces of land and holdings, directly and indirectly administered, which a great lord owned in a specific area, where other lords and even lesser allod-holders owned other pieces of land and holdings, intermingled with those of the first lord. Thus it happened that in the same village the cultivators were dependent on different administrative centres and on different lords, or that among the peasants some were dependent on lord's *curtes*, and others owned their own fields as small allod-holders. The patrimonial power of the great families and the great ecclesiastical bodies did not appear as a number of vast territorial lordships, internally coherent and ranged side by side, but rather as a network of landed lordships geographically and topo-graphically interwoven with each other and with the small allods. Through the traditions of life which had developed from collective resistance, through the agricultural practices that called for communal decisions for each common field, and through the use of the uncultivated common land, each peasant belonged in a certain way to a specific village community; and in another way, if he was not himself an allod-holder, he was dependent administratively on an estate centre which was sometimes distant.[32]

Hence the pressure, economic or more violent in nature, which the small allod-holders suffered from the lords who owned land in their village, and the concentration on peasants resident on a lord's land of burdens which did not derive solely from the lord of their own land. To this should be added public obligations, that weighed principally on small landowners, and on those dependent peasants who did not find in the lord whose land they worked a sufficient protection against violence and attacks from others. The capitularies testify to this widespread disorder in the exploitation of the rural classes every time that they instruct public officials to respect and protect the *pauperes* – that is, the free men, landowners or not, who do not own considerable property and who do not have effective *patroni* – or when they condemn particular abuses of power, attributing them generically to the powerful. In a capitulary of 850, issued at Pavia by the most energetic of the Carolingian rulers of the Italian kingdom, Louis II, King of Italy and Emperor, great-grandson of Charlemagne,[33] the counts are invited to

---

[32] Duby, *L'economia rurale*, vol. 1, pp. 7–90.

[33] P. Delogu, 'Strutture politiche e ideologia nel regno di Lodovico II', *Bullettino dell'Istituto storico italiano per il Medioevo*, 80 (1968), pp. 137–89.

ensure that the *potentes* abstain from carrying out the usual *oppressiones* around their own residences, and as an example the capitulary refers to the abuses of ruining others' meadows by pasturing one's own beasts there, and of afflicting the *pauperes* even in winter by demanding their participation in the maintenance of horses.[34] The concrete and specific nature of the text tells us a great deal about the customary exploitation already widespread in the Carolingian period, an exploitation which, radiating outwards from the residences of the powerful, passed beyond the limits of their own property and attacked the rural population not because of their personal or economic dependence but simply because they lived nearby. This is a first point of departure for the later development in the post-Carolingian period of a form of seigneurial domination, which was certainly based on the possession of houses and lands, but tended to create around them small, territorially coherent zones of local hegemony. The horses which Louis II chose to mention specifically are the undoubted sign of a military basis for local seigneurial power, the sign of a convergence between the vast and discontinuous landed base of the great lords and the groups of vassals that they armed and placed in their own houses, repaying the vassals with the concession of *mansi* in benefice, and through them commanding respect and fear within village communities.

If such was the form of coexistence between the various social classes and between these same classes and public and ecclesiastical power towards the end of the Carolingian period, it is easy to see how false is the picture of society supposedly resulting from the evolution of Carolingian institutions which was constructed by some of the historical writing of the nineteenth and twentieth centuries.[35] This interpretation presented a society divided into great territorial 'feudal lordships' side by side, which were in their turn divided progressively into lesser 'feudal lordships'; the hierarchy of fiefs and lay and ecclesiastical vassals thus formed culminated in the king and descended to include the entire working population in personal relationships of subjection. On the contrary, the Carolingian Empire already showed clearly within itself those contradictions which led the post-Carolingian kingdoms into a chaos of opposing and irrational institutions and customs.

In fact the Carolingians, aware of being at the head of a great unitary structure inspired by Catholicism, sought to satisfy the need, characteristic of the ecclesiastical culture of the period as well as of the military power-network, for a territorial pattern focused on well-defined

[34] *MGH Capitularia*, vol. 2, p. 85, c. 2.
[35] G. Tabacco, 'Fief et seigneurie dans l'Italie communale. L'évolution d'un thème historiographique', *Le Moyen Age*, 75 (1969), pp. 5–37.

centres of public and religious administration. This is even more apparent in the Italian kingdom than elsewhere. The royal palace of Pavia, still seat of the central administration, and the group of *consiliarii* working in the royal court supervised the comital districts which, since they substantially paralleled the diocese of the bishops, not unusually appear with precise borders, these latter also sometimes revealing the presence of sub-districts (the lesser districts entrusted to *sculdasci* or *centenari*) which satisfied a need for further division partly analogous to the subdivision of a diocese into parishes.[36] But on the other hand this political–administrative plan, and the commitment to realize it, contrasted with the inability to create – whether in the centre or at the periphery – a bureaucracy of freely removable royal agents, paid with types of remuneration that could be easily revoked. Agents were recruited from the military clientèles, which often included families powerful through their landed property and their own clientèles, and the functionaries were recompensed with gifts of land, sometimes in full ownership but more often in benefice. This procedure was prompted by the weak circulation of coin, but was destined, through donation or through gradual appropriation, to enlarge the landed base of the military families which collaborated with the king. At the same time the ruler sought to remedy the restless enterprise of the counts by calling the bishops into regular collaboration and by seeking effective points of support in the episcopal and monastic churches, as centres of moral influence and of accumulation of economic strength, in order to control the cities and obtain military provisions on the major communication routes. But the bishops and abbots were recruited from the same military aristocracy, and the loyal prelates were rewarded with donations of allods to the churches and the extension of immunity in perpetuity over their landed domain. The king built a network of

---

[36] H. Keller, 'Zur Struktur der Königsherrschaft im karolingischen und nachkarolingischen Italien', *Quellen und Forschungen aus italienischen Archiven und Bibliotheken*, 47 (1967), pp. 123–33; G. Arnaldi, 'Pavia e il "regnum Italiae" dal 774 al 1024', in *Atti del IV Congresso internazionale di studi sull'alto Medioevo* (Spoleto, 1969), pp. 175–87; C. Brühl, 'Das "palatium" von Pavia und die Honorantiae civitatis Papiae', *ibid.*, pp. 189–220; V. Fumagalli, 'Un territorio piacentino nel secolo IX: i "fines Castellana"', *Quellen und Forschungen aus italienischen Archiven und Bibliotheken*, 48 (1968), pp. 1–35; 'Città e distretti nell'Italia carolingia', *Rivista storica italiana*, 81 (1969), pp. 107–17; 'L'amministrazione periferica dello Stato nell'Emilia occidentale in età carolingia', *ibid.*, 83 (1971), pp. 911–20; A. Castagnetti, 'Distretti fiscali autonomi o sottocircoscrizioni della contea cittadina? La Gardesana veronese in epoca carolingia', *ibid*, 82 (1970), pp. 736–43.

friendships and protection which did not form a system, and which sanctioned or encouraged the development of nuclei of power with a basis of landed property within the persisting fabric of the public and ecclesiastical districts.

Thus the Carolingian Empire did not leave to following ages the inheritance of a hierarchy of vassal loyalties and 'feudal' lordships replacing public power, but on the contrary, through titles, offices and revenues that lasted for centuries, it left the memory of a tenacious effort to give to the territorial network the character of a public administration parallel to the ecclesiastical administration, sustained by the latter and in its turn capable of sustaining it. It was in truth a desperate effort, carried out with instruments which were often in contradiction with the end pursued, instruments that permitted each nucleus of lordship, lay or ecclesiastical, to emerge with domineering force, not at all as a 'feudal' institution (since the 'benefice', whose character was still formally precarious, could not constitute the foundation for any seigneurial autonomy), but rather as a power anchored to a variety of disparate bases: to scattered landed property, to the uncertain customary usages of exploitation and dominion over the cultivators distributed in hetero-geneous village communities, to the availability of armed men intro-duced on to the landed estates, to the traditional religious prestige of an ecclesiastical foundation, or to the vigour and renown of a given lineage.

LOMBARD AUTONOMIES AND THE BYZANTINE AND MUSLIM PRESENCE ON THE MARGINS OF FRANKISH POWER

The duchy of Spoleto, which in the Lombard period had survived somewhat on the margins of the kingdom, was intimately linked to the development of Frankish political power in Italy.[37] The fate of the duchy of Benevento was different: it remained in the hands of dynasties

[37] B. Ruggiero, 'Il ducato di Spoleto e i tentativi di penetrazione dei franchi nell' Italia meridionale', *Archivio storico per le province napoletane*, 84–5 (1966–7), pp. 77–116. E. Taurino's estimate in 'L'organizzazione territoriale della contea di Fermo nei secoli VIII–X', *Studi medievali*, ser. III, 11 (1970), pp. 659–710, that minor Lombard administrative divisions lasted longer in the duchy of Spoleto than in other regions of the Carolingian kingdom of Italy, must be modified by the results of the research of E. Saracco Previdi, 'Lo sculdahis nel territorio longobardo di Rieti (secolo VII a IX)', *Studi medievali*, ser. III, 14 (1973), pp. 627ff on the *sculdasci* of the territory of Rieti, which, in the Lombard and early Carolingian periods, do not seem to be distributed in lesser districts within the Rieti gastaldate.

of Lombard origin, who drew from the fall of the Lombard kingdom of Pavia a motive for a more determined affirmation of local autonomy, in the name of an ethnic and military tradition which had been overturned in northern and central Italy by the Frankish expansion. In the Carolingian period the duke bore the title *princeps gentis Langobardorum*, as if to declare the transfer of the theoretical centre of the Lombard people from Pavia to Benevento.[38] The duchy had to recognize formally Frankish supremacy on several occasions, promising in addition considerable tribute payments, but that had no real effect on the internal structure of the surviving power of the Lombards in southern Italy. At Benevento a *sacrum palatium* was organized, as the administrative centre of the *res publica* ruled by the prince, and the vast ducal territory still remained divided into circumscriptions entrusted to counts or gastalds, who were responsible for military protection and justice.[39] But the power of the prince was strongly modified by the strength of the aristocracy (*proceres*), who emerged from the ranks of the *exercitales* in a development consistent with earlier tendencies in the Lombard kingdom and in parallel with the experiences of the Frankish-dominated area of Europe. They were an aristocracy rooted in landed ownership, further enriched by the public lands of the duke, employed – and thereby strengthened – in the exercise of political power and episcopal authority and in the administration of the great abbeys, particularly Montecassino and S. Vincenzo al Volturno.[40] In short, a microcosm which presents on a smaller scale a structural analogy with the broad Carolingian area of the Latin–Germanic world.

In comparison with the Italian kingdom there was in fact an important variation; there was no Frankish element, no social group introduced at a high level above and within the *gens Langobardorum*; and there appears to have been only a slight infiltration of the type of military clientèle and the form of precarious remuneration for service given by commended warriors which have been discussed above in connection with the institutions of vassalage and benefices.[41] And yet, even though vassals and benefices were not particularly widespread in the Beneventan duchy in the Carolingian period, political disintegration

---

[38] O. Bertolini, 'Carlomagno e Benevento', in *Karl der Grosse*, vol. I, pp. 616–71; P. Bertolini, 'Studi per la cronologia dei principi langobardi di Benevento', *Bullettino dell'Istituto storico italiano per il medioevo*, 80 (1968), pp. 25–78.

[39] Poupardin, *Les Institutions publiques*, pp. 12–61.

[40] N. Cilento, *Le origini della signoria capuana nella Longobardia minore* (Rome, 1966), chapter 5, especially p. 166 note 38.

[41] See Leicht, *I problemi della civiltà carolingia*, p. 151.

revealed itself there even earlier than elsewhere. This is further proof that it was not the juridical institutions of *vassaticum* and *beneficium* that were at the root of territorial fragmentation in the Middle Ages, but rather the convergence of particular traditions of military or ecclesiastical command and a strong landed base. It was groups in conflict within the aristocracy that determined the secession of the principality of Salerno from Benevento in the course of the ninth century, and it was the enterprise of a gastald of Capua, Landulf, which gave rise to a powerful comital dynasty and the further secession of Capua from Salerno.

Particularly significant is the fate of the county of Capua in the last decades of the century, divided into gastaldates among the many descendants of Landulf as if it were a private patrimony.[42] The division made was not only of private property but also of a political territory, a 'fair distribution' (the expression used in a charter of 879) of the powers of command over the territory which belonged to the dynasty. But those public powers seemed to radiate outwards in each gastaldate from the estate centres of the Capuan dynasty and from the fortifications now appearing in its territory, similar to the castle which gastald Landulf had built decades before as the first sign of his desire for autonomy (such a clear sign that some gave the name of 'Rebellopolis' to the new stronghold). Landed goods and fortifications, populations of dependent peasants and nuclei of armed men in the castles; these were the centres of the material and human forces at the disposition of the many cousins who divided the county. Their territorial lordships arose from the 'distribution' of 879 through a political act, but in a form suggested by the customary division of inherited goods. The lordships constituted military and jurisdictional spheres of action, areas of public exploitation of the whole population of the territory, but they were based on the possession of property and the power to dispose of men who belonged to the comital family by patrimonial right. And besides, it should not be forgotten that the neighbouring papal rule over the Roman duchy, born as an officially autonomous government a century earlier through a series of Carolingian political decisions, had its concrete foundation in the co-ordination of the *patrimonia* of the Roman Church in Latium, and in the convergence around the 'apostolic see' of the military and ecclesiastical aristocracy of the region. Wherever wealth in land and militias, in the Germanic or in the Byzantine and Roman tradition, whether priestly or dynastic, found a centre around which it could co-ordinate itself, the preconditions were laid for territorial rule.

[42] Cilento, *Le origini*, pp. 155ff; see p. 31ff for the castles. For the principality of Salerno, see B. Ruggiero, *Principi, nobiltà e chiesa nel Mezzogiorno longobardo, l'esempio di S. Massimo di Salerno* (Naples, 1973), pp. 187ff.

The question which should be asked is why it was in this area, which was still Lombard and in which the institutions and power of the Franks were only marginally and intermittently present, that the military and landed aristocracy brought about an extreme political fragmentation earlier than elsewhere. One could answer that this was because it so happened that the Lombard aristocracy of southern Italy was operating within a complex network of forces in mutual conflict, which were pressing on the region from outside. The continual Muslim incursions, the expeditions of the Frankish kings of Italy to protect the peninsula against them, the interventions of the Frankish dukes of Spoleto and of the Roman Church, the Byzantine attempts at reconquest, all gradually threatened the autonomy of this last strip of Lombard land; but at the same time they offered the swarm of Lombard lords the chance to establish themselves in opposition to each other, and to survive by means of the boldest and most unscrupulous ties, since the most menacing external forces were at the same time both the most hostile to each other and the least capable (thanks to the complexity of their activities) of committing themselves consistently to the region.

The protagonists in the incessant movement of military forces across the south of Italy were the constant and many-pronged assaults on the region, which radiated from the Arab power-structure organized by the ninth century, by the Aghlabid dynasty in Tunisia. Tunis, conquered by the Arabs at the end of the seventh century, had very soon become the port and arsenal for attacks on Sardinia and Sicily. Long-distance Arab piracy had at the same time provoked the reorganization of Byzantine naval forces into one central fleet at Constantinople and a number of squadrons subordinate to the themes, the new military circumscriptions ruled by *strategoi* which were mentioned above in the discussion of Sicily. The military strength of Byzantium, enormously reduced on land in the various regions of the Mediterranean by the startling expansion of the Arabs, seemed to re-establish itself in a new form towards the middle of the eighth century, through the restoration of its predominance at sea, based on fortified strips of land around ports; it was an empire of 'dromons', the long fast Byzantine combat ships, which the Muslims imitated, as they did the fitting-out of arsenals and ports and the classic forms of sea combat, although without reaching the technical level and organization of their great opponent. In the West, the bulwark of the Byzantine bid for military survival in the Mediterranean was formed by the Sicilian theme centred on Syracuse, in that rich island with its protected bays on the northern and eastern coasts close to the Italian peninsula, where the remnants of Byzantine superiority over some coastal points still suggested the prospect of reconquest. Sicily was the target of the assault from the Aghlabid emirate, which had established itself in Africa at the beginning of the ninth century.[43]

The expedition of 10,000 infantry and 700 horse, with which the difficult Muslim penetration into Sicily began in 827, was imposed on the emir by the religious demands of holy war (it was led by a theologian, who died at Syracuse), and by the centuries-long Arab tradition of raids and conquests; it was a part of a much greater sea offensive in the Mediterranean, which was unleashed in the west and east under the aegis of Islam but which by its nature included and exalted the customary practice of piracy among certain local populations. Certainly Sicily, in the course of a war that stretched through the whole of the ninth century, saw its new capital, Palermo, become the centre of a coherent Muslim power-structure which was based on its own emirate even though subject to the Aghlabid emirate of Tunisia, and which involved a considerable immigration of Arabs and Berbers, particularly to the western zones of the island, where the pre-existing population also underwent a general process of Islamization. In Apulia and Campania, however, the stable presence of Muslim nuclei signified only a naval expansion, with the settlement of some coastal bases for periodical incursions into the interior of the peninsula and for the exercise of piracy by sea.

Actually Muslims from Sicily were first brought to Campania, eight years after their first landing in the island, by the duke of Naples himself, to face the threat of the Lombard prince of Benevento. Soon afterwards other Muslims, coming from Spain and Africa, were used by the Lombard princes in their struggles among themselves. Only at Bari, however, did an emirate form – and exist for more than twenty years – after the Lombard gastald of the city, subject to the prince of Benevento, had called a Berber military leader to his aid in 847. The latter then remained at Bari and made it the centre of his activity, turning it into a base similar to that of the Muslims at Taranto which had already been in operation for some years, but he organized it territorially and set up a political power which survived him until 871. All the same, the irradiation of the Muslim forces of Bari across a large area of southern Italy was never directed towards the construction of a regional power-structure of any breadth.[44] And so while in Sicily the various

[43] Eickhoff, *Seekrieg und Seepolitik*, pp. 42–99; 'Galeerenkriege im Mittelmeer', in *Ordinamenti militari*, vol. 2, pp. 979–1007.

[44] M. Amari, *Stori dei musulmani di Sicilia*, ed. Ç. A. Nallino (Catania, 1933), vol. 1, pp. 381–530; G. Musca, *L'emirato di Bari* (Bari, 1964), pp. 13–109; F. Gabrieli, 'Gli Arabi in Spagna e in Italia', in *Ordinamenti militari*, vol. 2, pp. 713–20.

phases of a violent, very slow and strongly contested conquest destroyed the whole social and political structure, resulting in military dominion based provisionally on violent religious opposition, the Muslims in southern Italy operated within political situations they had not created, merely sharpening conflicts and promoting political disintegration and local autonomy.

In truth, at certain moments, in reaction against the repeated violence, the Arabs provoked an alliance of forces which had formerly been hostile among themselves to expel them. Louis II of Italy sought several times to overcome the distrust of the Lombard princes of the south and induce them to accept the leadership of the kingdom against the nuclei of 'Saracens' (as the Muslims active in Europe were called in the West), and his last expedition in the south, undertaken in 871 with the purpose of expelling the Muslims from Bari, even gained the co-operation of the Byzantine navy. But the end of the emirate of Bari itself caused the collapse of these temporary motives for co-operation between the Empire of the Franks and the Empire of the Greeks, who were rivals for the imperial Roman title and thus rivals within an ideology which conferred on each empire a universal significance of ecclesiastical inspiration, and turned them both in the direction of the control of Italy.[45] Even though in the eighth century the failure of the papal plan for an Italian *res publica* based on Rome, and the spread of the Franks in various ways, in the Ravennate, Pentapolis, in the duchies of Perugia, Spoleto and Rome, including some influence even within the vast Beneventan duchy, guaranteed the Carolingians a solid hegemony over the peninsula and the 'apostolic see', this never brought Byzantium to renounce its ambition definitively. Indeed, when the Muslim advance in Sicily undermined the role of the 'theme' of Syracuse – that is, of the military province which should have arrayed around the *strategos* of Syracuse all the forces loyal to Byzantium in the island and in southern Italy – a new Byzantine plan was drawn up, that of carrying directly into the peninsula their greatest military effort against this threatened expulsion from the Italian world.

This plan was realized within the broader anti-Muslim offensive of the Emperor Basil I (867–86), founder of the Macedonian dynasty of Constantinople. The Frankish conquest of Bari had indeed weakened the Saracens locally but had not removed the Arab danger (indeed, Taranto

---

[45] P. Lamma, 'Il problema dei due imperi e dell'Italia meridionale nel giudizio delle fonti letterarie dei secoli IX e X', *Atti del III Congresso internazionale di studi sull'alto Medioevo* (Spoleto, 1959), pp. 155–253; W. Ohnsorge, 'L'idea d'impero nel secolo nono e l'Italia meridionale', *ibid.*, pp. 255–72 (see Ohnsorge, *Abendland und Byzanz* (Darmstadt, 1958), pp. 184–226).

became stronger, as a Muslim base for operations by land and sea), while on the other hand it had strengthened Lombard distrust of the Frankish empire. Basil succeeded in drawing the principality of Benevento within his own sphere of influence, occupied Bari, which had already passed from the Franks back to the Lombards who had held it before the emirate appeared, and expelled the Saracens from Taranto. This was the necessary preliminary to the reorganization of much of Southern Italy into the two Byzantine themes of 'Longobardia' and 'Calabria', ruled respectively by the *strategoi* of Bari and Reggio and destined to last until the eleventh century. The whole of Campania remained essentially outside this reorganization; here there survived, with conspicuous autonomy, not only the Lombard lordships but also the officially Byzantine cities of Gaeta, Naples and Amalfi, into which the Neapolitan duchy, which had already lacked territorial coherence, had disintegrated in the course of the ninth century. But Byzantine influence was felt in Campania as well, from the end of the ninth century, as a protection against the Saracens which replaced that of the Franks. Indeed one may say that in theory the theme of Longobardia in its widest sense included this region as well, although the direct power of, and government organized by, the Byzantines in Apulia were quite different from the overall supremacy they exercised over the lordships held by Lombards in Campania and over the autonomous Tyrrhenian cities with a Byzantine tradition, from Gaeta to Amalfi.[46]

These were the years in which the Carolingian Empire ceased to be a set of kingdoms entrusted to members of a single royal and imperial family. It is true that the post-Carolingian kingdoms of tenth-century Europe still existed within a Frankish tradition, and in large part the upper military aristocracy which struggled for their thrones was Frankish. This was the case in the kingdom of Italy as well. But the new presence of Byzantium meant the end, and some reversal, of the penetration into southern Italy which the Franks had repeatedly tried to carry out from Pavia or Spoleto. It meant for many decades a less unstable border, not between states confronting each other but between the zones of Frankish influence and the zones of Byzantine influence. The Italian kingdom as a political territory was breaking up, even though its structure and political developments remained analogous with those of the rest of formerly Carolingian Europe. The areas which lay between the populations that formed the Italian kingdom, living

[46] J. Gay, *L'Italie méridionale et l'empire byzantin* (Paris, 1904), vol. 1, pp. 79–163; Falkenhausen, *Untersuchungen*, pp. 18–44; A. A. Vasil'ev, *Byzance et les Arabes, II: La Dynastie macédonienne*, ed. M. Canard (Brussels, 1968), part 1, pp. 10–157, 221–44.

within the framework of the appeal to a public order which had been attempted by the Carolingians, and the populations that Byzantium sought to organize in Apulia and Calabria, were regions of transition differing among themselves. They ranged from those in which the Churches of Ravenna and Rome still wished to establish themselves on the political level, with greater or lesser efficacy and in persistent partnership with the aristocracy of Romano-Byzantine origin and the Franks,[47] to those regions in which Lombards and coastal cities evaded, if not the supremacy of Byzantium, certainly the order which Byzantium imposed on the provinces.

When one views the condition of the peninsula in general between the ninth and tenth centuries, it is noticeable how far the political dissolution already taking shape in the Lombard period had progressed, despite some vigorous attempts to halt it. But a more serious problem, which calls for a specific approach, is that of the varying meanings that anarchy took on in different regions and periods, in relation to the forms in which power was structured within the social system. The seigneurial development in the Italian kingdom now tended towards a profound disintegration of the public order. This, as we will see, was very different from the simple fragmentation of territory which took place in other regions of the peninsula from the ninth century onwards, whether this fragmentation was translated into the formation of territorial lordships linked to landed property, or whether such an autonomy was founded on centres of population with a Byzantine tradition, as in the cities of Campania noted above and in the remarkable composite centre of population which established itself with exceptional vigour on the Venetian lagoon.

[47] G. Buzzi, 'Ricerche per la storia di Ravenna e di Roma dall'850 al 1118', *Archivio della Società romana di storia patria*, 38 (1915), pp. 107–63; Simonini, *Autocefalia ed esarcato*, pp. 162–84.

4

POLITICAL ANARCHY

The autonomous territorial entities which emerged in Italy within the Byzantine tradition, from the Campanian coast to the Venetian lagoons, developed in a context of which violent sea warfare was an integral part. The great anti-Muslim offensive led by the Eastern Empire under the Macedonian dynasty in the late ninth and tenth centuries was not sufficient to re-establish the 'universal' hegemony of Byzantium over the seas, as the reorganization of its naval forces at the end of the eighth century had seemed to guarantee before the second wave of Arab corsair attack. The expulsion of the Saracens from the Adriatic and peninsular Italy was balanced by the consolidation of their position in Sicily. The new 'themes' organized between the Adriatic and the Ionian seas were of value to the Byzantines as a western protection for the forces concentrated on the Aegean, as a more organic and less ambitious defence of the central nucleus of the Empire. In any case, the expulsion of the Saracens from the Adriatic and the Italian peninsula had itself been the result of a temporary convergence of forces, in which it was difficult for Byzantium to play a pre-eminent co-ordinating role. On the contrary, it was at this time that the emphasis was on the multitude of initiatives by other political entities which had only a restricted range on land but could sometimes have very broad repercussions by sea.

This can be seen in parallel in both the Tyrrhenian and the Adriatic. In the case of the former, from the middle of the ninth century to the destruction of the Saracen colony of the Garigliano carried out in 915 the individual coastal cities of Campania alternated between alliance with the Muslims and anti-Muslim leagues, and between commercial exchange and military ventures. In the Adriatic, the Venetian fleet was faced with the extensive pirate activity of the Saracens of Apulia in the Carolingian period and the aggression of Croats and Narentani based on the eastern shore throughout the ninth and tenth centuries, but it not only managed to keep the lagoon area itself almost always intact, but, in its efforts to defend the lines of trade between the Veneto coast and Otranto, it seemed to offer itself as a force replacing both the Italic kingdom, which lacked any armed organization on the sea, and by degrees the Empire of Constantinople itself, which was gradually ever more deeply engaged in southern and eastern waters. The Venetian fleet was revealed as a political nucleus, presumably with a technological organization along the lines of Byzantine naval models. It showed an increasing determination to assail the very bases of pirate activity in the Adriatic, and through action against various sites along the coast it supported the political attempt of the Venetian duchy to co-ordinate around the interests of Venice itself the activity of ports of the exarchate, such as Comacchio, and of Istrian and Dalmatian centres; these harbours were either officially part of the dissolving Italic kingdom or within the peripheral and ephemeral domination of Byzantium.[1]

Thus the political fragmentation present in those parts of Italy where the development of Romano-Byzantine institutions had taken place with unbroken continuity was projected on to the sea as well, in the commitment to protect commercial routes and coastal security. But what was the structure of these political 'fragments', and what was their social basis?

If, beginning with the Campania–Lazio coast, we consider for example the case of Gaeta, we find a politically identifiable territory which stretched along the sea for about forty kilometres, from the mouths of the Garigliano as far as Terracina, and which was prolonged inland for another fifteen kilometres at the most, as far as the pre-Apennine watershed. Between the ninth and tenth centuries Gaeta, the capital of the territory, was a large stronghold; its walls protected a population formed mainly of landowners (the *viri honesti*, often also adorned with the title of *comites*), whose properties had substantially

---

[1] R. Cessi, 'Politica, economia, religione', in *Storia di Venezia* (Venice, 1958), vol. 2, pp. 110–247; *cf.* E. Sestan, 'La conquista veneziana della Dalmazia', in *Venezia del mille* (Florence, 1965), pp. 87–116; Eickhoff, *Seekrieg und Seepolitik*, p. 151.

benefited from the division of a papal landed estate lying within the territory. Its wealthiest family, by far, was one around which the landowning class gathered, and which had added to its private patrimony of lands and *coloni* the public administration of fiscal property and political power. The latter was obtained with full military and jurisdictional functions, through the favour of the imperial court of Constantinople and through ties with the ducal court of Naples, to which Gaeta was originally subject, and with the Church of Rome. A purely honorific Byzantine rank, *hypatos*, was at first sufficient to distinguish certain members of the leading family until its head, in a move to exercise political power and to protect the episcopal church, took on the title of *hypatos et dux* or (in imitation of the dukes of Naples) *consul et dux*. Succession became hereditary through the elevation of a son of the *hypatos et dux* or *consul et dux* to become co-ruler with his father, with the same title. In the course of the tenth century, even within the formal unity of the duchy, Gaeta's territory was dividing into districts, each resting on small centres gradually growing in population and fortified with castles. The lords of the various castles, most of them with the title of count (which now seems to have been restricted to them alone), were members of the ducal family or related to it, and the division of the duchy into several counties seems to correspond to the division of the landed patrimony of the ducal family, which was scattered among these districts.[2]

This is a social and political system clearly founded on landed property. The land supplied the small amounts of capital which were needed both by the ducal family, to arm flotillas, and by the better-off landowners, often members of the ducal court itself, to carry on a certain maritime commerce which was encouraged by ties with important centres of consumption for eastern goods, the See of Rome and the abbey of Montecassino. Only in the eleventh century does the clear evidence of a general increase in the traffic centred on the city suggest greater complexities in its social structure, which were reflected in the exercise of power. It is evident that in the city ducal power was now increasingly subject to control by the *nobiliores homines*, the *maiores*, a class possibly heterogeneous in their economic condition, and perhaps largely engaged in commercial and financial activities less rigidly subordinated to the power of landed property. This was a first step towards the commune, the *res publica* of the city, a civic order dominated by the *maiores* (the most influential individuals) but not without some participation by the *mediocres et minores* also living in the city; this order

[2] Merores, *Gaeta*.

is well attested at Gaeta at the beginning of the twelfth century, as it confronted the duke and the seigneurial powers scattered among the castles of the ducal territory. Thus over three centuries, within the exceptionally modest territorial limits of a political formation with a purely Romano-Byzantine origin, there appears to have been a wealth of experimental developments, in which local power kept pace with variations in economic and demographic conditions. A power which was organized dynastically to guarantee a stable social hegemony for the dominant landowning family and the class related to it had to commit itself to fortifying the territory, menaced on all sides, and to arming fleets to keep open the territory's access to the sea; by such means it laid the basis for the decomposition of the duchy into lesser lordships and for the concentration in Gaeta of new forms of wealth which, when accompanied by the military traditions of the *nobiles*, were destined to create a flourishing *res publica*.

Partly similar conditions appear in the still more limited ducal territory of Naples and in the extremely small territory of Amalfi, but with some important variations. Naples was an ancient city, the seat of an episcopal church with a long tradition, and was rich in Greek and Latin monasteries. Repeating an event of the eighth century, some of its bishops rose to a position higher than that of the ducal authority itself, as if imitating the power achieved in other regions by the Churches of Ravenna and Rome. But in reality this only occurred at Naples when the episcopal seat was occupied continuously by members of the ducal family itself, between the mid-ninth century and the first decade of the tenth century. And so, properly speaking, it was a ducal dynasty rather than an ecclesiastical body that imposed, even through the figures of energetic and sometimes ruthless bishops, a political will that persisted over the generations, capable both of associating the *militia* of Naples with its own interests and of organizing territorial and maritime defence. The *militia* was formed by the class of prominent landowners, which in its name and its military and bureaucratic functions maintained the purest tradition of the Byzantine cities of Italy.[3] Amalfi in its turn presents other peculiar features. It had no territory, like that of Gaeta and Naples, which might inspire a multitude of strongholds and of counties dependent on them; it was completely directed towards maritime commerce and gave rise to a political regime that appears only gradually

---

[3] F. Ciccaglione, *Istituzioni politiche e sociali dei ducati napolitani* (Naples, 1892), pp. 130ff; M. Schipa, *Il Mezzogiorno d'Italia anteriormente alla monarchia* (Bari, 1923), pp. 53ff; N. Cilento, *Civiltà napoletana del medioevo nei secoli VI-XIII* (Naples, 1969). See also G. Galasso, *Mezzogiorno medievale e moderno* (Turin, 1965), pp. 63–135.

to have become based on a single dynasty. But towards the Longobard principality of Salerno, in both the ninth and the tenth centuries, it developed a political and military response which was equal in intensity to its enterprise by sea; we need look no further than the successful rebellion of the Amalfitan population which had been forcibly transported to Salerno in 839, and the acquisition by the duke of Amalfi in 981 of nothing less than the principate of Salerno itself.[4]

How far can one compare this process, in which autonomous nuclei with their own naval power took root in a particular Romano-Byzantine territorial tradition, in a system of relationships contrasting with that of the Lombards of the hinterland despite certain undoubted *de facto* analogies, with events in the islands of the lagoon which organized themselves into the duchy of Venice?

The latter duchy had a most unusual territorial formation. In the Carolingian and post-Carolingian periods it stretched over about twenty centres of population; most of them were scattered on the islands and the sand-bars, but some were also in the middle of marshes or in a coastal area which extended from Loreo south of the Adige along ninety kilometres of shoreline to Caorle, and included also Grado, forty kilometres further east. Along the shore there was a mixture of systems of salt-pans, fishing basins, pasture, wooded areas with wild cattle, ports, agrarian towns, vineyards and orchards, suffering from some natural instability in minor lands still emerging from the sea, and with frequent protective embankments and man-made linking canals.[5] At the beginning of the Carolingian period such a territorial structure must have corresponded to a sort of federation between all these sites, a regime created through the action of an aristocracy of military and landed origin (the *tribuni* of the Byzantine tradition); this aristocracy was constantly developing through its participation in commerce and through the probable rise of new families, and though it culminated in the ducal power it was often also present on the mainland outside the duchy in landed properties of its own. From the ninth century onwards the aristocracy focused around the community of the island system of Rialto, which through a centuries-long process was in its turn co-ordinating itself as a city, and which was ever more dominant as a political, demographic and commercial centre. The ducal seat was at Rialto; it was formally subject to Byzantium until the eleventh century,

[4] M. Berza, 'Amalfi preducale (596–957)', *Ephemeris Dacoromana*, 8 (1938), pp. 349–444.

[5] L. Lanfranchi and G. G. Zille, 'Il territorio del ducato veneziano dall' VIII al XII secolo', in *Storia di Venezia*, vol. 2, pp. 3–65.

and politically linked both with Byzantium, with which it frequently co-operated and from whom it obtained notable commercial privileges, and with the Carolingian Empire and the Italic kingdom, with which, after some discord, it concluded and renewed for centuries treaties vital for the security of the lagoon, for the river communications of the whole duchy with the hinterland, and for the supplies of timber needed for naval construction.

The ducal power was developing its co-ordinating role with an outlook that was monarchical in tendency, and with its own small bureaucratic apparatus, but it was restrained both by the influence exercised over the person of the duke by the presence of bishops and *primates* or *iudices* (the official designation in the post-Carolingian period for the dominant aristocratic group) at the palace or in the duchy, and in the assemblies of the people summoned for the most important discussions. They were summoned primarily over the ducal succession, which was no longer influenced by the government of Byzantium and was normally arranged beforehand by the duke himself through the association of a son in his power – at least when factions of the aristocracy, palace conspiracies or popular uprisings did not cause the downfall of these incipient dynasties and the rise to the duchy of another powerful family.[6]

Here we have a limiting case, among the autonomous naval powers which emerged at this time from systems originally rooted in the *militia* and in landed property. The 'Venetian' territory, with its lagoon formation dominated everywhere by the presence of the sea, still permitted the evolution of a durable aristocracy of families furnished with a rich landed base. It was in competition, even military competition, for ducal power or for influence over the duke, and was intimately linked with episcopal churches and monasteries of the lagoon; it also possessed some properties beyond the duchy and maintained relations with groups of relatives and religious bodies on the mainland. This limiting case, however, should be interpreted with due caution. It would be unwise to assume too strong a resemblance between an aristocracy resident on small, often marshy islands, capable from the ninth century onwards of complex financial operations and involved in commerce by sea and river, and showing a clear tendency in the tenth and eleventh

[6] Kretschmayr, *Geschichte von Venedig*, vol. I, pp. 190–7. This view has been modified by more recent interpretations: C. G. Mor, *L'età feudale*, vol. 2 (Milan, 1953), pp. 162–9; *Aspetti della vita costituzionale veneziana*, pp. 127–38; R. Cessi, *Le origini del ducato veneziano* (Naples, 1951), pp. 323–32, *Venezia ducale I: Duca e popolo* (Venice, 1963), pp. 155–379.

centuries towards the monopolization of Adriatic traffic,[7] and that military and landed aristocracy on the mainland which crudely accumulated *curtes* and forests, guarded strongholds, dominated rural populations, rode tirelessly between the various scattered strongpoints of their power, demanded oath and homage from their client vassals, and recruited serfs to their armed entourage.

There was a shared adherence to certain bases and traditions of power, but none the less a notable variation in the developments and arrangements, in the political formations on which the naval forces of Gaeta, Naples, Amalfi and Venice were erected. There is a specific reason for laying this emphasis on the animation and strength of the 'fragments' of territory and maritime power which made themselves independent of the great Byzantine political framework. Here, on the border between great land-based power-structures in crisis and the declining predominance of Byzantium over the sea, these 'fragments' are the first evidence of the vigorous development that the collapse of the great military and political apparatus brought to areas with only a modest population. The disorder of southern *Langobardia* and of the Italian kingdom was the presupposition for these marginal developments, which did not take place in a uniform direction, but all of which are extremely significant indications of the capacity for initiative which was restored after a millennium to the local life of the population of Italy.

When one looks at the process of decentralization that took place in the post-Carolingian period in the duchy of Gaeta, and at the simultaneous process of demographic and political concentration of the scattered 'Venetian' lagoon territory, one can see how impossible it is to reduce the autonomous characters of those formations to a single model of evolution. Indeed, one may go further: if the lagoon and its affairs are considered in isolation, it is impossible even to measure how far the influx of aristocracy and lesser population to the islands of the Rialto combined to elevate the ducal power and to encourage it to take on a dynastic tendency connected with greater responsibilities of government and with consequent demands for a stronger stability, and how far on the other hand that same influx complicated the exercise of power by a single family, by creating around it several flourishing organizations of interests which were able to take on the shape of an anti-dynastic opposition. Hence in modern historiography there is an exceptional disparity in interpretations of the hesitant institutional development of

[7] M. Merores, 'Der venezianische Adel', *Vierteljahrschrift für Sozial- und Wirtschaftsgeschichte*, 19 (1926), pp. 193–237; G. Luzzatto, *Studi di storia economica veneziana* (Padua, 1954), pp. 125ff, 'L'economia veneziana nei suoi rapporti con la politica nell' alto medioevo', in *Le origini di Venezia*, pp. 151ff.

Venice from the ninth to the twelfth century. But it is precisely this uncertainty, and the new freedom of movement of the power-structures under the contradictory pressures of local society, which provide an advance warning of the historical fruitfulness of the anarchy which arrived in Italy and Europe during the period which is inaccurately called 'feudal'.

The process which took place very early in the areas considered above, through the accident of its marginal status both politically and geographically, had some very diverse parallels throughout the Latin–Germanic world, even where a more dramatic course of events, involving the highest levels of politics, might suggest to us that the great political frameworks were still effective. Those events were not without effect on lesser powers, but they left no mark on the structure of the 'disorder' through which those lesser powers everywhere emerged. In the shadow of ephemeral royal and imperial hegemonies, a struggle which gradually involved all social levels took place over the whole continent. This struggle also involved fleets; returning to Italy, the northern Tyrrhenian sea saw the formation of nuclei with naval strength (Pisa and Genoa) somewhat later than the 'fragments' of the Byzantine tradition, but the former had a vitality equal to that of Venice and superior to that of the Campanian nuclei, which were too quickly reintegrated by the Norman unification of the south into the 'order' of a broad and coherent dominion. In fact the Genoese and Pisans were already establishing themselves militarily in the Tyrrhenian at the beginning of the eleventh century. But the territories and social systems which produced these naval forces were not established in opposition to inland political formations with a different tradition: rather, they were intimately involved in the great affairs of the fragmented Italian kingdom, and so they bring us back to the transformations undergone by the post-Carolingian public order in the North.

THE METAMORPHOSIS OF ROYAL AND COMITAL POWER IN
POST-CAROLINGIAN ITALY AND THE DISINTEGRATION OF THE
STRUCTURE OF THE STATE

With the end of the Carolingian dynasty in Italy the kings of Pavia did not cease to be part of a Frankish political tradition; nor did they cease to claim Charlemagne's imperial title. This latter traditionally belonged to the Italian kings because of their responsibility (thanks to their geographical position) for the protection of the Church of Rome, the symbol of the religious universality which from the fourth century onwards had been connected with the idea of the Empire. Those great military families which for more than half a century (from 888 to the middle of the tenth century) contested the royal and imperial throne in Italy all dated back in their patrimonial power and public authority to the period of the Carolingians, to whom they were all related. Thus they were families of high royal officials, strengthened by their own client vassals, by the wide-ranging ties of kinship among the Frankish aristocracy of the Empire, and by their immense landed property, often situated on both sides of the Alps.

The case of the two first contenders for the Italian crown, King Berengar and King Guy, is particularly significant. They belonged to Frankish families which originated respectively near the lower Rhine and near the Moselle[8] and were therefore both from old Austrasia, homeland of the Carolingians. The Carolingian dynasty had entrusted to these two families the important border duchies, or marches, of Friuli and Spoleto, and then gradually allowed the succession in both duchies to rest within the respective families. Each of the two kings (in the years in which one or the other managed to reign) and their successors on the throne thus fitted automatically into the normal models of the world from which they came. At Pavia a central administration persisted, with its chancery, and the counties and marches continued to exist in the ambiguity which characterized them; they were public districts at the disposal of the king, but at the same time they were spheres of power within which particular families sought to define themselves, with a more or less obvious dynastic tendency. This tendency was reinforced by customary usage, although the latter was still ephemeral and was resisted by the king in the name of the public nature of the comital or marchesal office, whenever it appeared most useful to him in the interplay of ecclesiastical and military politics, and whenever a replacement appeared possible. This is apparent for example when King Hugh, who arrived from Provence at the request of the great aristocrats who elected him in Italy in 926, began after 930 to insert numerous new men, particularly of Provençal origin and mostly his relatives, into the counties and marches of the kingdom.[9]

Did nothing, then, really change with respect to the Carolingian period? On the contrary, one thing is certain: after 898, legislative activity stopped. In the capitularies promulgated in 891 by Guy of

[8] A. Hofmeister, 'Markgrafen und Markgrafschaften im Italienischen Kön-
    igreich', *Mitteilungen des Instituts für österreichische Geschichtsforschung*, 7, fasc.
    2 (1906), pp. 171ff.
[9] E. Cristiani, 'Note sulla feudalità italica negli ultimi anni del regno di Ugo
    e Lotario', *Studi medievali*, ser. III, 4 (1963), pp. 92–103.

Spoleto and in 898 by his son and successor to the kingdom, Lambert, one may still read exhortations to bishops and counts to proceed in agreement with each other in pacifying the provinces entrusted to them. The purpose of ecclesiastical tithes is recalled, the autonomy of parishes from lay exploitation is defended, provisions are made for restoration of public buildings, there are instructions on the validity of notarial documents verifying the transfer of property and on the right of women to dispose of their own goods, the *arimanni* (the class of small landowners) are defended against the abuses of public officials, and the *arimanni* themselves are warned to fulfil their military obligations. All this is in the purest tradition of Carolingian public order.[10] Then all is silence at the level of legislation. Nor is there any further mention of *arimanni*, except (for some centuries afterwards) in royal diplomas and notarial charters where they appear as groups, mostly very small in size, of *liberi homines*, distinguished from others by special ancient bonds with the public power. Throughout the ninth century the class of small landowners still officially appeared as the broad social basis of the kingdom, marked out by the name of *arimanni*, which referred to the Lombard people but in reality was open to any ethnic element economically capable of sharing in the military protection of the kingdom, maintenance of ecclesiastical and public buildings, communication routes and itinerant tribunals. Now, however, it ceased in the eyes of the king to appear as a unitary class, as a valid partner in dialogue or the immediate focus of public authority, or as the normal subject of the rights and duties which justified the existence of the kingdom. The semantic evolution of the term *arimannus*, as its broad social significance was gradually forgotten, and its narrow application to groups which crystallized in particularly conservative localities, demonstrate, not that small landholding was already disappearing (we have too much evidence for its perennial vitality and its mobility in the cities and countryside of Italy[11]), but rather that the king and the officials of the kingdom were losing their normal bond with it. They no longer perceived the affairs of landowners as a whole but only as local groups here and there, and ultimately they often interpreted these groups (in the zones in which tenacious customs maintained the name *arimanni*) as the heirs of some specific condition of dependence on the king.

The royal chancery continued to function, not in order to enact

[10] *MGH Capitularia*, vol. 2, pp. 107–10. See Tabacco, *I liberi del re,* pp. 37–66.

[11] See C. Violante, *La società milanese nell'età precomunale*, 2nd ed. (Bari, 1974), pp. 51–167; E. Conti, *La formazione della struttura agraria moderna nel contado fiorentino*, vol. 1: *Le campagne nell'età precomunale* (Rome, 1965), pp. 149–74.

general measures but only to draw up diplomas: privileges addressed to the most disparate individuals, particularly churches and friendly aristocrats, centres of force which the king sought to link to his own power. The network of heterogeneous relationships is, properly speaking, not a new development, but this feverish activity, even though it certainly has behind it centuries of experience of Lombard and Frankish kings, now seems almost to encapsulate the whole meaning of the kingdom.

To clarify this by an example, we should look at the diplomas promulgated by the chancery of Berengar I, the king who survived his rivals, Guy of Spoleto and Lambert, until 924. Berengar strengthened individual ecclesiastical patrimonies by extending his protection over them, renewed and conceded immunities, gave away serfs and tenant holdings, fiscal *curtes* and wooded mountains, extended fishing and navigation rights, gave exemptions from tolls, and conceded public revenues in ports, on bridges and roads, in market-places and from coinage. Following the example of his rivals Guy and Lambert, he permitted the bishop of Modena to dig moats, build gateways and fortify the territory within the radius of a mile around the city's church and the cloister of the canons, and permitted the bishop of Bergamo and his fellow-citizens to rebuild the towers and walls of the city, which was destroyed by Hungarians and (according to the document) 'oppressed by the counts and their agents'. He permitted a deacon of Verona to build a castle on the deacon's land and arm it with turrets, battlements and moats; he allowed the bishop of Reggio Emilia to build a castle in one of his parishes; he allowed a group of twenty-nine inhabitants of Novara and its territory to raise a castle on their own land as a defence against the Hungarians and *mali cristiani*; he permitted the bishop of Padua to build castles in his diocese wherever his church had lands, with full immunity from public intervention; and he permitted the abbess of a Pavian monastery to do the same on the land of the abbey 'wherever she will think it useful against the incursions of the Hungarians', with full immunity, donating to the same abbess on another occasion a part of the public walls of Pavia so that she could freely open gateways there or put up buildings. He confirmed to a parish of Voghera public revenues 'et districtum', that is, the power of command and coercion, to be exercised over the residents of the lands belonging to the parish. He donated to his own daughter Berta, abbess of the powerful monastery of S. Giulia of Brescia, a public road, with the right to dig moats and build fortifications, and donated other public roads to the episcopal church of Padua, together with a whole valley and every *iudiciaria potestas* over the *arimanni* and other *liberi homines* (those not descendants of the arimannic tradition of allod-holders) resident in that same valley. And he made similar donations and concessions to many other churches and other private individuals.[12] Perhaps the boldest privilege of Berengar's time is that conceded in 916 to the episcopal church of Cremona, which obtained perpetual ownership of all the rights due to the fisc in the city and surrounding territory for a radius of five miles, and the gateways and towers, with a ban preventing all public officials ('comes, vicecomes, sculdassio, gastaldio, decanus aut aliqua magna parvaque persona publice et imperialis aut regiae partis') from carrying out any act of authority or jurisdiction in the city and the aforesaid territory without the consent of the bishop. It also obtained the recognition of perpetual episcopal power over all castles built to protect parishes and *curtes* belonging to that bishopric, with full immunity from public authority. Equally significant, in the clarity of the terms used in the concession, is the diploma of 912 with which the king transferred from his own law and dominion, to the dominion and law of the patriarch of Aquileia and his successors in perpetuity, the castle of Pozzuolo in the county of Cividale, together with everything belonging to it and every right of justice and coercion in the fortress and within the radius of one mile around – exactly the power and rights, in short, that had been exercised by the holder of the count's office up till then.

These examples should illustrate the heterogeneity of the means used, and of the persons and organizations given privileges, in order to guarantee to the king a network of ties which might complement the unreliable collaboration of public officials. But the evidence presented above also shows how the public order was being undermined from the beginning of the tenth century. It is not only a matter of the obvious impoverishment of the fisc through exemptions and generous donations of goods and revenues, but also of explicit concessions in perpetuity, in particular sites and areas, of the exercise of the most purely public functions, military and judicial power, to the detriment of the kingdom's officials. Not only are officials again banned from entering lands economically subject to the holder of immunity in order to exercise directly acts of force and jurisdiction – a ban already serious in itself and a feature of the Carolingian diplomas of immunity – but all freedom of action is withdrawn from the kingdom's officials in whole fortified areas and cities, and in the territories centring on those fortifications or cities;

[12] L. Schiaparelli, *I diplomi di Berengario I* (Rome, 1903). See, more generally, V. Fumagalli, 'Vescovi e conti dell'Emilia occidentale da Berengario I a Ottone I', *Studi medievali*, ser. III, 14.1 (1973).

sometimes, indeed, the officials lose all right to summon the men of such areas out of them to make them answer for their deeds elsewhere before the public authority, and instead the recipient of the privilege (as with the castle of Pozzuolo) is given precisely the powers that previously belonged to the authority of the count.

This clear process of territorial breakdown differs from the forms of disorder proper to the Carolingian period, in the awareness with which the kingdom now accepted and promoted the formation of autonomous nuclei of power where comital authority displayed serious deficiencies in its operation. The disturbances denounced by the capitularies of the ninth century, arising from the 'oppressions' committed by public officials against the population, are quite different from this radical incapacity of the public power to guarantee local protection. Weaknesses of operation, already obvious in the Carolingian period in the connivance between counts or their subordinate agents and powerful families, were now aggravated both by the increased instability of royal power, the object of struggles which could no longer be moderated by an appeal to the shared solidarity of claimants as members of the same imperial family, and by the rapid and deep incursions of the Hungarians, who devastated the whole kingdom of Italy on several occasions from 898 to the middle of the tenth century.[13] Territorial defence could no longer be maintained by armies which, apart from the frequent paralysis of their operations provoked by disputes with the king, appear to have been disoriented on every occasion in the face of the Hungarian raids, which were quite unlike the forms of combat known in the Frankish world. It became necessary to fortify the territory in depth, and above all to protect the population centres most exposed to sack at the hands of both the invaders and the *mali cristiani* who profited from the confusion, and here the lack of comital authority is most obvious. The discredit to the royal power resulting from the armies' ineptitude in the face of repeated Hungarian incursions (to which in Piedmont were added Saracen raids) was matched by the discrediting of the counts and marquises, who were perhaps actively engaged in protecting their own *curtes* but were certainly not engaged with equal care, and with the readiness and vigour which were needed, in protecting the towns and cities. And, as the military discrediting of the king led to rebellions of the aristocracy or of factions among it and the search for a less 'inept' king, with the consequent reopening of struggles for the throne, so the obvious insufficiency or negligence of the counts provoked independent

[13] G. Fasoli, *Le incursioni ungare in Europa nel secolo X* (Florence, 1945).

initiatives of fortification (*incastellamento*) by lords and groups of landowners, religious communities and cities represented by bishops. It induced the king himself to authorize and encourage, sometimes by gifts of royal lands, private initiatives in fortification and the direct assumption of responsibility by bishops and their fellow-citizens for the restoration of city walls and the preparation of the outworks and moats needed for defence.

What is still surprising, though, even if every concession is explained by relating it to the Hungarians and the dissensions in the kingdom, is the definitive character taken on, even officially, by fortifications such as these, as constructions belonging to churches and private individuals and as centres of autonomous organization of the territory in perpetuity. It is particularly surprising that even a city like Cremona should assume such a status: here, rights of the fisc and public powers were almost abolished in favour of the episcopal church, on the grounds that the goods of the church had suffered serious damage from the 'incursions of the pagans' and that further burdens came from exactions and the exercise of jurisdiction by public agents, who frequently gave as a pretext the need to repair gates, towers and roads[14] – as if an emergency, such as the impoverishment of the church of Cremona through the incursions and the exploitation of them by the *publici ministeriales*, could justify a transfer of revenues and powers *usque in perpetuum*! Evidently the Hungarian devastation, like that of the Normans in Francia in the ninth and tenth centuries, provoked solutions towards which there were already strong tendencies.

For example, in the rural territory of the village of Cologno Monzese, a village six kilometres from Monza on the road to Milan with a territory of a few square kilometres, one can follow through the rich documentation the gradual expansion of the patrimony of the monastery of S. Ambrogio of Milan. This monastery, which was clearly a member of the old Lombard royal clientèle, had penetrated or extended into this territory at the beginning of the Carolingian period through a donation from a *gasindius*, and in the course of the ninth century it replaced many of the Lombard landowners in the area through a variety of economic operations, until it achieved an absolute pre-eminence in landed property and built a castle to protect it during the period of the Hungarian invasions. It owned the fortifications of the castle completely, whereas in the internal area, as with that of the land outside the walls,

---

[14] See C. Manaresi, 'Alle origini del potere dei vescovi nel territorio esterno delle città', *Bullettino dell'Istituto storico italiano per il medioevo*, 58 (1944), pp. 222ff.

its property was mixed with that of other allod-holders.[15] There is no trace of any royal intervention in the erection of the castle, nor of any royal rights over its operation. The economic hegemony attained by the Milanese monastery in the village was spontaneously translated (in the climate created everywhere by the spread of fear of the Hungarians, but doubtless also related to a more general search for territorial security) into a fortification, which was destined in its turn to attract population from other villages and to become a centre for autonomous reorganization of the territory.

Among these spontaneous tendencies a place must be accorded to the activity of the royal chancery in promulgating diplomas, an activity which was perhaps rather sporadic but none the less significant. The contrast which had characterized the action of the Carolingians, between a tenaciously pursued project for territorial administration, ordered by rational models, and the need to extend immunities to churches and to respect the traditions of power of the aristocracy, was now decreasing. In its effort to survive, the kingdom now recognized all the spontaneously-produced *de facto* situations of which it had knowledge, and contributed to their definition in terms which took on a new boldness, seeking to crystallize them in order to bind itself permanently to them. The vocabulary of private law, concerning the possession of goods and inheritance, was used to express transfers of power which were manifestly aberrant both with respect to the whole public tradition of Roman origin, and with respect to Germanic traditions of the organization of the people. For with the exception of a few brief impulses in this direction in the Carolingian period,[16] no king had ever been seen to donate with full property rights, in free and absolute possession, towers and fortresses, city gates and walls, public roads and judicial powers, with the same formulae that were used for landed goods whose significance was purely economic.

Nor was this the aberration of one king, or of some particular chancellor. Alienations of this kind continued throughout the tenth and eleventh centuries, and there were similar documents from north of the Alps as well, particularly from Germany, where the kings donated freely, *iure proprietario*, cities and fortresses, military districts and entire counties, sometimes with formulae that explicitly furnish the recipient

---

[15] G. P. Bognetti, 'Terrore e sicurezza sotto re nostrani e sotto re stranieri', in *Storia di Milano*, vol. 2 (Milan, 1954), pp. 805–41; G. Rossetti, *Società e istituzioni nel contado lombardo durante il medioevo: Cologno Monzese* (Milan, 1968), vol. 1.

[16] G. Tabacco, 'L'allodialità del potere nel medioevo', *Studi medievali*, ser. III, 11.2 (1970), pp. 567ff.

with the right to possess and hold, sell and exchange the powers he has received, 'doing with them whatever may please him'. This does not reflect a system of ideas with its basis in the relationship of vassals and benefices, in the so-called 'feudalism' which is too often referred to for an explanation of the medieval dissolution of public order; rather it mirrors a precise allodial conception of power and jurisdiction, conceived in connection with visible goods and property, with *curtis* centres, nuclei of habitation, and fortifications.[17] The case of the castle itself is typical. All the powers of command and jurisdiction over the men that lived within its walls, and in the territory that centred on it, appear inherent in the fortress, as if they were the personal property of whoever owned the fortress as an allod: the king, or a powerful family, or an ecclesiastical body, or even a group of men who had acquired it or founded it on their own land. The 'guardian' of the fortress, the castellan responsible for its operation, was generally not the same as its lord, but was an agent of the king, if the fortress was royal, or an agent of the powerful family or the ecclesiastical body, or even of the consortium of title-holders of the castle. So in general he was a functionary of a public or ecclesiastical authority, or of private persons, and as a functionary he might or might not be bound to the lord of the fortress by a bond of vassalage and receive from him in repayment a 'benefice', which was made up of property inside or outside the castle and even from revenues connected with the exercise of the powers entrusted him by the lord. The institutions of vassalage and benefice could thus appear in the context of the emerging powers of the territory; but, at least for most of the eleventh century, they underlined the tie between the agent and his lord, rather than signalling the autonomy of a seigneurial power whose guarantee, on the contrary, lay in a right of property.

This application of the law of property to the exercise of functions with a public character, while it had been suggested by the spontaneous formation of centres of force around visible and alienable elements of the territory concerned, suggested in its turn the most diverse forms of transmission of power, often even in the shape of shares distributed among the heirs which in their turn were ceded to different purchasers (for example shares of the castle, that is of revenues and powers connected with the fortification), and which indeed not uncommonly provoked the disintegration of the power itself into the separate elements through which it was expressed. Between the tenth and twelfth

---

[17] P. Vaccari, *La territorialità come base dell'ordinamento giuridico del contado nell'Italia medioevale*, 2nd ed. (Milan, 1963), whose purely Italian perspective needs to be allowed for.

centuries any element of a territorial power could be subject to independent donation, will, dowry, sale, pledge, lease, or any other private contract. Everything could be traded, every exaction and contribution connected with political protection, together with the specific activity that justified the exaction or contribution, thus including the taking of tolls related to the control of bridges, gates and roads, the right to promulgate orders and inflict fines, the power to judge and punish certain crimes, the use of *albergaria* (hospitality due to the lords who protected particular localities), the custom of exacting guard service in the fortresses or prestations of labour for their maintenance. The normal foundation of the right possessed or ceded was inheritance, or a preceding economic transaction drawn up between lords, but in the last analysis it went back sometimes to a royal gift and much more often to a local customary usage, whether or not it had taken shape through a process of successive demands and coercion. Thus not only were the *consuetudines bonae* conceded, but sometimes explictly the *consuetudines malae* or *iniustae* as well.

These private transactions concerning nuclei of power and their constituent elements were therefore interwoven with the formation of local customs that were preponderantly seigneurial. The process of disintegration of public power and new political elaboration at the local level were linked together; they overlaid and alternated with each other in a disorder which was all the greater where the dispersal of great landed property, the normal economic basis of local power, was more extreme and where as a result several lords were in rivalry with each other within the same zone, where they all had property. The divergence noted above in connection with the Carolingian period, between the structures of the countryside and the great landed property – that is, the disharmony between peasant settlement in villages and the distribution of landed estates into unconnected and mainly fragmented *curtes*[18] – tended to favour the formation of seigneurial customs which rivalled each other in the local protection they offered, and which were susceptible to mutual interference. In this case the political reordering of the territory around *curtes* and castles was slower and more precarious, and local seigneurial power was less capable of overcoming the deficiencies of public order in a crisis, and of resisting tendencies – encouraged by the allodial conception of power – towards its own

---

[18] For the tenth century, see V. Fumagalli, 'Per la storia di un grande possesso canossiano nel Parmense: la corte di "Vilinianum"', *Quellen und Forschungen aus italienischen Archiven und Bibliotheken*, 49 (1968), pp. 73–94.

disintegration into isolated instruments for the exploitation of the rural population.[19]

The clear connection which we have stressed between local political developments and the distribution of great landed properties should not, however, imply that one can deduce mechanically the distribution of power in the post-Carolingian period from the differing economic strength of the landed aristocracy. Possession of the land was the instrument necessary for any local political power-base, but this power-base was not precisely commensurate with the extent of the property. The multiplication of centres of power was influenced decisively by the individual traditions of authority and desires for autonomy and self-affirmation of families with a military background as well as those of the ecclesiastical organizations. The seigneurial fortress did not arise in a territory exclusively from the need to defend private property.

The subordination of castle-building (*incastellamento*) to economic interests is particularly evident where, for example, a monastery or convent of canons fortified sites around which its concentration of property was increasing, as in the case, described above, of the castle of Cologno Monzese, which arose through the initiative of the abbots of S. Ambrogio of Milan. For a bishop, on the other hand, the reinforcement of the city walls and the construction of fortresses in strategically important points of the diocese represented something more than the protection of property and landed income. Such construction set up a political–military framework for the centre and – in a partial and discontinuous fashion – even for the periphery of an ecclesiastical district, for purposes which were not only patrimonial but which also included the control of parishes, monasteries and other churches of the diocese, so as to intensify the episcopal presence in the religious and social discipline of the clergy, monks and laity, according to the authoritarian models of episcopal tradition. An idea of the nature and intensity of episcopal castle construction between the tenth and eleventh centuries is given by an imperial diploma conceded in 1041 to the bishop of Asti which confirms, among all the possessions of the episcopal church, thirty-seven fortresses, mainly connected with *curtes* but in part distributed according to purely strategic criteria along the banks of the Tanaro.[20] Such a military apparatus far exceeds the needs

[19] See R. Ripanti, 'Dominio fondiario e poteri bannali del capitolo di Casale Monferrato nell'età comunale', *Bollettino storico–bibliografico subalpino*, 68 (1970), pp. 109–56 (for the map see *ibid.*, 69 (1971), p. 507).

[20] See R. Bordone, 'L'aristocrazia militare del territorio di Asti: i signori di Gorzano', *ibid.*, pp. 358–74.

for protection of rents from tenant-holdings and pastures; it displays a political ambition in the service of ecclesiastical structures of power.

The purely political character of certain seigneurial fortifications, with that final aim of power which presupposes a taste for dominion over men, is clear above all in the dynastic interests of the most prominent families, which were not always sustained initially by any real economic base. A well-documented case of this kind is the Canossa (a Lombard family from the region around Lucca), whose fortunes can be followed from the time, around 940, when King Hugh endowed it with property around Parma, thus causing the family's transfer from Tuscany to Emilia.[21] At the root of the social rise of this family from the minor Lombard aristocracy to the great aristocracy of the kingdom, which up to the beginning of the tenth century was mostly composed of Frankish elements, there was no consolidated economic power, just a purely political relationship: the link between the interests of a new king from north of the Alps and the ambition of enterprising 'new' men among the Lombards, ready to range themselves alongside the king in action against the most dangerous men of the kingdom. This political ambition, however, was manifested not solely through a link with the king but also through the further acquisition of allodial lands, which were not extensive but were already fortified with castles, and through expansion by means of exchanges and purchase in the direction of the Po, into uncultivated zones of little economic interest but of great strategic importance, where castles were restored by the Canossa and by the peasants whom they attracted there. Meanwhile, during the tenth century, the Canossa took over, by royal command, the government of counties and bishoprics in the region, and so started to become the great dynasty of marquises which in the eleventh century gathered into its hands the counties of Brescia, Mantua, Reggio, Modena and Ferrara and the march of Tuscany.

This process of continual mutual influence between political ties, acquisitions of property, the multiplication of castles and the assumption of high official responsibilities in districts of the kingdom is noteworthy. The name we usually give this dynasty, drawn from the Apennine stronghold of Canossa, serves to symbolize the structure of its enormous seigneurial dominion, which was essentially built up from a large number of unconnected castles and rural estates, scattered among the estates and castles of ecclesiastical bodies and other lords, within and outside the great public districts which the Canossa held as officials of the

[21] V. Fumagalli, *Le origini di una grande dinastia feudale. Adalberto-Atto di Canossa* (Tübingen, 1971).

kingdom. Compared with the power of the aristocracy of the Carolingian period, the new element here is the intensity of fortification of estates and strategic strongpoints by means of fortresses; these were largely held as allods and thus connected not with the functioning of the kingdom but rather with the exercise of a plurality of local powers, even though in the case of counts and marquises these powers were gathered into the same hands to which the traditional public districts were entrusted. The districts, the countries or marches, were breaking apart and losing all significance, to the profit of all the ecclesiastical and lay lords, small and great, including the counts and marquises themselves, who held a personal title to the lordship of individual villages and cities, whether by royal donation or by local custom and through the presence of landed property and fortifications. So, for example, the Canossa constituted a strong and stable political force not so much through the high public offices they held as through a fine mesh of hereditary power, inserted into the local circumstances of countless towns and villages, through the obedience of the peasants to the local seigneurial 'ban' and through the personal loyalty offered them by the nucleus of vassals in each castle. This power was capable of placing itself in opposition to the kingdom and driving it gradually to acknowledge the strength of the Canossa, from one generation to the next, in the titles of count and marquis which dignified the family's territorial dominance.

In parallel with the construction of local powers on an allodial base, the hereditary tendency of public offices became more explicit, and there is no doubt that the title of count or marquis gave particular importance to the political aims of the great families. But in the actual exercise of power the most valuable element was military control of individual areas, strengthened by a more or less intense concentration of landed property. An interesting sign of the fundamental importance of the exercise of local powers for the overall strength of a great family, by comparison with the more formal dignities with which it was invested, may be seen in the case of the imperial diploma granted in 1001 to the marquis of Turin, Olderic, who was a member of the Arduinici, a family which had risen to great wealth through the acquisition of political power at a high level.[22] Two Franks following Salic law, Roger and Arduin, arrived as adventurers in Piedmont at the beginning of the tenth century and entered the clientèle of the count of Auriate, by whom Roger was designated heir to his landed estate and his successor as count, with the royal designation as count then following as well. From Roger

[22] G. Sergi, 'Una grande circoscrizione del regno italico: la marca arduinica di Torino', *Studi medievali*, ser. III, 12 (1971), pp. 661ff.

there descended the Arduinici, invested by the king towards the middle of the tenth century with the vast march of Turin, which absorbed a group of counties so that it reached from the valley of the Lanzo as far as Ventimiglia and Albenga. Within the march the Arduinici gradually acquired an important allodial landed patrimony, which in its turn became, when duly fortified with castles, a solid basis for autonomous hereditary power. This is apparent from the marquis Olderic's anxiety to receive in the diploma of 1001 the concession of immunity for his numerous possessions – a strange immunity, seeing that it was from interventions by the public power which was then represented by the marquis himself, as if to guarantee his property and local power against the eventuality that one day the authority of marquis might be withdrawn from himself or one of his descendants.

Faced with such a tangle of powers emerging from individual local conditions and from the political aims of churches and dynasties, competing among themselves to create economic and military strongholds, the royal and imperial authority none the less preserved its own uneven supremacy in the Italian kingdom. Although it was still anchored formally to the idea of public order, whose summit it represented, in reality it was progressively transforming itself into a power with nothing more than ambitions of generic hegemony over the territory of the kingdom. This power was incapable of guaranteeing territorial peace and security according to rational uniform models, but it was none the less just as much able to operate effectively, even if only in an episodic fashion, to strengthen or disrupt the activity of other centres of power, according to whether it met deference or resistance. The royal authority still functioned at individual points within the kingdom's territory, everywhere entering into rivalry or alliance with forces that recognized it as the supreme power, and which in their turn sought recognition from it but checked its interference.

This surviving royal authority constituted the centre for an irregular co-ordination of strength which up to the middle of the tenth century tried repeatedly and in vain to establish a dynasty. In the same way that the count or marquis held his title, not yet by a formally recognized dynastic or 'feudal' right, but by the king's choice of him to fill an office of the kingdom, even though the choice was mostly made within the family of the deceased official, so too the king acquired the royal title not by the hereditary nature of the crown but through election by the great lay and ecclesiastical lords of the kingdom, that is, by the members of precisely those powerful families from whom the kings drew counts, marquises, and even bishops and abbots. This pattern was further complicated after the German conquest of the Italian kingdom in 951.

The opportunity for German intervention was analogous to that of other lords fron north of the Alps, from Burgundy and Provence, who were summoned to Italy by one or other faction of the aristocracy in the first half of the century, supplied as it was by the usual internal struggles of the kingdom; but unlike other interventions there is no sign that Otto I, King of Germany, in entering Pavia in 951 was concerned to strengthen his own conquest by means of an election carried out by part of the Italian aristocracy. He seemed, rather, to act like Charlemagne after his military victory over the Lombards,[23] even though now there did not follow any settlement of German nuclei like that of the Franks and their allies who had emigrated to Italy to control the *gens Langobardorum*.

In the Italian and German kingdoms, which were both the product of the Carolingian tradition, a large part of the dominant aristocracy was still of Frankish or Alamannic origin, following the patterns of the Carolingian expansion across central and southern Europe – however numerous the great Bavarian, Thuringian and Saxon families might be in the political context north of the Alps (King Otto himself was of old Saxon stock), and however much the presence of Lombard families might make itself felt in the tenth century in the political context south of the Alps. The imperial title itself, which Otto I took care to assume in 962, having himself crowned by the Pope according to the traditions of all the Italian kings who aspired to empire, went further to place the two kingdoms theoretically within the same tradition inherited from Charlemagne. But the territorial and military dominance of the German armies was such as to render inevitable Italy's subordination to the decisions which were made north of the Alps over the choice of the king. At the beginning of the eleventh century, when the Ottonian dynasty became extinct, part of the Italian aristocracy attempted to escape from this subordination by electing as king the marquis Arduin of Ivrea; but the orientation of the German kingdom towards Italy and towards the imperial tradition, founded on coronation at Rome, was now too strong for it to be possible to cut the bond that the Ottonian dynasty had established between the two kingdoms.

The subordination of the Italian kingdom to German decisions, and the increased strength that the military might of the German royal dynasties seemed to give to royal power in Italy, none the less had no marked effect on the evolution of this power. Indeed one can say that the metamorphosis of royal authority after the Carolingian period, its transformation into a discontinuous territorial hegemony, became

[23] See Mor, *L'età feudale* (Milan, 1952), vol. 1, p. 174.

apparent in Italy in its full clarity only under the German dynasties, between the tenth and eleventh centuries. The appeal to Carolingian tradition, the ostentatious solemnity of the new Empire, the dynastic tendency of the House of Saxony, as of the House of Franconia which succeeded it in the exercise of royal authority simultaneously in Germany and Italy and in the imperial title, did not modify the process of disintegration of public power and its dispersal among the most disparate political foci. In particular there was a continuation of that annexation of political power by ecclesiastical bodies which had already appeared in outline from the beginning of the tenth century, in the remarkable activity of the chancery of Berengar I, and which requires analysis because it was interwoven with the increasing encroachment of the lay aristocracy on ecclesiastical life, and culminated in the papal attempt to resolve the political problem of Italy and Europe through a priestly theocracy.

THE CHURCHES AS INSTRUMENTS AND ACTIVE CENTRES OF POLITICAL POWER

The active participation of the churches in the general rivalry over territorial organization is the most striking aspect of their deep involvement in a closely-woven network of temporal interests. This involvement had two directions. The stability of ecclesiastical bodies, which was displayed visibly in the church building itself and found an effective symbol in the saint to which the church was dedicated, aroused an ever more intense bond between the kingdom, the military aristocracies and local population on the one side and the episcopal seats and more energetic canonical and monastic communities on the other. The latter accumulated landed wealth, clientèles of vassals and of lesser men in commendation, privileges, powers and material responsibilities, while individuals loyal to the king and members of the great families were placed as administrators or members of the communities. At the same time this stability prompted the multiplication of church foundations on the estates of powerful families.

This multiplication of monasteries and chapels, founded and endowed by prominent families and destined to be part of the landed inheritance of those same families, answered a tendency present in all the aristocracy of the Latin–Germanic world on both sides of the Alps, from the Merovingian and Lombard period up to the eleventh century.[24] The

[24] U. Stutz, *Die Eigenkirche als Element des mittelalterlich-germanischen Kirchenrechts* (Darmstadt, 1955, reprinted 1964); this reading should be complemented by H. E. Feine, *Kirchliche Rechtsgeschichte* (Weimar, 1950), vol. 1, pp. 135–45 and

foundations arose from religious preoccupations, from the aim to procure prayers in perpetuity for the founder, his family and all his descendants, but at the same time they constituted an important source of income. The patrimony with which the church was endowed, when it was entrusted to clerics or monks, tended to increase through the influx of donations inspired by the cult of the saint to whom the church was dedicated, and because the revenues from landed property were supplemented by offerings brought to the altar by the faithful; the offerings and property were destined for the church, but they were administered by the church's lord and protector, as the founder or the descendant of the founder. The idea that such churches belonged to the seigneurial family arose from the fact that the altar was built on ground included within the property of the family and from the conviction that the buildings and sacred objects, habitations of clerics and monks, lands and men dependent on the latter, and every type of revenue connected with the ecclesiastical role were appurtenances of the altar. This was taken to such a point that the patron of the land on which the altar was built not only interfered in the administration of goods and income, to his own great profit, but chose the person who officiated in the church, or intervened in the ordering and recruitment of the community to which the church had been entrusted.

Thus the possession of churches not only gave the lord a religious insurance and increased his income, sometimes to a notable degree, but it constituted one of the foundations of the social prestige of the aristocracy, together with the extent of the landed estate, the number of serfs and *coloni*, the availability of an armed clientèle and, from the tenth century, the fortresses built on the estates. Indeed, it gave those transient family groupings, which did not yet always manage to define themselves by clear lines of dynastic descent, a means of orienting the descendants of the founder around the stability of the churches founded and owned by them (and in particular around the favourite sanctuary of the family), so keeping alive the memory of a common descent. This happened for example, from the ninth to the twelfth centuries, with the family of the Berardenghi, a family which occupied the position of count at Siena in the Carolingian period but later lost it; it found instead its sense of direction, which enabled it to preserve later the memory of its own past, in the foundation in 867 of a nunnery, of which abbesses from the family of the founder were to be in charge. In time the nunnery shrank to the church alone, with its patrimony, until at the beginning of the eleventh

F. Kempf, H. G. Beck *et al.*, *Die mittelalterliche Kirche* (H. Jedin, *Handbuch der Kirchengeschichte*, III) (Freiburg-Basel-Vienna, 1966), vol. 1, pp. 296–301.

century the descendants of the founder restored a monastic community there, masculine this time, and subordinated it to the dominion of the Berardenghi. This dominion did not, however, remain unified but was divided in the course of the century among several members of the controlling family.[25] Thus, the process outlined above with regard to allodial fortresses took place in seigneurial churches as well; they were divided into shares among heirs, and also transferred into hands other than those of the founding family, through donations, exchanges, and sales of the church or part of it.

In this sense, as a way of increasing the status of the families that controlled them, the churches owned by a family, sometimes quite numerous, helped to make up the basis for the exercise of local territorial and political powers over the population. We may note that such churches, particularly the monastic churches, could sometimes attain a certain landed wealth and power in their own right, even though they were themselves included within the property and power of a great military family. Nor was it only the lay lords, beginning with the king, who owned allodial churches – the great abbatial, canonical and episcopal churches themselves sometimes owned over a hundred at a time; those were the churches whose power reached the greatest level of autonomy that was compatible with the interventions of the king. For these ecclesiastical organizations too the possession of minor churches, together with other property, fortresses and vassals, formed a sound foundation for the construction of political power, in which exploitation of landed wealth and dominion over churches, temporal jurisdictions and military force joined together to form an aggregate as heterogeneous as that of the great lay aristocracy. Thus the same economic and military, jurisdictional and ecclesiastical elements, although in different proportions, went into the composition of each prominent nucleus of power, whether it were an abbey, a bishopric, a cathedral chapter or a lay dynasty, and whether or not it were invested with dignities of public origin, comital or royal. And in each of these diverse nuclei, represented at its summit by an ecclesiastical or lay lord, the individual elements became stratified, one becoming subordinate to another through the persistent reference to the concept of property. For example a bishop or great family might possess in allod, among other goods, an abbey, which possessed in its turn within its own allodial landed patrimony lesser

---

[25] P. Cammarosano, 'La famiglia dei Berardenghi sino agli inizi del secolo XII', *Studi medievali*, ser. III, 11 (1970), pp. 103–74. See W. Kurze, 'Adel und Klöster im frühmittelalterlichen Tuszien', *Quellen und Forschungen aus italienischen Archiven und Bibliotheken*, 52 (1972), pp. 90ff.

monasteries and other churches, these in their turn owning goods and men. Thus there were patrimonies within patrimonies, spheres of economic action and power over men within other spheres with broader power.

None the less one should be aware that this patrimonial interpretation of the subordination of powers to powers, an interpretation in which churches played such an important part both as the culminating points and as links in the chain, never characterized the political and ecclesiastical framework as a whole, in the central centuries of the Middle Ages. It never became a concise system of hierarchical relationships. It only functioned as a series of internal relationships between particular organizations, particularly in those areas where ecclesiastical buildings and fortifications, standing on an allodial patrimony, suggested the idea that the power that radiated outwards from a building could be owned by another centre of power, on whose allod the building rose; as a result there developed a concept of property which allowed the seigneurial rights of intervention or command over churches or fortresses to be placed on the market, as objects of the most explicit private transactions. But applying the concept of private property to a power, although it placed that power itself at the disposal of a higher seigneurial authority, also assured that higher authority, whether ecclesiastical or lay, of the greatest autonomy with respect to the official public and ecclesiastical order. That is, it broke up any ordered political system, and became the instrument for opposition to the intervention of bishops and royal officials, and even for possible reciprocal opposition between kingdom and bishopric, since episcopal possession of a fortress in allod removed this element of military and political force from submission to the authority of the king and his officials, and royal possession of a church in allod withdrew it from rigid control by the episcopal authority.

The guardianship exercised by royal authority over bishoprics and the chapters of the cathedral churches was of an entirely different nature from the dominion of ecclesiastical bodies and lords over their allodial churches, although royal protection of the great abbeys sometimes tended to be confused with the rights of property that the king exercised over churches in the fisc. In the case of bishoprics and cathedral chapters the king did not consider them part of his patrimony, but he claimed the supreme responsibility which belonged to him within the territory of the kingdom, and appealed to the co-operation which the bishops, assisted by their canons, owed to the king in the government of the 'Christian' people. The bishops were often imposed on the diocese by the king, who either drew them from the circle of clerics loyal to him (clerics of the court, of his chancery and his 'chapel', or clerics of cathedral chapters which had a special relationship with the king) or chose them from the candidates of the upper local clergy; hence in the various sees of northern Italy and Tuscany there was a succession of bishops originally foreign to the diocese and the region (indeed, for most of the eleventh century they were not infrequently drawn from Germany), alternating with bishops drawn from the military aristocracy of the region or from the leading citizens of the episcopal city itself.[26] But whatever its origins and however deep its ties with the king, it remained impossible to confuse the Italian episcopate with a class of royal agents, since each individual bishop, even though a stranger or foreigner, necessarily found himself absorbed into the upper local clergy who surrounded him, and with whom he shared membership of the ecclesiastical order, a power-structure rooted in a tradition of priestly autonomy and religious superiority in apposition to the dominance of the king. So each time that the king enriched an episcopal church with goods, privileges and temporal jurisdictions, although he certainly promoted the development of an organization whose title-holder had usually been chosen by the king himself, he strengthened at the same time the bases of a local power which by virtue of canon law (the guarantor of the inalienable and perpetual nature of every new addition to ecclesiastical power, and of the sacred dignity of the bishops and their colleagues) did not permit harsh interventions by the king to the detriment of persons and goods within the church.

Thus, throughout the kingdom, in the context of the spontaneous interplay of local relationships and through royal calculation, the temporal structure of the great churches grew larger. They lay outside the normal public order (which was at the same time distintegrating to the advantage of the great seigneurial families) and remained under a royal control which was intermittent and not fully legitimate, due to the long absences of the German king from the Italian lands and to the official distinction between *regnum* and *sacerdotium*. While the loyalty of counts and marquises to the royal power dissolved into the political action of unstable seigneurial dynasties, the loyalty which the kingdom demanded from the bishops as a substitute was in its turn limited by the respect due to a morally and materially powerful priesthood, and to an ecclesiastical culture before which the royal power was almost

---

[26] G. Schwartz, *Die Besetzung der Bistümer Reichsitaliens unter den sächsischen und salischen Kaisern* (Leipzig-Berlin, 1913), pp. 1–25; E. Hoff, *Pavia und seine Bischöfe im Mittelalter* (Pavia, 1943), vol. 1, pp. 124–332; E. Dupré-Theseider, 'Vescovi e città dell'Italia precomunale', in *Vescovi e diocesi in Italia nel medioevo*, pp. 55–109; H. Schwarzmaier, *Lucca und das Reich bis zum Ende des 11. Jahrhunderts* (Tübingen, 1972), pp. 71–155.

defenceless. It would be enough to affirm, in the cultural currents which ran through the world of clerics and monks in the tenth and eleventh century, the need for a more rational discipline of ecclesiastical institutions, for the absence of any apparatus defining and constituting the royal power to be revealed. The great reforming movement, which divided the episcopate both north and south of the Alps and in the course of the eleventh century involved the Roman papacy as well, forcing it to take on the management of ecclesiastical reform at its most uncompromising, also threw into confusion the royal and imperial power. It overturned the hegemony exercised loosely by the kingdom over the ecclesiastical sees and abbeys and over seigneurial dynasties, and left the very person of the king undefended, as is shown by the humiliation of Henry IV at Canossa in 1077 before Pope Gregory VII.

The reform movement can indeed be interpreted as a vigorous defence of the religious experience against encroachment of the patrimonial and political strength of the kingdom's military and landed aristocracy. This is the significance of the polemic against the simoniac purchase of ecclesiastical offices by members of rich families, and against buying and selling of altars and churches, with their revenues. But although the reformers, struggling for the *libertas ecclesiae*, intended to found an order of monks and clerics which would be independent of any intervention by the laity (contrary to the whole tradition of the High Middle Ages), they did not renounce the economic and political power which was increasingly being incorporated into the patrimony of the churches. The attack on the mixing of sacred and secular, except for some marginal episodes, was in one direction only; wealth, temporal jurisdictions and fortresses, where they belonged to the churches, were *res sacra*. Only when we examine closely that strange tangle of elements of power which the eleventh century inherited from preceding periods, can we understand and reconcile the apparent contradiction between the laments of the reformers, who preached against the enslavement of the churches to the arbitrary power of the laity, and the papal aspirations to supremacy over the empire and the kingdoms, aspirations which presupposed in the priesthood an exceptional capacity for political action. The tendency towards a priestly, theocratic interpretation of power, in which the Roman pontifex replaced the emperor at the summit of every jurisdiction (hence the sentence deposing Henry IV, pronounced by Gregory VII[27]) would be inexplicable in a situation

---

[27] G. Miccoli, 'Il valore dell'assoluzione di Canossa', in *ibid.*, *Chiesa gregoriana* (Florence, 1966), pp. 203–23; G. Tabacco, 'Autorità pontificia e impero', in *Le istituzioni ecclesiastiche della 'societas christiana': papato, cardinalato ed episcopato, Atti della V Settimana internazionale di studio della Mendola*

where the priesthood really was subservient to the secular power. The dependence was mutual.

In reality it had been mutual from the Carolingian period onwards, but now it had taken on a different and more complex appearance. No longer was it a matter of a rich and influential episcopate co-operating with and protected by the public power; rather, it was a matter of a power acting as a political substitute for the secular state, in many well-defined zones of every kingdom in the formerly Carolingian Europe. We have already seen this in Italy in the course of the tenth century and afterwards, in the case of the fortification of *curtes* to protect ecclesiastical property, or of strategic points important for the political control of large areas of the diocese. Particular attention has been paid to the assumption of temporal responsibilities by the bishops of Bergamo, Cremona and Modena, replacing the insufficient or oppressive activity of the count and associated with Berengar I's distrust of his own officials. Now the emphasis must shift to the diffusion, during the tenth and eleventh centuries, of analogous extensions of episcopal power in many of the cities of the Italian kingdom which were the seats of bishops. But the new political power in these cities even though it might manifest itself as the development of a church, actually represented the interests of all the citizens and particularly the leading ones, in a manner which grew ever more apparent with the demographic and economic recovery of the cities.

Clear evidence of the significance for cities of some of these developments in episcopal power can be found in the diploma with which Lothar, King of Italy, when confirming in 945 the right of the bishops of Mantua to mint a public coinage which would be current in the cities of Mantua, Verona and Brescia, specified that such money in its weight and proportions of silver should conform to the expressed wishes of the assemblies of the three cities, 'secundum libitum et conventum civium predictarum urbium'.[28] This presupposes that in this respect the bishop of Mantua was operating as a prominent figure in the region, able to represent not only the interests of his own church but also

---

(Milan, 1974). For the tendency towards a more systematic organization of the landed power of the churches of the eleventh century, see O. Capitano, *Immunità vescovili ed ecclesiologia in età pregregoriana e gregoriana* (Spoleto, 1966), pp. 83ff.

[28] L. Schiaparelli, *I diplomi di Ugo e di Lotario, di Berengario II e di Adalberto* (Rome, 1924), p. 252. See C. G. Mor, 'Moneta publica civitatis Mantuae', in *Studi in onore di Gino Luzzatto* (Milan, 1950), vol. 1, pp. 78–85; R. S. Lopez, 'Moneta e monetieri nell'Italia barbarica', in *Moneta e scambi nell'alto medioevo* (Spoleto, 1961), pp. 83–8.

those of an active economic class in the city, a class which still did not possess an organization capable of establishing itself autonomously at the political level. In this example the convergence of ecclesiastical power and urban enterprise took place within a broad regional grouping but in a specific sector of the state, and thus contributed to break it down further into its constituent parts. More often, this convergence happened at first in smaller areas, in a single city and the suburbs belonging to it, but with a tendency towards the substitution of the entire public order by the bishop, supported by the citizenry. Thus there grew up areas which were immune from the power of counts, for other reasons than simply the development of seigneurial powers radiating out from *curtes* and from rural fortifications; and it was these urban areas which were the most important forces in the break-up of public circumscriptions. In fact as the city, the traditional capital of diocese and county, grew in economic importance, gradually made itself immune from the count's authority, and became subject to the temporal jurisdiction of the bishop, it constituted an exception to the Carolingian order which was too striking for the concept of a regular royal division into districts to survive.

The most conspicuous example in the Italian kingdom of development of the urban powers of the bishop is that of Milan, and it is significant that for Milan there is no royal concession of public jurisdiction over the city to the bishop. This demonstrates how spontaneous was the emergence of autonomous islands of power around the great urban churches. Naturally the archbishops of Milan also possessed a power sanctioned by royal concessions: in particular, over and above the usual immunities for their landed patrimony, they held a series of public fortresses in Lombardy donated by Otto I to the archiepiscopal church.[29] But the heart of their enormous temporal power, which radiated out into a large number of areas even beyond the boundaries of the diocese itself, was at Milan, where the most eminent citizens, distinguished by the name of *capitanei* and equipped with their own goods and clientèles in the city and its contado, were from the last decades of the tenth century bound to the archbishop by ties of vassalage and as a result endowed by him with benefices, which included ecclesiastical revenues and even pieval churches (the baptismal churches to which the rural population distributed through the diocese was subordinated).[30]

[29] G. P. Bognetti, 'Gli arcivescovi interpreti della realtà e il crescere dei minori ordini feudali nell'età ottoniana', in *Storia di Milano*, vol. 2, pp. 843–62.

[30] For the interpretation of an important passage by the chronicler Landulf Senior (*Mediolanensis historia* I. II, c. 17, in Muratori, *Rerum Italicarum*

174   The struggle for power in medieval Italy

Analogous situations developed in many other episcopal seats of the kingdom of Italy. But it is wrong to conclude from this, as is often done, that between the tenth and eleventh centuries the bishops generally took on the rank of count in the public districts of which their cities were capitals. What happened was that the public districts dissolved into a plurality of powers in the hands of laity and ecclesiastics. The bishops were among the holders of those powers, using as a basis their own strength in the cities where they resided; but as territorial lords they mingled with other organizations and lords. After the second half of the eleventh century some bishops began to assume the title of count in their own district (the first example is that of the bishop of Arezzo in 1059), but the pretensions of these bishop–counts[31] only pointed up the now obvious lack in much of the Italian kingdom of any comital co-ordination of the territory by the lay aristocracy, on the level of the divisions into Carolingian counties. The only great churches south of the Alps which managed to co-ordinate permanently the territories of former public districts, and added to this to a royal donation of comital powers, were those of the bishop of Trento and, in Friuli, the patriarch of Aquileia, from the eleventh century onwards.[32]

Naturally the bishop of Rome was an exception. In the post-Carolingian period he continued officially to govern the Roman duchy (not without occasionally recalling his rights over Pentapolis and the Ravennate), even though, once an effective royal political structure protecting the Roman See had disappeared with the end of the Carolingians, the local aristocracy increased its presence in the administration of the duchy and in the exploitation of the papal patrimony, uniting in the first half of the tenth century around the family of the senator Theophylact. The papacy itself became for some decades the monopoly of this same family. None the less, the central organs of Roman political government preserved the bureaucratic structure of the Romano-Byzantine tradition, and there was an attempt to co-ordinate through the central government the ambitions of the aristocracy over the lands dependent on Rome.[33]

scriptores, 2nd ed., vol. 4.2, p. 51), see P. Brancoli Busdraghi, *La formazione storica del feudo lombardo come diritto reale* (Milan, 1965), pp. 87ff, 178ff.
[31] Dupré-Theseider, 'Vescovi e città,' pp. 98–101.
[32] See F. Nicolai, *Città e signori* (Bologna, 1941), p. 94 note 1 (but the interpretation of the imperial concession of comital powers to the bishop of Trent in 1027 as feudal rather than allodial should be corrected); H. Schmidinger, *Patriarch und Landesherr. Die weltliche Herrschaft der Patriarchen von Aquileia bis zum Ende der Staufer* (Graf-Cologne, 1954), pp. 56ff.
[33] O. Vehse, 'Die päpstliche Herrschaft in der Sabina bis zur Mitte des 12. Jahrhunderts', *Quellen und Forschungen aus italienischen Archiven und Bib-*

In the tenth and eleventh centuries the imperial German interventions in the life of Rome, while they forcefully recalled the papacy to its ecclesiastical responsibilities towards Western Christianity and not infrequently placed on the papal throne prelates from north of the Alps who were deeply concerned with their official duties, were not able to repress the power of the aristocracy, which indeed developed precisely at that time on Roman territory the same tendencies which characterized the seigneurial development on a military and landed base in the Italian kingdom and in all post-Carolingian Europe. But when in the course of the eleventh century the papacy decisively placed itself at the head of the religious reform movement, it also showed its capacity for action in local political government. Ecclesiastical reform, which withdrew the papal election from any direct intervention by the Roman aristocracy, aroused strong reactions in the latter, but the Roman church knew how to use all the tools that its religious and temporal organization offered it in the region to create a local following and to take command, despite some setbacks, and so, in return, it came to affect considerably even the composition of the seigneurial class which was dominant in Rome and its territory.[34]

The affairs of the Roman region, in their association with the great European reform movement, show clearly the complexity of the connections which were present everywhere between the development of new ecclesiastical structures, strengthened according to rational models of religious autonomy and institutional centralization, and the temporal situations in which the life of the churches of the time was rooted. The transformation which the ecclesiastical order underwent, beginning with the last decades of the eleventh century, in the direction of a papal monarchy thus necessarily became incorporated, as a further complicating element, into the political chaos which had arisen after the Carolingian period. It was also to exercise a multiple and contradictory effect on political events. On the one hand, by presenting itself as a commitment to the rational reorganization of collective life, this transformation was destined to suggest analogous experiments at the secular political level in the reconstruction of power on coherent institutional bases; and by defining itself as a priestly organization suspicious of any lay interference, it was to drive the laity to form themselves into a secular body with the propensity to be hostile to

liotheken, 21 (1929–30), pp. 120ff; O. Gerstenberg, *Die politische Entwicklung des römischen Adels im 10. und 11. Jahrhundert* (Berlin, 1933), vol. 1, pp. 26ff; W. Kölmel, *Rom und der Kirchenstaat im 10. und 11. Jahrhundert bis in die Anfänge der Reform* (Berlin, 1935), pp. 18ff (but see K. Jordan in *Deutsche Literaturzeitung*, 57 (1936), coll. 1277ff.).

[34] P. Brezzi, *Roma e l'impero medioevale (774–1252)* (Bologna, 1947), pp. 231ff.

priestly interference. On the other hand, the strong awareness that the priesthood acquired of its own superiority, not only cultural and moral but institutional, over the world of the laity, nourished at the summit of western Christianity the vain papal aspirations to a theocratic construction which would juridically subordinate to him secular as well as episcopal power, and gave the pope further excuses for intervention and conflict in the multiple processes of political and territorial reconstruction. All this was taking place while old and new motives appeared, in diverse forms and to different extents according to local situations, for a convergence between the interests of churches and monasteries and the interests of the most varied secular social groups, particularly those prominent social groups from whose number the holders of ecclesiastical as well as of secular power were recruited, no less now than before the ecclesiastical reform.

FROM THE DECLINE OF BYZANTIUM TO THE NORMAN EXPANSION INTO SOUTHERN ITALY

The affairs of the Italian kingdom and of the empire, with the accompanying development of ecclesiastical power which was destined to emerge in the reform movement and in the theocratic aspirations of the pope, also had a profound effect on the fortunes of southern Italy, first offering the chance for Byzantine influence to expand in the peninsula, then forcing Byzantium to restrict its sphere of action, and finally permitting a completely new social and political settlement of the south of Italy, under Norman domination and the formal supremacy of Rome.

In the first half of the tenth century the persistent Byzantine presence in southern Italy was also reflected in Rome, where the papacy and the family that dominated it entered into quite intense relations with the imperial court of the East, as if moving towards a return to the old Roman recognition of Byzantine supremacy over the region, and promoted diplomatic relations with the kings of Italy, who were always insecure on the throne of Pavia in a kingdom where the public order was in the course of dissolution and who were anxious to raise their own prestige again through alliances and marriage ties with the dynasties that succeeded each other on the throne of Constantinople.[35] But in the same decades the reassembly of the Lombard lordships of Capua and Benevento into a single political unit under the Capuan dynasty posed serious problems for the Byzantine hegemony in southern Italy. This

[35] Gay, *L'Italie méridionale*, vol. 1, pp. 218ff; Falkenhausen, *Untersuchungen*, pp. 41ff.

prepared the way for the situation in the second half of the tenth century when southern Italy for some decades, up to 981, appeared divided (leaving aside the political nuclei of Byzantine origin along the Campanian coastline, and the Lombard principate of Salerno which was for the most part autonomous) into two great opposing blocks: the principate of Capua and Benevento, which also incorporated the powerful monasteries of Montecassino and S. Vincenzo al Volturno, and the vast Byzantine area which was administratively divided into the 'catepanate of Italy' (the catepan, resident at Bari, inherited the functions of the *stratego*s of the 'theme of Longobardia' and displayed in his new title the continuing Byzantine ambitions in the peninsula) and the theme of Calabria ruled by the *stratego*s of Reggio. The desire of the Lombard dynasty of Capua and Benevento to escape Byzantine control now found encouragement in the imperial ambitions of Otto I and Otto III of Germany, who from the kingdom of Pavia extended their own activity into Roman territory; from there, linking themselves with the Carolingian tradition, they looked towards southern Italy and there sought allies against Byzantium in the Lombard presence.[36]

The opposition between these two blocks mirrored the hostility between the two Empires, both Roman in name but with very different traditions, namely Frankish and Greek. Was it also a response to a difference in social and political structures? As far as the catepanate of Italy is concerned, one must conclude that the Byzantine reconquest and reorganization of Apulia in the last decades of the ninth century had not substantially modified the Lombard social organization of the region, which dated back to the time when the duchy of Benevento had reached its greatest extent in the seventh and eighth centuries. Certainly there was some infiltration of oriental elements, reinforcing the ancient Greek presence in the region, and indeed at Taranto, after it was reconstructed in the second half of the tenth century following the Arab attacks, we can ascertain a strong numerical prevalence of Greeks over Lombards from private documents.[37] But we cannot generalize from conditions in Taranto. The undoubted diffusion of some elements of Greek culture in the property-owning class of Bari and other cities did not disturb the continuing hegemony of Lombard law in private relationships. Besides, the general militarization, centuries old, of the propertied class in the Byzantine lands of Italy must have favoured the preservation, after the

[36] Gay, *L'Italie méridionale*, vol. 2, pp. 293ff; Falkenhausen, *Untersuchungen*, pp. 104ff (but see also A. Guillou, 'La Lucanie byzantine', *Byzantion*, 35 (1965), pp. 119–49); M. Del Treppo, '*Terra sancti Vincencii*'. *L'abbazia di S. Vincenzo al Volturno nell'alto medioevo* (Naples, 1968), pp. 45ff.

[37] V. von Falkenhausen, 'Taranto in epoca bizantina', *Studi medievali*, ser. III, 9 (1968), pp. 149ff.

Byzantine recovery of Apulia, of the Lombard social structure, which
was founded on the economic and social prevalence of an armed people
dominating the common population of the towns and countryside.

None the less, the catepanate of Italy certainly had some features
which were different from those of the Lombard principate of Capua
and Benevento. Stretching far along the Adriatic and Ionian seas, the
territory governed by the catepan was characterized by a substantial
number of coastal cities and fortified towns, which multiplied as a
defence against the Beneventan lands, especially in the northern region
which is still called the Capitanata. This structure of towns and cities –
all called *kastra* and entrusted to local militias, and all directly subject to
the catepan of Bari, a temporary official sent from Constantinople –
brought about a form of cohabitation, effective but not always
smooth,[38] between Greek officials and prominent local residents. There
were also tendencies towards forms of urban autonomy. These extended
even to the Lombard principates of Campania, but there they coexisted
with the autonomous lay and ecclesiastical seigneurial powers which
were founded on great landed estates and which re-emerged with new
vigour at the end of the tenth century, when the united power of the
principality of Capua and Benevento came to an end.

The spontaneous disintegration of this principality took place in a
period when violent Arab incursions were beginning again in all of
Byzantine Italy, from Calabria to Apulia. It coincided with the failure
in 982 of Otto II's military intervention in southern Italy, an intervention
which was simultaneously a response to Muslim aggression in the
peninsula and a desire to affirm the imperial Geman presence in those
regions of Italy which were still more or less focused on Byzantium.
Lombard disintegration, German failure, Byzantine difficulties (the
Eastern Empire was at the time deeply committed in the Balkans and in
Asia), all placed the Apulian *kastra* in direct contact with the Arabs,
forced them to defend themselves, and accustomed them to operate at
the political level with increasing autonomy from the catepan. Thus
from the beginning of the eleventh century a movement towards the
commune began to appear in the region, which paralleled the
development of urban collectivities functioning around their bishops in
northern Italy. It also paralleled conditions in Gaeta, where, however, as
we have seen above, the *nobiliores* were establishing themselves in
opposition to the ducal dynasty which was resident in the city and lord
of the territory; at Bari and in the other Apulian *kastra* the tendency to
autonomy was still taking shape within the Byzantine political context,

[38] A. Guillou, 'L'Italia bizantina', *Bullettino dell'istituto storico italiano per il
medioevo*, 78 (1967), pp. 11–20.

even though there were some violent rebellions against the behaviour of particular officials sent from the East.[39]

It was in these circumstances that nuclei of Normans – adventurers from the duchy of Normandy, where for a century the Vikings, of Scandinavian origin, had settled as a dominant group within the kingdom of France – began to operate in southern Italy, in the service of or associated with individuals among the rebellious Apulian aristocracy, with Lombard princes, with German emperors, with anti-Byzantine Roman popes.[40] They intervened with great freedom of action, passing rapidly from one side to another, provoking violent reactions in the population of the catepanate or making pacts with them, and gradually settled in both Campania and Apulia, in formal juridical subordination to the Lombard princes or to the German emperors but with increasing autonomous political weight. Nor were popular insurrections, Byzantine–Papal coalitions, German hostility or problems of co-ordination among the Norman leaders themselves sufficient to halt them. In the second half of the eleventh century they imposed their military supremacy on the whole of southern Italy and also expanded by sea, so that from Byzantine Calabria they attacked all Muslim Sicily and threatened the Balkans and Greece.

The penetration into the Balkans was only a brief venture. What is surprising, though, is the capacity demonstrated by the Norman leaders to replace, with stability, the Byzantine administration of Apulia and Calabria, the Lombard dynasties, the duchies of the Campanian coast and the Arab government of Sicily, and to overcome their own fierce disagreements. The kingdom into which they finally united themselves was the heir of the various Norman lordships, recognized by the Church of Rome in the second half of the eleventh century and subordinate to it through an oath of loyalty to the pope; it was officially born by papal concession in 1130 and had its capital at Palermo. This Norman enterprise is the more surprising because it involved bands of knights who flowed from Normany to southern Italy over several decades. It could only arise from a profound cohesion between these adventurers, which was stronger than any disagreement among their leaders because it was nourished by common origins and common traditions of action; this cohesion was reinforced by reasons, which were ever renewing themselves, for solidarity among the invaders in the face of the diversity and multiplicity of their adversaries.

[39] F. Calasso, *La legislazione statutaria dell'Italia meridionale*, vol. 1, *Le basi storiche cittadine dalla fondazione del regno all'epoca degli statuti* (Bologna, 1929), pp. 35ff.

[40] H. Hoffmann, 'Die Anfänge der Normannen in Süditalien', *Quellen und Forschungen aus italienischen Archiven und Bibliotheken*, 49 (1969), pp. 95–144; J. Deér, *Papsttum und Normannen* (Cologne-Vienna, 1972), pp. 37ff, 51ff.

The crises of the great Lombard duchy of Benevento and of the Byzantine co-ordination of the Campanian coasts, the latter reaching its greatest development by sea in the coastal duchies of Campania, had given rise to a certain freedom of political movement in southern Italy, which had, however, at the same time been checked by the new principate of Capua and Benevento. Now, in the tenth and eleventh centuries, this freedom continued its development in two directions. The Lombard disintegration into local seigneuries and urban autonomy within the Byzantine catepanate of Apulia was, however, soon reined in and repressed by the spreading Norman penetration, which was boldly reaching towards an ever more systematic exploitation of the local dynasties and a progressively stronger territorial co-ordination.

The Normans exploited the local conflicts in Campania, Apulia and Calabria and even those beyond the Lombard and Byzantine world – that is, in the no less complex world of Sicily. Here the definitive ordering of the Muslim domination in the island (a domination subordinate in the tenth century, after the collapse of the Aghlabids of Tunisia, to the Fatimid dynasty, which in the second half of the century shifted its centre of gravity eastwards, towards Egypt) had not led to the development of firm links between the various Muslim nuclei of settlement, composed of Arabs and Berbers of African origin, and the seat of the regional government, the emirate of Palermo. The religious conflicts within the Islamic world were reflected in Sicily and led to rebellions of the Muslims of Agrigento and Palermo, the two cities in which the Islamic population, particularly the Berbers, began to preponderate both numerically and politically over the Christians, whether of the Greek or Latin rite, and the persistent Jewish colonies. Finally, after some decades of greater tranquillity in the second half of the tenth century, there emerged in the eleventh century the autonomous Muslim lordships of Mazara, on the south-west coast, Agrigento, Syracuse, and Catania. These lordships were founded on the military enterprise of the leaders settled in the cities (for the cities remained in Sicily, no less than in Apulia or on the Campanian coast, the economic centre and focus of political power[41]), which were destined to assist the fortunes of the Normans in the island.

[41] I. Peri, 'Il porto di Palermo dagli Arabi agli Aragonesi', *Economia e storia. Rivista italiana di storia economica e sociale*, 5 (1958), pp. 422–37; 'Per la storia della vita cittadina e del commercio nel medioevo. Girgenti porto del sale e del grano', in *Studi in onore di A. Fanfani* (Milan, 1962), vol. 1, pp. 555–84; G. Fasoli, 'Le città siciliane dall'istituzione del tema bizantino alla conquista normanna', *Atti del III Congresso internazionale di studi sull'alto Medioevo*

When one considers the continuity and breadth of Norman activity, from the borders with the duchy of Rome to Sicily, and the seriousness of the conflict with German power in which the reforming pope found himself in these same decades, one can understand how the Church of Rome, even after committing itself militarily against the Normans, very unsuccessfully, yielded to this new and irremoveable reality and sought to draw from it the greatest profit with the smallest possible harm to itself. Did not the Norman adventurers recognize their dependence on Rome in the ecclesiastical sense, and could they not then become a very useful instrument to check the development in southern Italy of the monasticism and clergy of the Greek rite, which looked to the Byzantine East?[42] Were they not the liberators of Sicily from the Muslims? And so it was the papacy that took the initiative of incorporating the new Norman dominion into the power-structures of the West, although it did not fit into the ideal models of the two Christian Empires; rather, it fitted into the model of a priestly theocratic hegemony, which was exactly what the popes were then seeking to define in theory and to bring about in several areas of Christendom through a bond of loyalty sworn by the princes to the See of St Peter. Rome legitimized a great venture and encouraged its transformation into a political and territorial settlement, supported by the military loyalty of the Norman bands and by the deference of a Latin episcopate.

Its unitary orientation was thus beginning to contrast the south of Italy with the rivalry of the many nuclei of power which were acquiring increasing strength in central and northern Italy. Some of these nuclei, those which had formed in the cities of Genoa and Pisa, expanded their own sphere of action, after the beginning of the eleventh century, to the great Tyrrhenian islands of Corsica and Sardinia – over Corsica, formally entrusted for its military defence in the Carolingian period to the marquis of Tuscany, and over Sardinia, still officially dependent on Byzantium but in reality from the tenth century divided into autonomous 'judicati', perhaps of Byzantine origin.[43] The two islands, left to themselves, had continued until the eleventh century to suffer Arab incursions, which provoked the intervention of the fleets of Pisa and Genoa and the eventual political absorption of the islands themselves into the contests between the nuclei of power that had emerged in the Italian kingdom.

(Spoleto, 1959), pp. 386–95; F. Gabrieli, *L'Islàm nella storia* (Bari, 1966), pp. 57–67.

[42] Borsari, *Il monachesimo bizantino*, pp. 35–76; Guillou, *Grecs d'Italie*, pp. 83–7.

[43] G. Volpe, *Storia della Corsica italiana* (Milan, 1939), pp. 17ff.; F. Artizzu *et al.*, *La società in Sardegna nei secoli* (Turin, 1967), pp. 111ff.

5

CITIES AND FORTRESSES AS CENTRES
FOR HEGEMONIC DEVELOPMENT

THE FORMATION OF COMMUNAL GOVERNMENT WITHIN THE
SOCIAL STRUCTURES OF THE CITY

Well before the commune arose as an autonomous political organization,
social struggles were already flaring up in Milan in the first half of the
eleventh century. At first they were a continuation of the violent
conflicts which had exploded repeatedly in the city, from the last decades
of the tenth century onwards, over the complex activities of the
archbishop. The choice of person for their appointment and his methods
of co-ordinating civic life hinged on a varying relationship between the
influences of the imperial German court and the ambitions of the most
prominent families of the city, families which in their turn were
connected through landed wealth and clientèles with the Milanese –
and, more broadly, Lombard – territory. The enrichment of the
Milanese *capitanei* through ecclesiastical benefices, mentioned above in
the discussion of the general development of the power of bishops in the
cities, was in one respect an instrument of the ecclesiastical and temporal
predominance of the archbishop, who found in his link with the
dominant class of the city the fulcrum for his own heterogeneous and
vast network of power, which took the form of landed estates, churches
and fortresses through much of Lombardy. But in another respect it
brought about a decisive increase in the hegemony exercised by the class
of *capitanei* in Milan, a hegemony which was apparent as much in the
recruitment of the upper clergy as in the operation of political and
economic control in the city, gained from the archbishop through a slow

spontaneous evolution. This increase was such that, when evoking the decline of comital power which took place in Milan in the course of the tenth century, the chronicler Landulf Senior (a Milanese cleric of the second half of the eleventh century) omitted to mention the archbishop himself, even though he is elsewhere celebrated or criticized by that same chronicler for his energetic government or harshness of command, and laid out the facts as if little by little the power of the *duces* – that is of the counts or marquises in charge of the public circumscription that included Milan – had passed directly from their 'negligent' hands to those of the *capitanei*, who in their turn had used the collaboration of the *valvassores* to sustain the power they had acquired.[1]

This alternation between the archbishop and the *capitanei*, in Landulf Senior's description of the powerful in Milan, illustrates the complex nature of the power that was functioning in practice a hundred years before the commune arose in the city. We may note that in the first half of the eleventh century there is still occasional evidence for the presence in Milan of a 'marquis', 'count of the city' and 'count of the county', who presided over the judicial courts;[2] this means that not all record had yet been lost of a territorial jurisdiction which belonged to the office-holder of the Milanese public circumscription. But for some time the circumscription had been fading away because the power of the comital family, the Obertenghi, was oriented towards control of those zones of Lombardy, Liguria and Tuscany where its own profitable estates, with their associated fortifications and clientèles, were densest, both within and outside the public districts entrusted to the family. Meanwhile in Milan the power of the metropolitan church and of the leading residents of the city had grown as a whole, in a muddle of patrimonial and ecclesiastical interests and vassal relationships, which concentrated in the archbishop and *capitanei* the responsibility for military defence and urban policing, the responsibility for the direct administration of justice, and the control and exploitation of markets and tolls. The imperial court itself, in order to ensure that it had some control over the city and its territory, turned not to the Obertenghi but to the archbishop, in whose election it intervened, or to the military aristocracy of the city.

Within this aristocracy violent conflicts might break out when, as happened in the tenth century, the harshness of an archbishop, supported by the predominance of his kin group, provoked the formation in the

[1] *Landulphi Senioris historia Mediolanensis* I. II, c.26 (in Muratori, *Rerum Italicarum Scriptores*, new ed., vol. 4.2 (Bologna, 1942), pp. 63ff).
[2] C. Manaresi, *I placiti del 'regnum Italiae'*, vol. 2.2 (Rome, 1958), p. 624 (1021); vol. 3.1 (Rome, 1960), pp. 126 (1045), 129 (1045).

city of seditious sworn associations,[3] or when, as happened in the first half of the eleventh century, the greater and lesser *milites* (that is, the *capitanei* and the *valvassores*) clashed among themselves and drew the royal power and the archbishop into their conflict. These disagreements arose from the desire of the valvassors of Milan and other zones of the kingdom to gain formal recognition of the hereditary nature of the benefices conceded them by their *seniores*, as perpetual remuneration for a service that was now equally hereditary; recognition was finally obtained in the edict promulgated by Emperor Conrad II for the whole Italian kingdom in 1037. But soon other struggles arose with a broader social significance.

Landulf Senior tells of 'most serious wars in the city, the people fighting against the leading citizens to regain their lost liberty', the liberty which, according to the imagination of the chronicler, they had enjoyed at the time when Milan was still governed by the *duces*. It was a true conflict of opposing social classes which another Milanese chronicler Arnulf, a member of a family of *capitanei* and a contemporary of the events, recalled as a fight through the crossroads and squares of the city, accompanied by fires started by the mob to force the 'nobility' to surrender. For in the struggle almost all the military aristocracy, greater and lesser, had joined forces against the 'people' (*popolo*); when the *milites*, unable to suppress the popular violence, abandoned the city with their wives and children, Archbishop Aribert himself was not slow to follow them in seeking help in the Lombard region. But who made up this 'popolo'? Landulf Senior, with highly significant rhetoric, calls them 'strong in poverty, very strong in their aspiration for liberty, desiring wealth but more anxious to be free', guided in the struggle by Lanzo, *nobilis et capitaneus altus*. This 'people' had grown accustomed to fighting in the struggles of Aribert against Conrad II and perhaps also in those of the *capitanei* and archbishop against the valvassors, and so were a people who in those earlier struggles had been organized by the military aristocracy. But among the people, notwithstanding Landulf Senior's simplification, there was a disparity of economic conditions, since private documents in the tenth and eleventh centuries give copious evidence of the growing activity and acquisition of urban and rural lands by 'negotiatores' (merchants).[4] The mob that rose against the oppression of the *milites* was a population largely different from that which Landulf Senior assumed lived in freedom in the mythical age of 'ducal' government; it was more numerous, through the influx of

[3] *Arnulphi gesta archiepiscoporum Mediolanensium*, I.1, c.10 (in *MGH Scriptores*, 8, p. 9).

[4] Violante, *La società milanese nell'età precomunale*, pp. 137ff.

inhabitants of the contado, of every social condition, and it was more vigorous, through the possibilities for arming and action acquired by one section of society thanks to the availability of movable and landed property.

The sworn reconciliation of 1044 between the classes in conflict was the premise for the future commune.[5] With the return of the *milites* and their families to the city, there did not immediately arise any new institution embodying a government formally different from that of the archbishop, but the sworn agreement generally tended to produce an urban collectivity which was potentially able to provide itself with an autonomous political order, in the shadow of and in opposition to the power of the prelate. The stormy events of following decades, which had at their centre the Patarine agitation against simoniac clergy and clerical concubinage, were a part of the most extreme current of the great ecclesiastical reform movement; but at the same time, with their violence and the agreements which were sworn at intervals, they fitted into the development which was to result in the creation of the commune.

Late eleventh-century evidence for this in Milan, as in many other cities of the kingdom, is supplied by the mention of the consulate, the collegiate magistracy; this varied in number from one city to another and sometimes from one year to another, from a few individuals to twenty or more consuls, and appeared in the cities before the term *commune* came to be used in documents to describe the new political organization.[6] The expression initially used to indicate the consular magistracy, *consules civitatis*, demonstrates that the commune was not born as a private association of leading citizens, placing 'in common' the rights of each member insofar as they were individually invested with so-called 'feudal powers', as the historiographical tradition of this century has usually asserted. On the contrary, it was born with an explicit political and territorial significance, through the desire of the leading citizens to represent the whole urban collectivity. The consulate of the city presupposed an initial consensus, at least a formal one, around the *maiores*. And depending on how far it appeared to encompass

---

[5] G. Dilcher, *Die Entstehung der lombardischen Stadtkommune* (Aalen, 1967), pp. 137ff; *cf.* H. Keller, 'Die soziale und politische Verfassung Mailands in den Anfängen des kommunalen Lebens', *Historische Zeitschrift*, 211 (1970), pp. 50ff, 'Pataria und Stadtverfassung, Stadtgemeinde und Reform', in *Investiturstreit und Reichsverfassung*, Vorträge und Forschungen XVII (Sigmarigen, 1973), pp. 321ff.

[6] O. Banti, '"Civitas" e "commune" nelle fonti italiane dei secoli XI e XII', *Critica storica*, 9 (1972), pp. 568–84.

interests common to all the citizens in the various cities it gradually became a consulate of the *commune civitatis*, or, as it was sometimes called, of the *res publica civitatis*. The concepts of *civitas* and of *res publica* were the link between the communal idea and the earlier ordering of the city, which was founded on the local customs and political convergence of 'people' and 'nobles' around a lord invested with a public title or ecclesiastical dignity, the bishop, or more rarely the marquis or count or their representative, the viscount.

The lord of the city was not deprived of authority by the consuls by a sudden revolutionary act. At Milan the political substitution was perhaps particularly rapid, yet what gave rise to this sequence of alternate convergence and conflict between the archbishop and the consuls was not an abstract problem of rival powers, but rather the solution to concrete military and religious questions. We know from Landulf Junior, a Milanese cleric contemporary with the events he narrates, that in a great Lombard assembly which met in Milan in 1117 two platforms were set up: on one the archbishop, his suffragan bishop and certain abbots and rectors of churches took their place, and on the other the consuls with the experts in law and customs.[7] These two platforms, around which there crowded 'innumera multitudo clericorum et laicorum', symbolize the ecclesiastical and political supremacy of the city in Lombardy and the Milanese consulate's intention to co-operate with the multiform power of the archbishop. It was a co-operation all the more apparent in that the archbishops, like the members of the consulate, were mostly recruited in those decades from the military class which was still dominant in the city, the very class which coincided with the vassals of the metropolitan church.[8] There was no lack of mistrust and conflict, but they arose when the archbishop withdrew from active participation in the armed struggle of Milan against Como over control of the Alpine passes, or when he seemed less zealous in defending the privileges of the Ambrosian See against the invasive activity of the Church of Rome. The growing political and jurisdictional responsibility of the Milanese consulate was directly related to the fact that it was better suited to represent the interests and ambitions of the city than was a prelate who was ever more completely

---

[7] *Landulphi Iunioris historia Mediolanensis*, c.44 (in Muratori, *Rerum Italicarum Scriptores*, new ed., vol. 5.3 (Bologna, 1934), p. 27). See G. L. Barni, 'Milano verso l'egemonia', in *Storia di Milano*, vol. 3, pp. 318ff.

[8] For the archbishops, see P. Zerbi, 'La chiesa ambrosiana di fronte alla Chiesa romana dal 1120 al 1135', *Studi medievali* ser. III, 4 (1963), pp. 136–84. For the consuls, see the judgement of 1130, published in C. Manaresi, *Gli Atti del comune di Milano fino all'anno MCCXVI* (Milan, 1919), p. 7.

incorporated into the priestly hierarchy that culminated in the new monarchical papacy. There was even some convergence with the more radical Patarine movement, which was now developing an anti-hierarchical tendency in the face of the weakening of the Roman church's reforming intransigence, and particularly of the emergence of a wealthy mercantile class among the people. Among the twenty-three Milanese consuls named in an arbitration of 1130, five appear with the general qualification of *cives*, as distinct from the others who are listed as *capitanei* or *valvassores*.

Up to now we have used the Milanese example as an illustration because narrative sources contemporary with the events give the most reliable picture of the line of development which is crucial to our understanding of the complexity of the social relationships from which the urban commune emerged as an instrument for the coexistence of different classes and opposing groups. At Milan the consulate, from its earliest activities onwards, is clearly the new organ which represented simultaneously the old urban military aristocracy's desire to survive and consolidate itself and the interests of the more economically-enterprising stratum, against the background of the Ambrosian tradition which was able to unite the whole population in certain military, economic and religious policies. But while the consulate took on everywhere the significance of a tie between forces that had been linked too weakly by the preceding lordship, whether lay or ecclesiastical, only at Milan was it unequivocally the surmounting of a deep class conflict, which had already exploded at the time of Archbishop Aribert half a century before the commune was established; for at Milan, a robust economic centre in full expansion and the seat of a powerful metropolitan bishop who was surrounded by a large curia of clerics and vassals, the network of urban lordships which preceded the commune could form itself into a 'nobility' within the society, moving closer to the archbishop in opposition to an 'oppressed' people.

In other cities the political and social dynamic in the initial phase of the commune's formation is less clearly characterized by the opposition and reconciliation of nobles and people. The case of Genoa and Pisa is notably different from that of Milan: here the importance taken on by mercantile activity, which demanded the equipping of fleets, recruitment of crews and training for defence and attack by sea, had caused a convergence, well before the communal period, of the most diverse classes of the urban population, in order to carry out complex operations which were both economic and military. The classes involved ranged from the aristocracy furnished with landed revenues and armed clientèles, more or less closely tied to the bishop and viscount of the city (with the bishopric becoming increasingly interlinked, though not without serious conflicts, with the family in which the office of viscount became hereditary), to the class of the humblest property-owners and the poorest elements of the population.[9] In particular, at Genoa the consular commune was born at the end of the eleventh century as a *compagna communis*, from the 'companies' of the city districts – that is, of associations which presumably already in themselves united elements of different social origins, perhaps particularly for reasons of urban military defence, under the hegemony of the leading citizens.

At Milan, at Genoa, at Pisa, despite the diversity of the process of formation of the commune, there is clearly present in the twelfth century a consular aristocracy, the political class from which the consuls were usually recruited, made up of military and mercantile families which were variously linked or mixed among themselves, sometimes quarrelling in family feuds or power struggles but all marked out by their high level of social prestige with respect to the rest of the population. It is possible that elsewhere the social composition of the citizens was less complex, and the hegemonic group had a somewhat lesser importance. Sometimes indeed the commune appears to arise from an urban collectivity which was in complete agreement about defending itself against the arbitrary will of the local lord and his embryonic apparatus of government.

This seems to be the case in Mantua, where the citizens, still described as *arimanni* (the ancient name of the whole class of landowners in the late Lombard and Carolingian periods), obtained imperial privileges in the eleventh and twelfth centuries, before and after the creation of the consulate. These were clearly obtained as part of a dispute with the lordship of the Canossa, who were titular lords of the Mantuan county up to 1115 when the dynasty became extinct with the death of Countess Matilda.[10] It is not clear what the connections were between the city and

---

[9] G. Volpe, *Studi sulle istituzioni comunali a Pisa* (1902, 2nd ed. Florence, 1970), pp. 3ff; V. Vitale, *Breviario della storia di Genova* (Genoa, 1955), vol. 1, pp. 13ff; vol. 2, pp. 16ff; G. Pistarino, 'Monasteri cittadini genovesi', in *Monasteri in Alta Italia dopo le invasioni saracene e magiare* (Turin, 1966), pp. 242ff; G. Rossetti, 'Società e istituzioni nei secoli IX e X: Pisa, Volterra, Populonia', in *Atti del V Congresso internazionale di studi sull'alto Medioevo* (Spoleto, 1973), pp. 320ff.

[10] P. Torelli, *Un comune cittadino in territorio ad economia agricola* vol. 1 (Mantua, 1930) pp. 3ff, 49ff. This should be supplemented and corrected by V. Colorni, *Il territorio mantovano nel sacro romano impero* (Milan, 1959), vol. 1, pp. 45ff, and G. Tabacco, *I liberi del re*, pp. 167ff (see also Haverkamp, *Herrschaftsformen*, pp. 152ff).

the vassals of the Canossa, who were well rooted in the territory of Mantua and easily survived the disappearance of the comital dynasty. The seigneurial stock which descended from these vassals shared in the political management of the city in the course of the twelfth century, but the commune appears to have arisen not from some special initiative of theirs, but rather from that of all the *arimanni* with an urban background, who had for some time been anxious for the recognition by the emperors (and, in 1090, by the countess, who was besieged by imperial forces in the city and forced by them to annul the acts of her predecessors) of their common use of vast uncultivated areas along the banks of the Mincio and the possession of private property and numerous exemptions from the tolls imposed on the merchants. Indeed in the first document in which the Mantuan consuls appear, one of 1126 concerning a dispute between the commune and a monastery, the city is represented by five consuls and another twenty-six *arimanni*, all of them, as appears from several documents, fully linked with the interests of the bishop, who possessed an enormous patrimony and some revenues of fiscal origin even in the city but who had no political power nor even a notable clientèle of vassals.

So during the initial emergence of the commune at Mantua there apparently developed a collectivity of property-owners, who also extended into the lands of the church as tenants or benefice-holders and often participated at the same time in modest commercial activity as far away as Lake Garda and the great delta of the Po. This collectivity organized itself through the consulate to protect its multiple interests; certainly it gathered around a group that was dominant through its landed wealth, but perhaps the latter did not exclusively control the government and military defence of the city. Between the pattern postulated for the commune of Mantua and that of Milan, Genoa or Pisa all variations and nuances were possible in the political and social arrangement of the Lombard and Tuscan cities in the first decades of the twelfth century. These variations were interwoven with others, since the consulate co-existed with, or was modified by, more or less important remnants of jurisdiction and influence arising from the urban political structure that preceded the commune, and which varied according to whether those remnants were related to the past dominance of a bishop, as was usual, or of a comital dynasty or vicomital family, or to an old convergence of the episcopal and lay powers in the city (the most notable case being Verona).[11]

[11] C. G. Mor, 'Dalla caduta dell'impero al commune', in *Verona e il suo territorio* (Verona, 1964), vol. 2, pp. 149ff.

In every case the commune of the consuls appears to have had a remarkable institutional flexibility, without claims to exclusivity. It did not presume to monopolize the public functions in the city, nor did it challenge rights of exaction and control (over markets, weights and measures, and the sites of tolls) which belonged to ecclesiastical bodies or which were passed in inheritance within the comital or vicomital families. Even so the early commune already displayed a commitment to define itself juridically. The consulate, despite the instability of some of its internal structures, soon set itself up as the permanent magistracy of each individual city; it was sustained politically by the consensus of the popular assemblies which were summoned by the consuls and reinforced technically by the opinions of jurists, in the exercise of a jurisdiction which was not concerned solely with arbitration since it rested on the political capacity of the consulate to protect and guide the citizenry.[12]

The participation of legal experts was indeed essential to the commune, and represents the clearest cultural connection between the operation of the powers that preceded the commune and the activity of the consulate. A whole tradition of notaries and judges, called respectively to draft any document which had legal force and to draw up any judgement pronounced in the public and seigneurial courts, binds the Early Middle Ages to the communal period. This tradition was often embodied in particular families of the city, and from the end of the Carolingian period it gave rise to a stratum which was mostly sustained by landed wealth and should therefore be placed within the wider class of landowners,[13] but which was distinguished by its own prestige and by the official recognition accorded it by the kingdom and by seigneurial powers. The cultural progress of this class in the final pre-communal period played no small part in the transformation of the customs of civic freedom (that is, of the limitations on the public and seigneurial powers of the city that had spontaneously arisen through the pressure of the *cives*) into an autonomous order under the government of the consuls. The definition of a permanent civic magistracy in fact presupposes a new awareness of the need to translate the collectivity's tendency towards united action into the action of governmental institutions; such awareness could arise only from a meeting between the more stable political desires of groups or classes and the jurists' readiness to outline a suitable institutional model.

[12] Dilcher, *Die Enstehung der lombardischen Stadtkommune*, pp. 175ff.
[13] Schwarzmaier, *Lucca*, pp. 284ff.

THE DEVELOPMENT OF THE SEIGNEURIAL BAN AND OF THE RURAL COMMUNITIES

The experience of the urban commune, whose variety of development in its first phase has been outlined here, was not peculiar to the geographical area that corresponded to the Italian kingdom of Frankish–Lombard tradition. It is found also in the regions which from the eighth century onwards belonged to the Church of Rome, from the exarchate to the Roman duchy, regions where more than one aspect of Frankish-dominated Europe had spread with varying intensity through the greater or lesser presence of the Carolingians in each area; the standard developments of the military and ecclesiastical aristocracy took place here too (hence, for example, the 'capitanei et valvassores' of Ravenna and Cesena present at a Ravenna court of 1079[14]), and so did the concomitant processes of disintegration and reconstitution of local powers. Moreover, one may say that a communal tendency can be observed in the eleventh and twelfth centuries even in the regions of the purest Byzantine tradition, whether in southern Italy, where urban collectivities, called *universitates*, allied among themselves, carried out military actions and stipulated commercial treaties,[15] or in Venice, where the ducal government, formed by the doge and his 'judges', was complicated in 1142 by the institution of a *consilium sapientium* deriving from a popular assembly.[16] But the southern *universitates* were soon incorporated into a kingdom, that of the Normans with its capital at Palermo, which was far more efficient as a unitary dominion than was the Italian kingdom in German hands; in developing models of central and provincial political control, its domination was assisted by the traditions of regional organization which dated back to the time of the Byzantine themes. And the *commune Veneciarum*, an expression first recorded in 1152, however new some of its institutions, did no more than develop the formal dyarchy of *dux* and *populus* which was already the traditional framework for the public order of the lagoons. In Venice the interplay of political clientèles, stimulated by growing commercial interests, became broader, extending from the relations between ducal court and popular assembly into the institutionally intermediate zone of a new *consilium*. Here, however, unlike the cities of the Italian kingdom,

[14] Buzzi, 'Ricerche', p. 193; A. Vasina, 'Ravenna e Forlì nel secolo XII', *Atti e memorie della Deputazione di storia patria per le province di Romagna*, new series, 10 (1958–9), p. 97.

[15] F. Calasso, 'La città nell'Italia meridionale durante l'età normanna', (1959), reprinted in *Annali di storia del diritto*, 9 (1965), pp. 263–79.

[16] *Deliberazioni del Maggior Consiglio di Venezia*, ed. R. Cessi (Bologna, 1950), vol. 1, pp. 235ff.

there did not develop a complex relationship between the communal constitution and the juxtaposed remnants of those rights of a public or seigneurial origin which had been transformed into the estates of ecclesiastical bodies or powerful families. Nor were the communal institutions constantly involved in the city's relations with a turbulent territory.

By contrast, in the Frankish–Lombard area it is impossible to isolate the progress of civic institutions from the traditions of anarchy and rivalry for power that distinguished the whole territory. There are several reasons for this. The sectors that determined the life of the early commune, whether Milanese *capitanei*, Pisan ship-outfitters or Mantuan *arimanni*, already had an extensive presence in the territory as landowners, as collective holders of rights to uncultivated land, as patrons of churches and guardians or owners of fortresses, as leaders or members of vassal clientèles, and as merchants. An obvious consequence was that, in the first period of their emergence, certain communes were already undertaking military operations even at great distances from the city. For example, the Milanese destroyed Lodi in 1111 after a war of four years, although at one point they were simultaneously engaged against the Cremonese, whom they defeated in 1110 in open battle at Castelleone, fifty kilometres from Milan.[17] Furthermore, in these conflicts fostered by the multiple interests of the groups and classes which converged in the institutions of the commune, a part was often played by rivalries based on the traditions of other powers rooted in the city and competing in the territory. Thus in 1118, when Como and Milan engaged in a long war which was certainly fed by the strong economic competition between the two cities, the initial motive for the conflict was given by the activities in the contado of Como of Landulf da Carcano, a cleric of a noble Milanese family, created bishop of Como by Emperor Henry IV but driven from the city by the election of Bishop Guido by the papal party. The Comaschi occupied the castle in which Landulf was staying and killed his nephew, a Milanese 'egregius capitaneus'; the Milanese, further aroused by the archbishop in an assembly of *milites* and *cives* (the *contio* in which the people joined with the military aristocracy), rushed on Como and freed Landulf. When they were later expelled from the city the war – a war of consuls and popes, according to a chronicler[18] – was renewed, until Como was destroyed in 1127.

---

[17] *Landulphi Iunioris historia Mediolanensis*, c.24–8 (pp. 16ff).
[18] *Ibid.*, c.48 bis (p. 30). See Schwartz, *Die Besetzung der Bistümer Reichsitaliens*,
      p. 50; Barni, 'Milano verso l'egemonia', pp. 324ff.; R. Rossini, 'Note alla
      "Historia Mediolanensis" di Landolfo Iuniore', in *Contributi dell'Istituto di
      storia medievale* (Università Cattolica, Milan, 1968), vol. 1, pp. 418, 478ff.

It would be difficult, in the conflict just considered, to separate the antagonism between urban collectivities from the factors that set the two bishops against each other. The Milanese turned to war, says the chronicler, to avenge 'the many evils that the Comaschi had done to the goods and the men of the archbishopric', but at the same time they avenged the insult offered a family of *capitanei* and punished the insolence of a rival city. Nor did the conflict between the bishops have a purely ecclesiastical significance: the archbishop retained in his own hands, largely through imperial donations of the tenth century, the numerous castles that extended north of Milan into the diocese of Como as far as the lakes region.[19] Thus the action of the commune, the ambitions of the great families, and the diverse powers that belonged to the bishop and to the more influential colleges of canons and monks which had their seat in the city, radiated out widely from the city and were interwoven amongst themselves; everywhere they encountered other political nuclei formed by local conditions in the contado or in the territories of other cities, and those forces in their turn, even when they were subordinate, reacted on the life of the dominant city and on the way it operated in the territory.

A large part of the communal period, from the end of the eleventh century until well into the thirteenth century, consequently appears to be mainly a continuation of the earlier political anarchy of the Italian kingdom, even though in very different forms, signifying profound social changes. The cities exerted a powerful appeal on many elements of the rural world and so became centres of increasing strength capable of acting over a wide area, but until their decline into regimes of a monarchic character or rigid oligarchies, they did not create a strong and uniform territorial order, and conversely, any conflict or development in their own territory had repercussions for their still transient political structures. In the same way that in the tenth and eleventh centuries the dynasties holding titles to marches or counties had coexisted with the splintering of the territory into ecclesiastical and lay lordships which emerged from local situations, the political expansion of the cities now coexisted with the spontaneous reordering of the rural world around newly-forming nuclei of power.

But in what did this incessant reordering consist? We must return to the discussion of the multiplication of seigneurial nuclei of power, and their concomitant tendency towards disintegration. From the tenth to the twelfth centuries the peasant population, scattered in villages which sometimes included both small allod-owners and tenant cultivators,

---

[19] P. Zerbi, 'Ad solita castela archiepiscopatus exivit?' in *Miscellanea Gilles Gérard Meersseman* (Padua, 1970), pp. 107–29.

became in many places more and more clearly subject to the political protection of the one landed lord, among the ecclesiastical bodies or military families, who organized the defence and peace of the village, the *dominatus loci*, on the basis of his local economic dominance or of his military strength. The erection of a fortress was the normal route to construct a lordship like this over a village or several neighbouring villages; it was a territorial lordship of the 'ban', exercising powers of command and coercion, policing, jurisdiction, exaction of tolls and *albergaria* (enforced hospitality for the lord's men). In addition it had power to impose labour contributions for the maintenance of the fortifications, in connection with the role of the castle as 'protection' for all the peasants living in the village or in the area, whether or not they cultivated land belonging to the lord of the local 'ban'. In the main the fortress arose through the fortification of a *curtis*, the seat of the agents appointed by a landed lord to administer one of his complexes of property, or through fortification of the village in which the *curtis* was located.[20] And the castle helped the estate centre to establish itself at the same time as a centre of local political activity, so much so that documents of the twelfth century show that an interesting semantic change had occurred: the term *curtis*, rather than indicating a seigneurial complex of property distributed in a particular agricultural area, now indicated the area itself, as a compact rural territory dominated by the ban or *districtus* of the lord who had built or acquired the castle. And so the *curtis*, when understood in this new meaning, could incorporate allods which did not belong, in the sense of economic possession, to the lord of the said *curtis* or *curia*.[21]

However this process, which appears everywhere in the Italian kingdom, was none the less neither linear nor uniform. Often the most eminent landowners who lived in a village evaded the control of the lord who was developing, through customary usage, his *districtus* over the area, and they often obtained from the *dominus loci* explicit recognition of their own privileged condition;[22] not uncommonly the *dominus loci* was also opposed by the powerful families and ecclesiastical bodies which had property and peasants on the same site. The opposition of these great landed lords could be translated into the development of

[20] Vaccari, *La territorialità*, pp. 45ff.
[21] E. Balda, 'Una corte rurale nel territorio di Asti nel medioevo', *Bollettino storico-bibliografico subalpino*, 70 (1972), pp. 24–34, 105–13. See Conti, *La formazione della struttura agraria*, vol 1. pp. 45ff.
[22] R. Romeo, 'La signoria dell'abate di Sant'Ambrogio di Milano sul commune rurale di Origgio nel secolo XIII', *Rivista storica italiana*, 69 (1957), pp. 356ff; Balda, 'Una corte rurale', pp. 133ff.

banal powers to rival those of the *dominus loci*. This could take the form of rights of protection, justice and exaction, expressed by the terms *honor et districtus*, that the landed lord on the basis of his own customary usage (sometimes linked with ancient royal concessions of immunity) might claim to exercise over his own peasants, supplementing those rights with the rents and labour services due to him for the land; thus he withdrew these peasants from the local lordship and kept them entirely within his own control.[23] Or the process could take place through agreement between lords, in which provision was made for a division of the rights and income connected with the 'ban'. An example of this is the transaction drawn up in 1173 between the abbess of the monastery of Caramagna Piemonte and the lord of Luserna (her brother) for the villages of Caramagna and Sommariva Bosco.[24] It was agreed that the *fodrum* (a very widespread name in Italy for the new local exactions which applied to all the residents of a given area) should belong to the lord of Luserna in both localities, without excluding the men of the abbess, and that the seigneurial right to *successiones* (the right to inherit the goods of whoever died without heirs) should in Caramagna belong half to the lord of Luserna and half to the abbess, independently of the economic or personal subordination of the *homines* of either party, while in Sommariva the lord and the abbess would have the complete rights of inheritance each from their own men. The *placita comitalia*, the most serious judicial cases (here the document specifies murder, perjury, adultery, arson, theft, attack by treachery and duelling), would everywhere belong to the lord of Luserna, while the lesser cases would be judged by the abbess for all the men of Caramagna, and for those men of Sommariva who were dependants of the monastery; the *banna que banniuntur nomine castellanie* (the ordinances promulgated by the guardian of the castle, with the fines established for infractions) would belong to the lord of Luserna, while the other *banna que publice banniuntur* (other territorial ordinances with their respective fines) would belong half to the lord of Luserna and half to the abbess.

The document presented here illustrates very well the variety of the forms in which the seigneurial power of ban by virtue of customary usage was implemented, and the tendency to break it up into separate elements capable of being ceded, exchanged or sold. It is clear that the *honor et districtus* in the two sites considered did not belong exclusively either to the monastery of Caramagna or to the dynasty of the Luserna. The lordship of the Luserna took on a precise territorial orientation in

[23] Ripanti, 'Dominio fondiario', pp. 133ff.
[24] C. Patrucco, 'Le più antiche carte dell'abbazia di Caramagna', in *Miscellanea saluzzese* (Pinerolo, 1902), pp. 30–2; see also pp. 40–2, 48–50.

the area, but was obstructed by the customs developed by the monastery. The monastery too tended to exercise a local ban, at least at Caramagna, even though it had become limited to the exercise of a power under the clear jurisdictional and political dominance of the military dynasty; at Sommariva the monastery's ban tended to be restricted to the limits of its own landed patrimony. The result of this complex rivalry was not a rational division between the powers of a landowning lord and the powers of a lord of a territory, but an empirical distribution of rights of coercion and exploitation, listed individually, in accordance with the differing prestige of the monastery and its presumably different landowning position in Caramagna, where the monastery had its seat, compared with the neighbouring village of Sommariva. The settlement was the outcome of a long-standing unstable situation but not even with the transaction of 1173 did it attain a definitive character, since the controversy between the Luserna and the nuns was reopened repeatedly in the first half of the thirteenth century. Furthermore, according to a document of 1219 relating to the *successiones* of the men of the two villages, the result was complicated by the rights owned in the area by two military clientèles, those vassals of the monastery and of the Luserna who had benefices there.

The disintegration of the official public power into its elements – which explains the persistence into the communal period, in the very cities in which the consulate was organized, of rights of control and exaction of tolls on roads and markets in favour of churches and comital and vicomital families – thus has its counterpart in the ever-present danger of a similar disintegration of 'autogenous' seigneurial powers, which had developed spontaneously through customary usage to fill the gap left by the dissolution of the official public order. None the less it remains true that in the twelfth and thirteenth centuries ecclesiastical bodies and seigneurial dynasties appear, in general, to have been increasingly committed to defining their own rights in the rural world and to reinforcing the landed base of their own power through economic transactions, particularly where preceding concentrations of property had already prompted the formation of a seigneurial ban with a territorial orientation. The transaction of 1173 just analysed, although it witnesses to a situation where it would have been difficult to establish any coherent local power, at the same time demonstrates the effort expended by the rival lords to define minutely that situation and to crystallize it.

As far as economic transactions are concerned, let us consider the case of the canonical chapter of Asti, which in the course of the twelfth century developed over the *curtis* of Quarto, an area very close to the city and covering perhaps six square kilometres including woods and uncultivated land, a *dominatus loci* centring on a castle, which was recognized in its territory and its jurisdiction by the bishop and by the commune of Asti, by the pope and by the emperor. While up to about 1170 the acquisitions of the chapter were distributed fairly evenly among the various sites in the Astigiano where canonical lands were located, from 1171 for about a century the purchases made by the chapter in Quarto became four times greater than those known for all other areas of the contado put together.[25] In part it was buying allods, in order to prevent (where it was still possible) their acquisition by rich citizens of Asti, who would easily escape the territorial *dominatus* of the chapter. On other occasions the chapter bought back its own lands from peasants in Quarto, from those cultivators who held rented property from the chapter. The residence of peasant families over many generations on certain lands, which had been assigned to them from time immemorial, had eventually created a tenants' right to remain on those same lands for an undefined period and to sell them to others, including the lord himself, when the lord did not refuse his consent; they could sell, that is, the rights to exploit the lands, transferring to the purchasers the same obligations of rent in money or kind and labour services which had previously fallen on the vendor. So the chapter, in addition to acquiring allods, undertook to recover their own lands everywhere in Quarto where they feared the sale of exploitation rights to individuals who because of their social prestige or their economic strength could not easily be controlled.

These operations reveal in the landlord and the territorial lord not only the desire to resist the penetration into his landed property and the territory he dominated of economic and social forces foreign to the area, such as those which arose from the growth of a city, but also the capacity to react, to build a more solid and disciplined rural lordship, through the replacement of tenants, the modification of agrarian customs and the formal exclusion from the territory of any outsider not ready to take on the burden of strict submission to him. In the twelfth and thirteenth centuries this submission quite often took the form of a declaration of loyalty, a rural *fidelitas* which tended to be modelled on that owed to lords by their vassals in families of 'noble' military tradition.[26] And in

---

[25] Balda, 'Una corte rurale', pp. 34ff.

[26] P. Cammarosano, 'Il territorio della Berardenga nei secoli XI–XIII', *Studi medievali* ser. III, 10.2 (1969), pp. 293–300; Ripanti, 'Dominio fondiario', p. 144.

the case of the *curtis* of Quarto there is evidence that such a *fidelitas* was already sworn in the last decades of the twelfth century by all the men of the territory subject to the chapter, including allod-owners, with the exception of a few privileged individuals, and so was an expression of subjection to the *dominus loci*.[27]

But the commitment necessary for churches and lay families to arrange the submission of the rural population reveals a deeply significant factor which for some time had been decisively complicating the paths of power in the rural world. The interplay of customary usage, violence and commercial transactions was not confined to the composite class of warriors, clerics and monks which traditionally held power, and which furnished the example, given above, of the abbess of the monastery of Caramagna and her noble brother of the dynasty of the Luserna. The development of the *usus et abusus*, interwoven or mingled with rights of public origin, from which there emerged the powers of the ban connected with the exercise of patronal authority or embodied in a castle and local protection, had been imposed on a peasant population that was not purely passive. It too, in the disorder of these centuries, had developed its own usages. Although small allod-owners, coming little by little under the protection of the *dominus loci*, gradually suffered from more and more burdens and limitations, on the other hand they usually found themselves liberated from the no less burdensome relationship, which had now fallen into disuse, with the remnants of the official public power; one thinks of the *oppressiones* noted by the capitularies of the Carolingian period. But most important was the complex evolution of the *tenementarii*, who cultivated land that was territorially dependent on the *curtes*. They saw their banal burdens multiplying to the profit of the landlord or territorial lord as seigneurial protection gradually became organized, but in their turn they normally obtained, during the twelfth century, a fixed customary rent for the exploitation of the land, even when the rent became inadequate through the increase in value of lands and produce,[28] and at the same time they acquired (as we have seen with the cultivators of Quarto) a certain right to dispose of the goods in their possession. As the jurists of the thirteenth

[27] Balda, 'Una corte rurale', pp. 68ff, 108ff.
[28] Romeo, 'La signoria dell'abate di Sant'Ambrogio', pp. 473ff; G. Chittolini, 'I beni terrieri del capitolo della cattedrale di Cremona fra il XIII e il XIV secolo', *Nuova rivista storica*, 49 (1965), pp. 241ff; A. Kotel'nikova, 'L'evoluzione dei canoni fondiari dall' XI al XIV secolo in territorio lucchese', *Studi medievali*, ser. III, 9 (1968), pp. 601ff; A. Castagnetti, 'I possessi del monastero di S. Zeno di Verona a Bardolino', *ibid.*, 13 (1972), pp. 139ff.

century would say,[29] they held the title to a 'useful dominion' over the goods they held, as distinct from the 'high dominion' to which the property rights of the lord tended to be reduced whenever he did not redeem the land through purchase.

Customary usages had an effect on the status of the servile class itself, at first altering it economically and so subsequently weakening its juridical significance. Signs of this evolution can be perceived from the beginning of the Carolingian period. There is a well-known court case of 905 in which, under pressure from the judges, the numerous serfs of the *curtis* of Limonta, which was donated by the Carolingians to the monastery of S. Ambrogio of Milan in the ninth century, finally recognized their own servile condition but at the same time spelled out the precise obligations of service and rent which bound them to the *curtis*, with an implicit appeal to custom. From a later court action it appears that these serfs disputed their servile condition and claimed the status of *aldii*, an old traditional denomination for the semi-free among the Lombard people.[30] The spontaneous movement towards free status assumed such dimensions that Emperor Otto III, probably in a synod of 998 at Pavia, promulgated general measures to check it, in a century which is otherwise almost entirely lacking in legislation. The great ecclesiastics and laymen of the Empire and landowners in general, major and minor, complain that they cannot preserve the *obsequium* due to them from their serfs; the latter, when the vigilance of their masters is relaxed for a long time because of their involvement in other activities, neglect their servile duties and declare, when they have lived according to the usages of freedom, that they are free.[31] Therefore the emperor prescribes that from now on, in order that servile status should not become concealed, on the first of December of each year every serf should declare his condition through the payment of one penny to his master or to his deputed agent.

The interplay of local customs thus undermined the whole social and juridical system of the Early Middle Ages, with a strength that was gradually growing as political confusion increased. The dissolution of the public power, the centuries-long contradictory processes of the formation of customs and the tendency towards disintegration of the

[29] E. Meynial, 'Notes sur la formation de la théorie du domaine divisé (domaine direct et domaine utile) du XIIe au XIVe siècle dans les romanistes', in *Melanges Fitting* (Montpellier, 1908), vol. 2, pp. 409–61.

[30] Manaresi, *I placiti del 'regnum Italiae'*, vol. 1 (Rome, 1955), pp. 431ff, 456ff. See Violante, *La società milanese*, pp. 85ff.

[31] M. Uhlirz, *Die Regesten des Kaiserreiches unter Otto III* (Böhmer, *Regesta imperii*, vol. 2.3, Graz-Cologne, 1957), p. 697.

unstable nuclei of seigneurial power all operated as a most effective stimulus for the whole rural population no less than for the urban collectivities. The dispersal of political power prevented the uniform coercion of the population into the social structures of the Carolingian world, and created the abnormal situation in which not even the ancient separation of slaves from free men, which was as fundamental in the Roman world as among the Germanic peoples, managed to escape the confusion that affected every social relationship. Otto III and his bishops and princes were roused to anger by this. The serfs lie, he declares in the capitulary of 998. Faced with masters already negligent of their own rights, the serfs demand proof of their own servitude. And since proof cannot always be gathered (which suggests a broad solidarity among the peasants), the emperor provides for recourse to the judicial duel; the serf who *propter appetitum libertatis* declares himself free shall fight in the field (or if old or ill, shall designate his own 'champion') against the master or the freely-designated 'champion' of the master. And since the desire of serfs for freedom was strongest in the vast and scattered ecclesiastical patrimonies, the emperor forbids without exception the liberation of serfs belonging to the church: 'it will never be permitted to any serf of the church to leave his servitude; not even the prelate in charge of a church can free one of its serfs from servitude, and we ordain that whoever among such serfs shall be freed in whatever manner shall return to the right and servitude of the church'. According to ecclesiastical tradition the patrimony of the church is inalienable, and the emperor rigidly incorporates within the patrimony even the men who belong to the churches.

The Ottonian capitulary solemnly denounces the crisis of that social arrangement whose roots lay in the convergence of the Germanic military aristocracy with the power of the episcopate, that took place within the patterns of territorial order and economic organization supplied by the ancient model of the Catholic Roman Empire. The Lombard rupture in the history of Italy, although it permanently overthrew the senatorial tradition of the Romano-Italic world, had turned in the eighth century into a reconstruction of the social apparatus, according to stratifications which in large part matched the old ones and which corresponded perfectly with those which formed, by a different path, in the Byzantine regions of the peninsula. The prolonged post-Carolingian anarchy which lasted until the communal period constituted, however, a much deeper rupture, no longer in the sense of a violent replacement of the men and peoples in possession of land and of power, but in the sense of a gradual upheaval in the strongest systems of relationships between individuals themselves, through the free interplay of customs and local initiatives. This was accompanied by broad processes of cultural and economic transformation: a greater depth to various demands for rationality and coherence in ecclesiastical culture; a growing commitment among notaries and jurists to the definition of rights and powers; a more intense circulation of goods and men; the creation of new productive areas through land clearance; the increasing demographic weight of rural and urban centres. But none of these processes constitutes in itself the central fact which was capable of radically modifying the structure of the society of the Early Middle Ages. They all converged to produce a situation which was characterized, over several centuries, by a vacuum, thanks to the inability of any political centre to function fully and durably as a means of rigid co-ordination and uniform dominion.

It was thus useless for Otto III to denounce the serfs who were 'yearning for liberty'. Yet the disorder was not evenly translated into a general process of liberation. It created a thousand chances for establishing oneself, at all social levels, but those chances were seized in very different ways; on the other hand, it also gave rise to the powers of local constraint, banal impositions, new forms of exploitation of the peasants, and the tendency towards a new legal division of the population between *villani* (as they were called in parts of Tuscany) and those men who were free from the limitations and burdens imposed by the banal lord (whether a territorial lord or landlord). In a court case of 1183 between the cathedral chapter of Siena and a peasant who also owned allodial lands, the judge acting in the name of the Sienese consuls gave the verdict that, despite the possession of allods, that peasant should be defined according to the custom of the area 'villein of the clerics and not an allod-owner', because of the canonical *tenementum* on which he lived and for which he had long rendered the services 'which villeins are accustomed to do to their lords'.[32] This legal division was certainly drawn at a higher level than the traditional one between free and serfs, but it too invoked local custom as grounds for ensuring each lord the exploitation of persons resident on seigneurial land or in a given territory, as the counterpart to the protection exercised over them, and thus it was in addition to the prestations which corresponded to the exploitation of the land; it aimed to prevent the play of economic forces from freeing the protected individual, through the acquisition of allods, from the bonds of a traditional subjection.

But at this point the possibilities offered by political interaction intervened, to prevent rural subjection from moving constantly in the

[32] Cammarosano, 'Il territorio della Berardenga', p. 299.

direction of greater rigidity and heavier burdens; those possibilities appeared where a plurality of powers was present (in the case just considered, the canonical ban and the urban jurisdiction of Siena), powers which were not always in harmony among themselves, and where the nucleus of seigneurial strength with which the peasants as a group were in immediate contact was small in size. For the peasant was not isolated before the lord. He belonged to a *vicinia*, a community of the village, which was sometimes of ancient origin.[33] According to a centuries-old tradition he was accustomed to reach decisions in agreement with his own *vicini*, residents in the same *vicus*, concerning the problems of living together, the farming of lands in the village territory, and the exploitation of common uncultivated land. These were decisions which in themselves had originally no polemical significance, either against the lord (if there was one) of the land conceded to the peasant, or his agents in the *curtis* to which the land was subordinate, or against the political authorities; but after the break-up of the kingdom in the tenth and eleventh centuries, when the political context with which the peasant collectivity had to contend took on local dimensions and a seigneurial character, it thus became more directly involved in the problems of the land and its exploitation. The seigneurial power of the ban was intended to draw the greatest possible profit from the protection exercised over the subject peasants, while at the same time it was constantly limited by the competition of other lords and threatened with disintegration by its internal crises, either the religious crises of an ecclesiastical body or the patrimonial crises of an aristocratic family divided within itself. It was then that the peasant collectivity began to operate as a means of resistance and expressed its own political will, encouraged to do so by the hated growth of the *consuetudines pravae*, which were not supported by any organic political force of repression. The development of the seigneurial ban stimulated the whole social body, because it penetrated it in a capillary network and provoked it to react, without possessing the means necessary to stamp out those reactions.

In 1058 the men of Nonantola, in the Modena plain, obtained a charter from the abbot of the monastery of Nonantola in which, while they recognized the seigneurial jurisdiction, *iustitia domnicata*, which belonged to the abbot, they were guaranteed the integrity of their

---

[33] G. P. Bognetti, 'Sulle origini dei comuni rurali del medioevo', *Studi nelle scienze giuridiche e sociali pubblicati dall'Istituto di esercitazioni presso la facoltà di giurisprudenza* (University of Pavia), 10 (1926), pp. 136ff; 11 (1927), pp. 51ff, 'I beni communali e l'organizzazione del villaggio nell'Italia superiore fino al mille', *Rivista storica italiana*, 77 (1965), pp. 486ff.

persons and goods, which would not be imposed upon by the abbatial agents except in the ways customary to the legitimate exercise of justice. In 1091 the *vicini* of Bionde, in the diocese of Verona, obtained from the cathedral chapter of Verona the right to elect a local gastald, subordinate to the deacon placed in charge there by the chapter, and the penalties provided for certain crimes and the gifts due to the canons each year were specifically stated. In the course of the twelfth century the evidence for the vigour of rural communities multiplies. They conclude pacts with their lords to determine the amount of *fodrum* due, the frequency of the judicial courts held by seigneurial agents, and the limits to the exercise of seigneurial coercion, and they demand the reduction of burdens connected with the *albergaria*, refusing to shelter a seigneurial retinue over a certain size or to feed its horses. They take a common oath of solidarity, elect their own rectors who are often designated by the name of consuls in imitation of the urban commune, and give them, whether or not in agreement with their lords, powers of local jurisdiction which are usually subordinate to the seigneurial powers. They pay for advocates who invent proofs and arguments in the litigation carried on with lords over the settlement of obligations and jurisdictions, before a superior jurisdiction (which is usually that of the city which is spreading politically in the contado), and they buy parts of the banal rights, offering considerable sums to the lords for them.[34] In the thirteenth century they sometimes also buy out the entire seigneurial jurisdiction, making themselves directly subordinate to the dominant city.

In this manner the old *viciniae* transformed themselves into rural communes, took on a precise institutional form, the consulate, and developed their autonomous action within the interwoven seigneurial and urban jurisdictions. The phases of the passage from primitive collective action to the first vindications of rights, and from these to a properly communal organization, stretch from the eleventh to the thirteenth centuries, but with an enormous chronological variation from one place to another. The rural communes did not always emerge from

[34] L. Simeoni, 'Il comune rurale nel territorio veronese', *Nuovo archivio veneto*, new series, 42 (1921), pp. 171ff; 'Communi rurali veronesi', *Atti e memorie dell'Accademia di agricoltura, scienze e lettere di Verona*, ser. V, 1 (1924), pp. 137ff; E. Besta and G. L. Barni, *Liber consuetudinum Mediolani anni MCCXVI* (Milan, 1949), pp. 198ff.; Mor, 'Dalla caduta dell'impero al commune', vol. 2, pp. 197, 205ff; G. Fasoli, 'Castelli e signorie rurali', in *Agricoltura e mondo rurale in Occidente nell'alto medioevo* (Spoleto, 1966), pp. 562ff; H. Groneuer, *Caresana. Eine oberitalienische Grundherrschaft im Mittelalter (987–1261)* (Stuttgart, 1970), pp. 84ff.

the old tradition of a neighbourhood association, either. Settlement changes sometimes caused them to appear simultaneously with new villages. This is the case with the *villa nova canonicorum* which was founded in the first half of the thirteenth century by the cathedral chapter of Vercelli in the forest of Gazzo as the centre of a new territory, cut out of the old *curtis* of Caresana and furnished with a castle and moat. The men drawn to the new village and supplied with land by the chapter swore loyalty as 'vassals', recognized the canons' rights to *honorem*, *districtum*, *fodrum*, *bannum* and *successiones*, and governed themselves through three consuls who were chosen by election by the rural community and with the consent of the canons.[35] Gazzo was thus a small commune supplied with a minimal autonomy, an organization which arose through the choice of the canons who were faced with the turbulent commune of Caresana, always ready to ally itself with the powerful commune of Vercelli against its own lord, the chapter. The commune of Caresana in its turn had arisen in the middle of the twelfth century from an old *vicinia* protected by a castle, subordinate to the *dominatus loci* of the chapter and largely, though not exclusively, composed of holders of concessions of canonical lands; among the *vicini* there were also allod-owners and among the latter some knights, who possessed a military tradition and were of Lombard and Frankish juridical descent.

The example of the villages of Gazzo and Caresana does not simply demonstrate the disparity of the historical processes through which the rural communes arose – it reveals the great variation in social composition, autonomy and political weight which differentiated such communes amongst themselves. In the shadow of the same lord, the cathedral chapter of Vercelli, very different rural situations came about.

The example also serves to demonstrate how the presence of fortifications was not in itself sufficient to make the commune of the village socially and politically important, since both Caresana and Gazzo were supplied with fortifications and none the less appear in the thirteenth century with very different levels of communal autonomy. Even so, it remains true that the castle made the conditions of life of a rural collectivity more complex. While on the one hand it could operate as a seigneurial instrument of domination, on the other hand it could be transformed into an element of strength for the population that depended on it. This happened whether it was a purely seigneurial fortress, within whose shelter and near whose defences the *vicinia* and

---

[35] Groneuer, *Caresana*, pp. 115ff. See *Bullettino storico-bibliografico subalpino*, 69 (1971), pp. 617–22.

village grew in population and strengthened their organization, or whether it was a circular wall destined from the beginning to protect a rural collectivity, through its origin in the joint initiative of the collectivity and a landed seigneur. The first process may be illustrated by the castle of Caresana itself. In the twelfth century it had a circumference of 500 metres, beyond which the village (*villa*) stretched, surrounded in its turn by ditches, which a further expansion of the settlement subsequently passed beyond; finally, soon after the middle of the thirteenth century, the old seigneurial *castrum* was incorporated into the walls destined to surround the entire site, now with a population of 600 and raised juridically to the status of free *borgo* and so freed from a whole series of seigneurial burdens. The second process can be illustrated by the castle of Cerea, erected around 923 in the southern contado of Verona in the face of the Hungarian threat. The archdeacon of the episcopal church of Verona conceded to over sixty *liberi homines*, who were then fortifying Cerea, the right to free alienation of the houses built within the area of the castle, forbidding them none the less to alienate houses to individuals from outside the collectivity and obliging them to pay a small annual rent to the archdeacon and to offer hospitality to any seigneurial messenger who came.[36]

In any case, the erection of a castle attracted population. It created a small inhabited centre or provoked a demographic increase in the pre-existing site, and consequently more complex social and economic activity and a certain social stratification, which related to the military operation of the fortress as well, so that later in the communal period the castral commune not infrequently came close, in its organization and the composition of its controlling class, to situations which were characteristic of the urban commune.[37] Thus there was an ever greater separation between the leading residents and the other members of the collectivity, with the important presence of a small dominant group of landowners of seigneurial tradition who were called *domini*, inasmuch as they were rich in both landed goods (not infrequently owned with *honor et districtus*) and in churches or tithes; these lords participated in the life of the commune and in its consular aristocracy but at the same time were often also linked as vassals to the lord to whom the commune was subject, or to other lords. At Biella, for example, the *vicinia* which occupied the *locus Bugellae*, which was subject in the communal period to the *dominatus* of the episcopal church of Vercelli, owner of the estate-

---

[36] *Codice diplomatico veronese*, ed. V. Fainelli (Venice, 1963), vol. 2, pp. 247ff; see especially p. 316.

[37] See G. Volpe, *Toscana medievale* (Florence, 1964), pp. 397ff. for the castles of the Lunigiana.

centre at Biella from at least the tenth century, was in 1160 invested in fief, by the bishop of Vercelli, with a neighbouring hill, the present-day Biella Piazzo, for the construction of a castle which was entrusted to the care of those among the *vicini* of the *locus* who should move there. It was this castle which complicated the formation of the communal organism of Biella, in which responsibility for the consulate was taken on from the end of the twelfth century by families of both pure seigneurial character and pure 'popular' origin. An example of the former were the Collacapra, who were possessors of property at Biella Piano and at the Piazzo and generally in the Biellese territory, holders of titles to tithes and powers of jurisdiction connected to landed property, influential canons in the church of S. Stefano in Biella, vassals of the bishop of Vercelli and of some aristocratic families, and in their turn *seniores* of other seigneurial families. An example of the latter is provided by the Gromo, powerful in the corporation of butchers but also owners of land at Biella Piano and Biella Piazzo, who finally merged in the thirteenth and fourteenth centuries into a close *consorzio* with the Collacapra themselves.[38]

Indeed one may say that a commune like Biella, even though sprung from a rural *vicinia*, goes well beyond the idea of the rural commune and clearly matches the social and political models of the urban commune. A whole range of local developments thus provoked the transformation of villages into centres endowed with a varying autonomy and social composition, from the most humble, still rigorously subordinated to the local seigneurial power and operating internally in almost egalitarian forms, to those which took part in the subsequent range of urban communal developments. But can this complex movement of rural populations towards autonomy have taken place entirely in response to the developments of seigneurial power?

On the contrary, the point must be clearly made that we normally do not find rural communities residing entirely on land received in concession from a particular lord within his own complex of property. The double meaning of the term *curtis*, which we have discussed above, which was used in the Early Middle Ages for a centre of estate administration with its agricultural appurtenances but came to signify in the communal period the coherent territory over which the *dominatus loci* was exercised, has suggested in the past the idea of a peasant

---

[38] *Monumenta historiae patriae*, vol. 4 *Chartarum tomus secundus* (Turin, 1853), coll. 633ff; N. Irico, 'Il problema della presenza signorile nei primordi del comune di Biella', *Bollettino storico-bibliografico subalpino*, 69 (1971), pp. 449–504.

movement which took place within a single landed estate.[39] The actual process was quite different. The movement was centred on the village, which in the main was not compactly incorporated in one estate but included within itself small and not-so-small landowners and the cultivators of lands of different lords, even when hegemony was established over the village by a militarily enterprising seigneurial family or an ecclesiastical body endowed with a rich landed patrimony in the area. Only in this sense, that is insofar as one considers the development of seigneurial powers of the ban and their tendency to cover individual villages, well beyond the boundaries of simple landowning, is it permissible to say that the movement towards peasant autonomies is almost completely conditioned and stimulated by the stormy affairs of lords. Indeed, it is necessary to stress this political conditioning, even if in some instances, which we will consider next, it so happened that the rural commune arose outside any seigneurial framework.

These latter were *viciniae* completely composed of allod-owners, the *arimanni* of the Carolingian period, in the areas where neighbourhood collectivities had escaped the pressure exerted by the development of the great landed estates. In 983 Emperor Otto II conceded to eighteen men living in the territory of Lazise, on the eastern coast of Lake Garda, fishing rights and exemption from tributes, permission to extend the existing fortification on the site as far as the lake, and the collection of local transport duties.[40] Almost a hundred years later, in 1077, Henry IV repeated the concession with explicit reference to the whole collectivity of Lazise, which in the twelfth century appears to have been constituted as a commune and administered, at the end of the century, by its own podestà. The *pauperes homines piscatores* of Lazise (as Henry IV calls them, even if their poverty is only relative by comparison to the *potentes*) thus organized the commune without any threat from a lord and linked themselves directly with the royal power as a privileged group, not unlike the cities when they escaped the power of the count and the bishop. And this happened everywhere where the free rural collectivity was favoured by its geographical situation (Lazise was on the route used by the German kings when they descended into Italy) or protected by the nature of the landscape – particularly, therefore, in the valleys among the mountains, in sites similar to those in which certain Swiss liberties first developed.[41] But it still remains true that in these cases too

---

[39] See P. Schaefer, *Il Sottoceneri nel medioevo* (Lugano, 1954), pp. 203ff.

[40] Tabacco, *I liberi del re*, pp. 151ff. See Simeoni, *Comuni rurali veronesi*, pp. 218ff.

[41] See P. S. Leicht, *Operai, artigiani, agricoltori in Italia dal secolo VI al XVI* (Milan, 1946), pp. 82ff; Schaefer, *Il Sottoceneri*, pp. 231ff, 236; G. Santini, *I*

the strengthening of the rural *viciniae* was linked indirectly to seigneurial developments, that is, to the disintegration of the counties and marches provoked by the political development of the military and ecclesiastical aristocracy. Only the post-Carolingian disorder allowed the *pauperes homines* to organize themselves as autonomous nuclei of power, parallel to those which developed from or were provoked by seigneurial hegemonies.

CO-ORDINATIONS OF FEUDAL AND TERRITORIAL POWER, AND THE FAILURE OF THE EMPIRE

At every level of society in northern and central Italy, political initiatives were increasing at such speed in the twelfth century that it suggests that new methods were being increasingly used to ensure the survival of each emergent power within the highly fluid institutional and territorial structures. One of these methods was the ever more systematic use of jurists and their subtle tools, to define relations between centres of power and to calculate roughly the state of play within the tight network of interests and ambitions. This was grafted on to existing features: a lively dual (Lombard and Roman) legal tradition, the spreading ties of clientship, which were expressed through the solemn symbolism of vassalage, and the notarial production of charters recording the transfer of goods which (particularly if they were churches and castles) often implied the exercise of power over collectivities. However, the original features of each aspect of the legal tradition were now clearly being surpassed, and personal ties and economic transactions were transformed into political agreements drawn up with full legal rigour between forces which respected each other's spheres of autonomy.[42] It was in this cultural climate that the institutions of vassalage and benefices, and the allodial conception of power, modified each other and were translated into political feudalism.

This was the feudalism that one generally thinks about today when talking of vassals and fiefs, and which many still wrongly suppose to have been born, together with its political significance as a system of territorial seigneurial power, in the early Carolingian period. This presupposes that the many *vassi dominici* and *vassi comitum* and

comuni di valle del medievo (Milan, 1960), pp. 12ff, 225ff, *I comuni di pieve nel medievo italiano* (Milan, 1964), pp. 190ff.

[42] G. Tabacco, 'Potere e cultura nell'età precomunale', *Filosofia*, 18 (Florence, 1967), pp. 410ff; 'Ordinamento pubblico e sviluppo signorile nei secoli centrali del medioevo', *Bullettino dell'Istituto storico italiano per il medioevo*, 79 (1968), pp. 44ff.

episcoporum, abbatum and *abbatissarum* to whom the capitularies often refer held in fief respectively from the king, or from counts and bishops, abbots and abbesses, within a pyramidal system of clientship, autonomous political and territorial powers, which extended downwards, through successive infeudations and sub-infeudations, to form a hierarchy of the powerful throughout the whole area of the Frankish Empire, over all circumscriptions and districts. We know already that bonds of vassalage in the Carolingian period were not universally used; they were used to guarantee the dependence of public officials on the king and the loyalty of military clientèles to the king and to other powerful individuals, and the benefice, as remuneration for the vassal, was his stipend for the public office he held or for his professional armed service. We know that the economic significance of the benefice was complicated in the course of the Carolingian period by applying the concept of *beneficium* to the office of the count itself and to public power in general, which was conceived as a source of income and social prestige for the vassal who occupied it, but we also know that this did not corrupt the idea of public office as a revocable royal concession, since the benefice connected with vassal service still had a precarious, and not patrimonial, character. And we know that the tendency of the high public offices to become hereditary arose not from their absorption into the concept of the benefice, but rather from a tradition dating back to the Merovingian and Lombard periods, and so predating the institutions of vassalage and benefice. One should add here that the vassal benefice, as an economic remuneration, showed at an early date an equally strong tendency to become hereditary, thanks to the opportunity open to every powerful individual to preserve more easily his own military clientèle by receiving as vassals the sons of existing vassals, and thanks to the interest that these sons had in conserving by this means the benefice conceded to their fathers by the *senior*.[43]

In the course of the post-Carolingian period the customs which had encouraged the appearance of hereditary vassal benefices finally took on a definite form, which gave vassals increasing economic autonomy from their *seniores*. The usage was strengthened in Italy by the edict promulgated by Conrad II in 1037, during the siege of Milan, in favour of the lesser vassals, in order to check the power of counts and marquises, bishops and abbots, their *seniores*.[44] Thus the vassal benefice became a legally hereditary holding, conditional only on loyalty to the *senior*, the commitment to help him in case of need, and on the formal renewal of

[43] Mitteis, *Lehnrecht und Staatsgewalt*, pp. 167ff; Leicht, 'Il feudo in Italia', pp. 93ff.

[44] *MGH, Diplomata regum et imperatorum Germaniae*, vol. 4, n. 244.

investiture with the fief (now the prevalent denomination for the benefice, from the eleventh century onwards) at every change of *senior* or *vassus*. In the twelfth and thirteenth century the holding was defined in legal theory, in its rules of inheritance and in its obligations, through the jurists' exegesis of customary usage and of the repeated imperial legislation.[45] In this new legal form the feudal possession took on a patrimonial character which was very similar to that of allodial property, even though it was less absolute. The similarity appears not only in the inclusion of economic rights conferred over property, but also in the expression of the patrimonial character of any power which had been conceded; a measure of political domination was thus incorporated into the hereditary power of a family, or of an ecclesiastical body or a commune. The fief, as a legal concept, thus acquired at the political level a tendency analogous to that formerly apparent in the allod, whenever there had been a concession in allod of a castle with its connected jurisdiction, or of the power of a count or marquis, or of the locally-formed customs of coercion, exaction and justice, or of any fragment of rights with a public character. That is, it tended to suggest that the exercise of such powers or rights was not due to a revocable concession, but belonged autonomously to the family or organization.

By this we mean that feudal investiture of a power of a public nature was now, in the communal period, clearly distinct from the normal conferring of a delegated office by the king or another territorial power. Hence for example the care shown by the bishop of Asti in documents of the twelfth and thirteenth century to specify that among the castles confirmed to the lords of Govone with certain jurisdictions, the castle of Monticello was not the subject of a feudal concession, and, referring to the lords of Vezza, to specify that the castle of Vezza itself had never been assigned to them in fief because they had always held it 'tamquam custodes et guardatores predicti castri pro Astensi ecclesia'. Thus he distinguished the normal office of guarding a castle, and exercising jurisdiction over its territory exclusively in the name of the bishop, from a guardianship wholly or partly enfeoffed – that is, transferred as a patrimony into the hands of a seigneurial dynasty.[46] One may note that the lords of Govone were vassals of the bishop and as such held in fief, among others, the castle of Govone, with part of its revenues and

---

[45] Brancoli Busdraghi, *La formazione storica del feudo lombardo*, pp. 127ff; *cf.* Tabacco, 'L'allodialità del potere nel medioevo', pp. 604ff.

[46] Bordone, 'L'aristocrazia militare', pp. 409ff. See G. Morello, 'Dal "custos castri Plocasci" alla consorteria signorile di Piossasco e Scalenghe', *Bollettino storico-bibliografico subalpino*, 71 (1973), pp. 23ff.

jurisdictional powers, but since such dependency no longer excluded – indeed rather it implied – seigneurial possession as patrimony, the bishop resisted the tendency of his subordinates to include within the same feudal relationship (in the act of renewing the oath of loyalty to the prelate) all the goods and powers committed to them, and he refused to use feudal formulae in re-committing to the Govone family the castle of Monticello and to the Vezza the castle of Vezza. These are distinctions as subtle as they are emphatic, and presuppose suggestions to the bishop by jurists. None the less they are distinctions which answer precise practical needs: the occasion to recognize the stability attained by those rights traditionally conceded through solemn feudal investiture of a vassal (that is, to respect the freedom of their exercise of lordship and the rules of transmission elaborated by the jurists), and at the same time the opportunity to check the progressive creation by custom of new islands of political and military autonomy. The importance given to explicitly feudal investiture was enough to mark the boundary between the autonomous, even though subordinate, seigneurial disposition of powers and rights, and the exercise of a delegated power subject to intervention and control by the delegating authority. This boundary had not existed in the Carolingian period, when the assignation of a public *honor*, county or march or duchy, as a benefice to a loyal subject of the king coincided with the concession of the office.

The importance given to explicitly feudal investiture was also sufficient to mark the limits of autonomy in that seigneurial disposition of rights. For the fief, however close it came to the allod, was not confused with it. The patrimonial quality of the fief was restricted, whether it concerned property or power, by loyalty and service, by the investiture and by specific rules of succession. So while it might be expedient for a king or bishop or some other territorial power to confine certain of their agents to a sphere of action not protected by feudal law, at least for some of their functions, it was equally useful, where the agents had in practice already attained full autonomy, to preserve at least the symbols of a formal subordination. These symbols were the bonds of vassalage and feudal investiture, to which it was always possible to appeal in requesting aid or abstention from hostility, in the name of loyalty; they were also the bonds from which was derived the *senior*'s right (when a castle was the object of the investiture) to have the enfeoffed castle opened to him, a right which was highly valued during military operations. And since, in the intensification of the rivalry between all powers, political isolation became ever more dangerous for each of them, the feudal bond was often a highly valuable one, not only for a territorial power trying to keep within its control the nuclei of strength that were emerging within its territory, but also for those nuclei themselves, which were certainly eager to establish themselves with the greatest possible autonomy but which were at the same time involved in an increasingly difficult struggle for existence.

The feudal bond was even sought by lords who had built a castle on their allodial land, or who had earlier transformed into an allod a castle entrusted to their forebears by some church or lord. With increasing frequency they sought or accepted a feudal bond with a more powerful lordship in order to have its protection, tolerance or alliance. Often the castle was handed over, in a purely formal donation, to the more powerful lord, and then received back as a fief. In this way the possession of the allod was transferred to a new *senior*, but the original lord, now a vassal, still held the castle as part of his patrimony, his rights now taking a feudal form. This legal expedient is usually called an oblate fief; it was also applied to property without political significance. In the communal period the oblate fief was increasingly used, in the various regions of the Italian kingdom and in the papal territories, to express a form of political autonomy which recognized another power as superior.[47] As a result, the conception of seigneurial power as based on allods began to decline, since this tendency to transfer allodial possession to a higher lord appeared in the Italian kingdom (just as in the kingdoms north of the Alps) at every political level, up to that of the king. In the second half of the twelfth century, when Frederick I of Swabia attempted, by various means, to re-establish royal and imperial authority in the kingdom, he too often used the fief of lordship, that involving seigneurial power emanating from a fortress or radiating over a broader territorial dominion, in order to renew or set up an explicit legal link between the Empire and the local lordships, either on the basis of pre-existing ties of vassalage between comital dynasties and the kingdom, or in relation to powers based solely on local customs. This was the 'feudal' significance of the policies of Barbarossa. In the bonds that he established in specific political circumstances with the marquises of Monferrato or with the counts of Biandrate, with the Malaspina marquises or the marquises of Este, or even with the small seigneurial dynasties such as the

---

[47] K. Jordan, *Das Eindringen des Lehnswesens in das Rechtsleben der römischen Kurie* (1931, new ed. Darmstadt, 1971), pp. 42ff; Volpe, *Toscana medievale*, pp. 339ff, 366, 407; Brancoli Busdraghi, *La formazione storica del feudo lombardo*, p. 161; G. Tabacco, 'La costituzione del regno italico al tempo di Federico Barbarossa', in *Popolo e Stato in Italia nell'età di Federico Barbarossa* (Turin, 1970), p. 170; Haverkamp, *Herrschaftsformen*, p. 319; Toubert, *Les structures du Latium*, vol. 2, pp. 1,089ff.

lords of Robbio in the area of Vercelli,[48] Frederick was generous with investitures *nomine feudi*; but this was in order to bring the seigneurial autonomies into a relationship with the Empire, rather than to restore for the benefit of rural lords some earlier feudal order of the kingdom which had been damaged by the development of the urban communes. For it has now been shown that his alliances with seigneurial dynasties were never constant or inflexible; they were, rather, episodes of varying importance in a political struggle which generally aimed to intensify imperial protection over the whole area of the kingdom. And in pursuing this feudal policy within a broader plan, Barbarossa was simply taking part in a spontaneous movement within the Italian world, which in its turn was part of a broader European tendency.

In reality, when the counts of Biandrate in Piedmont first linked themselves with Frederick in 1152, he renewed a diploma earlier conceded to them by the Empire in which were confirmed all the places belonging to the Biandrate, in order that 'they should hold them and enjoy them in perpetuity according to the *ius proprietarium*, concerning things that are their own property, and according to the *mos beneficiarius* concerning benefices'.[49] This was evidently not a feudal investiture, but rather a generic imperial guardianship of the whole patrimony of the Biandrate in the double form, allodial and feudal, assumed by aristocratic landed property, together with the usual formulae of ownership which were traditionally applicable as much to allods as to fiefs, and which concerned castles, villages and chapels, houses, fields and vineyards, *fodrum* and *albergaria*, jurisdictions and landed revenues, all listed without order as if to display the range and diversity of the economic and political power of the comital dynasty. Thus the diploma seemed to reflect precisely a situation produced by a complex set of events over the centuries; economic goods and public powers were intimately linked and both were absorbed into the patrimony of a family, while the benefice and allod had gradually been drawing closer together until they now ensured a strong hereditary basis, the foundation of seigneurial autonomy. But the distinction that emerges in the small print of the diploma, between goods possessed in allod and those held in benefice, is open to another interpretation; it could suggest that among the properties held by the Biandrate some were of such a nature as to require the feudal bond. Actually, in those years, the imperial court was very

---

[48] R. Manselli, 'La grande feudalità italiana tra Federico Barbarossa e i comuni', in *Popolo e Stato*, pp. 345ff; Tabacco, 'La costituzione del regno italico', pp. 169ff; Haverkamp, *Herrschaftsformen*, pp. 373ff.

[49] *Carte valsesiane fino al secolo XV*, ed. C. G. Mor (Turin, 1933), pp. 26, 29; see Haverkamp, *Herrschaftsformen*, p. 88 note 16.

clearly making known its desire to separate the seigneurial jurisdiction, which had a public character, from the material possession of allodial property.[50] In the Diet of Roncaglia in 1158, in the presence of great lords, consuls of cities and jurists, the Empire claimed the overall monopoly of public power, expressly prohibiting anyone, when selling his allod, from selling with it the *districtus* and *iurisdictio* of the emperor. Public jurisdiction could indeed pass into seigneurial hands in connection with fortresses or landed property, but the Empire must be recognized as the source of this jurisdiction, recognition being expressed through the symbolism of fief and vassalage. The spontaneous movement of the seigneurial powers towards a system of feudal ties, in which the equilibrium between a need for autonomy and a need for co-ordination was able to overcome political chaos and to guarantee the survival of all parties, thus fitted in with a newly mature legal culture, which directly or indirectly drew on the constitutions of the ancient Roman Empire and which was therefore intolerant of the centuries-long disorder through which power had multiplied and been dispersed.

Traditional respect for the fluid environment of contradictory customs was altered by the formulations which were founded on a strongly rational nucleus of ideas. However, this respect was not undermined as long as the emperor functioned within a feudal outlook, since through the patrimonial fief of lordship the power of greater and lesser families was protected, together with its eccentric territorial pattern in which marquisates, counties, and castle districts were interwoven with each other and with the ecclesiastical and communal territories, stretching without any continuity over different areas and regions, and having by now nothing in common with the marches and counties of the Carolingian division into public districts. The ecclesiastical dominions themselves were absorbed into the feudal concept. Following the Concordat of Worms, which in 1122 had ended half a century of struggle between the German kings and the Roman See, and which distinguished between the properly ecclesiastical element in the power of the churches (where the interference of the lay and of royal investiture was now forbidden), and the temporal patrimony which was integrated into secular political structures, the notion that everything was allodial which belonged materially and politically to the churches was increasingly undermined; a tendency appeared, to interpret in a feudal sense (against the literal and original meaning of the diplomas earlier obtained by the churches) the complex of goods, rights and powers which had come to them from the king. These were the so-called

---

[50] Brancoli Busdraghi, *La formazione storica del feudo lombardo*, pp. 178ff.

'regalia', to use the legal language that was first employed in the twelfth century. The expression was used initially to designate all that had been conceded by the king, and then to distinguish from the goods and rights of a private character those powers of jurisdiction and government, repression and exaction, and those rights over roads and waters, vacant goods and coinage, which were held to be peculiar to the public powers.[51]

Even Barbarossa's opposition to the power of the Lombard communes seems on occasion to conform to this well-balanced tendency towards the feudal, whenever he brought himself to recognize their power in forms analogous to feudal relationships or – in exceptional cases – even in forms that were explicitly feudal. In this too he was part of a development prompted by the Italian powers themselves. In fact, even though the urban collectivities constituted centres of power unlike those of the seigneurial families, and could therefore less easily be assimilated into a web of personal relationships such as that presupposed by the feudal network, it was often the case that vassal subordination was from the first adapted to certain communes, together with the related conferral of a fief. The consuls of Asti in 1095, in the first document which mentions them, receive in the name of all the citizens the castle of Annone *in beneficio* from the bishop, and in their turn in the course of the twelfth century confer fiefs in order to build up a seigneurial clientèle around the commune of Asti.[52] There are even more unusual instances in which the legal bond of clientship is used to indicate the political dominance of one commune over another, as happened when in the twelfth century the powerful commune of Vercelli, formally subject to the bishop, extended its sphere of action westwards to the Eporediese, so that every ten years the citizens of Ivrea had to renew their oath of loyalty towards Vercelli for two fortresses *tamquam vassalli faciunt dominis suis*.[53] In such a context it is easy to understand how, for example, Barbarossa enfeoffed the cities of Genoa and Pisa with broad territorial powers in 1162. And it is also possible to understand how, even where the vocabulary of vassalage and benefices is not explicitly used, the reciprocal obligations assumed by the emperor and the commune could be spontaneously set out in parallel with feudal agreements. In 1183 the Treaty of Constance, which halted the wars of Frederick with the cities and lords of the Lombard League, recognized

[51] Haverkamp, *Herrschaftsformen*, pp. 85ff, 436ff, 522ff.
[52] *Codex Astensis qui de Malabayla communiter nuncupatur* ed. Q. Sella (Rome, 1880), vols. 2 and 3, particularly n. 635.
[53] *Documenti dell'Archivio Comunale di Vercelli relativi ad Ivrea*, ed. G. Colombo (Pinerolo, 1901), pp. 19ff.

that the 'cities', 'places' and 'persons' constituting the League held *in perpetuum* the *regalia et consuetudines*: all the powers that legal doctrine considered to be founded on royal and imperial authority and which lords and communes exercised *ab antiquo* through a process of spontaneous acquisition; rights of jurisdiction 'in causes both criminal and pecuniary'; rights to an army and fortification; rights of *fodrum*, toll, and exploitation of uncultivated land and waters. This was on condition that the customs that favoured the kingdom be equally respected – that is, that the emperor on his entry into 'Lombardia' should be paid the *fodrum consuetum et regale*: that roads and bridges should be maintained in working order for his arrival and return; that imperial vassals should request investiture of their fief and should take the oath of loyalty 'as vassals', while 'all the others' should swear 'as citizens'; and that the consuls of the city should be loyal to the Empire and should receive from it a periodic formal investiture of their office.[54]

Even in the distinction between the oath of the *vassalli* and the oath of the *cives*, between feudal investiture and the investiture of the consuls, the parallels are clear between the seigneurial autonomies and the communal autonomies, which Frederick confirmed to the members of the Lombard League on a contractual basis. There is a clear tendency towards the construction of a feudal kingdom, similar to that which was taking shape in France in the twelfth and thirteenth centuries. This was the classic period of feudalism, something wholly different, on the political level, from the spontaneous convergence in previous centuries of public order and bonds of clientship: it was an ill-defined system of autonomies which had grown in a disorderly fashion into a knot of juxtapositions and superpositions, and which was now brought into a formal hierarchy converging on the king. But it is equally clear that the tendency towards feudalism was soon blocked in Italy. The exceptional development of communal power, and the violent actions through which Barbarossa attempted several times to undermine it, created insuperable obstacles to the attainment of a feudal and parafeudal equilibrium in Italy. Strong and autonomous cities were not lacking north of the Alps, but there they remained a politically marginal presence or were contained within narrow territorial boundaries, and were therefore an element that could be moderated by the formation of feudal principalities within kingdoms with the same tendency. In Italy the communal cities themselves became in the twelfth and thirteenth centuries the protagonists of new territorial developments, which

---

[54] *MGH, Constitutiones et acta publica*, vol. I, pp. 412ff; Manaresi, *Atti*, pp. 199ff.

tolerated subordinate or juxtaposed seigneurial nuclei and were in harmony with the rapid growth of the rural communes, and which therefore took their place within a complex framework of autonomies; but these developments centred on urban realities which were too economically dynamic and too different in nature from the seigneurial tradition to be able to adapt themselves to the dominance of feudal institutions, vassalage and benefices. On the political level the cities took the form of lordships with a collective structure, which could in theory be linked among themselves and with other powers through oaths of loyalty and investitures *per feudum*; but, since they were collectivities with a large membership, they were unable to sustain purely personal relationships, such as the privileged friendships and mutual affection between *seniores* and vassals, without radically denaturing them. All the more so since Barbarossa had no inclination to implement a *mutua dilectio* with them!

Nor did he have any inclination even to offer a convincing parafeudal structure, adapted to the realities of the Italian communes, which would decisively replace the feudal structure. He did indeed draw up a whole series of agreements and distributed privileges to reward special co-operation, and at Constance even drew up a peace treaty of great breadth; but he was not convincing, because his concessions, even though made *in perpetuum* in precisely the feudal manner, were too clearly subject to the political circumstances, and contrasted with his formulation of solemn general principles. That every *districtus* and every *iurisdictio* should rest with the emperor and that all judges should receive rights of administration from him, as was expressly declared in 1158 at Roncaglia,[55] was a principle of Roman law which Barbarossa reserved the right to interpret in very different ways. At one moment he enfeoffed or conceded in perpetuity the *regalia* to certain lords and cities, and thus adapted it to a reality of local autonomies which was very far from the ancient Roman world, and at another moment he limited the concession to certain *regalia* alone. At other times he refused the *regalia* as a punishment and imposed heavy exactions, as well as sending podestà and other German officials here and there to govern castles and cities or impose harsh control on their local government. Even in the Treaty of Constance he refrained from stating a principle of general respect for autonomies. He presented his recognition of customs as a privilege conceded to the Lombard League and its members alone, and in fact in the years that followed he pursued in several areas of Tuscany the same

[55] V. Colorni, 'Le tre leggi perdute di Roncaglia (1158) ritrovate in un manoscritto parigino', in *Scritti in memoria di Antonino Giuffrè* (Milan, 1967), vol. 1, pp. 143ff.

policy of reducing local forces and replacing them with a direct imperial administration which he had earlier attempted in central Lombardy, in connection with some of his military campaigns.

The imperial court, in pursuing in such diverse and ephemeral forms its broad ambition to dominate the equally diverse and ephemeral world of Italy, was in fact following the example of the most powerful cities of 'Lombardy'. These cities, each operating over a wide surrounding area, made use of agreements of the most diverse kinds in their relations with other seigneurial and communal territories, sometimes going so far as to destroy the centre of greatest resistance. This happened to Lodi in 1111: after years of war the Milanese brought it to total ruin, 'funditus destruxerunt',[56] and scattered its population, and for more than forty years, up to the time of Barbarossa, they prevented the nucleus of inhabitants who re-formed themselves into a commune and centre of population from carrying out their own political policies or from administering themselves with effective autonomy.[57] Nor was this political development characteristic only of the larger cities. In Piedmont, for example, the commune of Alba laboriously built up its territory in the twelfth and thirteenth centuries through the most diverse means. It removed castles from its own bishop with violent *coups de main* and then reached compromises with him, drove back the menacing Aleramic family of marquises and the interference of the commune of Asti through military preparation and agreements for coexistence and containment, and brought into vassalage a multitude of minor seigneurial families, whose allodial possessions the commune bought or received as donations, restoring to them their goods and jurisdictions as fiefs. These and other families were forced to become citizens, swearing to observe the formal agreement drawn up between the *cives* of Alba, with its related rights and duties (*cittadinatico*). The inhabitants of entire settlements were also drawn into citizenship, with Alba promising to respect both the internal structures of the community and any surviving tie of subjection to local lords, while other small communes became subject to the city through agreements which excluded the local organs of seigneurial rule. And in this whole incessant policy of co-ordinating the territorial autonomies of lords and communities Alba followed no

---

[56] *Landulph Iunioris historia Mediolanensis*, c. 28 (p. 17).

[57] H. Simonsfeld, *Jahrbücher des deutschen Reiches unter Friedrich I*, vol. 1 (Leipzig, 1908), pp. 170ff, 593ff, 631ff; Barni 'Milano verso l'egemonia', pp. 287ff, 296; 'La lotta contro il Barbarossa', in *Storia di Milano*, vol. 4, pp. 10ff, 27ff, 36. See, now, also L. Fasola, 'Una famiglia di sostenitori milanesi di Federico I', *Quellen und Forschungen aus italienischen Archiven und Bibliotheken*, 52 (1972), pp. 116ff.

unitary criteria, nor was it concerned to exercise its supremacy with the same degree of intensity wherever it could.[58]

The analogy between the forms of imperial action and the complex political co-ordination pursued by the urban communes can even be extended to a consideration of the geographical frameworks in which such activity took place. The imperial power in Italy officially took on the framework supplied by the tradition of the kingdom, but the borders of the kingdom were no longer very clear; this uncertainty dated, in the north and north-east, from the time when the vast Teutonic kingdom had been united through the Ottonian conquest with that of Italy under the same kings and emperors, and in the north-west from the time when Conrad II inherited and conquered (in the name of the German kingdom and the empire) the kingdom of Burgundy after the royal dynasty of the Rudolfings died out in 1032. In the south, too, the empire exercised a traditional protection over territories which the pope governed or laid claim to, and this official protection and interference survived despite the formal 'restitutions' sworn by the German kings from the Ottonian period onwards in favour of the Church of Rome. In their turn the communal cities operating in the kingdom, cities which were episcopal seats and had been centres of comital circumscriptions since the Carolingian period, saw as the legitimate framework for their own political expansion (wherever they might have the military and economic strength capable of realizing it) the boundaries of the diocese and the old borders of the county; they appealed to one or the other according to whether the greatest scope of their own ambitions was offered by the ecclesiastical boundary or the now theoretical and often poorly known boundary of the administratively defunct county. In fact, by the second half of the twelfth century the political district that centred on the city, the *districtus*, *posse* or *podere*, the *virtus* or *forcia*, as the sources significantly say – that is, the more or less broad and irregular territory placed under the more or less intense hegemony of the urban commune – had now, after a whole series of wars and treaties reached an extent which often approximately matched that of the diocese or county.[59] But the theory developed by the urban communes to justify

---

[58] D. Albesano, 'La costruzione politica del territorio comunale di Alba', *Bollettino storico-bibliografico subalpino*, 69 (1971), pp. 95ff, 152ff, 165ff. For the interesting case of Alessandria, founded by the Lombard League and at once intent on constructing its own political territory, see G. Pistarino, 'Alessandria nel mondo dei comuni', *Studi medievali*, ser. III, 11 (1970). pp. 24ff.

[59] G. De Vergottini, 'Origine e sviluppo storico della comitatinanza', *Studi senesi*, 43 (1929), pp. 402ff, 'I presupposti storici del rapporto di comitatinanza e la diplomatica comunale', *Bullettino senese*, 60 (1953), pp. 1ff.

their territorial dominance, the appeal to the *civitas mater* to which the *filii comitatini*, the population, lay and ecclesiastical lords and rural communes scattered in the county, owed respect and obedience, is only the ideological cloak for that knotted tangle of pacts, conventions and violent submissions which brought the forces of the contado to centre on the city. So, too, the designation *sacrum imperium* was frequently used from the time of Barbarossa to indicate the 'Roman Empire' of Carolingian origin[60] and to signify, as well as the universal role of the highest political guide of Christendom, the concrete political power that belonged to the emperor in the kingdoms of Italy, Germany and Burgundy. In Italy the *sacrum imperium* was the ideological cloak for a concentration of German military might, united with allied Italian forces, and for the control which they tried to exercise over the whole territory of the kingdom through a multiplicity of political ties and – in some areas – through a direct presence in government.

None the less the parallel only goes so far. The Empire in Italy lacked a centre of gravity, an economic support, a social base. When the emperor was in Italy no one could ignore the presence of the nucleus of forces travelling with him across the peninsula, but the ties remained transient. He entered into a political contest which he could not dominate except episodically, and in which he was only a useless and costly complication.[61] Imperial action was, in some of its phases, effective in reducing and humiliating the major centres of political concentration, particularly Milan, and therefore moved in a direction which seemed to lead towards a greater equilibrium among the various Italian forces. But the ruinous 'punishments' and heavy interventions in the lives of some cities finally showed the Empire to be a force of subversion; they provoked the formation of the Lombard League, so creating for a destroyed Milan the chance to rise again as an expanding hegemonic power, and determined the tie between the League and the papacy. Papal authority, busy consolidating the success of the ecclesiastical reform movement, became the constant point of appeal for all the opponents of the imperial ambitions. The Concordat of Worms had officially recognized the hybrid legal shape of episcopal power, present in both the ecclesiastical order and the seigneurial order (which we can now legitimately call 'feudal') of the Empire. Thus it had not extinguished, but only covered over, the inevitable tension between the imperial power, which was still connected to a considerable extent with the activity of bishops and was therefore disposed to interfere in their

[60] H. Appelt, *Die Kaiseridee Friedrich Barbarossas* (Vienna, 1967), pp. 7ff.
[61] See C. Brühl, 'La politica finanziaria di Federico Barbarossa in Italia', in *Popolo e Stato*, pp. 197ff.

operation, and the Roman Curia, which was resolved to strengthen the ties between the episcopal sees and Rome and was therefore distrustful of any intensification of imperial power, above all in Italy where a concentration of German forces could directly affect papal activity. The network of ties in Italy which centred on the emperor was thus spontaneously counterbalanced by a network of opposing interests co-ordinated with the Roman Curia.[62] The ideology of the *sacrum imperium* was set against the ideology elaborated by those canonists who, in connection with the idea already expressed by Gregory VII in the Investiture Dispute, had established with varying significance the supremacy of the priesthood, culminating in the papacy, over any other power.[63] The activity of the Roman Curia, which deprived the Empire of its monopoly over theoretical programmes for 'justice' and 'peace', contributed powerfully to demythologize the royal and imperial power. It stripped the latter of its own peculiar function and revealed it as purely a political complication, without succeeding on the other hand, despite all its own theocratic display, in presenting persuasively the papacy as the focus for a balanced political order. Indeed the imperial rivalry demythologized in its turn the priestly theocracy.

This holds good for the period of Barbarossa and Henry VI, his son, and is still valid in the first half of the thirteenth century for Henry VI's son, Frederick II, who was to bring the Empire to ruin when faced with the converging forces of the papacy and the Lombard communes. At the political level, the complicating effects of the Empire and the papacy remained on the surface of a development which was centred on the communal cities. Certainly, for much of the thirteenth century, the latter did not create uniform territorial networks, nor did they manage to render the ideology of the *civitas mater* credible as they co-ordinated within their own *posse* the *posse* of seigneurs and lesser communes. There was all the more reason for this since the more powerful cities, such as Milan, Genoa and Pisa, had from the first half of the twelfth century passed well beyond the borders of diocese and county, including, in the base of Genoa and Pisa, even the great Tyrrhenian islands of Corsica and Sardinia, and thus they were not interested in appealing to the theory of the relationship of *comitatinantia*. Nor, obviously, could new urban centres, such as Chieri in Piedmont and Prato in Tuscany,[64] appeal to it,

---

[62] M. Pacaut, 'La papauté et les villes italiennes (1159–1253)', in *I problemi della civiltà comunale* (Bergamo, 1971), pp. 33ff.

[63] *Ibid.*, *Alexandre III* (Paris, 1956), pp. 336ff.

[64] L. Cibrario, *Delle storie di Chieri*, 2nd ed. (Turin, 1855); E. Fiumi, *Demografia, movimento urbanistico e classi sociali a Prato dall'età comunale ai tempi moderni* (Florence, 1968).

since they were not in the communal period, and had never been, the seats of bishops and counts, and yet they too eagerly built themselves their own political territory. Each of these old and new cities represented, as an expanding political force, not the realization of a theoretical programme but the natural centre of attraction and co-ordination of economic activities, of patrimonial interests, seigneurial and ecclesiastical ambitions and demographic growth. They also represented the natural epicentre of conflicts between classes and factions which involved both the city and the territory, and compromised the stability and institutional unity itself of the urban communal organism.

INSTITUTIONAL INSTABILITY AND THE STRUGGLE FOR POWER IN THE DOMINANT CITIES

In a large part of the Italian kingdom the city functioned in the communal period as a strong centre of attraction, as can be seen from the growth of the urban area itself, demonstrated everywhere by successive enlargements of the city walls. For Florence it has been calculated that the population grew in two centuries from several thousands to several tens of thousands of inhabitants.[65] Immigration to the city, fed by all the social classes of the contado,[66] complicated urban life. It supplied new clientèles for the *consorterie* into which the consular aristocracy was divided, drew into the conflicts between urban noble factions those powerful families which the commune had forced into association and citizenship, and spread even within the city the use of private towers for defence and attack (there were 150 at Florence at the beginning of the thirteenth century[67]), similar to those to which the immigrant seigneurial families were accustomed in their castles in the contado.[68] It introduced small and middling rural landowners into urban artisan activity, into trade, and into money-changing, contributing to the formation of guilds which were intended to protect the exercise of crafts, the small

---

[65] K. J. Beloch, *Bevölkerungsgeschichte Italiens* (Berlins, 1940), vol. 2, pp. 127ff. But see also E. Fiumi, 'La demografia fiorentina nelle pagine di Giovanni Villani', *Archivio storico italiano*, 108 (1950), pp. 78ff.

[66] G. Luzzatto, 'L'inurbamento della popolazioni rurali in Italia nei secoli XII e XIII' (1939), reprinted in *ibid.*, *Dai servi della gleba*, pp. 414ff.

[67] R. Davidsohn, *Forschungen zur Geschichte von Florenz*, vol. 1 (Berlin 1896, reprinted Turin, 1964), pp. 121ff; P. Santini, 'Società delle torri in Firenze', *Archivio storico italiano*, ser. IV, 20 (1887), pp. 25ff.; see B. Stahl, *Adel und Volk im Florentiner Dugento* (Cologne-Graz, 1965), p. 78.

[68] F. Niccolai, *I consorzi nobiliari ed il comune nell'alta e media Italia* (Bologna, 1940), pp. 40ff.

enterprises of workshop masters, and commercial enterprise, so that it helped greatly to change the shapeless *populus* of the eleventh century into a complex and vigorous, even though inharmonious, organization of interests. Immigration also increased the population of individual urban quarters and suburbs, permitting the development of aggressive armed popular companies based on the quarters, in reaction to the violence and guerrilla warfare of the nobles' *consorterie*.[69]

This growth of the city at every social level emphasized its internal tensions, in the same decades of the twelfth and thirteenth centuries when even the most recently formed urban communes were largely freeing themselves from all residual protection by or burdensome symbiosis with episcopal power. The Treaty of Constance in 1183 had appeared to confirm officially this episcopal protection in some instances, since it allowed that the responsibility to invest consuls chosen by the city belonged to the bishop rather than the emperor, whenever that reflected local custom and when the bishop held comital powers confirmed by a royal or imperial privilege.[70] As the commune took full political and jurisdictional authority over the city (and as a result the city controlled its *posse* in a more unitary fashion) new communal organs were created with specific roles, in addition to the 'consuls of the commune' and the *arengo* or general assembly of the citizenry. For example, the 'consuls of justice' appeared, and cities began increasingly to elect a single 'rector' or 'podestà' who would replace the 'consuls of the commune', or be placed over or alongside them; this practice was influenced by similar appointments previously made by the emperor. At first the podestà was mainly chosen from among the citizens themselves, up to the 1220s, and then normally among foreigners, as a better guarantee of impartiality.[71] But it was precisely in the first phase of the regime of the podestà, when he was of local extraction and alternated with the consuls, that the communal organism showed itself unable to represent politically the whole citizenry, now so much larger in numbers and ever more differentiated in social and economic terms. Thus one can say that the urban commune, even though it defined itself as *res publica* and functioned as a territorial organization, took almost a century to complete the construction of institutional arrangements of its own, with respect to the residual rivalry of episcopal power or comital or vicomital

[69] G. De Vergottini, 'Problemi di storia della costituzione comunale', *Rivista storica italiana*, 59 (1942), pp. 225–38; *Arti e popolo nelle prima metà del secolo XIII* (Milan, 1943).

[70] Manaresi, *Atti*, p. 199 c. 8.

[71] E. Cristiani, 'Le alternanze tra consoli e podestà ed i podestà cittadini', in *I problemi della civiltà comunale*, pp. 47ff.

power in the city.[72] But the commune reached this point only at a time when its institutions were already under violent attack from within the city's own structure; new forms of struggle among old factions were accompanied by an explosion of forces capable of generating foci of power with an entirely new structure, as if to show once again, after centuries of the free growth of political nuclei, how precarious any order would be which tried to enclose medieval society in a single organization of power.

The office of podestà, even though it was of short duration (usually lasting for one or two years, or even only six months), in fact represented the aim of creating a more efficient and more significant political focus for civic unity than the consulate had been. But this greater efficiency at the top was countered by the strengthening of the nobles' *consorterie*, fed by immigration, which was organized within the city itself in imitation of the urban 'commune', with their own 'rectors', 'consuls' or 'captains' or with their own 'podestà'.[73] These *consorterie* were strengthened by drawing up agreements, such as those made in 1179, 1180 and 1181 between the members of some of the towers in Florence,[74] agreements just as precise and rigorous in their definitions as were those drawn up for the alliances and peace treaties made in the contado between seigneurial families or between the latter and the commune. Hence the old urban quarrels among the nobles were transformed into harsher struggles, more dangerous for the life of the city. Thus juridical culture could work in two opposing directions in the operation of the collectivity, according to whether it was applied to the communal organism or to the individual groups of urban nobility, since it tended to confer cohesion on both the 'commune' and the forces that placed it in crisis.

It gave this cohesion not only to the forces that placed the commune in crisis from within the dominant aristocracy, but also to those forces that were vigorously growing up against the nobility. In fact it so happened that the class conflict already clear in Milan in the eleventh century, which had then seemed to be resolved through sworn agreements and in the creation of the consulate as a unifying leader by the side of the archbishop, broke out with equal force and with much greater effectiveness from the last years of the twelfth century onwards, and not only at Milan but extensively in the cities of the Italian kingdom

---

[72] See W. Goetz, *Le origini dei comuni italiani* (1944; Milan, 1965), pp. 100ff.
[73] Volpe, *Studi sulle istituzioni*, pp. 394ff.; Niccolai, *I consorzi nobiliari*, pp. 32ff.
[74] Niccolai, *I consorzi nobiliari*, pp. 155ff.

and the papal territory.[75] The *nobiles* or *milites* (*milites* in the sense of horsemen, contrasted to the *pedites*, the infantry which mostly coincides with the *populus* in the sources of the early thirteenth century[76]) had constituted in the tenth and eleventh centuries, under the seigneurial regime of the bishops or of some comital family, the framework that shaped the city's army, and this was still the case in the consular period and in the early period of the podestà. The *milites* were marked out by their type of military life and a rich base of landed property, following the whole aristocratic tradition of the Early Middle Ages. In the eleventh century they frequently used the institutions of vassalage and benefice to express their military traditions, their ties with the bishop and their bonds of internal solidarity, and in opposition to this class the rest of the population in Milan had already rebelled before the communal period began. In the twelfth century the *milites* in every city of the Italian kingdom were reinforced by the gradual immigration of *domini*, that is of the small and great rural lords (even in the cities such as Mantua which had been less oppressed by noble dominance or had been less completely incorporated into its system in the precommunal period[77]); the formation of *consorterie* also strengthened the *milites* as a class, and the *consorterie* were now accustomed to dispute the commune's magistracies among themselves. At Milan and elsewhere, at the end of the twelfth century and the beginning of the thirteenth, a large part of the remaining citizenry rebelled or offered resistance in various ways to these developments among the *milites*.

Not all the citizenry rebelled, however; for the mercantile and financial strata, even though now organized in their own guilds of merchants and money-changers and governed by their own 'consuls', remained intimately related to the noble *consorterie*, as in the period of the consular commune. It has been noted above that the consular aristocracy, understood as the political class from which the 'consuls of the commune' were recruited, had in many cities been formed above all by *capitanei* and *valvassores*, but that the richest merchants were also absorbed into it, and indeed at Genoa and Pisa, and to some extent also elsewhere, the activity of traders and arms merchants was not incompatible with membership of families and of associations of *milites*. Hence the wavering behaviour of the associations of the money-

[75] Davidsohn, *Forschungen*, vol. 4 (Berlin, 1908), pp. 8ff.; G. Franceschini, 'La vita sociale e politica nel duecento', in *Storia di Milano*, vol. 4, pp. 116ff.
[76] Volpe, *Studi sulle istituzioni*, p. 272 note 1.
[77] For the immigration of *domini* to Mantua see Torelli, *Un comune cittadino*, vol. 2 (Mantua, 1952), pp. 88ff, 103ff.

changers and merchants in the struggles between the nobles and people in the early podestarial period, at Milan as at Bologna, at Cremona as at Piacenza, at Florence as at Siena;[78] their hesitation did not detract from, but rather emphasized, the fully class-based nature of the social conflict, since those uncertainties reflected exactly the ambiguous social position of the class that dominated commerce in goods and money.

A further complication in the class struggle of the early thirteenth century was the frequent presence of nobles at the head of the popular movement. This had already occurred in the eleventh century at Milan at the time of Lanzo, a *capitaneus* warring against *capitanei*, and simply meant that in the course of the struggle the non-noble population needed to choose leaders of a militarily more expert class, exploiting the latter's internal discord. Besides, the conflict between the noble factions competing for political dominance could not be kept apart from class conflict, which was a sign of social tension but also took place at a purely political level. This was particularly the case since opposition to the noble class was fed by the need to check the violence with which the *consorterie* struggled to obtain power in the commune; in this connection we need only consider the years of guerrilla warfare, barricades and fires which afflicted Florence from 1177 to 1179, when the *consorteria* of the Uberti rose up against the long dominance of the coalition led by the Donati.[79] On the other hand the popular desire for a political presence, which was intended to force the nobles to adopt new methods of struggling for power, was usually complicated by a specific request for effective participation in city government and a balanced division of communal offices. Sometimes this request was translated into a complete, though still temporary, conquest of the communal institutions by the people; this happened at Piacenza in 1220, when the *milites* abandoned the city, and only returned more than a year later, thanks to the peacemaking intervention of a papal legate.[80]

The opposition between the *pars populi* and the *pars nobilium* can thus be interpreted in some respects as the intervention of popular forces in the struggles for access to the governing organs of the communal *res publica*. But it is not this which represents the peculiar feature of the popular struggle, a feature that distinguishes it from any other historical situation ancient or modern and which sets it among the exceptional political experiences characteristic of the central centuries of the Middle Ages. The peculiarity of that struggle, for a large part of the thirteenth

[78] De Vergottini, *Arti e popolo*, pp. 43ff, 81ff; Stahl, *Adel und volk*, pp. 130ff.
[79] Stahl, *Adel und Volk*, pp. 59ff.
[80] De Vergottini, 'Problemi di storia', pp. 234ff, *Arti e popolo*, pp. 6ff.

century, lay in the ways in which a complex armed organization of the 'people' (*popolo*) began to take shape and operate politically in every city. The *popolo* developed into an autonomous power, that coexisted with the 'communal' power and was capable of self-government and extensive action in the city; it was therefore institutionally ambiguous with respect to the 'commune'. It could not be seen as simply an instrument of rivalry with the nobles, aiming to introduce the popular classes into the 'commune's' institutions as they were already constituted and officially operating in the name of the city. The nobles' urban *consorterie*, continuing or repeating in a new form the seigneurial experiences of the tenth and eleventh centuries, shaped themselves in the second half of the twelfth century into autonomous centres of power, as they contended among themselves for control of official civic power; in the same way, the *popolo* appeared on the political scene, in imitation of the seigneurial groups, as a body with its own military strength, able to produce immediately effective discipline of its members, direct the confrontation with the noble *consorterie*, and establish a more or less organic relationship with the offical power of the civic *res publica*. And in this capacity to organize itself with its own particular form and its own statutes, the *popolo* made use of that same legal culture which tended contradictorily to confer cohesion both on the 'commune' and on the 'associations' of nobles.

But what was this formation of the 'people'? It did not arise from some sudden transmutation of a shapeless population into a unitary body. It had its roots in associations already active in the economic sector or in pre-existing geographical or military divisions of the city, associations of craftsmen and divisions of city quarters, which around 1200 were already exerting pressure on the nobles and the commune even in those places where they had not yet merged into a unitary organization. A well-known example illustrates how it was possible to arrive at an organization of the *popolo*.

At Bologna an ephemeral federation of 'guilds' (*arti*) is first recorded in 1228, when its leader, a powerful merchant, and the rectors of the artisan' societies entered the palace of the commune while the people were rioting, and asked the podestà to give the 'communal council' a broader base; both the 'consuls of the merchants' and the 'consuls of the money-changers' thus took no direct part in the action. The requests were refused and the guilds reacted by breaking up tables and chests, destroying registers, and occupying the palace. This violent action forced the commune to set up a 'general council' alongside the pre-existing one, now called the 'special council'. This revolutionary action had certainly broken out suddenly, but it had been preceded and was followed for decades by initiatives and agitation from both the guilds and the armed companies based in the city districts. After 1228 the *popolo* of Bologna reassembled in such a way that it also appears as a unification of the armed companies; the latter, except for the presence of some nobles, had the same social base as the guilds that were confederated in the first formation of the *popolo*, but differed from them in the forms of association and in their immediate military purpose. The *popolo* then organized itself under a council of 'anziani', in which the federated guilds and the armed companies both took part, and linked itself in its turn by a further oath of federation with the powerful guilds of the merchants and money-changers, who were still governed by their own consuls.[81] Soon after the middle of the thirteenth century a 'captain of the popolo' and a 'council of the popolo' were created, to co-ordinate and unify this whole complex of societies; the organization as a whole not only became so powerful that it influenced decisively the activity of the commune, which was still governed by its podestà and general and special councils, but it also took on a completely official position in open symbiosis with the commune itself in the exercise of civic powers. It was then that the nobles, more than one of whom had already been operating in the armed companies, infiltrated the guilds as well, intensifying their own presence in the *popolo* as it became more organized, while the commune of the podestà became politically weaker. In their turn the formations of the *popolo*, especially the armed companies, became involved in the continuous struggles between the noble *consorterie*, which were party struggles connected with the great Italian factions that used the names of Guelf and Ghibelline.

Here was a typically medieval tangle, formed not only of ambitions, interests and forces but of institutions of differing and sometimes very uncertain stability. Thus the communal period continued, in the heart of the dominant cities themselves, the stormy centuries-long process of adjusting political power to social developments by continually creating new structures. As always, the process rested on customary practice and competition, but now, in the thirteenth century, there was a far more conscious commitment to legal definition and determination by statute, even though this still failed to check the alarming fluidity of institutions. The emerging structure of the *popolo* faced a double constitutional problem within the interplay of extremely disparate pressures and stimuli; on the one hand there was the problem of its formation as a

---

[81] G. Fasoli, *Le compagnie delle armi a Bologna* (Bologna, 1933), pp. 11ff, *Le compagnie della arti a Bologna fino al principio del secolo XV* (Bologna, 1936), pp. 6ff; De Vergottini, *Arti e popolo*, pp. 15ff.

political body out of different societies, which despite their confluence in the *popolo* retained their own organs and autonomous operation, and on the other hand there was the problem of its juxtaposition with and introduction, by means of certain of its organs such as the 'anziani', the 'captain of the popolo' and certain 'councils', into the context of the organized urban forces and the 'communal' government.

This highly fluid interplay of institutions should not be confused with certain ambiguous formations – both of the state and factional in character – which arise from the violent but imperfect union of distinct bodies; these latter formations are found as part of political experiments both in ancient times and quite recently, and, indeed, in some contemporary political contexts as well. The medieval structures were both composite and mutable. Their distinguishing characteristic was the completely spontaneous interaction of a multiplicity of armed movements (visible, for example, in the public towers and the towers of the *popolo* and the *consorterie*), by which they were incessantly generated and altered. And this process took place not through the simple *coups de main* of a small inner circle, but through a lasting bond with very specific interests of classes or broad factions, even though this bond often took unpredictable and flexible forms. These classes and factions were groups that were powerful because of their economic strength or social importance; no institutional force could constrain them to compete in a fashion that would respect a stable constitutional framework. As yet there was no political apparatus with such institutional force, even though in the thirteenth century the idea of the *res publica* coinciding with the city was flourishing. The concept appears to underlie part of the urban legislation, as well as to operate in the network of conventions which had subjected the churches and lords scattered over the dependent territory of the city (the *posse*) to the payment of the *fodrum*, to the control of superior jurisdiction and to a loyalty which implied participation in the military defence of the dominant city against other *res publicae*. One may wonder how, in the conditions of conflict in the city, it was possible to develop a general civic capacity for defence, and indeed for expansion and territorial domination. But here, within limits, a certain solidarity emerged between the urban forces even though they were struggling amongst themselves for power; their solidarity was fed not only by the myth of a common fatherland, but also by the practical convergence of the interests of merchants, artisans and nobles. While the ambitions of powerful families with a knightly tradition were satisfied by the exercise of public activities which fitted their military calling, such as guarding fortresses belonging to the commune and managing the commune's war operations and the diplomatic negotiations connected

with them,[82] the merchants and financiers in their turn needed freedom
of transit and a communal prestige that would protect them even in
distant lands. The artisans, like the *cives* in general, saw the political
expansion of the city as improving conditions for the distribution of
their products and as the best guarantee for the provisioning of the
city.[83] On the other hand civic solidarity had very clear limits, even in
the face of the enemies of the city. In 1275, according to information
collected by the Florentine chronicler Giovanni Villani, the Bolognese
were defeated by the Romagnoli when their cavalry abandoned the
battle 'almost without striking a blow', because the *popolo* of Bologna
'treated the nobles badly'.[84] It is well known, besides, that the harshness
of the political conflict and the tendency of hostile groups to act
autonomously produced links between the factions of different, rival,
cities, which made use of the models offered throughout Italy by the
great conflict between the Swabian imperial dynasty and the papacy,
Guelf versus Ghibelline. The factions which were expelled from their
own cities were thus able to pursue political and military activity with
the support of castles in the contado and of the allied forces of other cities.

   The extreme complexity of this picture has provoked a lively debate
among historians over the interpretation of these factional struggles,
ever since Gaetano Salvemini's emphasis, at the end of the last century,
on the ideological inconsistency of Guelfism and Ghibellinism (which
echo through all the chronicles of the Italian communal cities) and on the
divergence of those factions from the contemporary class conflict, which
he considered to be primarily based on the opposition of the interests of
nobles, as landowners, and those of the bourgeoisie, as consumers of
agricultural produce.[85] During a debate which has lasted for decades, the
polemic against schematic interpretations has sometimes led to the
emptying of meaning of the very concepts of nobility and people, as if
they were (or became in the course of the thirteenth century) merely

---

[82] See L. Salvatorelli, 'La politica interna di Perugia in un poemetto volgare della
       metà del Trecento', *Bollettino della Deputazione di storia patria per l'Umbria*, 50
       (1953), pp. 5–110; Franceschini, 'Vita sociale e politica', p. 333; N. Ottokar,
       Il comune di Firenze alla fine del dugento (1926, 2nd ed. Turin, 1962), pp. 97ff;
       G. Martini, *Siena da Montaperti alla caduta dei Nove* (Siene, 1961), p. 47; E.
       Cristiani, *Nobiltà e popolo nel comune di Pisa* (Naples, 1962), pp. 135ff.

[83] See F. Carli, *Storia del commercio italiano II: Il mercato nell'età del comune*
       (Padua, 1936), pp. 263ff; G. Luzzatto, *Storia economica d'Italia: il medioevo*,
       (2nd ed. 1963, reprinted Florence, 1967), pp. 152ff.

[84] G. Villani, *Cronica*, I. VII, c.48 (Florence, 1823), vol. 2, p. 219.

[85] G. Salvemini, *Magnati e popolani in Firenze dal 1280 al 1295* (1899; new ed.
       Turin, 1960), pp. 48ff.

names intended, in the same way as Guelfism and Ghibellinism, or the Florentine 'White Guelfs' and 'Black Guelfs' of the time of Dante, to cover the complex conflict between powerful families, each with a following of clientèles.[86] The arrival of the regime of the *popolo* in the various cities, rivalling or replacing the regime of the podestà, would then lose any class significance, particularly if one considers the powerful families of the *popolo* (whose structures were not very different from those of the noble *consorterie*), and the way they designed electoral practices to maintain their dominance in the institutions of the *popolo*, which had become instruments for their ambitions. But how can it be seriously argued that class was not a significant element in this conflict? Without doubt, it was never purely on the basis of class; one thinks, for example, of the traditions of associations extremely hostile towards each other, or of the interests of the different sectors represented by the individual guilds, which not uncommonly involved deep divergencies and open opposition, as well as of the hostility between certain of the armed companies based in the city quarters. But a constant point of reference in the conflict throughout the thirteenth century was the ostentatious and repeatedly-denounced arrogance of the 'nobles and great men', and the most difficult problem for the formations of the *popolo* was the impossibility of doing without the aid of the 'nobles and knights', who provoked disagreements and inextinguishable violence but who were expert in war operations and peace negotiations, accustomed to command and to the pragmatic compromises of peace.

The military style of life which marked out the nobility was in keeping with the idea, valid for so many previous centuries, of political power as the capacity to constrain and exercise dominion, over the *rustici* as over the *cives*, even if in reality the dominion became less rigorous and uniform as the clashing centres of such power became more numerous. And the nobility, precisely because it was the political class,[87] also had its own particular position in the 'economic system', which is sufficient to characterize it. In examining this position, we should consider not only the extent of cultivated and uncultivated land in the nobility's

[86] Ottokar, *Il comune di Firenze*; Cristiani, *Nobiltà e popolo*. See G. Masi, 'La struttura social della fazioni politiche fiorentine ai tempi di Dante', extract from the *Giornale dantesco*, 31 (Florence, 1930); J. C. Marie-Vigueur, 'Les Institutions communales de Pise aux XIIe et XIIIe siècles', *Le Moyen Âge*, 79 (1973), pp. 519ff.

[87] See, on the nobles' conviction 'that through hereditary privilege they were the repository of the right to administer power', M. Luzzatti, 'Le origini di una famiglia nobile pisana: Roncioni nei secoli XII e XIII', *Bullettino senese di storia patria*, 73–5 (1966–8), p. 67.

allodial and feudal possession, but the operation of the peasant population in areas which were largely still dominated by different local lords, even when the latter were often resident in the city. In short, these lordships formed a flexible framework for villages and rural communities not only as centres of settlement but as centres of a specific type of labour and production. The exploitation of the peasants through the imposition of banal rights arising from the seigneurial *honour* and *districtus*, rather than through requests for heavy agricultural rents, testifies to the exceptionally 'political' nature of the 'economic' bases of so much of the nobles' power. This economic basis permitted the nobles to broaden their sphere of action in the cities, build up clientèles of urban and rural origins, take over responsible positions in ecclesiastical bodies and religious communities (new sources for social elevation and enrichment of families, with further complications of vassalage and feudal ties), and construct efficient kinship consortia and broader *consorterie*, sometimes linking together areas within the city and the edge of the contado itself by means of a network of strongholds.[88] This confused and dissonant pattern of noble powers found itself at the same time both in perennial tension with the communal movements of the rural population and in violent conflict with the armed groups and societies of the guilds of the *popolo*. The simultaneous appearance of these problems was not translated into convergent and coherent action, since the powerful nobles, in the contado and in the city, did not always merge their interests with those of the nobility still resident in the contado, but it was displayed in the repeated interventions by the city to free the serfs *de persona* and *de terra*, for example in the great manumissions decided on in 1257 at Bologna and in 1289 at Florence, during the political dominance of the *popolo* and the guilds.[89] Although these manumissions were often prompted by the conflict between the city and seigneurial dynasties, they weakened the structures of rural domination as a whole, and favoured a social and economic osmosis between countryside and city. In short, they were certainly part of a spontaneous process of liberation from the bonds of servitude, a process linked with the confused multiplication of rival nuclei of power, but they were also significant in the general struggle, both rural and urban, against a centuries-old hegemonic seigneurial structure.

[88] See R. Frankovich, *Geografia storica delle sedi umane. I castelli del contado fiorentino nei secoli XII e XIII*, Università di Firenze, Facoltà di Magistero, Atti dell'Istituto di geografia 3 (Florence, 1973), pp. 75ff.

[89] Leicht, *Operai*, pp. 136ff; E. Fiumi, 'Fioritura e decadenza dell'economia fiorentina, II: Demografia e movimento urbanistico', *Archivio storico italiano*, 116 (1958), pp. 485ff. See Ottokar, *Il comune di Firenze*, pp. 187ff.

The subsequent emergence from the non-noble strata of powerful new families, which tended to remain within the organizations of the *popolo* but which none the less showed strong tendencies to imitate the noble *consorterie* by enlarging their own landed base and sometimes forming armed clientèles and erecting towers, undoubtedly altered the pure significance of the *popolo* as the instrument of a class conflict; it strengthened the presence in the *popolo* of elements which were not popular, elements which had already been introduced through the exigencies of the struggle. But the problems of the 'nobles and great men', and of their vocation for the monopoly of political power, were not forgotten as a result. Indeed the struggle became further inflamed, even though it took place within an extraordinary confusion of forces. In the second half of the thirteenth century it led to the daring anti-magnate legislation, which spread from one city to another with the aim of excluding from any responsibility in government what was in fact the political class *par excellence*, the 'great', or 'magnates', or 'powerful', or, as they were usually still called, the *milites* and *nobiles*; the variety of names mirrored the clear absence of a legal definition.[90] The exceptions that the various anti-magnate laws made, in favour of a series of noble families which had placed themselves on the side of the *popolo*, as well as in favour of the powerful individuals who already belonged to the *popolo* by origin or by previous admission, ultimately give the impression that the criterion for exclusion from the organs of city government, of the *popolo* and of the 'commune', rested on an opposition between *popolo* and magnates which was now fictitious, and which was suggested only by the hatred between factions which were without any specific social orientation. This aspect was certainly present, since we are dealing with conflicts that ranged powerful *consorterie* against each other, but it does not account completely for that opposition; the abundant range of measures which attacked the 'magnates' in their political rights and freedom of action, even if they did not include them all, still characterized them according to the criteria of military nobility, with some stress on the possession of strongholds or the rank of knight, and on the reputation of being 'great',[91] all of which had already been features characteristic of the noble *consorterie* of the early thirteenth century. The base-line of action of the organized *popolo* thus remained constant, and with all the more reason since the *consorterie* in the course of the century revealed themselves, despite everything, to be very strong and sometimes took the form of associations of exceptional breadth.

[90] G. Fasoli, 'Ricerche sulla legislazione antimagnatizia nei comuni dell'alta e media Italia', *Rivista di storia del diritto italiano*, 12 (1939), pp. 53ff.

[91] *Ibid.*, pp. 55ff; Cristiani, *Nobiltà e popolo*, p. 90ff.

This was so particularly in the case of the purest and oldest nobility, such as the Gualandi, Sismondi and Upezzinghi at Pisa;[92] they could not be confused with the new powerful families of the *popolo*, whose mercantile origin was mostly well-known, even when they were also rich in land.

Ottokar, disputing the old model of Salvemini, argued that at Florence in the last decades of the thirteenth century the struggle against the magnates was at the centre of the internal life of the city; he explained the Ordinances of Justice of 1293 as being the result of a broad popular movement, which did indeed aim at violent persecution of the 'magnates', but which attributed to them all the negative features of a governmental oligarchy which in the years immediately preceding had in reality been largely formed by powerful members of the *Arti maggiori* (first among them the dominant guild of the merchants and bankers, called the Calimala). In fact, between 1293 and 1295 the principal families of the Arte di Calimala were indeed included among the more than seventy urban 'magnate' families which were proscribed from political life.[93] But this only demonstrates that the concept of 'magnate' was also being extended to the most overbearing elements of the *popolo*: membership of the guilds was no longer sufficient to safeguard the 'influential', who were in any case often descended from noble families or linked to them through kinship, friendship, and above all, business. And so the legislation against the magnates was truly part of a class conflict, and included under that designation political groups which in social terms certainly qualified, through the solidarity which bound them to magnates, even if they did not always descend from the *pars nobilium* of the beginning of the century and even if they differed from the latter by being less clearly distinct from the organisms and guilds which flowed together into the *popolo*.

On this subject, to go back in time, it should be clearly emphasized that the 'nobility' from which the 'magnates' – within and outside the official organisms of the *popolo* – only partly derived, was linked in its turn with the tradition of the military and political aristocracy of the High Middle Ages, but despite this it did not constitute *ab antiquo* a 'legal class' which was formally hereditary and externally protected by ancestral privileges, as has often been assumed in the past. The aristocracy of the Early Middle Ages knew no formal boundaries except the reputation of 'greatness' of each family, following the model of a

[92] Luzzatti, 'Origini dei Roncioni', p. 35. See Cristiani, *Nobiltà e popolo*, pp. 370ff.

[93] R. Davidsohn, *Storia di Firenze*, vol. 2.2 (Florence, 1957), pp. 633ff; Ottokar, *Il comune di Firenze*, pp. 159ff, 199ff; Stahl, *Adel und Volk*, pp. 174ff.

'strength' which was visible in dominion over rural populations and military clientèles, in the possession of fortresses and churches, and in possible ties of vassalage with the more powerful. In short, as a concept it was not very different (when one leaves aside problems of ancestry and includes among such power bases also the towers and clientèles of the 'great' in the city) from the 'magnates and powerful men' who were attacked by the legislation of the *popolo* at the end of the thirteenth century; indeed, those old nobles had already often been called *magnati* and *potentes*. But something had changed in the twelfth and thirteenth centuries with the flood of new seigneurial elements from the contado, and with the tendency noted above towards the stiffening of distinctions between the lesser *popolo* and the great into opposition between organized bodies. On one side seigneurial clans were absorbed into *consorterie* and federations of *consorterie*, often included overall in a *societas militum*, while on the other the companies of arms and of the guilds were in various ways also federated to and associated with the mercantile guilds in a general *societas populi*. This new capacity brought about a social conflict of a persistence, political dimension and breadth such as had not been known for more than a millennium in Italy, and such as was not to be known again after the struggles of the late fourteenth century for at least four centuries.

Clear instances of the creation of official and legal boundaries for the urban nobility coincided markedly with the tracing of more rigorous definitions of clan groups. At Milan, for example, where political and social processes seem to anticipate those of other cities by some decades, the opposition between the 'credenza di S. Ambrogio', an organization of the *popolo* which had arisen since 1198, and the association of the nobles (with the 'Motta' manoeuvring between the two, probably acting as a focal point linking minor dissident nobility and mercantile families) was expressed in controversies not only over the division of fiscal burdens and of the powers of government, but also over the custom of admitting into the cathedral chapter almost no one other than members of the families of *capitanei* or their vassals. This question concerned the archbishop and his canons for decades and led in 1277, when the nobility dominated the city in association with Archbishop Otto Visconti, to the redaction of a *matricule nobilium familiarum Mediolani*, which included 189 families to which was guaranteed the privilege of being able to accede to the Metropolitan See.[94] This privilege, too, except for the additions and exclusions suggested by

[94] Franceschini, 'Vita sociale e politica', pp. 119ff, 288ff, 331ff; A. Bosisio, 'Milano e la sua coscienza cittadina nel duecento', in *La coscienza cittadina nei comuni italiani del duecento* (Todi, 1971), pp. 56ff.

factional criteria, essentially descended from the powerful families' traditions of command, but until then it had never been so precisely defined; and this took place at a time when elsewhere in Italy the popular movement seemed to burst out of the limits of its own organization, and to concentrate in the concept of nobility a hatred of every oligarchic tendency and every privilege connected with it.

These were opposing orientations in a complex society, whose capacity for elaborating new models of action revealed broad and disquieting perspectives.

6

PROCESSES OF STATE FORMATION IN ITALY DURING THE DECLINE OF THE POLITICAL-SOCIAL DIALECTIC

·

FORMS OF UNITARY RULE IN SOUTHERN ITALY

While the fortresses and cities of the Italic kingdom became bases for autonomous power, in a period of development which was both communal and feudal, and brought about the exhaustion of the vigorous political experiments of the imperial Staufer dynasty, southern Italy saw the growth of its own peculiar royal power. This power was, in legal terms, created in 1130 by a papal decision, but was in reality constructed by the dynasty which in the course of the eleventh century had taken on the leadership of the nuclei of adventurers who had arrived from Normandy and entered the highly fragmented milieu of the Mezzogiorno. The coronation of the Norman Roger II took place at Palermo in 1130. Ten years later he was already responsible for a law code, although this has come down to us in a controversial text which may have undergone amendment in the thirteenth century.[1] The very fact of a commitment to co-ordinated legislation appearing in the Norman kingdom of Sicily and southern Italy in the middle of the twelfth century is such a novelty in the European West, after the Carolingian period, that it arouses considerable surprise in historians, all the more so in that the so-called *assisae regum regni Siciliae*, the laws of

---

[1] See L. R. Ménager, 'La législation sud-italienne sous la domination normande', in *I Normanni e la loro espansione in Europa nell'alto medioevo* (Spoleto, 1969), pp. 461ff, with the related discussion on pp. 601ff. See now also the *Atti del Congresso internazionale di studi sulla Sicilia normanna* (Palermo, 1973).

the kingdom promulgated as a body in the twelfth century, were flanked, no less remarkably, by a network of central and local officials, which guaranteed political and juridical control and considerable revenues, kept under firm control the aspirations of lords and cities for autonomy, and began the development of a state, covering the whole of southern Italy, from the Abruzzi to Sicily. This state took on the shape of a true monarchical absolutism in the first half of the thirteenth century under Frederick II of Swabia, grandson of Barbarossa, of the family which had succeeded the Norman dynasty in 1190 through the well-calculated marriage of Henry VI, son of Barbarossa.

The problem can be resolved by considering both the traditions of the Normans and the ethnic, social and cultural conditions of southern Italy. The Vikings who settled in Normandy among the Frankish population at the beginning of the tenth century, thus introducing themselves into the kingdom of Francia as 'guardians' of the northern coasts of the kingdom, gave birth to a duchy in which political power, even though the result of large-scale pillage and perhaps precisely because of its recent origins in simple aggression, was much firmer than elsewhere in repressing violence and plunder and in controlling its own representatives, the powerful viscounts, to whom the duke entrusted the custody of the territories of the duchy and of his own fortresses.[2] In Normandy, as elsewhere in post-Carolingian Europe, castles built by seigneurial initiative were springing up in the first half of the eleventh century, but their multiplication was checked; the military aristocracy, after some attempts at rebellion, found its equilibrium as loyal vassals of the ducal power, obliged as *milites* to do knightly service and as a result remunerated in general by benefices. All of this was in accordance with Carolingian tradition, to which the Norman duchy tied itself despite the foreign origin of its founders. The aristocracy found its equilibrium, indeed, in fealty to a dynasty which in 1066 led it to the conquest of England, and the reorganization of the kingdom in which the vassal fealty of the Norman barons, enriched with fiefs in the island, was modified by the royal and social traditions of the Anglo-Saxons, by the public obligations of judicial subordination and military service and by the duties of free men as a whole towards the public power.[3]

Thus in the Norman tradition in France and in its transposition to England there was a model for a political schema in which seigneurial

[2] J. Yver, 'Les Premières Institutions du duché de Normandie', in *I Normanni e la loro espansione*, pp. 299ff.

[3] J. Le Patourel, 'The Norman Colonization of Britain', in *I Normanni e la loro espansione*, pp. 409ff; A. Marongiu, 'I due regni normanni d'Inghilterra e d'Italia', *ibid.*, pp. 504ff.

development remained within an exceptionally strong network of vassal obligations, and found its limits and its complement in the direct relationship between the duke and his subjects as a whole. When we consider the origin of the Norman nuclei of Italy and the cordial relations which the kingdom of Sicily maintained with England in the twelfth century, we can easily recognize the effectiveness of a common tradition in which the dominant motive, north and south of the English Channel and in the Mediterranean, was the need of the conquerors to transform themselves into a stable apparatus of power. Hence the solidarity between local military aristocracies and their ruler and their acceptance of the latter's territorial dominance, thanks to long experience of the pirate enterprises and war which for centuries had characterized the world of the Vikings and its extension in the form of the Normans.

However this common tradition did not assume identical forms in the various regions where it existed. In Italy the Norman kingdom had its stable capital at Palermo, a centre once prevalently Muslim, and controlled territories which, though they had different cultures, were chiefly oriented, in their conception of a supreme political power, towards Byzantium. Around Roger II, who was a man of culture well beyond what was then normal for the education of princes and the military aristocracy in the West, Arabs and Greeks worked side by side with Normans and Latins, both at the cultural level and, above all, on the political and administrative level.[4] Hence the particular form taken on by the Norman domination in Italy compared with the Normans of France and England. The apparatus of power was based on concepts of monarchy strongly inspired by the East, with the ostentatious use of pomp in the royal court and in the presence of Arab and Greek titles, from the admiral to the protochamberlain and the logothete, alongside Frankish and Latin ones, and with a legislative ambition and a capacity to organize a central bureaucracy such as could not yet be found elsewhere in the West.

All this was used eclectically, in both the symbolism of power and the ordering of offices, to bind together under the rule of the king populations which were very different from each other. They were different by faith and by rite, and included Christians of the Latin and the Greek rites (with the corresponding development of Benedictine

---

[4] E. Caspar, *Roger II (1101–54) und die Gründung der normannisch–sicilischen Monarchie* (1904, reprinted Darmstadt, 1968), pp. 37ff, 435ff; F. Chalandon, *Histoire de la domination normande en Italie et en Sicile* (1907, reprinted New York, 1960), vol. 2, pp. 98ff, 708ff; R. Herval, 'Eclectisme intellectuel à la cour de Roger II de Sicile', in *Atti del Congresso internazionale di studi ruggeriani* (Palermo, 1955), vol. 1, pp. 73ff.

monasticism and the persisting and powerful Basilian monasticism[5]) and Muslims, with a strong Jewish minority as well. They were different in their language, speaking Romance dialects, Arabic and Greek, and in ethnic origin and legal customs; here it is worth emphasizing the considerable presence of the Lombard people, formerly subordinate to the Byzantine province of Apulia or grouped into the autonomous Lombard principalities. But above all they were different in their political and social customs, ranging from the Latin and Greek populations of Sicily previously for a long time under the firm control of the Arabs, to the cities of Apulia and Campania, accustomed throughout the eleventh century to make decisions for themselves quite freely. The court of Palermo superimposed itself over this complex of peoples, culturally heterogeneous and with very different levels of social activity, with remarkable tolerance for the diversity of religious and legal usages but with the clear intention of imposing a unitary political discipline. This intention was signalled even by the distinctions made between types of land in every region of the kingdom. Firstly there were the allodial ecclesiastical lands, with generous privileges according to the usual models in the West, and the autonomous temporal jurisdictions of bishops and abbots.[6] Secondly, the feudal seigneurial lands were linked with territorial powers that extended beyond them but remained mostly without geographical continuity; they varied greatly in extent, from the counties, which also included cities, to baronies, including at least one castle, down to the fiefs of ordinary knights. Thirdly there were the lands of the demesne, where they were numerous, together with the lands belonging to the fisc, castles and cities; here any seigneurial intermediary between the subjects and the king was excluded.

The demesne lands, which had an important urban component, were interwoven with the feudal and ecclesiastical territories in a manner which would seem at first little different from the dense thicket of civic and seigneurial jurisdictions of imperial Italy. In reality, however, there were profound differences. The cities which were immediately dependent on the king, even though they had often, at least in Apulia and Campania, drawn up pacts with the Normans which guaranteed local customs and autonomous government, found their own freedom of action strictly limited by restrictive and partial interpretations of these agreements, for example through the subsequent royal claim to distinguish between good customs and *malae et pravae* customs; in the

[5] A. Guillou, 'Inchiesta sulla popolazione greca della Sicilia e della Calabria nel medio evo', *Rivista storica italiana*, 75 (1963) pp. 55ff, 'Grecs d'Italie', pp. 87, 94ff; Borsari, *Il monachesimo bizantino*, pp. 82ff.

[6] C. Cahen, *Le Régime féodal de l'Italie normande* (Paris, 1940), pp. 127ff.

end, the city officials of various denominations, judges and turmarcs, catepans and *strategoi*, even when they were locally elected, came also to acquire the character of representatives of the king and to depend on his official nomination.[7] On the other hand, a network of bailiffs in charge of small local districts, and of provincial chamberlains and justiciars, was gradually introduced into all the regions of the kingdom to exercise in the king's name general rights of control and appeal, high justice and taxation, as well as the administration of fiscal property. They were in direct subordination to the court of Palermo and operated in circumscriptions which tended to possess a certain stability and territorial coherence, so that each one might include, together with lands and cities of the demesne, feudal territories and perhaps ecclesiastical lordships. The provincial officials were often chosen from among the most loyal vassals, who were equipped with feudal property and seigneurial jurisdiction in the same regions where they exercised by royal delegation the office of justiciars and chamberlains,[8] thus there was no fundamental conflict between this newly formed royal bureaucracy and the feudal fabric of much of the kingdom. But there was no confusion at all between the exercise of functions temporarily delegated by royal authority and the exercise of that power which, in the legal forms of the fief and the allod, had become part of the patrimony of seigneurial families and ecclesiastical bodies. The power of feudatories and prelates was exercised in its turn through agents who (as with the bailiffs, for example) were chosen and acted in a manner parallel to that of the royal officials in charge of demesne lands or districts of the kingdom; this was particularly the case in cities belonging to feudal or episcopal lords, where local *strategoi*, viscounts and catepans were nominated by their lords. It appears that alongside these latter officials the court of Palermo placed urban judges, who were, once again, nominated by the king even though they might have been elected locally.[9]

In short, the Norman kingdom did not create a uniform system of government, but none the less the royal presence was assured everywhere, with varying intensity, over prelates, barons and cities. It was a political system constructed empirically through the simultaneous and constant use, in very different forms, of royal agents, vassal relationships, and traditional ties with the churches. At any rate it was certainly a system, since the heterogeneous means employed did not

[7] Calasso, *La legislazione statutaria*, vol. 1, pp. 61ff; G. De Vergottini, *Il diritto pubblico italiano nei secoli XII–XV* (Milan, 1959), vol. 2, pp. 64ff; M. Caravale, *Il regno normanno di Sicilia* (Milan, 1966), pp. 325ff.

[8] Cahen, *Le Régime féodal*, p. 113; Caravale, *Il regno di Sicilia*, pp. 234, 240ff.

[9] Caravale, *Il regno di Sicilia*, pp. 356ff, 378ff.

remain simply juxtaposed: they were integrated and, in principle, co-ordinated in the ways indicated above, and all together enabled the royal court to express its paramount will. Such a system does not permit a simple solution to the current historical debate as to whether the kingdom was 'feudal' or a 'bureaucratic state', because both the method of using the personal loyalties of an ecclesiastical and lay aristocracy, privileged and respected by the king in its economic base and its autonomy, and the method of government exercised by replaceable agents both at the centre and on the periphery were equally important to the kingdom. It is, however, certain that the kingdom of Sicily, despite its approximate and sometimes contradictory developments, was both much more 'feudal' and 'bureaucratic' in tendency than was Italy under the Empire in the same century, whether before, during or after Barbarossa. This was so notwithstanding the fact that even in the chaos of the Italian kingdom there were impulses in both of these directions, coming sometimes from the emperors, but more often from more local centres.

The Norman kingdom of Sicily can be interpreted as a military dominion which was developing in the direction of a state; this gives us a means of understanding the central role which feudal institutions maintained in the kingdom despite the remarkable apparatus that was emerging. In fact the hierarchy of vassal loyalties formed the structure of this kingdom seen as a military dominion, that is, of the kingdom in its original form, resulting from the conquest. None the less, not even on the military level was the arrangement of the kingdom entirely feudal. Not all the knights owed military service in exchange for a fief conceded by the king or by a baron or a count, according to the customs that the Normans had brought from northern France; there were also *milites* who were bound to provide mounted military service on the basis of an allodial landed possession, through a custom which dated back to Lombard or Byzantine traditions,[10] just as in the kingdom of England during the same period Anglo-Saxon traditions of the military service of free men persisted side by side with the Norman feudal knighthood.[11] All the same it remained true that the Norman court of Sicily conceived the military strength of the kingdom in a perspective which was essentially feudal, so much so that the 'Catalogue of the barons', that is, a register of those among the vassals of the king who had vassals in their

[10] Cahen, *Le Régime féodal*, pp. 123ff.
[11] M. Powicke, *Military Obligation in Medieval England* (Oxford, 1962), pp. 31ff; C. W. Hollister, *The Military Organization of Norman England* (Oxford, 1965), pp. 268ff; 'Military Obligation in Late-Saxon and Norman England', in *Ordinamenti militari*, vol. 1, pp. 184ff.

turn and who brought the king a number of knights proportionate to the size of the barony, also included those *milites* who owed service as a burden on their allods, and thus there was a tendency to assimilate such patrimonies to the knightly fiefs.

This kind of general registration of the services due to the king in war demonstrates the methodical way in which the royal court was capable of proceeding in the most delicate areas. Similarly in the field of the fisc, relying on the Sicilian–Muslim and Italic–Byzantine traditions of land cadasters, it was able to organize central offices called *dohanae*, responsible for administration of fiscal goods and the collection of all the king's revenues, in the same period in which Barbarossa was extorting contributions in central and northern Italy intermittently and often haphazardly. The feudal organization of the militia and the meticulous administration of the property of the fisc were the most notable instances and the strongest instruments of royal efficiency. This efficiency was such that, between 1154 and 1160 in the reign of Roger II's successor William I, when the central government was ruled by his chancellor and 'great admiral of admirals' Maione (son of a royal 'protojudge' of Bari) it began to look as if the kingdom was moving towards tyranny, with more than a slight shade of the Orient – a sumptuous life and eunuchs at court, together with a rich literary, intellectual and artistic culture. A dangerous tension arose between the high bureaucracy of the capital – within which and on which there worked the most diverse elements, from Muslim functionaries to the archbishop of Palermo and other members of the insular and continental upper clergy of the kingdom – and the great feudal lords linked with several of the cities of Apulia and Campania.[12] There were insurrections, and agreements with the Byzantine forces that intervened to restore the dominion of the Greek Empire, until a conspiracy in Palermo provoked the assassination of Maione and the temporary imprisonment of the king. Palace conspiracies and the rebellion of vassals and cities both acted as indicators in moments of crisis of the composite nature of this political system.

Within the system the strengthening of the central power (the modifications which followed the affair of Maione of Bari, particularly at the time of the 'good' King William II, left untouched the general tendency of the Norman kingdom towards bureaucratic structures) was also apparent in attempts to make the social order more rigid. Legislation sought to make hereditary (always excepting possible intervention by the prince) the *militia*, that is, the status of knight,

[12] Chalandon, *Histoire*, vol. 2, pp. 167ff; A. Ancora, 'Alcuni aspetti dell politica di Maione di Bari', in *Studi storici in onore di Gabriele Pepe* (Bari, 1969), pp. 301–16.

important at the social level, and the ranks of judge and notary.[13] The framework of the state was scarcely sketched out, and already it displayed tendencies towards social crystallization which were worthy of the late Roman Empire. Within this context of royal ambitions, which aimed to control ever more strictly the public life of the population, we must also place the problem of the southern cities. Undoubtedly they did not have the good fortune to live in an easy relationship of trade and exchange of experience with the central regions of the Latin–Germanic world, like the cities of Lombardy or Tuscany. But the cities of Campania and Apulia had themselves been the first to demonstrate, in the disorder of the pre-Norman period, the capacity to establish themselves as centres of economic life and political autonomy, and even under the Normans they still lost no opportunity to appeal to the pacts drawn up with the conquerors and to their erstwhile customs of liberty. They repeatedly obtained recognition and promises; but the royal structure, even where it meant a guarantee of rights rather than repression, ended the need for self-defence and political initiative which, until Roger II's accession to the kingdom, had driven them, and still drove the Lombard and Tuscan cities, to elaborate a series of new forms of self-government. The southern cities were confined within a protective regime, on the margins of political life, in contrast to the counts and barons, who, however much controlled by the royal administration, formed the basic structure of the kingdom whose military strength they constituted.

The baronial power, operating in the line of Norman tradition, was able to display itself in all its might in the stormy decades which at the end of the twelfth century found the Staufers intent on succeeding the dynasty of Roger II. The resolute introduction into the South of German elements by Henry VI, king of Sicily and emperor, the subsequent intervention after Henry's death of the Roman church as guardian of his son Frederick and of the kingdom (by virtue of that vassalage of the kings of Sicily to the Roman church which in the time of the Normans had remained essentially theoretical), and finally the divisions within the feudal order of the kingdom which followed as the Sicilian problem was complicated by the problem of the Empire, permitted the Staufers to establish themselves in Sicily and, with Frederick II, to restore the political system of the Norman kings. Indeed they stressed decisively its commitment to legislation and the importance of the bureaucracy. But if Frederick was able to impose himself once he returned to Sicily after his elevation to the German throne and to the Empire, that was possible

---

[13] See Cahen, *Le Régime féodal*, p. 126.

only because the baronial anarchy had never destroyed the political framework created by the Norman royal tradition which had its focus in a capital city, Palermo, and in its central government.[14] The barons of Sicily and the south of the peninsula, although they had appropriated fiscal rights and property, still lived within the horizons of the kingdom. The desire to preserve and increase seigneurial power thus tended to become a struggle of influences over the king, as was apparent at Rome in 1220 when quite a few barons of the South hastened to the imperial coronation of Frederick.[15] The interest of the barons in the fortunes of the kingdom survived, even after thirty years of crisis and disorder, to a much greater extent than the episodic interest fostered in the Lombard and Tuscan world for the Empire. The latter was an empire which for at least two centuries had no longer had a visible and stable centre in Italy, no longer possessed an efficient social order or even, now, the memory of its old social order, and which was essentially a concentration of itinerant military forces which, in its empty aspirations to create a new imperial structure, was annoying and dangerous for the more effective territorial constructions centred on the cities.[16]

On to this persistent tendency towards unity shown by the kingdom of Sicily it was possible to graft the remarkable capacity for repression and administrative organization displayed by Frederick's government. This was, clearly and unequivocally, a resumption of the preceding Norman experiment,[17] but it took place more self-consciously, as a political programme, with frequent appeals to a legal culture which was deeply marked by Roman imperial absolutism. Its legislation, very ambitiously, claimed for the king and for his power apparatus the entire responsibility for public life. It was particularly intolerant of civic autonomies, of those cities which had found in the thirty decades of anarchy the most stimulating conditions in which to imitate the Lombard and Tuscan communes, with free election of consuls and podestà and the establishment of commercial and political agreements even with cities outside the kingdom, such as Ragusa, Venice and Pisa.[18] Frederick's legislation was directed against the possibility, not yet

---

[14] For the period of the Papal regency, after the death of Henry VI, see F. Baethgen, *Die Regentschaft Papst Innozenz III. im Königreich Sizilien* (Heidelberg, 1914), pp. 6ff.

[15] E. Kantorowicz, *Federico II di Svevia* (Milan, 1939), vol. I, pp. 85ff.

[16] See F. Bernini, *I comuni italiani e Federico II di Svevia. Gli inizi (1212–19)* (Turin, 1950).

[17] See E. Mazzarese Fardella, *Aspetti dell'organizzazione amministrativa nello Stato normanno e svevo* (Milan, 1966), pp. 52ff, 69ff.

[18] Calasso, *La legislazione statutaria*, pp. 103ff.

extinct, of a less restricted development; this is visible, for example, when the regional justiciar sought to apply to Messina the 'Constitutions of Melfi' of 1232, the great codification which remained the foundation of the law in force in the Mezzogiorno and Sicily up to the Napoleonic period. The city rose in rebellion, but Frederick dealt with the insurrection in purely military terms, even betraying a formal promise. There was a certain excess in legislation and repression here which reveals an inadequate bond with the society Frederick sought to control.

The various 'constitutions' were sometimes inspired by the need to be free from irrational customs, as when the fisc renounced its rights to shipwrecked goods. But the great body of the measures promulgated was essentially dominated by a meticulous and wide-ranging desire to control, to pacify the kingdom completely and to construct a machine which would produce profits for the ruling power and which would also be a basis for the costly imperial policies followed in other parts of Italy; these measures thus involved a careful determination of taxes and customs receipts and an increase of monopolies, monetary innovations, and the creation of state warehouses for cereals and various goods. To such ends the law everywhere reinforced the hierarchy of functionaries and at the same time demanded, under threat of heavy penalties, that they be incorruptible, which was the more difficult to ensure as the spontaneous interplay of local forces was ever more repressed by the law. The example of the Lombard city communes and the organization of their guilds was the source for the regulation by Frederick of artisanal work and mercantile activities, a regulation which showed remarkable zeal on behalf of consumers,[19] but the commitment to such minute instructions again reveals the tendency towards a uniform discipline, imposed from the centre and from above. This was completely antithetical to the regulations that arose and were amended in the Lombard and Tuscan cities through the local initiatives of groups and classes, where economic activity and the development of regulations did not occupy separate spheres.

In such a political climate, among courtly celebration, rigid constraints and intense bureaucratic activity, together with the methodical multiplication of royal fortresses and the recruitment of mercenaries, it was the aristocracy of barons and prelates which managed best to preserve its own autonomy. The king watched carefully over them, confiscating fortresses and forcing into flight or destroying disobedient or rebellious barons, but he respected their rights of exaction and

[19] J. M. Powell, 'Medieval Monarchy and Trade', *Studi medievali*, ser. III, 3 (1962), pp. 472ff; see the discussion by M. Del Treppo in *Rivista storica italiana*, 76 (1964), pp. 1092ff.

jurisdiction, and in the control of the population the aristocracy co-existed with the powerful bureaucracy of the royal court and the provincial justiciars, who were mostly recruited from the lesser aristocracy of knights and judges but in some cases even from Muslims or foreigners.[20] In their turn, the royal apparatus and the great landed aristocracy co-existed in reasonable harmony (despite political conflicts) with the merchants of Pisa, and for the most part with those of Venice and Genoa as well. All these merchants had some time before discovered an important market in the South and in Sicily, where they bought agricultural goods, the produce of private and royal estates, and sold luxury goods, a commerce very useful for the customs revenues of the kingdom. Here too the initiatives of the southern cities, which some decades earlier had been in direct contact with these and other republics, were replaced by the intervention of the kingdom as a protecting and unifying force. It is difficult to say how much this intervention, which was heavily influenced by the calculation of royal income, encouraged productive activity. But we can hardly suppose that it was more stimulating for the Apulian, Sicilian and Campanian cities than that direct and complex relationship with the most active centres of the Mediterranean which they had experienced in the period of disturbance and agitation in the kingdom, a relationship which had its dangers but offered many exciting possibilities.

These structures, after some years of crisis, were inherited by Manfred, the last Staufer king at Palermo (1254–66), and by Charles of Anjou, the papal candidate for the kingdom of Sicily, of which he took control in 1266 after the defeat of Manfred. Charles took control after entangling half of Italy in a Guelf alliance, which allowed him to carry out the difficult transfer of suitable military forces from France to southern Italy, and after contracting huge debts with the Tuscan bankers for the maintenance and employment of these forces. Those debts, guaranteed by the tithe whose collection in the churches of France was ordered by the pope for the 'crusade' against Manfred, were taken on with the prospect of notable advantages for the Tuscans in the kingdom once the conquest had taken place.[21] The venture of Charles of Anjou thus conditioned the whole financial and commercial activity of the kingdom for the future. The Venetian, Genoese and Pisans were joined

---

[20] E. Pontieri, *Ricerche sulla crisi della monarchia siciliana nel secolo XIII*, 3rd ed. (1950, reprinted Naples, 1965) pp. 7ff; P. Colliva, *Ricerche sul principio di legalità nell'amministrazione del regno di Sicilia al tempo di Federico II*, vol. 1, *Gli organi centrali e periferici* (Milan, 1964), pp. 180ff.

[21] E. Jordan, *Les Origines de la domination angevine en Italie* (Paris, 1909), pp. 537ff.

in the search for privileges by the Florentines, Sienese and Lucchesi, until, by the reign of Robert of Anjou in the middle of the fourteenth century, the concentrated mercantile and banking strength of the Florentine companies of the Bardi, Peruzzi and Acciaiuoli attained an absolute predominance in the Mezzogiorno in the commerce of money, and dominated the public finances, lending to the court and the barons, to cities, merchants and local proprietors, receiving deposits from ecclesiastical bodies, and managing tolls, mints and taxes farmed out by the king, and sometimes even providing pay for the troops. They operated without scruples in buying raw products and provisions even at politically very delicate moments, and in selling expensive goods, under the protection of their own mercantile clientèle, as well as introducing to their own profit individual members of their families directly into the court, as councillors, household members and chamberlains.[22] The apparatus of power which the Norman and Staufer kings had constructed with increasing zeal to furnish considerable financial and military resources in the service of their great political projects in the Mediterranean or in the Empire, had become in the twelfth and especially the thirteenth centuries (and still was at the beginning of the fourteenth century)[23] a kingdom which was exceptionally profitable for the prince and a suitable base for satisfying further ambitions; it was now a factor in the calculations of the mercantile companies, and became a field for exploitation by creditors. This apparatus of power does not, we should note, represent the South as a society capable of opening itself to new economic experiences; rather it is the 'kingdom' of the South, seen as a reliable system of obtaining funds, a system which was in its turn susceptible to exploitation by others. The celebrated wealth of the kingdom, in the political judgement of contemporaries, had essentially a fiscal meaning.

It had this sense for the king, for the Tuscan bankers, and also for the Roman Curia. In the pacts drawn up between the papacy and Charles of Anjou provision was made for the annual payment of a huge sum, 8,000 gold ounces (the ounce as money of account corresponded to five gold florins), in recognition of the feudal superiority of the Roman church; this was around thirty times more than the sum paid annually to the Roman Curia by the Norman kings and Frederick II.[24] The papal

[22] R. Caggese, *Roberto d'Angiò e i suoi tempi* (Florence, 1922), vol. 1, pp. 536ff, 567ff.

[23] Jordan, *Les Origines*, p. 606 note 1; E. G. Léonard, *Les Angevins de Naples* (Paris, 1954), p. 280.

[24] Jordan, *Les Origines*, p. 431; E. G. Léonard, *Histoire de Jeanne Ire, reine de Naples, comtesse de Provence*, vol. 1 (Paris, 1932), pp. 56ff; *Les Angevins*, pp.

calculation was in reality suggested by an offer which had been made in precisely these terms by Manfred shortly before, in the hope of placating the Roman church and retaining the kingdom, but this demonstrates only that the Staufers, the popes and the House of Anjou were in agreement in valuing the 'kingdom' in terms of ample fiscal profit. It was not always possible to pay the annuity, particularly because of the war which followed the Sicilian rising of 1282 and the loss of Sicily to dynasties of Aragonese origin, so that the Angevin debt to the Roman Curia had become enormous by the time of Charles II, successor of Charles of Anjou. Only King Robert, by carrying out drastic economies, managed to pay the annuity regularly and even to wipe out within a few decades the debt he had inherited. Following some very approximate calculations one may estimate the total annual income of the Angevin Crown at the time of Robert of Anjou (1309–43) at perhaps around 100,000 gold ounces, when certain trading operations carried out by the king had been successful, a sum that should be compared to the slightly more than 200,000 ounces income of the Crown of France at that time.[25] The confusion provoked during the tormented reign of Robert's daughter Joanna I (1343–82) by the dynastic wars between various branches of the Angevin house naturally placed public finance in crisis and with it the payment of the annuity, so much so that Pope Innocent VI at Avignon in 1355 excommunicated the queen and her husband, Louis of Taranto, and placed an interdict on the kingdom, in punishment for the long delays and postponements.[26]

In short, when it was not committed to serious operations of war or shaken by dynastic crisis, the kingdom as an administrative and fiscal system continued to function under the Angevins as well. If Pope Innocent launched interdicts and excommunications, that was not the irresponsible action of the Avignon Curia against a kingdom whose constitution was in radical collapse so much as the result of the indignant conviction of the pope that Louis and Joanna, in the years of respite between the disturbances that afflicted the kingdom, did not know how to make good use of the administrative devices at their disposal; King Louis, the pope repeatedly declared, was wasting the lands and rights of the demesne through his abundant and irregular alienations and donations. Besides, it was well known that the king preferred, even at

52ff, 281; S. Borsari, 'Il pagamento del censo del regno di Sicilia alla curia romana', *Annali della facoltà di lettere e filosofia dell'università di Macerata*, 5–6 (1972–3), pp. 167ff.

[25] Caggese, *Roberto d'Angiò*, vol. 1, p. 627; Léonard, *Histoire de Jeanne Ire*, pp. 59ff; *Les Angevins*, p. 282; Borsari, 'Il pagamento', p. 183.

[26] Léonard, *Histoire de Jeanne Ire*, vol. 3 (Paris, 1936), pp. 41, 110, 122ff, 169ff.

moments of tension, the pleasures of the hunt to planning for the future, somewhat to the despair of his councillors and ministers, including the powerful 'grand seneschal' Niccolò Acciaiuoli.

But the Angevin kingdom, in its most complex sense, was not only a fiscal system. It inherited from the Norman and Staufer period a military establishment which was largely sustained by the 'loyalty' of the barons, despite the Frederician tendency to multiply royal castles and employ militias which were partly mercenary. This establishment was the level at which, from the time of the Norman kingdom's foundation, political power took the form of a hegemonic social structure. The cities of the royal demesne had never been absorbed into the official apparatus of power, nor, except in times of crisis in the kingdom, were their customs of free government ever more than tolerated; and this tolerance, indeed, had been withdrawn during the most 'glorious' period of Frederician absolutism. The Sicilian Vespers of 1282 split the kingdom of Charles of Anjou into two parallel and opposing regional units, with their capitals at Palermo and Naples, destined to perennial conflict even though the possibility of reunion under a single royal dynasty was maintained, but this could happen because the Vespers took place at the delicate moment when baronial 'loyalty' was passing from the Staufers to the Angevins; it did not radically modify the social–political system, which remained the same in the regions on either side of the Straits. This is clearly apparent in 1354, during the years when King Louis did not pay the annuity to the Roman Curia; the enterprising diplomacy and the personal financial and military commitment of Niccolò Acciaiuoli, who held notable fiefs in the Angevin kingdom and had hopes of acquiring more in Sicily, led him into an agreement with the Sicilian faction of the Chiaramonte, formed by a large part of the so-called 'Latin' barons with an island tradition (in contrast to the 'Catalan' faction which included the Sicilian nobles of Spanish origin and their supporters). In a few months Niccolò obtained the return of two-thirds of the island, including Palermo and Syracuse, to the Angevin dynasty of Naples. It was an ephemeral success, but a significant indication of the continuing community of the social–political structures in the two kingdoms.

This community of structures should not, however, be understood as the mechanical continuity of a uniform tradition. It was the product of the persistent political co-existence of very different peoples and regions. The feudal structure of the South in the twelfth century, when seen as a legal relationship between the seigneurial autonomies and the royal power, often signified on the mainland that the earlier chaos of numerous independent political bodies, with their various origins and natures, had been overcome through their incorporation (where ecclesiastical immunities or civic liberties were not involved) into the Norman military fabric of vassal subordination. In Sicily, on the other hand, not only the model of military vassalage but the seigneurial establishment itself arose as entirely new creations in relation to the preceding Muslim regime, to the benefit of the Normans themselves. It should be emphasised that during the whole Norman and Staufer period the power of the barons was always adequately counterbalanced. The extensive jurisdictions of institutions with immunities were supported by ecclesiastical prestige and royal protection, but the organization of the vast demesne was also an important agent, either when the efficiency of the royal administration enabled bureaucratic activity to penetrate from demesnal centres of power into the feudal territories, or even, to a certain extent, during the crises of the kingdom, when the demesne was eroded by the barons but the cities of the demesne re-acquired a lively capacity for defence and self-affirmation against any other power.

It is true that the accession of Charles of Anjou did not at first substantially alter this equilibrium, but this lasted only for the years 1266 to 1282, which preceded the Vespers. In those years the return of barons who had emigrated earlier because of hostility to the Staufers, and the imprisonment or flight of barons once too closely tied to the Staufers, amounted only to a replacement of individuals.[27] Even the extensive introduction of French immigrants into the baronies, the high offices of the court and the justiciarates, although it greatly disturbed the indigenous feudal lords, kept alive the composite system of government, both bureaucratic and feudal, which dated back to Roger II, by employing trusted individuals. A good number of the royal cities had revolted in the years of crisis of Staufer rule, and had allied among themselves and asked the Roman church to assert its feudal authority over the kingdom in the attempt to recover their old 'customs' and imitate the communal liberty of other parts of Italy. Charles of Anjou had to take into some account the promises he had made to the pope, to restore conditions in the kingdom to those before the period of Staufer absolutism, when the 'good' King William II ruled; his was the mythic age to which barons and cities used to appeal in defending themselves against royal despotism. Charles therefore recognized that the cities (as *universitates*, that is, as collective entities) possessed some administrative autonomies.[28] It does not seem, however, that in those first years of the Angevin dominion the royal court was very eager to

[27] A. Nitschke, 'Der sizilische Adel unter Karl von Anjou und Peter von Aragon', *Quellen und Forschungen aus italienischen Archiven und Bibliotheken*, 45 (1965), pp. 241ff.

[28] See Calasso, *La legislazione statutaria*, pp. 181ff, but compare the information and discussion in De Vergottini, *Il diritto pubblico*, vol. 2, pp. 89ff.

respond to the aspirations of the cities. Everywhere in the kingdom the king relied above all on the nobility which had come from France, and which was immediately incorporated into the bureaucracy and feudal structure of the kingdom. When the Vespers occurred the traditional system survived, but not without suffering considerable changes on both sides of the Straits, changes which moved in roughly the same direction. Let us consider first of all the changes that took place in Sicily.

The insurrection of the island against Charles of Anjou was largely the result of broad projects and political planning, in which the kingdom of Aragon's capacity for expansion in the Mediterranean joined with the desire among the lords who had fled from the Angevin kingdom to regain their position.[29] None the less, it is certain that in the spring of 1282 a true revolution took place in Palermo and spread to the other cities. The *communitas Siciliae* which then formed was a league of cities, which sought to control the entire island and to obtain papal protection. This is yet another demonstration, although a temporary one, of the animation and breadth of political perspective of which the cities of the South were still capable, despite the regime of varying repression to which their rulers had almost continuously subjected them. But papal indignation against cities which had rebelled against the Guelph king, a vassal of Rome, led them to take part in the Aragonese plans and thus to allow the resumption, first under the king of Aragon and then from 1296 under a Sicilian Aragonese dynasty, of the old system centred on the royal bureaucracy and the military collaboration of the barons. This collaboration was now all the more essential since the island lived under constant threat from the Angevin kingdom and was exposed to continual piracy and periodic invasions, to which it responded by attacks on Calabria. The collaboration of the barons seems at first to be part of an organic political collaboration of all the island's forces with the royal court, in keeping with the manner in which the Aragonese domination had been created; indeed, in 1296 it was prescribed in a 'general colloquium' or parliament of the island that this assembly, in which barons, prelates and delegates of the royal cities participated, should be reconvened each year to co-operate with the king. But the dominance of the barons, partly Sicilian by tradition and partly originally from the kingdom of Aragon and thus Aragonese or Catalan, was displayed from the start both in the royal court and in the parliament, thanks to the almost continuous state of warfare; it continued to grow as the king conceded to one or another vassal land and even cities drawn from the

---

[29] See F. Giunta, *Medioevo e medievisti. Note di storiografia* (Caltanissetta-Rome, 1971), pp. 270ff.

demesne, and all rights of high jurisdiction in certain feudal territories, in order to maintain himself in the midst of his feudal system.

And so baronial power gradually extended territorially and at the same time increased in strength, so that the royal administration and cities were reduced to the margins of political power. This was all the more marked since the 'captaincies of war' were often entrusted to the owners of neighbouring baronies. These were set up in the course of the fourteenth century by the kings in cities which had remained in the demesne, in connection with the obvious military needs of the island threatened from outside but also in a certain jurisdictional rivalry with the elective urban magistracies. This office thus became a basis for the tendency, under cover of a royal office but to the further benefit of the baronial power, to superimpose a seigneurial structure over the most important cities, which were also those outside the feudal territories.[30] After the reign of Frederick III (1296–1337), who was recognized king of the island in 1302 by the papacy as well, with the title of King of Trinacria as distinct from the official title of the Angevins of Naples, 'King of Sicily', the power of the kings to co-ordinate the politics of the island weakened almost to vanishing point, and was replaced by the innumerable ties between the feudal families; organized factions struggled for control of the island and also drew into their power the major cities of the demesne, either in the way described above or by attracting the support of groups in the cities. Yet the surviving royal activity and the hierarchy of officials, which at least in their legal form were independent of the feudal system's power,[31] retained an undoubted effectiveness; they influenced developments in the direction of a possible restoration of the collaboration between the royal court and barons, a collaboration which would return more closely to the Norman and Staufer traditions of the kingdom. Hence, after the dynasty descended from Frederick III had died out, Sicily embarked on new political experiments at the end of the fourteenth and in the fifteenth centuries.

In more than one respect, the parallel evolution of the Angevin kingdom of Naples is surprising. In reality it sprang from the same previous situation and developed for very similar reasons. In 1283, as a necessary remedy for the tensions which the Sicilian insurrection had revealed in the Angevin political system, the son of Charles of Anjou, the future King Charles II, summoned to a 'general parliament' prelates,

[30] V. D'Alessandro, *Politica e società nella Sicilia aragonese* (Palermo, 1963), pp. 253ff; S. Tramontana, *Michele da Piazza e il potere baronale in Sicilia* (Messina-Florence, 1963), pp. 279ff.
[31] See, for example, G. Di Martino, 'Il sistema tributario degli Aragonesi in Sicilia (1282–1516)', *Archivio storico per la Sicilia*, 4–5 (1938–9), pp. 107ff.

barons and delegates of the royal cities, and was generous with concessions and recognitions.[32] Thus on the mainland too there was an attempt, in competition with the Aragonese experiment in Sicily, to construct a regime which would be organically sustained by all the forces capable of political will and autonomy. But on the mainland too the recognition of urban autonomies, with assemblies of *cives* and elective magistracies, remained in effect marginal in the face of the need to keep the loyalty of the military forces of the barons, beginning with the princes of the royal house, who were provided with appanages that included whole provinces and with jurisdictional powers that included criminal justice; the territorial seigneuries of the members of the Angevin family became the highest model of baronial lordship.[33] The cities of the demesne were given generous privileges where it was a matter of important centres capable of political initiative, such as Naples and Gaeta; elsewhere, however, the royal 'captain', residing in the city to supervise its administration and jurisdiction, passed beyond the limits of his competence at the expense of the elective magistracies, or else the city itself was ceded in fief to a baron exactly as happened in Sicily, even though in the fourteenth century royal power was never, even at the time of Queen Joanna, overwhelmed by baronial power for as long as it was in Sicily under the successors of Frederick III.[34]

On the other hand it seems to have been demonstrated that the capacity for resistance by the cities and towns against the encroachments of royal officials and feudal agents, through disputes and rebellions, was very considerable during the Angevin period. Also considerable was the capacity of groups and classes within each collectivity to demonstrate through conflict with each other their intolerance towards moves to establish dominance, which were continually taking place, even though there was no spontaneous military organization of the *popolo* comparable to the Lombard armed companies of the thirteenth century.[35] Hence it seems permissible to say that throughout the fourteenth century the South showed itself to be, at every social level, far from passive in the face of other levels of political organization. In this sense the South perhaps prolonged its Middle Ages, that disorder which hindered the

---

[32] Nitschke, 'Der sizilische Adel', pp. 254ff.

[33] R. Moscati, 'Ricerche e documenti sulla feudalità napoletana nel periodi angioino', *Archivio storico per le province napoletane*, 59 (1934), pp. 227ff.

[34] Calasso, *La legislazione statutaria*, pp. 217ff; De Vergottini, *Il diritto pubblico*, vol. 2, pp. 84ff.

[35] See in particular Caggese, *Roberto d'Angiò*, vol. 1, pp. 273ff, 467ff; C. Carucci, *Un comune del nostro Mezzogiorno nel medio evo: Salerno (secoli XIII–XIV)* (Subiaco, 1945), pp. 191ff, 216ff.

construction of great and lasting despotisms, beyond the limits reached by the better-known areas of northern and central Italy in their communal autonomies. And it is truly extraordinary that it was precisely this century, which elsewhere witnessed vigorous developments in the formation of structures which were state-like in nature and coherently despotic, should have seen in the South the crisis of the unitary systems perfected in the thirteenth century by Staufer absolutism. We may place at the beginning of this process the rupture which was provoked by the Vespers. This was always felt by the Angevin dynasty and by southern legal culture[36] (at least until Queen Joanna in 1373 made an agreement with the 'kings of Trinacria', obtaining their legal subordination in feudal form to the 'kings of Sicily' of Naples) as an unacceptable break in that unity which from the time of Roger II had seemed in itself to justify the presence of a 'kingdom' in the South. But the difference in significance which the 'disorder' of the South seems to have in the fourteenth century still remains a problem, when compared with the deeply-rooted movements of repeated alliance and fragmentation, within the heart of the communal cities and within a rural world which was still complex and thriving, which were characteristic of imperial Italy in the thirteenth century. Beyond making the simple observation that in Lombardy and Tuscany the effective territorial hegemonies were normally centred on cities, and not on royal dynasties or baronial lordships, may we not perhaps be anticipating a verdict suggested by the subsequent course of southern history, by the later, much-criticized 'passivity' of Southern social institutions? Or was it the case that in the fourteenth century, among economic and demographic crises and plagues that attacked the whole West, and wars that became more murderous with the alarming arrival, even in the Italian South, of paid military 'companies' of well-trained soldiers roaming across Europe in search of employment, this 'disorder' could no longer take on the same significance that it had in the thirteenth century? Historical research, if it wishes to pose these questions, must commit itself to the discovery and methodical analysis of all possible sources, and to the cautious comparison of results with other periods of the history of the South and with other regions of Italy and western Europe.

[36] For the commitment of southern jurists to maintaining the rights of the kingdom, see G. M. Monti, 'La dottrina anti-imperiale degli Angioini di Napoli', in *Studi di storia e diritto in onore di Arrigo Solmi* (Milan, 1941), vol. 2, pp. 13–54.

The centuries-long history of the 'kingdom of Sicily' never developed in isolation from two broader contexts: the commercial and military activity of the naval powers of the Mediterranean, from Byzantium and Muslim Africa to the Italian republics and the Catalan cities of the kingdom of Aragon, and the imperial and papal aspirations to set Italy within a political framework. The aspirations of German kings and Roman popes were already in open conflict from the eleventh century within the great struggle for the reform of ecclesiastical institutions. Already, at that time, it brought the Norman adventurers to make the choice which led in the third decade of the twelfth century to a southern kingdom which was in theory feudally subordinate to the Church of Rome, although this process reversed direction as a result of the succession at the end of that century, for dynastic reasons, of the Staufers to the kingdom. From then on, throughout the thirteenth century, there was a titanic papal struggle to detach the kingdom of Sicily from the empire, which from time to time drew the kingdom into involvement in the two party alliances into which all the political forces of central and northern Italy gradually divided from the 1230s onwards. Some forces, forming a *pars imperii*, linked their own interests with the imperial and dynastic ambitions of the Staufers, formerly called in Germany the lords of Waibling and therefore in Italy the 'Ghibellines'; the others polemically proclaimed themselves the *pars ecclesiae* and later called themselves 'Guelfs', both to indicate, by appealing to the papal struggle or old German (Welf) hostilities to the Staufers, their own aversion to the Empire and the Staufer dynasty, and in order to benefit from the support of the Roman church.[37] Thus the kingdom of Sicily found itself drawn into a great ideological controversy, for the 'honour of the Empire' or for the 'liberty of the Roman church', and into a tangle of highly contradictory and changeable interests which grew out of the clash of power between the two supreme 'political' centres of western Christianity, the *sacrum imperium* and the *ecclesia romana*. Both of these were clothed in a charismatic authority and equipped with very different but equally effective means of action, down to the internal guerrilla warfare in the communal cities, between noble *consorterie* and between groups aiming at local power.

This chaos of interests has brought some historians to ridicule those other scholars who believed that the two sides could each be seen as a united body, and to recall that the famous jurist Bartolo of Sassoferrato,

[37] Davidsohn, *Forschungen*, vol. 4, pp. 39ff.

towards 1355, had already demystified the conflict in his *Tractatus de guelfis et gebellinis*, where he declared that the names of the two parties had no relation 'either to the church or to the Empire, but only to those factions which exist in a city or in a province'.[38] That is undoubtedly true, and is something that often happens when political organizations with a broad equilibrium of power divide into separate parties, but it does not deprive the parties of their tendency to suggest types of behaviour which tended to persist over time and to be transmitted from one generation to the next with a progressive enrichment of language and myth, whenever they were not undermined by too extensive a change of interests. This tendency was all the greater since in that period, when interests and institutions were extremely confused, loyalty to a traditional party allegiance supplied a minimum guarantee of survival, whatever the outcome of individual local episodes in the struggle. The adherence of individuals, *consorterie*, cities and dynasties to a *pars* acquired in this way, through its usefulness in replacing or supplementing other forms of political cohesion, a role analogous to that which had caused and still caused the success of the bond of vassalage. The names of Guelf and Ghibelline thus took on, in the last decades of the thirteenth century, a generalized political significance in Italy – indeed a significance which became peculiar to Italy, as if to give the country a vague unitary form even in the shape of a violent division between hostile factions. When, in the thirteenth and fourteenth centuries, certain powers in the Mediterranean and in northern Europe also called themselves Guelfs and Ghibellines, it was only in so far as their political action also extended on to the chessboard of Italian affairs.

Frederick II died in 1250, and the imperial power was absent from Italy for many years (the Empire was then vacant for decades in Germany as well). But it was at this time that the two parties 'of the Empire' and 'of the Church', far from dying away, established themselves firmly; from now on the local forces that joined the various sides conferred on them a vitality independent of the conflict between the two supreme powers. This vitality was an autonomous force, but the pope could not remain passive in the face of it; to do so would have meant renouncing the papal project which had been born almost two centuries earlier in opposition to the Empire, the project to base the church's action on its own specific political clientèle. This renunciation

---

[38] L. Simeoni, *Le signorie* (Milan, 1950), vol. I, pp. 39ff. See A. Marongiu, 'Il regime bipartitico nel trattato sui guelfi e i ghibellini', in *Bartolo da Sassoferrato. Studi e documenti per il VI centenario* (Milan, 1962), vol. 2, pp. 335ff, and also H. Baron, *The Crisis of the Early Italian Renaissance* (Princeton, 1955), vol. 2, pp. 445ff.

would have been the more intolerable since, even while the Empire itself was silent, the parties remained, their names and their vocabulary speaking emphatically for or against the power of the Church of Rome. In addition, King Manfred emerged as an extremely effective leader of the supporters of the *pars Imperii* up to 1266, so that that party was still led by the Staufer court of Sicily, which was by far the strongest military and political organism present in Italy. The Angevin victory abruptly placed this organism at the disposal of the whole *pars Ecclesiae*; but it was soon damaged irremediably by the Vespers, so that radical antagonism between the courts of Palermo and Naples became the most natural basis for the opposition between the two Italian parties, which was already radical and violent in its own right.

This general outline of interconnections was as resonant in rhetorical expressions as it was lacking in any meaning for specific social structures, when considered on its own, and it could therefore be applied anywhere, to any object or individual. Within this adaptable framework, disagreements of very different kinds, which were usually specific and well-defined, took their place, as if to find a broader justification. At Florence, for which we have the oldest evidence (dating back to the 1230s and 1240s) of a division of the nobility into two factions, named Guelf or Ghibelline in the sense of adherence to the papacy or to the empire, the two factions soon began to imitate the individual seigneurial *consorterie* and the 'commune' of the podestà, and appointed their own 'captains' and 'councils'. They functioned both militarily and diplomatically in the city and its territory, competing for the official organs of the 'commune' and exercising decisive pressure on those organs from within and without; they also competed for the support of popular elements, and for alliance with the organism of the *popolo* itself when the latter acquired a unified constitution at Florence, in the 1240s, on the basis of the urban companies-at-arms.[39] It is worth noting the extreme complexity of such a coexistence, in the same city, between a 'commune', a Guelf Party, a Ghibelline Party and a *popolo*, all four with their own rectors and their own councils and armed formations, not to mention the individual organisms of the *consorterie*, guilds and city districts, all capable of varying degrees of political activity. In the most violent forms of conflict, the two parties did split the city in two; but at the same time, although they alternated as the dominant party among the nobles and over the commune were often in exile from the city itself, they functioned as powerful agents of cohesion among seigneurial

[39] Davidsohn, *Forschungen*, vol. 4, pp. 60ff, 100ff *Storia di Firenze*, vol. 2.1 (Florence, 1956), pp. 332ff, 410ff; Stahl, *Adel und Volk*, pp. 76ff, 108ff.

consorterie (thus reaching beyond the limits of the city with their own military forces), and between a particular seigneurial grouping and the formations of the *popolo*.

Let us consider the example of the complicated juridical acts that were involved in the formation of the bond between Florence and Arezzo in 1256, in order to illustrate the organic quality of the parties' action, their presence in the links between city and contado as well as in the relations, purely public in character, between several city communes. On the 9th of March the 'councillors of the party of the Guelfs of the city of Arezzo and the entire body [*universitas*] of the men of the said party' were summoned by the town crier and by the sound of bells (a summons which was also customary for the meetings of the communal councils) to the parish church of S. Maria in Arezzo, and the two 'captains of the said party of the Guelfs of the city and county of Arezzo', with their own councillors and all the men of the party convened there, appointed a procurator to make perpetual peace with the procurator of the 'party of the Ghibellines of the city and county of Arezzo', with the power to constrain the goods of the party and of its individual members, to swear peace on the soul of all the Aretine Guelfs, and to draw up a deed forgiving all offences. In the same way the Ghibellines were convoked on the 10th of March in the episcopal palace of Arezzo (the bishop was the Ghibelline Guglielmino degli Ubertini, who none the less maintained good personal relations with the commune of Florence dominated by the *popolo* and the Guelf party), and the 'captain of the Ghibelline party of the city and county of Arezzo' proceeded with his own councillors and the *universitas* convened there to nominate the Ghibelline procurator. On the 19th of March, when peace had been made between the two parties, the two procurators, with the 'podestà of the city of Arezzo' representing the 'commune and the men of the city', met the representative of the commune of Florence in the Aretine parish church of S. Maria in order to guarantee the Florentine commune against the losses it might suffer from the action that it had promised to take to maintain the peace achieved between the two Aretine parties, and to pledge the goods of the commune of Arezzo and the goods of the parties themselves to this end. On the 21st of March in the church of S. Donato in Arezzo there convened the twelve 'anziani of the *popolo* of the Aretine city' (the magistracy that headed the organism of the *popolo*, made up of three members for each of the four quarters of the city), the 'rectors and leaders of the Arts [guilds] and societies of the city of Arezzo' with their 'councillors', and the 'general council of the city of Arezzo' – in short, all the organs of the *popolo*, both those that represented it as a whole and those that made up its

autonomous divisions. All these together, in the name of the *universitas*
of the Aretine *popolo* and in the presence and with the consent of the
'podestà of the city of Arezzo' (the leader of the commune), appointed
a procurator to draw up the agreements of alliance, which also involved
substantial subordination to the *popolo* of Florence. The agreements
were drawn up near Arezzo on the 24th of March, between the
representatives of the *popolo* and commune of both Florence and Arezzo,
in the presence of the two podestà, and on the 26th of April in the parish
church of S. Maria the twelve anziani of Arezzo and the 240 councillors
of the *popolo* subscribed to the treaty.[40] The *popolo* and commune of
Arezzo thus bound themselves to the *popolo* and commune of Florence
with the preliminary consent of the two Aretine parties, Guelf and
Ghibelline, which had been reconciled expressly with the assistance of
Florence.

This temporary reconciliation under the aegis of Florence in collusion
with the *popolo* did not in reality signify a crisis in the structures of the
parties, nor a weakening of their activity. The regime that resulted at
Arezzo was an association of commune and *popolo* with Guelf support,
the Guelfs of Arezzo and of Florence. Hence, some years later the
Ghibellines went into exile from Arezzo, but they continued to function
as an entity on Aretine territory, maintaining diplomatic relations with
the communal organisms and the parties, Ghibelline and Guelf, of other
Tuscan cities, since they still constituted the *universitas* of the 'party of
the Ghibellines of the city and county of Arezzo', operating with their
own captain and council.[41]

A similar co-ordination between the *universitates* of Ghibellines or
Guelfs and between the latter and the individual *universitates* of the
commune or popolo is increasingly apparent in most of northern and
central Italy in the second half of the thirteenth century, and shows how
dense was the network of party institutions within which cities, towns
and social classes carried on their political activity, all of these
universitates, whether based on territory, social class or a party, being also
linked with the more powerful and autonomous seigneurial families.
The latter were as ready as were the citizen bodies and lesser *consorterie*
to cloak themselves in the name of one or the other party, even though
there was some variation over time and frequent disagreement among
the individual members of the families,[42] which included the marquises
of Monferrato, the Guidi counts and the Aldobrandeschi counts in

40 Pasqui, *Documenti*, vol. 2 (Florence, 1916), pp. 303ff; vol. 3 (Florence, 1937),
    pp. 293ff.
41 *Ibid.*, vol. 2, pp. 359ff.
42 For such disagreements see E. Sestan, 'I conti Guidi e il Casentino', in Sestan,
    Italia medievale (Florence, 1967), pp. 371ff.

Tuscany, the royal dynasty of Sicily and, after the Vespers, the royal dynasties of Palermo and Naples.

Indeed at the end of the thirteenth century and in the first decades of the fourteenth, we can see use of the Guelf and Ghibelline names within each seigneurial family and each urban collectivity becoming less flexible, so that they changed into a basic component of the particular traditions of a family or a city. Normally this was associated with the development of entrenched hostility between individual cities or *consorterie* which were rivals in territorial expansion (due to their location or to competition in commerce) or in the struggle for local power. But at the same time it should be noted that, even when the division into two parties was influenced by individual conflicts, the outline of a general distinction between them was gradually emerging, one which could not be reduced to a more or less chance reference to imperial or papal power. Guelfism often appears to be associated with the development of the institutions of the *popolo*, although exceptions are frequent and sometimes remarkable, as in the cases of Genoa and Pisa, and despite the fact that, like Ghibellinism, Guelfism originated in conflicts between the nobles.

This association is first apparent at Florence, from the time of the *popolo's* first period of dominance in the decade 1250–60, and can be explained by the earlier harshness of imperial government in Tuscany and by the abolition of the 'captains of the *popolo*', only recently set up, which had been ordered by the representative of Frederick II in 1246.[43] But this abolition in its turn was connected with the anti-imperial attitude of some captains of the *popolo* and showed the unpopularity of the restrictions set on civic autonomy by Staufer rule. In Florence, the *popolo's* first favourable leanings towards the Guelf nobility essentially arose from a strong popular desire for civic autonomy, a feeling which was more widespread among the people than among the nobles in general despite the predominance of the nobility in the communal government. This could be explained by arguing that the nobles could not easily unite to resist the Empire in a way that would reflect the opinions of the citizens, precisely because they were traditionally engaged in struggling for urban power; they were, as a result, divided into opposing and deeply-rooted factions, and were strongly tempted by the contemporary conflict between Empire and papacy to create external military and political ties. A process like that in Florence must have occurred in other cities, such as Bologna. Here, indeed, the division between two old noble factions became linked with the conflict between the Staufers and the papacy at a time when the *popolo* was already

[43] Davidsohn, *Forschungen*, vol. 4, pp. 25ff.

operating as a political body; the *popolo* could thus express the city's desire for autonomy side by side with the faction of nobles which was later called, under Tuscan influence, 'the Guelfs'.[44] At Siena, though, the Guelfism of the *popolo* appeared more than a decade later than at Florence, and arose from a collusion of financial interests between the Roman Curia and the bankers. The collaboration between the Ghibelline nobility and the *popolo* in the government of Siena was upset by the excommunication and interdict issued by the Church of Rome against the city and above all by the papal decision in 1262 not to repay the credits held by Sienese merchants. There followed negotiations between the Roman Curia and the 'consuls of the merchant guilds' of Siena (the heads of the guilds of banking and cloth-making), disagreement between the merchants and the commune and *popolo*, and the departure of many of the merchants from the city. The latter approached the party of the Guelfs of Siena, which was operating in exile, and the return in force of all the exiles to the city was followed by the constitutional reform of 1271; under the cover of the Guelf party and the *popolo*, this reform established a durable political regime of the upper bourgeoisie which lasted until after 1350.[45]

And so Guelfism's significance as the papal faction tended to be complicated by the ideology of those autonomous cities where the *popolo* was dominant, in the same decades in which powerful seigneurs of old families, feudally bound to the institutions of the Empire, were serving on the Ghibelline side, particularly in 'Lombardy' through the authority and activity of the marquis Guglielmo VII of Monferrato,[46] thus implicitly suggesting a more strongly aristocratic interpretation of Ghibellinism. In those decades, too, the Empire was at first in eclipse and then, after an exhausting struggle in Germany, began to flourish again in 1273 with Rudolf of Hapsburg; it was now under the papal aegis and friendly with the Angevins,[47] and so paradoxically took on a Guelf

[44] V. Vitale, *Il dominio della Parte Guelfa in Bologna* (Bologna, 1901), pp. 17ff; R. Caggese, 'Su l'origine della Parte Guelfa e le sue relazioni col Comune', *Archivio storico italiano*, ser. V, 32 (1903), pp. 265ff; A. Hessel, *Geschichte der Stadt Bologna von 1116 bis 1280* (Berlin, 1910), pp. 227ff, 336ff.

[45] G. Francini, 'Appunti sulla costituzione guelfa del Comune di Siena secondo il Costituto del 1274', *Bullettino senese di storia patria*, 46 (1939), pp. 11ff; Martini, *Siena*, pp. 6ff.

[46] A. Bozzola, 'Un capitano di guerra e signore subalpino: Guglielmo VII di Monferrato (1254–92)', *Miscellanea di storia italiana*, ser. III, 19 (1920).

[47] O. Redlich, *Rudolf von Hapsburg. Das deutsche Reich nach dem Untergange des alten Kaisertums* (Innsbruck, 1903), pp. 170ff; L. Gatto, *Il pontificato di Gregorio X (1271–76)* (Rom, 1959), pp. 163ff.

form, in such a way as to confuse the significance of Ghibellinism as the *pars Imperii*. But the two parties remained too mixed in character to be able to construct an ideological opposition founded on social conflict, and this set on one side the myth of the just prince or the liberating papacy. Therefore in these years the Italian Ghibellines, under the direction of the marquis of Monferrato and with the support of Genoa, upheld the claims to the Empire of Alfonso X, king of Castile, who had already been elected years before to the German kingdom but had soon been forgotten by the Germans; not only did the Ghibellines need an ideological cover, but they set up at the same time a military link with the most important political centre in Europe. Faced with the failure of Alfonso's plans, the Ghibellines then approached Peter III of Aragon. In reality they sought him as a candidate not for the Empire but for the kingdom of Sicily, and yet the approach was made within the lines of a tradition that was still purely Staufer and so anti-papal; in 1280 the marquis of Monferrato went in person to negotiate with King Peter in Aragon.[48] This focus on the Aragonese dynasty was the tie between the Ghibellines of imperial Italy and the barons exiled from the kingdom of Sicily, or those still within Sicily but hostile to Angevin rule. It is true that the successor to King Peter in the island and then also in Aragon, James II, reached a compromise with Pope Boniface VIII, renouncing Sicily and obtaining the papal enfeoffment of Sardinia and Corsica; this provided legitimation for the future Aragonese conquest of the two islands, at the expense of the Pisans and Genoese who dominated them. But the compromise was not accepted in Sicily, where the brother of James, Frederick III, was proclaimed king and became the official symbol of the Ghibellines, even being described in a prophecy, that of Fra Dolcino, leader of the rebel religious community of the 'apostolics', as the future emperor.[49] The entire Staufer, Sicilian and imperial tradition flowed together into the myth of the 'new Frederick'.

The two parties thus became so clearly opposed that they could drag into renewed conflict an emperor and a pope such as Henry VII and Clement V, who agreed on the idea of pacifying Italy under the sign of a restored and autonomous collaboration between papacy and Empire. The conflict broke out in 1312 through the intense diplomatic activity of Florence and the Angevins, particularly of Florence,[50] aimed at strengthening and extending the network of Guelf alliances in

[48] Bozzola, 'Guglielmo VII di Monferrato', pp. 126ff.

[49] A. De Stefano, *Federico III d'Aragona, re di Sicilia (1296–1337)*, 2nd ed. (Bologna, 1956), pp. 97ff.

[50] W. M. Bowsky, *Henry VII in Italy. The Conflict of Empire and City-State (1310–13)* (Lincoln, Nebraska, 1960), pp. 109ff.

the face of the dangerous reinforcement of the Ghibelline side. The latter was strengthened by the mere presence of Henry in Lombardy, independent of any intention of the prince himself. Equally instrumental in the conflict was the agitated activity of Frederick III's court and the anti-Angevin barons in Italy,[51] which produced embassies and offers to the King of the Romans (the title which the German king took after his election in Germany until his imperial Roman coronation), and resulted in agreements and military pacts between the two princes. But the increasing distrust and hostility between Henry VII and Robert of Anjou culminated in a sentence of Robert's formal deposition, solemnly pronounced by the emperor in 1313 in the Ghibelline city of Pisa, in the name of a concept of the Empire as world dominion in which the doctrine of the jurists of Henry's court accorded with that of the jurists in the Sicilian court.[52]

The political division of Italy between the two parties now reached its height, so much so that it suggested a compromise which would crystallize the division. This was in 1316. The empire and the papacy were both now vacant, and in Germany the kingdom was contested between Frederick of Hapsburg and Louis of Bavaria. Frederick, in the search for recognition, tolerance and friendship in Italy, signed an agreement with Robert of Anjou. He conferred on the prince Charles, son of Robert, the vicariate of the empire over the Guelf lands of Italy, that is, over those lands, as the treaty explains, that were governed by Guelfs at the time of Henry VII.[53] It was an interesting official recognition of two political clientèles no longer conceived as instruments of war (in truth, instruments of war so autonomous and strong as to condition Empire and papacy and sometimes force them into conflict), but rather as spheres of hegemony now worthy of mutual respect; the Guelfs under an Angevin protection legitimated by the imperial power itself, and the Ghibellines in an immediate bond of loyalty to the Empire. The treaty had no real effect, since the two spheres of action were not juxtaposed but intimately interwoven with each other; they could not be treated as defined units without losing their particular importance as spheres of conflict that stretched across Italy and expressed a thousand different struggles. Yet Robert and Frederick's vision of

---

[51] E. Haberkern, *Der Kampf um Sizilien in den Jahren 1302–1337* (Berlin-Leipzig, 1921), pp. 35ff.

[52] *Ibid.*, pp. 47ff; F. Schneider, *Kaiser Heinrich VII*, vol. 3 (Greiz in Vogtland-Leipzig, 1928), pp. 282ff; De Stefano, *Federico III*, pp. 170ff.

[53] Monti, *La dottrina anti-imperiale*, vol. 2, p. 51 note 1; G. Tabacco, 'La politica italiana di Frederico il Bello, re dei Romani', *Archivio storico italiano*, 108 (1950), pp. 22f.

imperial Italy as a whole is historically significant, since, as we know, Italy's divisions were in their turn connected with the splitting of the kingdom of Sicily.

When the new pope, John XXII, was elected, the theme of the 'pacification' of Italy was taken up again with a very different significance. The 'Roman See', now functioning from Avignon with a tranquillity and security which it had never known in Rome, energetically resumed command of the Guelf front.[54] The combative Pope John (1316–34) placed the Italian problem within the European context. The solution to the Italian problem was to be Guelf and Angevin, in a Europe directed by the papacy and the House of France (*domus Franciae benedicta*); to this house belonged both the Capetians ruling at Paris and the Angevins of Naples, the former descendants of Saint Louis IX, the latter descendants of his rash brother Charles of Anjou. For Pope John the recent conflict between Philip the Fair of France and the impetuous Caetani pope Boniface VIII had been no more than a brief episode and a papal error. The papacy could not rule over all Catholicism, or spread to Byzantium and Jerusalem, by founding itself on an uncertain and precarious political equilibrium and on the arrogance of Roman barons such as the Caetani and the Orsini. It had to work loyally with powerful and faithful friends, and therefore no longer with the 'Teutonic' Empire, which for centuries had followed a profoundly anti-papal line, but rather with the many 'faithful and devoted' powers which, under Angevin management and with French assistance, had freed the papacy from the Staufer nightmare. At Avignon one day at the beginning of 1324 the pope found himself in lively conversation with Cardinal Napoleon Orsini, who supported the plans of James II of Aragon against Sardinia; the island had been enfeoffed to him, 'stupidly', by Pope Boniface VIII in return for a renunciation that (albeit against James' will) had turned out to be a mockery, when Frederick III became king at Palermo. The pope could contain himself no longer and said to Orsini, 'But you are all Ghibellines, and by Our Lady it is monstrous that a cardinal should be a Ghibelline!' Soon afterwards he added, bluntly expressing his way of thinking, 'Why do you not love King Robert like the other kings?' When the cardinal protested, the pope smiled and answered, 'So you are a Guelf!'[55]

The vast and complex plan of Pope John apparently failed. The Ghibelline 'heresy' and the Visconti, who had become lords of Milan and many other cities against the Guelfs, could not be 'wiped out' from

[54] G. Tabacco, *La casa di Francia nell'azione politica di papa Giovanni XXII* (Rome, 1953), pp. 152ff.

[55] H. Finke, *Acta Aragonensia* (Berlin-Leipzig, 1908), vol. 2, p. 615.

Lombardy by excommunications and interdicts, nor by the military forces employed by the Avignon Curia or the exhausted Angevin presence. Nonetheless the 'French' direction consciously imposed on the papacy by John XXII turned out, until the Papal Schism of the late fourteenth century, to fit in with the way that all Europe, from the Atlantic to the Danubian basin, gravitated around the French–Angevin world despite the latter's military and political crises. The Empire, involved for some years through Louis of Bavaria in the struggles of Lombardy and Tuscany and of Rome itself, did not come into the possession of the King of France (as Pope John would have wished from the German Electors) but rather, after the final exclusion of Louis, into the hands of a nephew of Henry VII, Charles IV King of Bohemia (1346–78); Charles, however, was French in culture and was a 'Guelf' emperor in Italy and in Europe.

It is true that Guelfism and Ghibellinism had already lost in the course of John XXII's pontificate a large part of the dynamic significance they had taken on in Italy in the thirteenth century. Essentially they expressed support for, or aversion to, that political system which centred in Europe on the collaboration between the courts of Paris, Avignon and Naples. In Italy, during the Avignon pontificate of Benedict XII (1334–43) and even subsequently, the tradition of the Guelf cities, centring on Florence and its tie with the Angevin dynasty of Naples, emphasized from time to time the liberty of the communal 'republics' as opposed to the territorial development of the 'tyrannical lordships' of northern Italy, occasionally suggesting a programme of restoration of the local autonomies which had disappeared.[56] But in Italy now the two party-names, in the region which was not dependent on the political desires of the papacy and the House of France, were largely becoming fixed as symbols of the purely formal loyalty of cities and families to their own particular past. Bartolo of Sassoferrato in the middle of the fourteenth century, in the treatise mentioned above,[57] made a fourfold distinction between firstly, cities such as Florence or Pisa, in which the support of all citizens for the Guelf idea or the Ghibelline idea was assumed, and no disagreement about the party to which the city belonged was tolerated; secondly, those cities (for example the Guelf Perugia) in which there was a party officially recognized by everyone but which none the less permitted families with a different ideological

[56] G. Tabacco, 'La tradizione guelfa in Italia durante il pontificato di Benedetto XII', in *Studi di storia medievale e moderna in onore di Ettore Rota* (Rome, 1958), pp. 97–140. For further and later developments of a similar 'Guelfism' in opposition to the Visconti expansion in central Italy, see Baron, *The Crisis*, vol. I, pp. 11ff.   [57] See Marongiu, 'Il regime bipartitico'.

ancestry to keep faith with the idea of the party followed by their forebears,[58] thirdly those (such as Todi) in which the two parties participated equally in the political regime, presupposing that each individual or family in the city or town was either Guelf or Ghibelline by tradition or choice, and finally those cities (such as Orvieto) in which the political regime now left out of consideration any appeal to Ghibellinism or Guelfism. In short, according to this model, the party was no longer an instrument of political struggle anywhere, not even where the two parties coexisted in the government, since their past violent rivalry had not been replaced by any other form of competition using the same names. The stability of the parties in the Italian setting which the treaty between Robert and Frederick had foreseen in 1316 had thus been realized spontaneously by one city after another. Was this only the decline of a particular way of giving political expression to the will of groups and classes, through formations with traditional names that were widespread throughout Italy, a way that was now outmoded? Or did it indicate a political closure, separating the organization and exercise of power from any competition between groups that continually changed in size and interests?

FROM THE STRUGGLE AGAINST THE MAGNATES TO THE CONSTRUCTION OF STABLE APPARATUSES OF POWER IN THE CITIES

The instability of the institutions in the communal cities in the thirteenth century was the consequence of the need for direct links between the groups emerging from urban society, or the groups merging into it strengthened by resources drawn from the contado, and the exercise of political power. It has been noted above that constitutional changes did indeed arise from struggles that were often very violent, but that these struggles were not a contest of military skills between a few individuals only, observed by a passive population. Even so, *coups de main* were frequently used in the struggles for power, in which every citizen could take part. The movements of the city district companies-at-arms and popular insurrections were themselves profoundly interwoven with the initiative of *consorterie* of knights, with the activity of the Guelf and Ghibelline parties and with the wars between city and city. Even the broader and more tenacious resistance and opposition between classes were translated into or mixed with episodes of convulsive

[58] For the Guelfs and Ghibellines in Perugia in these years, see Salvatorelli, 'La politica interna di Perugia', pp. 70ff.

guerrilla warfare, and with the sudden expulsion or return of armed groups, before they gradually took the form of the creation of new organs of power, of brief or not so brief duration.

Florence can be taken as an example, since its model of development, roughly applicable (with suitable caution) to many other cities, can be analysed much better than elsewhere through the wealth of sources and studies, and because 'signorial' interruptions occurred less frequently. At Florence the progress of the *popolo* from the time of its first formation in 1244 inside a prevalently Ghibelline regime can be considered as typical of the shapes that class tension took in the thirteenth century. The creation and subsequent elimination of the 'captaincy of the *popolo*' was accompanied by disturbances and violence associated with heretics, thus arousing the reaction of the Inquisition; the *popolo* was then re-formed after an insurrection which broke out in 1250 in the middle of the repression, insurrection, exile and return of the Guelf nobles. The expulsion of the Ghibellines was followed by wars in Tuscany and reconciliation between the parties in Florence, and the podestà was later expelled by the *popolo*. The aggressions of the Uberti led to an attack by the *popolo* on the Uberti property and was followed by the exile of the Ghibellines from the city. This lasted until the Guelf defeat at Montaperti in 1260 which violently ended the Guelf dominance in Florence and the regime of the *popolo* which was now associated with it.[59] This class tension was incorporated into conflicts of a very different nature which proceeded from more or less organic political divisions in the magnate class; these tensions and conflicts were further complicated by the rise of a powerful mercantile class within the institutions of the *popolo*, and especially in the magistracy of the Anziani,[60] a class receptive to magnate influence.

This general situation led to violent episodes of an intensity already familiar in the Italian world, and all the European West, for centuries. But however similar these episodes were to the clashes which disturbed the contado as well, and which had also disturbed the cities themselves in earlier times, they now acquired greater importance in the Lombard, Umbrian and Tuscan cities. The population was now denser and the guerilla warfare of the nobles between their towers more highly co-ordinated, while the noble *consorterie* now employed in greater numbers bands recruited from the peasants of seigneurial lands and the 'mob' of the city,[61] which fought alongside the knights. At the same time both

---

[59] Davidsohn, *Storia di Firenze*, vol. 2.1, pp. 411–703.
[60] *Ibid.*, pp. 642ff.
[61] See Salvatorelli, 'La politica interna di Perugia', pp. 88, 105ff.

the legal culture of notaries and judges[62] and the great merchants' carefully calculated method of working (when their lifestyle did not simply imitate the violent knightly traditions of the magnates[63]) suggested more rational and more stable solutions to the problems of public taxation, participation in power, and even the power-structure of the city. In the course of the thirteenth century and after, the size and conspicuousness of the destruction grew in the very urban agglomerations where changes in culture and custom were making the destruction most intolerable. Thus began the crisis, not of the communal order, which had always been in crisis because the constant transience of civic institutions was ingrained in it, but of the political struggle which, through 'disorder' itself, enabled groups that were rising socially or increasing in number to enter into competition with other groups that had an older tradition of power.

The legislation against the magnates, whose class significance we have affirmed (even though it was complicated by the influence of the factions among the 'great and powerful'), also had another aspect which was no less important. It acted in the name of the *popolo* and often also of the commune, in effect continuing the struggles of decades against the nobles, although it also showed a tendency to strike at certain groupings of magnates rather than others. It answered the need to repress vendettas and coups, to restrain those combats which for centuries had given substance to a large part of the life of *milites*, *nobiles* and *domini*, the nobles who were united by the bonds of kinship, *consorteria* or loyalty to a *senior* or leader of a party. Indeed it demonstrated repeatedly this need for civil 'pacification' in the clearest terms.

At Florence the first measures towards this end, included in a 'proceedings of the commune' of March 1281, appear under the rubric *de securitatibus prestandis a magnatibus civitatis*; each magnate, when requested by the podestà, the 'captain conserver of the peace' and the magistracy of the Fourteen (who at that moment represented the various districts of Florence), would have to give a guarantee not to cause harm, and not to provoke injuries.[64] The provision, even though it followed a period in which the struggles between Guelfs and Ghibellines had again been interwoven with serious social tensions, does not appear in

---

[62] See S. Calleri, *L'arte dei giudici e notai di Firenze nell'età comunale e nel suo statuto del 1314* (Milan, 1966), pp. 29ff.

[63] N. Rubinstein, *La lotta contro i magnati a Firenze*, vol. 2, *Le origini della legge sul 'sodamento'* (Florence, 1919), pp. 49ff; M. B. Becker, *Florence in Transition*, vol. 1 (Baltimore, 1967), pp. 6ff.

[64] Salvemini, *Magnati e popolani*, pp. 96ff; Ottokar, *Il comune di Firenze alla fine del dugento* (Turin, 1962), pp. 7ff.

this case to be a specific instrument in the struggle against the nobles; rather, it was for the protection of public peace. Similarly in the following July the Fourteen, considering that men of evil condition, accustomed to taverns, gaming, thefts and murders, and without a craft or goods of their own, threatened to subvert the 'peaceful condition of the city and district of Florence' and also to arouse 'magnates and the powerful of both parties' in order to provoke scandals and wars that would permit them to plunder more easily, caused the 'councils' of the podestà and captain to approve the attribution of full powers to the podestà himself, so that he might proceed with severe penalties against the disturbers of the peace, imprisoning some, expelling others from the city and district, and restraining others, who were evidently the subject magnates, *sub securitatibus* – that is, demanding from them the guarantees already provided for in March. Concurrently with this deliberation an armed body of 1, 000 citizens was set up to assist the podestà and captain each time that serious disturbances of the peace should call for it. This armed body was different from the political and military companies-at-arms, which years before had carried out the autonomous will of the district organizations of the people and entered into the very constitution of the unitary organism of the *popolo* functioning in the city in competition or co-operation with the organs of the commune. The civic militia was now separated from any organism of the *popolo*, even though a possible opposition to the militias of the magnates surfaces when the provision is made that during its convocation no one, especially if 'magnate and powerful', may summon armed men from other city districts or leave his own.

In this legislative episode of 1281 we can see an aim of 'pacification' which passes beyond the idea of conciliating opposing forces, and which claims the use of militias exclusively for the commune, as the co-ordinating body of urban life and not simply as the expression of a dominant part, even of a large majority, of the people. At the same time we can perceive a link with the earlier polemic against the nobles, and with the later developments of an apposite legislation directed against the magnates. Finally, we can glimpse the existence of a class of propertyless individuals capable of colluding with the forces of the magnates, even if the collusion, according to the July provision, is expressed in the singular shape of a provocation of the magnates by idle people. The social tensions which would find a means to express themselves in the following years and decades in much more striking ways coexist with the tendency towards a type of government more clearly structured as a state, indeed one which would gradually render more difficult the autonomous movement of groups and classes at the political level. For the Middle Ages knew almost no other means of entering into competition for political power except through an organization capable of physical self-defence and violent attack.

It is true that the great Florentine merchants and bankers succeeded after this 'pacification' in reinforcing their own political influence in the officially impartial commune, inasmuch as they did indeed make use of the Arti maggiori, from whom the new magistracy of the Priors was drawn in 1282, but at the same time they largely drew closer to the magnates of the Guelf party and often became more clearly magnates themselves, when they were not already such through noble descent (as was the case with the Adimari, Tornaquinci and Abbati).[65] Popular agitations favoured the tendency to include the craft guilds among the organs of power, but for some years this inclusion was limited to those same seven Arti maggiori, to the almost exclusive advantage of the most prominent elements among them. The seven corporations were linked with the persistent military power of the magnates through the Arte di Calimala (defined among other activities by the importation of foreign cloth destined to be finished and re-exported), that is, through the guild which still exercised an economic hegemony over all the others. Certainly the artisan formation no longer had in those years the support of the companies-at-arms of the past. When, later on, the wars in Tuscany brought the political class into a broader contact with the artisan formations, the old armed associations of the *popolo* arose again,[66] significant forerunners of the revolutionary disturbances of 1293. In that year the reaction against the oligarchy of Guelfs, magnates and merchants which had substantially lasted until then took the form of the famous Ordinances of Justice, which were uncompromisingly and explictly hostile to the 'magnate' class in criminal and civil law as well as on the level of civic government. The Ordinances were applied for two years so inexorably, and with such a desire to punish whoever was accused, that even Ottokar, the historian who was most committed to arguing against the 'classist' statements of Salvemini, refers repeatedly to a 'popular dictatorship', albeit a stormy one. He describes an 'initially firm union of the artisan world' and its rush 'into public life', interpreting the hasty and heavy sentences as 'de facto reprisals by the

---

[65] Stahl, *Adel und Volk*, pp. 58ff.

[66] It occurred to none other than Ottokar, *Il Comune di Firenze*, p. 188, to suggest that, with the importance given to the external politics of Florence, the broadening of the 'popular base' of the government was far from spontaneous. For the reorganization of the military societies of the *popolo*, see Davidsohn, *Storia di Firenze*, vol. 2.2, pp. 418ff.

aroused masses of the *popolo*'. The evidence of the chronicler is unequivocal in any case: he states that 'many deformed justice for fear of the people'.[67]

This was the justice of the *popolo minuto*, organized in substantial numbers (according to the definition given for the term *minuto* at the end of the thirteenth century) in the Arti minori, against the 'great' of every party and every lineage, from the nobles or the people. The 'justice' that was thus 'deformed' referred particularly to the complex of procedures (defined as *cavillationes* by a provision of 1294 concerning a case brought against Corso Donati) which in the Florence of the late thirteenth century guaranteed the accused against an arbitrary verdict by the judges. But on the other hand it is clear that the Ordinances of 1293 (leaving aside here the considerations already set out on the objective significance of anti-magnate legislation, as a challenge to very solid and particular seigneurial structures) sprang from indignation, which had already surfaced several times in the legislation since 1281, against the violence of the 'great' and their *consorterie* and against the abuses of the oligarchy in the exercise of power. With all these moves for and against the magnates, and in the midst of social struggles for the acquisition of political power, the need for a better ordered *res publica* – and one which was better ordered in every sector – became pressing. The oligarchy which had been functioning in the decade before the Ordinances of Justice had itself proposed several times, with the agreement of the artisan groups, improvements in the taxation system and in the administration of public finances, with the introduction of more exact accounting, a more rational structure of offices, and a less benevolent supervision of officials, of the goods belonging to the commune and of fiscal evasion. And in this respect the years 1293–5 constituted not a reversal but an intransigent and enthusiastic continuation of the preceding years, with ambitions for general reform of legislation for and systematic codification of 'statutes' and 'ordinances' as well – that is, of both the permanent measures and of the more or less temporary provisions.

The end of the brief revolutionary regime signified in its turn the restoration of the complex movement towards oligarchy. This movement tended towards institutional stability, and to the disarming of forces capable of compromising that stability, by means of a hegemonic 'Priorate' originating largely from the more prominent Arts, and the interlinking of durable magistracies such as the 'podestà of the commune' and the 'captain of the *popolo*', and of various councils

---

[67] Ottokar, *Il Comune di Firenze*, pp. 199ff.

of the commune and of the *popolo*. The Ordinances of Justice were in fact not revoked, even though in 1295 steps were taken to mitigate the procedural and criminal measures against the 'magnates' out of respect for criteria of greater 'equity';[68] for the Ordinances, while proceeding from the rising of the *popolo minuto*, were at the same time in large part a harsher version of the anti-magnate measures which had already surfaced in provisions for the public peace. At the same time there disappeared once more, for several years, the military formations of the people. Under the guise of a political constitution, formally founded on respect for the various origins of commune, *popolo* and artisan guilds, a practice of government was established which became progressively more disengaged from the tumultuous accumulation of political forces at the institutional level. Not that institutional changes did not take place; indeed on several occasions they resulted in the creation of some new magistracy or the correction of electoral procedures, and between 1328 and 1329 the traditional four councils disappeared, 'and one council of the people was created, of 300 men chosen from the people and approved as capable and Guelf, and similarly a council of the commune, where 250 men were approved from men of great families and men from the people'.[69] We should note the desire to simplify these councils, even while the forms respected the forces which the new institutions should have represented, in accordance with thirteenth-century tradition and as a replacement for the preceding four councils. The latter, in fact, had not been born from a conscious reform, as were their successors, but rather gradually, in order to express on the political level the pre-eminence of classes and armed groups.

None the less, we must avoid anticipating events. The Florentine oligarchy of the fourteenth century still operated for a long time in a difficult equilibrium between opposing forces, in whose diverse nature it also participated in certain respects. The construction of a fully state-like structure, which was now beginning, had not as yet frozen social forces in a definitive form, even though it was checking their movement on the political level. In accordance with the purest communal tradition, that movement was still usually directly related to the capacity of groups and classes to conduct themselves as militarily autonomous forces. Indeed at first, around the year 1300, the cleavage between 'White' and

[68] On the political aspect of the 'ordinances' of 1295, see *ibid.*, 'A proposito della presunta riforma costituzionale adottata il 6 luglio dell'anno 1295 a Firenze', (1933), reprinted in Ottokar, *Studi comunali e fiorentini* (Florence, 1948), pp. 125ff.

[69] Villani, *Cronica*, 1. x, c. 108 (vol. 5, p. 147). See Davidsohn, *Storia di Firenze*, vol. 3 (Florence, 1960), p. 1, 184.

'Black' Guelfs reproduced with renewed violence the traditional divisions between the *consorterie* of the magnates, with their complications in the world of the merchants and bankers and with their clientèles at all levels of the social hierarchy.[70] With this cleavage the 'vendetta' between great families, conducted in contempt of the Ordinances of Justice, was a sign yet again of the competition (already, in itself, a crudely political one) between the *consorterie* for hegemony in that very particular type of 'civil' society constituted by the magnate aristocracy. This hegemony, if attained by one or the other faction, was capable of shifting in its turn, through further rivalries, on to the higher political level of the governing class of the city, with a decisive impact on the most delicate problems of Florence in those years, and in particular the problem of the co-existence of Florentine 'liberty' with the broad papal projects for Tuscany. But the White–Black conflict between the factions of the Donati and the Cerchi provoked the reconstitution of the companies-at-arms 'in the manner of the ancient *popolo vecchio*', wrote Giovanni Villani, referring to the events of 1306 and 1307, 'since it seemed to the common people of Florence that the great and powerful had acquired might and boldness'; and 'for the strengthening of the *popolo* they caused to come to Florence the executor of the Ordinances of Justice, who was to inquire and proceed against the great who should offend the common people'.[71] The institution of the 'executor of the Ordinances', chosen from among foreigners (as was already the case, since the previous century, for the podestà and the captain), was designed to impose a better order on jurisdiction over offences committed by 'magnates' or by men connected with them, and on the vigilance over magistrates and functionaries of the commune.[72]

We may note that although constitutional 'reforms' now took on a very different shape from the improvised proceedings which had characterized the creation of autonomous political organs in the middle of the thirteenth century, the re-arming of the people in opposition to the disdain of the magnates for the Ordinances was limited to retracing the course of an old experience, and in effect provided an armed and officially recognized counterbalance to the irrepressible violence of the *consorterie*. The various forces operated according to traditional models and therefore lacked the unpredictable quality which had characterized them in their rise; while they remained in equilibrium the city was ruled by a government oligarchy which relied on the wealth of experience of

[70] Masi, 'La struttura sociale delle fazioni politiche fiorentine ai tempi di Dante', pp. 14ff.

[71] Villani, *Cronica*, I. VIII, cc. 69, 87 (vol. 3, pp. 119, 164ff).

[72] Davidsohn, *Storia di Firenze*, vol. 3, pp. 465ff; see vol. 4.1 (Florence, 1962), pp. 134ff, 150ff, 160ff.

some of the Arti maggiori, and personified the tendency which we would call state-like. However the oligarchy itself, by its very composition, presented the most serious problem for the regime which it represented; the Ordinances of Justice had officially placed in crisis its composite nature, which had included both merchants and magnates and was strengthened by the no less complex Guelf ideology which was at the same time papal, Franco-Angevin and republican.

One can say more. The official ideology of the city of Florence now attained a complexity which surpassed that of Guelfism, and came to appear bitterly contradictory, involving as it did, as its essential elements, the struggle of the *popolo* against the 'magnates' and simultaneously a Guelf intransigence. The Guelfs still had a very distinct shape in the supervisory institution which survived and was still called by the old name of the Guelf party; this had a rich patrimony of its own which had originated in the confiscation of Ghibelline goods,[73] and was almost monopolized by magnate families. These families were unequivocally of magnate status, since they are well-known for their earlier conflicts with the *popolo*, and were then constrained by the civic government to 'guarantee' – that is, to give certain specific guarantees, required in various contexts in the provisions that followed each other from 1281 up to the Ordinances of 1293 and beyond[74] – not to harm or provoke harm against any member of the *popolo*. It was for this reason that provision was made in 1323 to reform the Guelf party, which was to be governed by six captains, three of them knights and three of them from the *popolo*.[75] But in this way the Guelf party became the symbol of the old tendency of the *popolani grassi* and magnates to converge at the political level; this tendency was all the more natural since it had reflected for some time the composite structure not only of the highest social level considered as a whole but also of the economic basis, life-style and clientèle formations of individual families and *consorterie*. This was carried to such a point that some magnate *consorterie*, for example the Bardi (a great family included in the official list of 1293 among the magnate families north of the Arno, who were also bankers enrolled in the Arte di Calimala and supporters, at the beginning of the fourteenth century, of the 'Black' Guelf faction[76]), almost seemed to interpenetrate certain powerful banking companies.[77]

---

[73] For some weakening of the traditional thesis of the great wealth of the institution of the 'Guelf party', see G. A. Brucker, *Florentine Politics and Society (1343–78)* (Princeton, 1962), p. 99 note 182.

[74] See Rubinstein, *La lotta*, vol. 2, pp. 5ff, 48ff.

[75] Davidsohn, *Storia di Firenze*, vol. 3, pp. 957ff; vol. 4.1, pp. 196ff.

[76] Masi, 'La struttura sociale', p. 25; Stahl, *Adel und Volk*, pp. 149ff.

[77] See Masi, 'La struttura sociale', pp. 20ff.

In the light of this it is possible to understand how Villani could write
that the 'Guelf members of the *popolo*', towards 1325, 'ruled the city
with the counsel of a large part of the great and powerful'[78]. The
political class was indeed centred ever more clearly on a stratum which
was simultaneously mercantile, industrial and financial, involving not so
much the Arte di Calimala now, in the course of the fourteenth century,
as the Arte di Lana, which was highly specialized in all degrees of cloth-
working and was, according to some calculations, capable of employing
perhaps a quarter of Florentine workers.[79] But the political class, thanks
to old and new constitutional arrangements concerning the Priorate and
other organs of government or of inspection, had an opening on to a
considerable part of the world which was properly speaking artisan,
while on the other hand it felt with even greater intensity the pressure
of the entire magnate class. To this class not a few of the merchant
entrepreneurs belonged or could be assimilated, through the interweaving of kinship and the persistent temptation in individual wealthy
families, even those with a more recently-made fortune, to build up
their own autonomous military defence[80] in the manner of the old noble
consorterie – paralleling in other respects the armed city district companies
of the *popolo*, including the entire artisan class. It was during those years
that the Ordinance of Justice, hitherto an expression both of class conflict
and of a gradual process of state construction, began to be nothing more
than a tool in the discrimination and rivalry between powerful groups.
The ordinances had artificially crystallized the social and political
division in the form of a list of names of families prominent at a specific
time, thus preparing the way for the ambiguities which Villani
underlines in relation to measures taken by 'arbiters' created in Florence
in that same year, 1325; 'among other things, they withdrew from the
number of the great and powerful ten of the slightest and most
powerless houses of Florence and twenty-five lineages of nobles of the
contado, and relegated them to the *popolo*'.[81] The economic decadence
of certain magnate families and their interest in escaping the
discriminations laid down by the Ordinances explain their request to be
declared 'of the *popolo*', and the fact that they welcomed it. However
Villani adds that many people criticized the action of the arbiters

---

[78] Villani, *Cronica*, I. IX, c. 333 (vol. 4, p. 296).
[79] N. Rodolico, *I Ciompi* (Florence, 1945), p. 12; V. Rutenberg, *Popolo e
movimenti popolari nell'Italia del '300 e '400* (Bologna, 1971), p. 17.
[80] See Brucker, *Florentine Politics*, pp. 35ff; Becker, *Florence*, vol. 2 (Baltimore,
1968), pp. 103ff.
[81] Villani, *Cronica*, I. IX, c. 287 (vol. 4, p. 248); see too I. XII, c. 23 (vol. 7, p.
75).

(presumably as being insufficient), 'since some of the powerful and offensive lineages who were members of the *popolo* were fit to be placed among the great, for the good of the *popolo*'. The arbiters, in the judgement of many, should thus have placed many families which were legally of the *popolo* – the *grandi di popolo*, as they were called (that is, the powerful members of the *popolo grasso*), among those who were legally 'great' or 'magnates'.

At a difficult moment (owing to certain serious military reverses in Tuscany) the competition between the two powerful groups, of which only one could exercise power fully and directly without the restrictions that were imposed on the other by the Ordinances, was displayed in a dramatic fashion. It took the form of a highly significant collusion between the forces set at the extreme ends of the political range and of the social hierarchy, the 'great' with their 'armed bands' (not without the support of some *grandi di popolo* as well) and the Arti minori together with 'certain carders and lowest rabble'.[82] These latter elements were not even part of the Arts except when they were trades subordinate to one of the twenty-one guilds recognized politically (in particular, to the Arte della Lana), or except as 'subject' salaried workers. The collusion that took place centred on a French captain of war, who was acclaimed as *signore*. This was the brief tyranny of Walter of Brienne, between 1342 and 1343; he excluded the *popolo grasso* from the government of the city, 'ruling with butchers, wine-sellers and carders and minor artisans', but at the same time he wanted to centre the dictatorship on an autonomous military force, the bands of his own French knights, scorning the armed bands of the 'great' and suppressing the armed companies of the people.[83] The alternative to government by the *popolo grasso* thus ended

[82] Villani, *Cronica*, I. XII, c. 3 (vol. 7, pp. 9ff.).
[83] *Ibid.*, c. 8 (vol. 7, p. 22):

he annulled the office of the Gonfaloniers of the companies of the *popolo* and took away their banners, and any other office or order of the *popolo* that there was, he removed, ruling at his own pleasure with butchers, wine-sellers and carders and minor artisans, giving them consuls and rectors as they wanted, dismembering for them the orders of the Arts to which they had been subject because they wanted a larger salary for their labours.

The action of Walter towards the various strata of the *popolo* was complex; he sought to suppress the military formations of the *popolo*, which were under the hegemony of the artisans of all the autonomous Arts, and lowered the political prestige of the Priorate, dominated by the Arti maggiori. He freed certain crafts ('dismembering') from subordination to an Arte maggiore, and from other sources this appears to concern, for example, the dyers; see Rodolico, *I Ciompi*, p. 35. He permitted certain salaried workers to organize

not with the accession of the other powerful group, the so-called 'great' in the full sense, under the cover of a 'signorial' and broadly popular government, but in an autonomous signorial experiment which aimed to bring about the disarming of all the traditional organized social groups and to make use of the new social tensions in order to paralyse at the political level those groups which were economically pre-ponderant. This was a means, of which the Lombard world offered examples at the same time, of overcoming with one blow the remnants of the medieval 'anarchy', a means of accelerating the installation of a centre of state power, thus conferring on the government a clumsy stability and a 'superior' impartiality. In short, it was a political short-cut, but one which in Florence was too brutally far from the practice of government which had found its centre of gravity in the 'great of the *popolo*', and too much lacking an anchorage in Florentine society despite the shrewd moves of that 'ungracious' and 'very cunning' lord, Walter, and his improvized ties with certain social groups: he was 'playing the whore' with the lowest citizens and with certain individuals among the 'great', who had already rebelled against the city and were 'recently returned to Florence'.[84]

Soon afterwards Walter was driven out through three conspiracies of the 'great' and the *grandi di popolo* and by popular uprising (the *popolo* being at that time, in the broadest sense of the term, 'very noble and powerful and united', as our merchant chronicler Giovanni Villani says in referring to that tumult[85]); but the old magnate class, which had contributed more than the others to the fall of the harsh *signore* and which had finally obtained the revocation of the Ordinances of Justice, did not know how to exercise its hegemony in government with the same flexibility as the *popolo grasso*. This shows that the osmosis and the kinship between the two powerful groups had not yet completely deprived them of the characteristics which had distinguished them in the past, especially since the Florentine houses with a magnate tradition (particularly strong in the city north of the Arno) appear to have a special relationship with certain famous Tuscan aristocratic dynasties such as the Guidi counts, and thus with the highest level of the military aristocracy, which had centred its old territorial rule on the basis of a

themselves, perhaps in a form parallel to the Arts which were already recognized, as may be the case with the carders, and relied not only on this lowest social class, of crafts formerly subordinate and salaried workers, but also on some Arts which were not the more economically influential ones; hence Villani's reference to butchers and wine-sellers.

[84] *Ibid*, I. XII, c. 8 (vol. 7, p. 22, 26ff).
[85] *Ibid.*, c. 17 (vol. 7, p. 48).

landed patrimony. Yet again, as in Florence in the thirteenth century, the political struggle erupted in the city at the end of September 1343 in a clash between armed formations, this time between the armed bands of the 'great' and the re-established armed companies of the *popolo*, for yet again the rivalry between socially dominant groups – in the thirteenth century between Guelf and Ghibelline *consorterie* and now between 'great' and *grandi di popolo* – was interwoven with the ancient class conflict between the magnates and the formations of the *popolo*. This conflict was still deeply felt, as is apparent from the account of the companies of the city districts, with their banners, assaulting the 'garrisons' and the 'strong enclosures' of the Donati and Cavalcanti or the Bardi, Rossi and Frescobaldi; and the growth of the 'large crowd of the *popolo*', concentrating its forces against the Bardi, who were 'well-equipped and fitted out on horse and by foot and with many retainers', the burning of 'great and rich houses', until the resistance of the Bardi, the most hated 'for their great arrogance', was overcome for ever. It was overcome not just in the piazzas and in the streets, because the Ordinances of Justice were re-established; and as many as 500 magnates, 'certain lineages of the great, less powerful and not harmful', sought, after such a great defeat, to be 'withdrawn from among the great and translated to be members of the *popolo*', and had their request granted. Thus, within an urban patriciate which was still quite violently excitable, there took place definitively, on a wide scale, that fusion between Guelf nobility and 'powerful' merchants which had been foreshadowed a century earlier in certain convergences within the aristocracy of the 'commune' and between the communal institutions and the organisms of the *popolo*.

In reality others among the magnates also asked to be made members of the *popolo* but were refused: 'through envy they were not accepted'. Was this clash then merely an anachronistic conflict, purely an instrument in the struggle between groups at a high social level? The magnates who had driven out Walter of Brienne had shown themselves, with renewed ostentation, to be the grouping which was most arrogantly convinced of its own military and political calling, which set them within the purest tradition of the lords of estates and castles even though with all the financial complications characteristic of *consorterie* living in a big city. Let us say, rather, that the epilogue of that old conflict had been arrived at, a conflict which had never been exclusively an opposition of classes but whose class character had been most evident from the Ordinances of 1293, when the most influential families of the Arte di Calimala were added to the official list of the magnate *consorterie*. Now the earlier lists were brought up to date, limiting the circle of magnates to the most

dangerous or powerful, but they did not include any *grandi di popolo*;
'note well, that several lineages and houses of members of the *popolo*
were more worthy of being placed among the great than the larger part
of those who remained the great'.[86] There sprang from this the
government of a lively urban patriciate, which certainly continued
directly the action pursued by the *popolo grasso* before the brief signorial
tyranny of 1342–3, but which was much less hindered in its political
manoeuvres by the old Ordinances and which also emphasized the
participation of all the recognized guilds, the old 'twenty-one Arts' of
the late thirteenth century, to all of which the civic constitution now
officially entrusted, through complex procedures, the supreme responsibility of government. This eliminated a large part of what
remained of a specifically knightly class[87] and thus simplified public life;
the slow process of constructing a state, without dictatorial short-cuts,
was resumed under the hegemony of a class which had formed
spontaneously through a broad experience of commerce and industry,
linked with the artisan world, and through the acquisition of a style of
noble life which still felt the effects of certain knightly traditions of
violence but which no longer raised them to a normal criterion of
political behaviour. Despite the persistent superfluity of political
magistracies, whose competences overlapped and whose office-holders
were rotated too rapidly, the practice of government was being
strengthened by the increasing importance taken on by the notaries as a
group, as the stable bureaucracy of the 'commune'; salaried officials
increased by a factor of five in the half-century following the signoria
of Walter.[88]

A tendency towards a general reconciliation and collaboration? But
a society in continual development, such as the Florentine and Italian
urban world generally still was in the fourteenth century, could not but
express new tensions, even when one sets aside the specific financial crises
in connection with the failure of the bank of the Peruzzi and the Bardi,
which had ventured on grandiose loans in Europe, and the demographic

---

[86] Villani, *Cronica*, I. XII, c. 23 (vol. 7, p. 75).

[87] See Becker, *Florence*, vol. I, pp. 205ff.

[88] *Ibid.*, 'The Florentine Territorial State and Civic Humanism in the Early
Renaissance', in *Florentine Studies. Politics and Society in Renaissance Florence*
(London, 1968), p. 117, *Florence*, vol. I, pp. 99ff, 231. For the interesting
figure of the notary Piero di Ser Grifo da Pratovecchio, influential in the
financial policy of the commune and therefore hated by the Ciompi, and for
the family *consorteria* that formed around him 'in the heart of the Florentine
burocrazia', see O. Banti, 'Noterelle sul tumulto dei Ciompi', *Bollettino storico
pisano* (1959), pp. 8ff.

crisis provoked by the plagues which towards the middle of the century greatly reduced the population of Florence (which before then may already have reached almost 100,000 inhabitants[89]). The demographic crisis intensified as a result of the usual influx of new population from the contado, of every social condition, with notable consequences both in the world of the artisan and workman and in the bureaucratic and political class of the entrepreneurs.[90] The problem, however, concerns the way in which a regime which was consolidating itself at the institutional level was able to, or sought to, settle or express political rivalries and social tensions, now that the latter could no longer affirm themselves through violence, as in the thirteenth century, and through the incessant construction of autonomous organs of political and military power.

And here the increasing inadequacy of that political regime appears, precisely as it was gradually strengthening itself bureaucratically. It is not wrong to envisage the period 1343–78, from the signoria of Walter to the rising of the Ciompi, as a period of increasing and ever more complex social tension,[91] at least by comparison with the calmer years after the humiliation of the 'great' families. But persistent and intense conflicts had always been woven into the life of the city. The remedy envisaged for certain problems was gradually taking on a different shape, and we can glimpse not far off the accession of some great family, the Albizzi or the Medici, to a more stable power, but this was a result not of the greater seriousness of conflict or its more irreparable nature, but rather of a greater intolerance of it and of a growing ability to repress conflict within a power apparatus that sought a more stable centre on which to base itself definitively.

But before that came about, and Florence's 'Middle Ages' came to an end, the city was still experiencing spontaneous political disagreements, and social conflict of a completely new type. In the governing class there were important divergences (mixed, it must be understood, with the ambitions of influential families) between an intransigent desire for conservation and a display of political open-mindedness and social openness; this was perceptible both in external politics, where the construction of a firm and dangerous territorial power by the Roman

---

[89] E. Fiumi, 'La demografia fiorentina nelle pagine di Giovanni Villani', *Archivio storico italiano*, 108 (1950), pp. 78ff; 'Fioritura e decadenza dell'economia fiorentina', *Archivio storico italiano*, 116 (1958), pp. 463ff. But see too Beloch, *Bevölkerungsgeschichte Italiens*, vol. 2, pp. 129ff.

[90] See Brucker, *Florentine Politics*, pp. 40ff; Becker, *Florence*, vol. 1, pp. 177ff; vol. 2, pp. 93ff.

[91] As does Brucker, *Florentine Politics*, pp. 50ff.

papacy placed the official Guelfism at Florence in crisis, and in internal politics, where a problem was created by the new population which had flowed into the city, while at the same time there emerged the other, wholly new, problem of the proletariat. The conservatives in their external and internal policy made use of the old institution of the Guelf party, whose task of ideological supervision had already been used in the past by the magnate faction to influence the activity of the government; by issuing 'admonitions' against those suspected of Ghibellinism, it was now admirably suited to hindering the anti-papal policy, and to removing from responsibility new citizens coming from the contado who had origins that were ideologically obscure or who, if they were of higher social descent, were often openly suspect. In this context, in the tension created by the enthusiastic activity of the Guelf Party, there occurred in 1378 the uprising of the Ciompi, of the proletariat.

It was a 'primitive proletariat', if we accept the use of a term which is suitable for those 'pre-capitalist' forms of production which were emerging from the development of certain of the Arti maggiori, particularly the Arte della Lana.[92] For the unorganized salaried workers, who in the thirteenth century were still a somewhat marginal presence among the working classes (the latter at that time being largely incorporated into guilds which were either autonomous or subordinate to the Arts of entrepreneurial merchants), grew, at Florence during the fourteenth century, to perhaps one-third of the population. They found themselves for the most part subjected to the iron discipline of the Arte della Lana, which was equipped with its own jurisdictional and coercive powers over questions relating to work and to the discipline of the workmen. The uprising was grafted on to the political action of a restless patrician, Salvestro de'Medici, who unsheathed again the old weapon of the Ordinances of Justice – a dangerous one for some of the nobles entrenched in the structure of the Guelf party. Ordinances and Guelf party, the old opposing instruments of class conflict between *popolo* and magnates, reappeared (with an old-fashioned language now directed against nothing more than the shadows of the magnate nobility and Ghibellinism) in the new role of legal weapons in the struggle between families that represented different orientations of the patriciate in the government of the 'commune'. These latter, however, found themselves drawn into a new class conflict generated by an entrepreneurial development which could no longer be completely incorporated into the old guild tradition.

---

[92] Rutenberg, *Popolo*, pp. 5ff. See too E. Werner, 'Der Florentiner Frühkapitalismus in marxistischer Sicht', *Studi medievali*, I (1960), pp. 661ff.

The link between the purely political action of the Medici and the proletarian uprising was formed by the dissatisfaction of the world of the lesser artisans with the ultra-conservative course which depended on the Guelf party. The action of the Medici was in fact complicated by the insurrection of the armed companies of the *popolo*, and the latter in its turn by the Ciompi rising. This was rather more than a rising since it led the Ciompi to demand their social and political incorporation into autonomous artisan groupings, and in this they were briefly successful. The corporate order's incipient decline was indicated by the presence of the Ciompi themselves in disputes over salaries and working conditions, so that their claim to their own Arts within that order perhaps appears to be an anachronism, lacking in 'innovatory dynamism'.[93] The new Arts were, however, a powerful tool for a radical transformation of the conditions of labour and power in the city of Florence, stronger than were the Guelf Party and the Ordinances as means of struggle at a high social level. They were certainly an instrument which, if we consider names and forms, dated back to the thirteenth century; but their content was by now entirely different, precisely because they were Arts of salaried workers, which placed themselves on a level of political equality with the pre-capitalist Arts and therefore took on a role of social resistance within a single production process. They were able to take on this character as a specific result of the strongly political nature acquired by the Arts in the thirteenth century, even through in the earlier period the Arts had achieved this political nature with different aims. In that instance the Arts had been in conflict with the magnate *consorterie* and in competition amongst themselves, in a struggle for power in the city between juxtaposed groupings which represented autonomous processes of production. That is, this new development arose from the purely 'medieval' and 'anarchic' nature of political power.

The anachronism, if any, lies in quite another area. The Arts at Florence in the second half of the fourteenth century were still an instrument of political power, but the political power now functioned in a unitary structure. Florence was now truly a republic, very different from those *res publicae* which more than a century before had meant, in the high-flown language of chanceries and notaries, forms of political co-operation that were in reality rather transient and often still functioned in symbiosis with other, institutionally heterogeneous, powers. The armed companies of the *popolo* still had a place in the insurrection which culminated in the Ciompi rising, but the Ciompi

---

[93] M. Mollat and P. Wolff, *Ongles bleus, Jacques et Ciompi* (Paris, 1970), p. 160, but see p. 162.

could no longer form themselves into an armed political nucleus which could be accepted by other militarily similar forces in the city, as had happened in the middle of the thirteenth century. Factional organizations had learnt through the experience of a century to operate in a different manner. Florentine society was ridding itself of the 'crudeness' of the endemic violent self-affirmation of organized groups. The waning of magnate violence, which disturbed the peace and provoked all the strata of the people to imitation, was followed by the 'pacification' of all levels of society. The monopoly of violence, after so many centuries of medieval dispersion of power, was definitively restored to the official political authority. The magistracy of the Guard of Eight, set up in 1378 immediately after the failure of the Ciompi revolution with the purpose of supervising the public order,[94] can be taken (with the developments which it underwent in later years) as the symbol of a new desire to 'guard' peace and repress violence, following in a tradition which had begun with the anti-magnate legislation but which now had the ability to translate the state-like orientation of that old legislative activity into the construction of a sizeable nucleus of forces, a military and policing order, institutionally separated from society.

The construction of such an order, after passing through a phase during which it was gradually more narrowly oligarchical, was to become an instrument of social cystallization around a 'civil' despotism. This came about because the inclination to construct the state apparatus 'rationally' was linked with the 'culture' of the hegemonic patriciate, a patriciate which had increasingly found in the progress of the public debt, its expansion and organization into the *monte delle prestanze* in the fourteenth century, a form of carefully-calculated and profitable investment; this gave them a new reason to recognize their own interest in a solid and well-administered republic, and their affinity with such a structure of government.[95] Equally, the easiest way to stabilize political power appeared to be reduction of political discord, and, eventually, its suppression, when faced with a *signore* who respected the titles and forms of the republic.

Florence is not the whole of Italy, and its affairs cannot reflect exactly the developments of the other communal cities. But the anti-magnate

[94] G. Antonelli, 'La magistratura degli Otto di Guardia a Firenze', *Archivio storico italiano*, 112 (1954), pp. 3ff. See Becker, *Florence*, vol. 2, p. 221.

[95] B. Barbadoro, *Le finanze della repubblica fiorentina* (Florence, 1929), pp. 629ff; M. Becker, 'Problemi della finanza pubblica fiorentina della seconda metà del Trecento e dei primi del Quattrocento', *Archivio storico italiano*, 123 (1965), pp. 433ff; *Florence*, vol. 2, pp. 151ff.

legislation,[96] the evolution of the 'great' and of the *grandi di popolo* towards a patriciate which was gradually more composite in origin and more homogenous in its life-style (although complicated by some collusion between *popolo minuto* and magnates[97]), the tensions provoked by the influx of new population to the city and the expansion of the working class,[98] and the move towards more stable and repressive communal structures, towards a public finance connected with well-calculated private operations,[99] and towards a more rigid social structure sanctioned by legislation – all this can be found again elsewhere, even though factors such as a lesser degree of pre-capitalist development, external interference, and variations or changes in timing can make it less intense in nature. The whole process was very widespread in central Italy and also, up to a certain point in its development, in many cities of northern Italy, wherever and as long as the spontaneity of these processes was not prevented, interrupted or deflected by the sudden rise and subsequent consolidation of the signorial tyrannies.

For 'tyranny' was the other route followed by the communal cities in the thirteenth and fourteenth centuries, in order to resolve problems of internal coexistence and to orient themselves towards a state structure and the social crystallization associated with it. In Lombardy, in particular, they followed this route so frequently that the period of the passage from a regime centred on the competition of autonomous powers in the city, at one moment co-ordinated among themselves and at another in violent conflict, to a regime which was properly speaking state-like is called, according to an old historiographical tradition (and not without reason when one considers its most visible aspect), the period of the urban *signorie*, as if the 'signoria', and not the general consolidation of institutions, were the historically central fact.[100] We could say, rather, that the spontaneous nature of the process of state construction can be perceived much better in cases where the signoria appeared after the process itself was fully mature, and as its consummation, as in the Florentine case, than in cases where it was grafted on to the initial phase of the process. It remains true, none the

---

[96] Fasoli, 'Ricerche'. For Pisa see Cristiani, *Nobiltà e popolo*, pp. 71ff. For Padua see J. K. Hyde, *Padua in the Age of Dante* (Manchester, 1966), pp. 217ff, 238ff.

[97] Particularly interesting in this respect is Salvatorelli, 'La politica interna di Perugia', pp. 104ff.

[98] For Perugia and Siena see Rutenberg, *Popolo*, pp. 115ff.

[99] See Barbadoro, *Le finanze*, pp. 673ff.

[100] See G. Chittolini, 'La crisi delle libertà comunali e le origini dello stato territoriale', *Rivista storica italiana*, 82 (1970), pp. 999ff.

less, that the more or less precocious arrival of the signorial regime had a strong impact on all urban institutions and on urban society, so much so that it brought about a particular series of events somewhat different from that of the 'republican' type.

This particular series of events did not arise from the violent means, the *coups de main*, with which the signoria was very often installed.[101] In thirteenth-century cities *coups de main* were almost a normal way to proceed in the harshest moments of political struggle, when the conflict between concentrations of interest broke down the ephemeral framework of institutions and created, replaced, or added new organs of power sustained by an armed will. The novel occurrence was when the holder of an eminent civic magistracy (such as the 'podestà', 'captain of the *popolo*', *anziano della credenza* or 'general captain', 'conserver of the peace' or 'lord'), which was already one of the organs of the commune of *popolo*, or had been created à propos to overcome a difficult situation, was formally given by the councils of the commune or popolo the powers belonging to his office or other extraordinary powers, not simply for a period of months, but for five or ten years or for life; the extraordinary powers of the *balia* were sometimes conferred on collective organs to resolve certain serious internal or external problems or, in the form of a *balia generale*, for an exceptional period of supreme rule over the city. In other words, at this point the practice of very brief periods of office in the highest magistracies began to break down, and the magistrate or lord was given the means of consolidating his personal power and preparing its transmission to other members of his own family. The urban signoria of several years was usually (either as *balia* or *balia generale*) a temporary expedient, for which the instability of the power and its institutions offered a thousand opportunities. But in certain cases or periods, while it maintained its original character and represented with particular efficiency, through its special importance, the dominance of a group or a class, or a need for internal reconciliation or for co-ordination with external forces, it did not preclude further changes as circumstances or relations between social groups altered. This happened in Florence itself several times, first in the thirteenth century, when in 1266 Charles of Anjou was made podestà for six years in connection with his imminent conquest of the kingdom of Sicily and for the clear purpose of co-ordinating the Guelfs in Italy. In the fourteenth century the Florentines acted more freely on their own initiative when in 1313, while Emperor Henry VII was still alive, they responded to an

[101] This violence is demonstrated by many examples collected by F. Diaz, 'Di alcuni aspetti dell'affermarsi delle signorie', *Nuova rivista storica*, 50 (1966), pp. 116ff.

external situation which called for anti-imperial action and internal reconciliation. The Florentine 'councils' gave a generous *balìa* for five years, and then for a further three, to the king of Naples (officially 'king of Sicily') Robert of Anjou, who sent to Florence a vicar, changed every six months, to act as supreme moderator. Again, in 1325, when the threat of Castruccio Castracani, lord of Lucca and Pistoia, was becoming more serious, the 'councils' of Florence elected as 'lord, governor, defender and protector' for a decade the son of King Robert, Charles, Duke of Calabria, who held a splendid court in the city for two years. Despite 'all that his stay in Florence cost overall', 'he was indeed a sweet seigneur';[102] he then had to leave Tuscany because of the needs of the Angevin kingdom and soon afterwards died. Finally, in 1342, Walter of Brienne was acclaimed by the people and confirmed by the 'councils' as 'signore for life', but he interpreted his signoria in a very different way from Duke Charles and was driven out after a year, as seen above.

From the Florentine examples it is already apparent how the 'signoria' could be differently interpreted in the internal and external political life of a communal city. King Robert and the Duke of Calabria did no more than stress with their personal presence or through vicars, not only in Florence but in other threatened cities as well, the protective role which the Guelf party in Italy, in parallel with the opposing Ghibelline party, had exercised for some time towards the organizations that supported it. At the same time they granted their political support within the city to the group of merchants dominant in the organs of the commune and the *popolo*, and resisted, in the case of the Duke of Calabria in 1326, the pressure of the magnates, who offered a signoria of unlimited duration in order to influence the duke by their friendship and obtain a reversal of the power relations in the government of the city, through the abolition, in particular, of the Ordinances of Justice. But Walter did not want to resist such pressure, and believed he could combine it with the opposing pressures of the *popolo minuto* to construct a permanent autonomous signoria analogous to those of Lombardy. In Florence the project failed, and so the signoria, even in the case of Walter's rise and fall, functioned in practice, independently of his plans, as an instrument of the usual manoeuvres between social groups. Elsewhere similar projects succeeded and 'communal liberty' – that is, the ability of groups to exert influence with varying degrees of violence directly on the political level – came to an end.

But these purely communal experiments with the signoria did not happen only in Florence, nor only in cities such as Lucca and Pisa,

---

[102] Villani, *Cronica*, i.x, c. 49 (vol. 5, p. 63).

Genoa, Asti and Bologna, which for much of the fourteenth century and with varying difficulty still used the signoria in the disputes between local forces as well as for protection against external dangers. Those powerful cities (of which Milan is a notable example) in which a signorial regime was precociously established generally present a phase of public life in which the signoria functioned within, and not above, the civic political world: that is, it was not yet able to suppress political activity under the weight of the signoria's own apparatus, but, rather, functioned as one of the recurring institutional elements of the city. For example, the difficulty in identifying precisely the beginning of the signoria of the della Torre at Milan in the central decades of the thirteenth century arises from the presence of the family in the organs of the *popolo* in prominent positions, which were occupied at first for their normal duration (although not without some significant renewals). They had a political role that was clearly still connected with the real needs of the popular classes for the struggle against the nobility, needs which took the form both of concrete questions such as those of the tax valuation, the public debt and the physical security of the members of the *popolo*, and of questions which were prevalently, though not exclusively, matters of prestige, such as the social recruitment of the cathedral chapter.[103] The incipient signoria of the della Torre was indeed still so rooted among the Milanese communal institutions that not only could it be interrupted, or alternate with others, but it could appear simultaneously with another personal signoria with a different title and different official function. In 1259 Martino della Torre was proclaimed *anziano del popolo*, thus influencing through the popular body of the *credenza di Sant'Ambrogio* all the political activity of the city, but in the same year, also in Milan, the condottiere Oberto Pelavicino, a member of the pro-imperial party and already lord of several Lombard cities, was raised to the 'general captaincy of the *popolo*' for five years, through the initiative of the della Torre and while the latter's anti-imperial signoria still continued. In these years Oberto, through a compromise of co-existence with the della Torre, exercised not only a military role to protect the city but a precise political power, that of removing and choosing the podestà of the commune. The two signorie, with their extraordinary powers, were incorporated into the context of the multiple civic organs of government, complicating them yet further both in their formal aspect and as real expressions of the specific political demands of the city and of the groups organized within it.

[103] Franceschini, *Vita sociale e politica*, vol. 4, pp. 248, 257, 264ff, 294ff, 312; R. Romeo, *Il comune rurale di Origgio nel secolo XIII* (1957, 2nd ed. Assisi, 1970), pp. 88ff.

After the five years of the 'captaincy general' of Oberto had ended, the signoria of the della Torre continued in Milan, as usual with 'popular' complications and with a Guelf flavour, and co-ordinated with the dominance in Italy of Charles of Anjou, to whom was offered the power to nominate the podestà of the city. But the title of 'permanent *anziano* of the *popolo* of Milan', which began to be used to designate the office that was passed through formal deliberations of the *credenza* from one member to another of the family, now clearly signified a power which was not only dominant in the city in the shape of the official administration of an organism of the *popolo*, but which was directed towards overcoming the usual instability of the civic order. Support was also sought for this latter aim from the imperial authority, when in 1275 Rudolf of Hapsburg, King of the Romans, was asked to recognize the liberties of Milan and the official position attained by the della Torre in the city, and to undertake not to assist the Milanese exiles (a large part of the nobles, including Archbishop Otto Visconti) to re-enter the city.[104] The imperial authority, after the failure of the political project which the Staufers had attempted in Italy, thus displayed its last marginal effectiveness in the history of the Italian kingdom; it added legitimization from above to the powers which had sprung up spontaneously in the Italian cities, and which were already legitimized by customs and local intiatives – that is, by the complex structure which gave shape to the civic constitutional order, however elastic and vulnerable to fractures that structure might be.

The expression of this imperial legitimization at the time of Rudolf is unknown, but twenty years later it took on a very clear form in the concession of an 'imperial vicariate' in favour of the signore (at that time, in 1294, the lord of Milan with the title of 'captain of the *popolo*' was Matteo Visconti, and the King of the Romans was Adolf of Nassau[105]). Can such a legitimization be paralleled to the feudal (or quasi-feudal) investitures that were used in the twelfth century by Barbarossa when he was constrained to recognize the powers that were emerging through spontaneous developments in Italy? The parallel is possible with two provisos: first we should bear in mind the very feeble political weight of a Rudolf or an Adolf in Italy, compared with the possibilities of action that the Staufer emperors still possessed; and secondly, conversely, we should note that, in its formal aspect, the

---

[104] *Die Regesten des Kaiserreichs unter Rudolf, Adolf, Albrecht, Heinrich VII* vol. 1, ed. O. Redlich (Böhmer, *Regesta imperii*, vol. 6.1, 1898, reprinted Hildesheim, 1969), n. 324, 354ff. See Redlich, *Rudolf von Hapsburg*, p. 198.

[105] *Die Regesten*, vol. 2, ed. V. Samanek (Böhmer, *Regesta imperii*, vol. 6.2, Innsbruck, 1933–48), n. 389.

'vicariate' was clearly distinct from a vassal invested with public powers in a fief. The 'vicariate' did not realize the concept of an autonomous hereditary property; it was, rather, a delegation of authority which was now transmissible, or, for much of the fourteenth century, a delegation transmissible within a family only when the emperor explicitly approved each instance.[106] But when one looks closely, there is no contradiction between imperial weakness and a cautious legitimation through vicars; in fact, as long as the German king was not present with a strong armed force in Italy (as he still was occasionally in the fourteenth century), this legitimation more or less fitted the imperfect status attained by the *signore* in the city and on the level of local law. It was limited to strengthening the *signore*'s threatened stability through a solemn appeal to the empire, which was presented in the imperial diplomas as the source of the powers exercised by the *signore*.

Nevertheless, the increase in institutional stability still did not mean at Milan, in the years in which the della Torre entered into relations with the 'Guelf' empire of Rudolf, that the signorial power was as yet autonomous of its specific social base and clientèle. Soon afterwards, in fact, the della Torre were overthrown by the nobles and the archbishop, who re-entered the city. And although Archbishop Otto Visconti, proclaimed *signore*,[107] proceeded with some moderation, his government immediately revealed the imprint of the victorious noble party when the official list of noble families was drawn up (even though the list only concerned admission to the cathedral chapter, which had been an issue vigorously debated for decades in the city's social and political conflicts), and when a new 'society' of nobles was set up for the defence of the city.[108] Not without reason Milan, unlike so many other cities, thus did

---

[106] See F. Ercole, *Dal comune al principato* (Florence, 1929), pp. 280ff, with the modifications called for by the documents re-examined in G. Tabacco, 'Sulla distinzione fra vicariato politico e giuridico del sacro impero', *Bollettino storico-bibliografico subalpino*, 46 (1948), pp. 31ff (and for the vicariate as legitimation, see the conclusions on pp. 65ff). For the real political efficiency of some imperial vicariates, see G. De Vergottini, 'Vicariato imperiale e signoria', in *Studi di storia e diritto in onore di Arrigo Solmi*, vol. I, pp. 43ff. For the change of civic mentality in the consolidation of the signorial regime, assisted by the imperial vicariate, see P. Torelli, 'Capitanato del popolo e vicariato imperiale come elementi costitutivi della signoria bonacolsiana' (1923), reprinted in Torelli, *Scritti di storia del diritto italiano* (Milan, 1959), pp. 377ff.

[107] For the lack of clarity in the legal position of the new *signore*, see E. Salzer, *Über die Anfängen der Signorie in Oberitalien* (Berlin, 1900), p. 117 note 74.

[108] See the opinion of Bozzola, 'Guglielmo VII di Monferrato', p. 116, on the archbishop's behaviour.

not have anti-magnate legislation: under the della Torre the nobles largely emigrated, and under the Visconti they were the support of the new signoria. Meanwhile, between the two signorie, a regime was being formed which, however much it was still influenced by factions and classes, tended to depress the capacity for autonomous action of both the organs of the *popolo* and those of the noble *consorterie*. As a result the regime also blocked the political development of that class of merchants and entrepreneurs who elsewhere, manoeuvring between inclusion in the *popolo* and imitation of the nobles, were at this time acquiring a central role in the orientation of public life towards state-like structures. Despite the exceptional mercantile and industrial prosperity of Milan, particularly in the sectors of wool and metal-working, the political function exercised by the *popolo grasso* elsewhere in Milan fell to the *signore*.

For some years Archbishop Otto had to co-ordinate his predominance with another signoria in the city, conferred on the Marquis Guglielmo VII of Monferrato to meet the needs of the war, in a fashion not very different from the co-ordination between the della Torre and the captaincy of Oberto Pelavicino. But he then procured for his great-nephew Matteo Visconti a five-year 'captaincy of the *popolo*', which was subsequently renewed each five years. The leader of the nobles and of the upper clergy felt the need to present his political heir as a representative of the *popolo*. After the alternation between Visconti and della Torre in the first decade of the fourteenth century, the Visconti re-established themselves for the rest of the century, despite intermittent crises provoked by papal or imperial policies in Italy or by bitter internal rivalries within the signorial family itself; the Milanese signoria was now clearly a very solid political regime. The phase in which the signoria functioned at Milan as an instrument of political struggle, in a society divided among organized and armed groups, had been wholly left behind. The 'councils' of the city were recruited through procedures in which the tendency to co-opt blended with designation from above, and were subordinate to the will of the *signore*. The political character of the various organs of the commune and of the *popolo* was watered down to become consultative and administrative, in the service of the lord and of his court. The number of functionaries grew. A chancery of the *signore* was formed and towards the end of the century, at the time of Gian Galeazzo, there appeared a 'secret council', for the purpose of political management and high criminal jurisdiction.[109]

[109] F. Cognasso, 'Istituzioni comunali e signorili di Milano sotto i Visconti', *Storia di Milano*, vol. 6 (Milan, 1955), pp. 456ff.

Meanwhile, in the middle of the fourteenth century, measures were promulgated for the succession to power within the Visconti family. Thus the dynasty was officially recognized as such, and the 'imperial vicariate', which had been repeatedly requested and obtained in the course of the century, now appeared inadequate for such a condition of permanent supremacy. Hence in 1395 Gian Galeazzo received an imperial enfeoffment of power with the title of prince and duke, comparable with the surviving Italian marquisates and counties and the German territorial principalities, which were autonomous de facto and de jure, and bound to the emperor only by the oath of vassal loyalty and by the form of feudal investiture. Once more the Empire functioned as a further instrument of legitimization for signorial power. But now the imperial legitimization of the dynasty did not replace the legitimization supplied by the 'councils' of the city only in theory (that is, in the formulae of the imperial diplomas) but replaced it completely, since the signorial dynasty, parading its ducal title which was in tune with the growing princely ceremonial of the court, now ignored its communal origin totally. Were these simply forms and symbols? Undoubtedly yes, but those forms and symbols expressed a robust reality, the arrogant operation of a political power no longer within, but above society. Certainly it was not isolated from society, but it had such a capacity to attract the classes which were prominent for their ancestry or wealth that it powerfully assisted that society to re-mould itself into an hierarchical structure which increasingly developed rigid social divisions. A patriciate of 'notables' was marked out by its relations with the court and by its presence in the civic institutions that the prince controlled, and tended to act as a barrier between the prince himself and the remaining population.

In short, by routes which were notably different but with results that were substantially similar, both in the cities with a signorial regime and in those with a more resilient communal tradition, there took effect the construction of a more stable power and a more highly-ordered administration, accompanied by a growing acceptance of inherited social status.[110] It is exceptionally interesting to observe that these developments and social closures were not limited to the cities which had experienced the clash between political–military organisms of

[110] For a case which is intermediate between communal tradition and seigneurial orientation in the course of the fourteenth century, but which moved in the usual direction towards more stable powers, see M. Tangheroni, *Politica, commercio, agricoltura a Pisa nel trecento* (Pisa, 1973), pp. 49ff. For the last phase, before the definitive crises of Pisan autonomy, see O. Banti, *Iacopo d'Appiano* (Pisa, 1971), pp. 79ff.

knights and of the *popolo*, but had their counterpart in the Venetian republic, which, because of its Byzantine descent and the topographical conditions of the city itself, experienced a less adventurous development of political power. In the twelfth and thirteenth centuries the 'duchy' broadened institutionally into a 'commune' which gradually became more articulated and complex but was nevertheless always unitary as a structure of government; in those years it repeatedly displayed the tendency towards a broader social participation in power (which would no longer consist only in the acclamations or uprisings of the *popolo*), in parallel with and in opposition to a 'noble' circle which founded its predominance on the political tradition of particular families and on a wealth which was now fed in large part by commerce. But the social tensions were resolved by the gradual assimilation of new economically powerful families into the circle of the 'nobles', or by their participation in the government even while their recent orgin was remembered – which, through their designation as *popolari*, guaranteed them a certain favour with the people.[111] No conflict broke out which was comparable to those of the mainland cities, since in Venice there were no specific autonomous organisms of the *popolo*, nor was the nobility divided into violent knightly *consorterie* of a type that would feed an anti-magnate polemic. And therefore, despite some temptations in that direction in the fourteenth century and despite the many examples given by the mainland cities, there was no turning towards a personal regime which tended to the dynastic, even though such a regime had already been experimented with in the 'duchy' in times of simpler political structures. Political development centred not on a *popolo grasso* oscillating between its inclinations towards the magnates and its links with the guilds of the Arts, but rather on the graduated social differentiation between a modest artisan class and a class that possessed great wealth in movables and also in real estate. This wealth was increasing through substantial investments, from the thirteenth century onwards, in the public debt of the republic, which was extensively engaged in the dominion of the Adriatic and the eastern Mediterranean; and also, above all, through still more substantial investments and active participation in commercial enterprises of great

[111] Kretschmayr, *Geschichte von Venedig*, vol. 2 (1920, reprinted Aalen, 1964), pp. 68ff, to be modified by Merores, 'Der venezianische Adel', pp. 213ff. See *Deliberazioni del Maggior Consiglio di Venezia*, vol. 1, pp. ixff, for constitutional changes. See G. Cracco, *Società e Stato nel medioevo veneziano* (Florence, 1967), pp. 54, 75, 84ff, 176ff, 202ff, 217ff, 229ff, 254ff, 264, 325, for the social composition of the institutions of the republic and of the electoral colleges which designated the doge, and pp. 108ff for the noble title in the twelfth and thirteenth centuries.

breadth. At the same time, landed patrimonies spread in the Venetian hinterland, outside the political boundaries of the republic, as a further support for the prestige of this class and as a guarantee of stability.[112] This social class, which had arrived at political power by virtue of an incomparable economic power and was practically without rivals either 'above' or 'below', managed in the thirteenth and fourteenth centuries to render gradually more difficult the access of the *homines novi* to power. Finally, in 1323, they sealed themselves into a closed hereditary political class, using forms which attained a rigidity known by no other political class in Italy at the time and which were able to create the most extreme model of an inflexible legal definition of the patriciate, with, as a result, the inevitable problems of rearranging power within a class which was officially static but which would none the less alter in its economic structures.

In selecting the most notable examples of the development of the commune in the direction of the state, we have purposely set to one side the great territorial complications which accompanied them in Lombardy, in Tuscany and in the East in the thirteenth and fourteenth centuries. But is it really possible to isolate the growth of an apparatus of power from its extension far beyond the walls of a city? It would certainly be a mistake to reduce the construction of new state formations to the simple perspective of territorial expansion. The examples proposed demonstrate that the crisis of the mobility of power in the Middle Ages was initially born within every social system capable of expressing itself with vigour; it was born from an experience of struggle and organization, from the gradual acquisition of techniques of internal 'pacification', and from the choice made by the most highly-regarded classes, in the most respected cities, of a type of security in which the need for a constitutional framework was transformed into the repression of political impulses. The Florentine example, which can be followed continuously through two centuries, leaves no doubt in this respect. And in Milan itself, always involved in the broader affairs of Lombardy, personal and dynastic power developed not from the 'captaincy general' of Oberto Pelavicino or from the 'signoria' conferred with full powers on Guglielmo VII of Monferrato, but rather from the *anzianato di popolo* of the della Torre, from the noble and ecclesiastical pre-eminence, purely Milanese, of Otto Visconti, and from the composition of the urban forces around Otto's great-nephew Matteo. It remains true, none

---

[112] G. Luzzatto, 'Les Activités économiques du patriciat vénetien (xe-xive siècles)' (1937) reprinted in Luzzato, *Studi di storia economica veneziana*, pp. 128ff; *Storia economica di Venezia dall'XI al XVI secolo* (Venice, 1961), chapter 2. For the artisans, see also Cracco, *Società Stato*, chapter 3.

the less, that della Torre and Visconti represented at the same time interests broader than those of the city, and that Florence had constantly to place its own internal disagreements in a regional and Italian context.

TOWARDS THE ORDERING OF ITALY INTO REGIONAL STATES

As we have seen above, the class which was prominent in the great and smaller cities (through its landed wealth, military tradition or mercantile activity) was already, at the time of its first close association around the 'consulate', operating both politically and militarily, in fluid coalitions of interests, in a territory which stretched far beyond the limits of the city both materially and socially. And so, as the political class organized itself within the dominant city, as it developed the 'commune' and promoted legislative activity, it reflected in the redaction of 'statutes' and 'customs' not only interests peculiar to the city, as a centre of activities clearly distinct from those of the countryside, but also the preoccupations of those in the seigneurial class who were simultaneously active in both the city and the contado.

The *Liber consuetudinum Mediolani*, which was compiled in 1216 by a commission of experts formed for this purpose at the direction of the podestà and by the unanimous wish of the power centres of the city ('inter capitaneos et valvassores et suam partem et Mottam et credentiam et populum Mediolani'[113]), presents some very interesting measures on the duties of *rustici* of the Milanese territory towards their local lords. Already, in introducing the measures, the *Liber* declares respect for the seigneurial powers of constraint and jurisdiction, which is moderated only by an explicit commitment to guarantee the certainty of law and the action of lawyers and also, one must suppose, by the need not to jeopardize the peaceful submission of the rural population, which had shown very clear signs of its capacity for independent initiative.

Through the ignoble avarice of certain lords, who negotiated agreements with their *rustici* over matters of bans [the fines for infraction of the seigneurial ban] and of other dues, the power to *distringere* [to command, judge and punish] is now reduced, as can be observed in almost all the localities under our jurisdiction. Hence the holders of the *districtus*, animated by aversion to such pacts and conventions drawn up by their

---

[113] Besta and Barni, *Liber consuetudinum*, p. 136. Thus there are listed the three political and military organs which, in harmony or disagreement, dominated the city: the nobles of knightly tradition, the 'credenza' which arose in 1198 as an expression of the *popolo*, and in the middle the so-called Motta, in which there seem to converge certain noble and mercantile elements.

ancestors who, after receiving money from the *rustici*, freed them and remitted some of their own rights, molest the *rustici* themselves in disregard of the legal order, and seek to throw their own guilt, or that of their forebears who suffered from blind avarice, on to the legal representatives of the cases in which the rights of the *rustici* are defended, and spitefully accuse those who in reality are worthy of esteem for the honest labour they perform of defending the law.[114]

This strenuous defence of the lawyers and of the legal conditions brought about by negotiations is followed by measures that are quite in accordance with the irritation displayed over the observed pliancy of the local powers; permission is withheld from any diminution of seigneurial rights made by simple decree, the rural population is forbidden to set up its own consuls or other officials without agreement with the lords, particular note is made of the duties of the *rustici* to maintain the castle, attend the seigneurial tribunal, and pay the customary contributions owing to the lord (assessed either by number of families in the village or in proportion to the fields and oxen owned), and it is specified that the ownership of the common uncultivated land in each village belongs half to the local seigneur, as holder of the *districtus*, and half to all those who own land in the site of proportion to the land owned (the latter again including the local lord as a proprietor, it should be noted).

It should not be surprising that the obvious defence of seigneurial interests (which chiefly concerned the *capitanei*, who had decided with the valvassors, the Motta and the *popolo* that the customs should be drawn up, or the ecclesiastical bodies, in which archbishop, canons and abbots were mostly recruited from among the noble families of the city) is accompanied by insistence on the respect due to agreements and to the legal order in general, in a society which seemed founded on the violent capacity of groups and individuals to assert themselves. Vendetta between families and *consorterie* was exercised as a right. The constitution of the groups of forces, consorterial or popular, was shot through with legal rules. The relations between communes, and between communes and territorial lords, were disciplined by conventions, pledges of loyalty, peace treaties; even if war very frequently violated the pledges and treaties it was only in order to draw up others, with abundant use of formulae and sub-sections. Now we may consider how such a network of reciprocal obligations, even if they were able in some ways to check the abundant wealth of political impulses obvious in the thirteenth century in every class and every locality, could be translated into a

[114] *Ibid.*, p. 109.

territorial order; such an order was indeed extremely composite and diverse, but it tended to become more rigid as the juridical consciousness of this social world (fed by lawyers and jurists, of whom the Milanese commission of 1216 may be taken as example and witness) gradually confronted the growing inclination of the power groups, which were increasingly concentrated in the cities, to develop organically and to proceed to compromises among themselves wherever mutual interests were not harmed.

In the eleventh and twelfth centuries, as has been noted above, many opportunities had opened up for the rural populations to imitate their own lords and their *consorterie*, who were often divided or in violent internal conflict, by forming themselves in their turn (as the structure of settlement in villages suggested) into groups which were gradually better organized, and capable of negotiation, defence and attack, both physical and legal. But this ability to establish themselves was closely tied to the modest dimensions of the power that the peasants were confronting, and to its lack of strong co-ordination. In certain regions this was still the case for the whole of the thirteenth century. In the region around Turin, for example, there was no city that co-ordinated the many local lords or attracted them within its walls. At Turin, which was demographically quite weak, the commune still coexisted in the thirteenth century with an episcopal power that conserved its own important seigneurial clientèle in the region, a region menaced by the progress of the power of Savoy but at the same time open to interventions by the commune of Asti and the marquises of Monferrato.[115] In such a context, where the most important territorial powers were still in a very fluid phase, not only could the local lords maintain their own autonomy but the rural populations subject to those lords could oppose the seigneurial power with resolution, precisely because there was no superior ruler present to intervene in the name of 'law' and guarantee the 'peace'. Thus the seigneurial family grouping of the Piossasco, which extended south-west of Turin over a considerable patrimony of castles and jurisdictions and which fleetingly collaborated through a plurality of feudal relationships with the dynasty of Savoy, the marquises of Saluzzo, the marquises of Romagnano, the commune of Turin and the bishop, found in its turn that it had to contend with the communes that arose in the shadow of its own castles, in the sites of Piossasco, Scalenghe and Castagnole. These communes were very lively, as documents from the end of the thirteenth century show, and were not

[115] T. Rossi and F. Gabotto, *Storia di Torino* (Turin, 1914), pp. 324ff; F. Cognasso, *Storia di Torino* (Milan, 1959), pp. 136ff.

at all ready to submit passively to seigneurial decisions in matters concerning the organization of the communities, the rights over woodland and pastures, and the exercise of justice and seigneurial dues.[116] But it was at that time that the dynasty of Savoy was consolidating its position, and it intervened; in 1291, for example, it sent a vicar to Piossasco after the lords and their men had come armed among the communes. The following year several judgements, still, one may note, in the form of arbitrations, settled the controversies in Piossasco as well as in the other two communes. And it is interesting to observe how the *homines* met a favourable response over economic questions and over the removal of seigneurial abuses in the exercise of justice, while certain requests were rejected which would have implied a greater autonomy of the communities, whether in their internal functioning or in their relations with other persons or collectivities. Thus the incipient territorial framework of the Savoy already shows signs of being translated into a safeguard for the 'law', destined to give a more rigid shape to power and conditions of life. Certainly in the future there was to be no other occasion such as that witnessed in a dispute of that period, when the lords of Piossasco boldly and arbitrarily repealed the application of criminal law through notarial documents, extending, 'against God and against the law', written concessions to commit certain offences without penalty of fine! The population would no longer be provoked to react by such a crude exercise of the seigneurial *districtus*. They would no longer rise in arms against the local power, but would be 'pacified' within a broader apparatus of power that would protect the whole social hierarchy.

This means that where power did not become concentrated in the city, as it had at Milan at the beginning of the thirteenth century, the process of territorial reconstruction normally took place under the aegis of the great military dynasties, which mostly bore the title of marquis or count, and so were dynasties which could be linked with those old traditions of public order which had been disintegrating in the post-Carolingian period. A counterpoint to the commission of experts which officially set down in writing the customs of Milan and its territory can be read in the action of the jurists who drew up the statute promulgated by Count Pietro II of Savoy after 1262, which, by disciplining the activity of judges and notaries, was to provide for 'the benefit of all the nobles and non-nobles, clerics and religious, town-dwellers and peasants, and every other person of the county of Savoy'.[117] This county was

---

116 Morello, 'Dal "custos castri Plociasci"', pp. 36ff, 76ff.
117 G. Tabacco, 'Forme medievali di dominazione nelle Alpi Occidentali', *Bollettino storico-bibliografico subalpino*, 60 (1962), pp. 349ff; 'La formazione della potenza sabauda come dominazione alpina', in *Die Alpen in der*

not either territorially or institutionally the simple extension of a political–administrative district of the Early Middle Ages, but rather a new and autonomous political construction resulting from an agglomeration of local lordships and of valleys spread along the two great roads, across the Mont Cenis and the Great St Bernard passes, which unite Italy with the transalpine world. The local domination of the Savoy, rooted in those valleys and passes in order to exploit merchants and pilgrims through the appropriate tolls, was being transformed into a more ambitious entity; a circle of experts encouraged its interpretation as an institution that could legislate and function over an increasing area of territory in the service of all, set above all, disciplining the various social classes and pacifying the population. This was the comital power that in the years around 1190, when Amedeo V was count, came to be superimposed in the Turin region over various local lords, over the remains of the episcopal domination and over the commune of Turin, and that presented itself as the highest jurisdictional and political court of appeal for all the rural population, whether or not they were already gathered in communal collectivities endowed with their own modest autonomy and subject to intermediate seigneurial powers.

In other words, from the thirteenth to the fourteenth centuries, over different time-scales in different areas, either the powerful communal cities or the seigneurial dynasties (wherever the latter, as was the case with Piedmont, were not shackled by a vigorous urban development) made use of feudal bonds and multiple contracts, drawn up with the lords of fortresses and with communities of towns or modest cities, in order to end, through their own military strength, the political mobility of the rural territories; they imposed permanently on the latter new rights of exaction (particularly the *fodrum*, a recognition of the supremacy of the dominant power), and constructed a superior jurisdiction which was at first an arbitrator and then a compulsory tribunal, whether for appeal proceedings or for disputes directly involving the interests of seigneurial powers or subordinate communes. At the same time, when there were no intermediate seigneurial powers, the lesser communes received a podestà or rector chosen by the dominant territorial power. The latter, referring to the need for co-ordination, justice or the confirmation of customs, issued general regulations for the subordinate territory, which had been developed in the court of the dynasty or in the governing councils of the powerful commune. On occasion, the dynasty also created districts (sometimes given the name of castellania) whose appointed officials received the mixed income due to the dominant power for the administration of property, for tolls, and for dues both

europäischen Geschichte des Mittelalters (Vorträge und Forschungen X, Constance-Stuttgart, 1965), pp. 240ff.

negotiated and imposed, and supervised the peace of the territory and the activities of the various subordinate powers. All this did not signify a uniform legislation or administration, but certainly represented a movement towards a much less temporary set of relationships than that which relied only on sworn fealty and loyalty towards friendships and agreements.

Here too, as within the larger cities, the crisis of political mobility and institutional fluidity arose from a long experience of struggle and from the acquisition of methods of co-operation which were suggested partly by the development of juridical culture but essentially by practical procedures, which, when they succeeded in one place, were rapidly imitated everywhere. One may wonder only whether it is possible to suggest a parallel between the need for security which was felt in the cities, above all by the elites with a mercantile tradition and the prosperous artisans, and that need for an orderly justice and peace which was certainly not absent from rural centres. The urban notables in fact emerged with varying importance within the social system of the powerful centres, and spontaneously took the standpoint of greater stability, whereas the rural population and their leaders constituted a political world which was barely outlined and whose development was interrupted by the establishment of a hierarchy of seigneurial and urban forces weighing upon their territory. Political fragmentation, while it appeared as a liberating force when accompanying political instability, became an accumulation of different rights, of landed possession, of local protection and of a broader territorial framework, wherever it was crystallized in the name of a 'right' that was guaranteed and controlled from above.

Such accumulations, to tell the truth, could in some respects take on their own internal coherence. This was the case with the locality of Origgio (twenty-three kilometres north-west of Milan), where the *dominatus loci* exercised by the Milanese monastery of S. Ambrogio over the *rustici* and their commune, after it had been challenged and undermined by the rural population in the time of greatest disorder in the middle of the thirteenth century, became consolidated again in the thirteenth and fourteenth centuries alongside a powerful expansion of the landed patrimony of the monastery, which extended to about half the agrarian territory belonging to this *locus*, and a reorganization of the administration of their property through the introduction of short-term contracts.[118] Such contracts reconstructed the monastery's full ownership of its lands; they marked the breakdown of the distinction made on a

---

[118] Romeo, *Il comune rurale di Origgio*, pp. 39ff, 61ff, 72ff.

single piece of land between eminent domain, which belonged to the owner of the property, and useful domain, belonging to the peasant tenant, from which, owing to a slow development of customary rights, the dependent cultivators had drawn their economic autonomy. The economic and jurisdictional pressure of the abbot, supported by the intervention of the commune of Milan when confiscations of goods were carried out, was such that in 1313 the peasants rebelled, using every sort of weapon – spades, spears and knives – against the Milanese official, the officers of the abbot, and their armed escort. But Milan was now capable of guaranteeing the 'peace' and 'law'. The confiscations were carried out in the following years.

And so the dominant city with its 'anti-magnate' orientation succeeded in rooting out the political bases of the seigneurial lineages over a wide radius, and drew the rural communities into closer dependence not only sporadically but systematically, as happened in a large part of the Florentine contado. At the same time, the economic penetration of the prosperous citizens into the countryside increased, as did the political protection that the government of the city guaranteed to citizens who owned land in the contado, whether it was a matter of new landed acquisitions, in allod or in tenancy, or of the old landed base of notable citizens who had often only recently become urbanized.[119] Here, peasant customs and the corresponding forms of bargaining entered a crisis even more quickly than elsewhere; something of the animated activity of the city was reflected on to the countryside. But the political monopoly thus attained by the city over the contado objectively favoured the clear victory of economic initiatives of the citizens, and of the legislative activity of the political regime established in the protecting city (including, it should be understood, norms to protect forests, pastures and livestock, or to contain the flooding of rivers, or to re-establish a more ordered taxation policy[120]). This regime, with its ever more narrowly oligarchical orientation, or the seigneurial structure it had acquired, and with its growing capacity for restriction, without counterbalances, could not establish a serious exchange with the society

[119] E. Fiumi, 'Sui rapporti economici tra città e contado nell'età comunale', *Archivio storico italiano*, 114 (1956), pp. 37 note 1, 62ff, 'Fioritura e decadenza dell'economia fiorentina', pp. 497ff; Conti, *La formazione della struttura agraria moderna*, vol. 3, parte 2, *I catasti agrari della repubblica fiorentina e il catasto particellare toscano* (Rome, 1966); G. Cherubini, 'Qualche considerazione sulle campagne dell'Italia centro-settentrionale tra l'XI e il XV secolo', *Rivista storica italiana*, 79 (1967), pp. 127ff.

[120] See Fiumi, 'Sui rapporti economici', pp. 25ff, 41ff.

that was subject to it, considered as a whole, and above all with the rural world.[121]

This incorporation of the peasant population into more rigid political structures through the action of the territorially-dominant communes, of lords installed in the city and of great dynasties, through the preservation or partial replacement of the lesser seigneurial powers and a more alert control over the autonomies of towns and village communities, was paralleled by the signs of a growing co-ordination between the greater and the lesser urban centres. The collaboration showed itself in the fluid forms of participation by the cities in one or the other of the two parties which involved all Italy, but which were truly alive for less than a century, from the middle of the thirteenth to the first decades of the fourteenth centuries; increasingly, however, it also showed itself, in a very different way, in the unification of several neighbouring city territories. The two forms of linkage, that of the party and that of the territory, were in many cases antithetical. The former reflected, on the whole, the individual cities' desire for autonomy, each city behaving defensively towards its neighbours, which often tended to take on the colour of the party opposite to that dominant in the first city; the latter resulted from the breakdown of this unstable equilibrium, which favoured a force capable of broad and permanent attraction. The crisis of mobility of the parties which we have noted above, following Bartolo da Sassoferrato, as being a sign that their political role as indicators of the internal tensions of each social system was exhausted, had its counterpart in the weakening of those same parties when faced with the problem of balance and collaboration between the centres of power which had acquired responsibility for controlling more or less coherent territorial districts.

As within each city, and as in the rural world which now focused around cities or dynasties, so on this further level of wider territorial ties the centuries-old dual tendency, simultaneous and contradictory, towards ever new forms of disintegration, and towards new structures which were always unstable and provisional, was replaced by the creation of bureaucratic and financial tools which gave the centres of power a new capacity to resist emerging desires for fragmentation and autonomy. As always, this change of direction was due to the spread, from one centre of economic and political power to another, of

[121] For the 'class' concept of rustic life in the dominating class, see P. J. Jones, 'Per la storia agraria italiana nel medio evo: lineamenti e problemi', *Rivista storica italiana*, 76 (1964), pp. 340ff 'Italy' in *The Cambridge Economic History of Europe*, vol. 1, *The Agrarian Life of the Middle Ages*, ed. M. M. Postan, 2nd ed. (Cambridge, 1966), pp. 419ff.

knowledge about the attempts which had succeeded best in the continual fierce struggle. And perhaps at the same time it was due to the richer range of possibilities for action, reflection and satisfaction open to individuals of the middle and upper levels of society, for whom it was now more difficult to resist official power – as compared with the past centuries of a more basic existence when there had been no alternative to the urgent need to establish oneself through command and violent conflict other than the ascetic and spiritual total renunciation of power.

How were the regional links realized? It is customary to go back to the time of Emperor Frederick II and his decline, when, in the clash between the imperial and communal forces and in the midst of papal condemnations, the chance appeared for the figure of Ezzelino da Romano, monstrous in his coherent ferocity, to place himself in power over several important communal cities at once. He belonged to a seigneurial family of Frankish origin, rich in goods and allodial and feudal fortresses, local jurisdictions and armed followers in many parts of the Veneto; it was linked as a vassal to several episcopal sees and to canonical and monastic organizations, and sustained by a small apparatus of *visdomini* and viscounts, gastalds and *villici*, captains and judges, with which he controlled the rural populations and the artisans of the large town of Bassano and of the many rural communities subject to him.[122] He controlled a whole world, geographically scattered, present in several counties and so in different urban communal spheres of influence, but one which was quite capable of forming the autonomous basis of an economic and military power for the various members of the family, who were not always in agreement among themselves. And so family members could take a leading position in those associations of *consorterie* which were operating as rival factions both in a particular city and in its territorial district, and which in their turn established relations with Frederick II or with the Lombard League that was hostile to the Empire. With this multiple base, juridically weak but politically strong, Ezzelino became for long years the master, though not officially the *signore*, of the city of Verona, and also expanded from there to the cities of Vicenza, Padua and Treviso. This was a territorial grouping with considerable geographical coherence, which came to focus, although not continuously, around the power of a noble of the old autonomous military tradition, who had entered into the political context of several communal cities simultaneously.[123] The cities preserved their own

[122] G. Fasoli, 'Signoria feudale ed autonomie locali', in *Studi ezzeliniani* (Rome, 1963), pp. 7ff.

[123] R. Manselli, 'Ezzolino da Romano nella politica italiana del secolo XIII', *ibid.*, pp. 35ff; C. G. Mor, '"Dominus Eccerinus". Aspetti di una forma

ordinances, but the podestà, when not imposed by the emperor, were largely imposed by Ezzelino. When Frederick II died the power of Ezzelino did not decline, but a military defeat was sufficient to shatter it. In 1259 Ezzelino died and his family was wiped out by his enemies.

This failure did not arise from the heterogeneous nature of the forces, seigneurial and urban, on which Ezzelino relied, for that did in fact correspond perfectly to the conditions of central and northern Italy in general in the thirteenth century; rather, it arose from the over-bold character of his civic policy. This was analogous to the experience of Oberto Pelavicino at more or less the same period. We already know Oberto as 'captain general' at Milan at the time of the della Torre; he started from a patrimonial base scattered in several counties south and north of the Po, at the centre of the Po plain, and also took advantage over several years of the office of 'imperial vicar' and then of the friendship of Manfred, king of Sicily and of various urban podestà. Eventually, as one of the more prestigious and autonomous leaders of the party of the Empire, he dominated militarily a dense and compact group of cities, from Parma via Cremona, Piacenza and Pavia as far as Milan, from Brescia to Alessandria and Tortona. But everything fell apart, even before he died in 1269, in the face of the counter-offensive from the church party, when Charles of Anjou was summoned to Italy.

A third grouping of communal cities was then forming in western Lombardy around Marquis Guglielmo VII of Monferrato, from Ivrea and Vercelli to Acqui, Alessandria and Tortona – that is, all around his marquisate, which stretched as a huge agglomeration of local lordships, territorially almost always continuous, along the Po and in the Tanaro basin, from the Canavese to the territory of Acqui. The grouping extended in certain years to include Pavia as well, and Milan too, in the form of the 'signoria' co-ordinated with the power of Archbishop Otto which has been mentioned earlier in relation to the formation of the Visconti regime in the city. And while the collaboration with Pavia had the character more of an alliance than of a dominion, and the lordship over Milan could not be established without the recognition and acceptance of Visconti rivalry, the remaining grouping had an impressive appearance, with its focus around the marquis's patrimonial power. The ties with the various cities, though, were not juridically uniform, involving in one instance a full political and jurisdictional lordship, and in another a captaincy of war; and the means used to attain supremacy differed from one environment to another, with the marquis

presignorile', *ibid.*, pp. 81ff; G. Arnaldi, 'I cronisti della marca travigiana', *ibid.*, pp. 128ff.

setting himself up at one moment as leader of a party, at another moment, though more rarely, as a conciliator, or again as a force protecting a city against external dangers.[124] Compared with Ezzelino or Pelavicino, his power appears to have been centred on a more sizeable zone of attraction, the marquisate, which in turn had its own small capital at Chivasso on the Po. But although it certainly offered the marquis the military base which permitted him a broad range of political manoeuvre in Lombardy, the marquisate did not constitute a centre of economic force and administrative co-ordination comparable to communal cities of any importance. The forebears of Guglielmo VII had been engaged for a long time, up to the beginning of the thirteenth century, in the attempts to ensnare Asti, seat of an extensive episcopal lordship and of a very animated commune, exerting themselves to penetrate that centre of intense mercantile activity and to limit its political expansion,[125] but the commune of Asti had shown itself the stronger; and now Guglielmo VII suffered the consequences of the forced renunciation of his ancestors, for Asti, if it had belonged to the marquisate, would have been the true centre suited to the military and political perspectives of this tireless war captain. And so Guglielmo too failed in his attempt at regional co-ordination, he was finally captured by the Alessandrines who had risen against his lordship, and died in prison in 1292.

Of a different character was the expansion carried out in Piedmont from 1259 by the House of Anjou as counts of Provence, before and after the conquest of the kingdom of Sicily; they drove their dominion like a wedge east of the Alps between the dominions of the marquises of Saluzzo, the counts of Savoy, the commune of Asti and the marquises of Monferrato. This dominion reached from Cuneo as far as cities such as Alba and Alessandria, Turin and Ivrea, but it tended to co-ordinate above all a dense number of communes and seigneurs of small or middling importance who were mostly threatened by the advance of Asti, and so it took on a character which was essentially rural, analogous to that of the subalpine marquisates. On the other hand, where it reached cities such as Ivrea and Alessandria the lordship of Charles of Anjou became little more than a formality, just as in the highly transient grouping of Lombard cities which interpreted Charles' supremacy in the individual cities as no more than an expression of the Angevin political direction of the Guelf party in Italy – interpreting it, that is, in a sense which was neither regional nor coherently territorial. In south-western

---

[124] Bozzola, *Guglielmo VII di Monferrato*, pp. 96ff.

[125] D. Brader, *Bonifaz von Montferrat bis zum Antritt der Kreuzfahrt (1202)* (Berlin, 1907), pp. 11ff.

Piedmont the Angevin domination persisted for more than two decades, with considerable variations, and then disappeared. When it arose again at the beginning of the fourteenth century at the desire of Charles II of Anjou (who indeed conferred on it the title of 'county of Piedmont' as if to stress its unitary character), it then extended to include, in the time of King Robert, even Asti, which surrendered in 1312; but the surrender of the city only took place in the context of the mobilization of the whole Guelf party in Italy, both Guelf cities and Guelf parties in exile from Ghibelline cities, against the Ghibelline ambitions aroused by the arrival of Henry VII. Although, even after this time, Asti remained incorporated in the Angevin county for another twenty-five years, the city and its territory were only an advance stronghold, and were always threatened by the subalpine dynasties and by the Visconti.[126] The 'county of Piedmont' was governed by a seneschal who was placed over the many local seigneurs and, through vicars, bailiffs and castellans, interfered in the communal ordinances of the few small cities, such as Cuneo, Mondovì and Albi, and those towns which had handed themselves over to the Angevins with agreements that retained autonomous 'councils' and preserved customs and statutes while giving the Angevins control of local legislative activity. Asti was the exception, and here the royal 'vicar' was chosen by the king or the seneschal among candidates elected by the 'general council' of the city.[127] When in 1339, through an internal upheaval in the continually restless city, Asti passed from the Angevin lordship to that of the marquises of Monferrato, the 'county of Piedmont' was eventually reduced to a modest appendage of the county of Provence and in 1385 its remains disappeared into the hands of the Savoy dynasty.

In contrast a purely spontaneous regional grouping of cities can be seen in the surrender to King John of Bohemia between 1330 and 1331 of Brescia and then of a series of other neighbouring 'Lombard' cities, from Bergamo and Como to Pavia, Novara and Vercelli, from Cremona to Parma, Reggio and Modena, with the addition of Lucca beyond the Apennines, through the initiative of communal councils or of the lords placed above them in some cities. John was the son of the Emperor Henry VII, and maintained highly ambiguous relations on the one hand with the German King Louis of Bavaria (crowned emperor at Rome in 1328, in a revolutionary procedure, by a Colonna as representative of the Roman people) and on the other hand with the House of France and with Pope John XXII. The rapid movement in

---

[126] G. M. Monti, *La dominazione angioina in Piemonte* (Turin, 1930), pp. 69ff.
[127] *Ibid.*, pp. 273ff.

favour of King John was provoked by the desire of the various cities, of the parties and the seigneurs who ruled them, for defence against the lords and the cities which threatened them, either directly or in connection with the political and military organizations of the exiles. The Emilian cities also sought a defence against the cardinal legate who had been sent to Lombardy from Avignon, with military forces, some years earlier to destroy Ghibellinism.[128] The success of King John was also assisted, as the zeal of certain citizen bodies shows, by a real desire for a less stormy political life, and was such as to induce even Azzo Visconti to submit the city of Milan to him, although in a purely formal manner, which caused the king to confer on him the title of his 'vicar' in the signorial control over the city. Azzo's was a purely provisional welcome, in order to remove the pressures which were on the increase all around the Visconti lordship now that they had found a common meeting point in the king, since the Visconti themselves were, for many of those cities, the danger against which they were uniting behind the person of the king. But already between 1333 and 1334 this unforeseen and improvised political formation was breaking up with equal speed. King John's commitment to steer prudently among the various agreements to pacify each city and each territory, and his need to stay in some way faithful to the political parties, heterogeneous among themselves, which had summoned and acclaimed him, could not withstand the coalition of the many forces that had been threatened or harmed; these included the Lombard lordships of Ghibelline affiliation (the Visconti, formally subordinate to the royal lordship, and the signori from cities bordering on the royal grouping, such as the Scaligeri of Verona and the Gonzaga of Mantua) or those formerly of the Guelf tradition but now of uncertain affiliation, such as the Estensi of Ferrara, as well as the extremely Guelf Florentine republic, hostile to the king over the question of Lucca.

The Italian adventure of John of Bohemia was the last and most dramatic demonstration of the impossibility of organizing a vast territorial dominion in Lombardy or Tuscany for anyone who did not have deep roots in a powerful urban centre, as long as the cities maintained their intense rhythm of economic life and their active social development. But at the same time that adventure, with its thirteenth-century antecedents, and the prevalently signorial structure of the coalition that brought it to an end, demonstrated how much easier it was for the signorial families than for the cities which remained loyal to a

[128] C. Dumontel, *L'impresa italiana di Giovanni di Lussemburgo, re di Boemia* (Turin, 1952), pp. 33ff; Tabacco, *La casa di Francia nell'azione politica di papa Giovanni XXII*, pp. 281ff.

communal model of government to conceive of a territorial political framework which passed decisively beyond the immediate sphere of action of a single city. In the course of the fourteenth century Florence did indeed establish control several times over Pistoia, Volterra and Arezzo, but with great difficulty, alternately advancing and retreating, and under pressure of threats from signori installed in north-western Tuscany or of tensions arising from the city's opposition to the Ghibelline Party in Italy. Not that the Florentines were insensitive to the temptations of power: 'the said acquisition of the city of Arezzo', wrote Giovanni Villani, narrating events of 1337, 'although it cost much money, aggrandized and raised greatly the magnificence of the commune of Florence, which far off had great fame among all the Christians that heard of it, and nearby was more honoured and feared by the neighbouring communes'.[129] And Florence had ample means of employing militias and buying rights, and had experience of territorial administration, with vicars, captains, podestà and well-tested methods of taxation.[130] But the commitment to the permanent organization of a vast territory was more difficult to carry out in political regimes such as that of the Florentines or Sienese which were directed by the multiple interests of a complex hegemonic social class,[131] than in the signorial regimes, which were sustained by a more harshly linear ambition for dominion and external greatness.

More generally, one should say at this point that signorial government, when it was completely integrated into an urban context which could finance military action and draw on the qualifications and experience derived from the complexities of city life, appeared particularly well suited to carry on a highly co-ordinated policy of defence and offence towards organizations outside its own territory. Without doubt this aspect, as well as the spontaneous movement of urban society towards more stable forms of government as analysed above, was a powerful factor in the consolidation of the signorial regime in the communal cities. At the same the *signori* of the more effective cities were then particularly able to realize the opportunities for territorial expansion beyond the city's own contado; in such cases it was as if the

---

[129] See Villani, *Cronica*, I. XI, c. 60 (vol. 6, p. 128). See Pasqui, *Documenti*, vol. 3, pp. viiff.

[130] Becker, *Florence*, vol. 2, pp. 214ff. For a parallel with the republic of Siena and its contado, see W. M. Bowsky, *The Finance of the Commune of Siena (1287–1355)* (Oxford, 1970), pp. 225ff, and A. K. Chiancone Isaacs, 'Fisco e politica a Siena nel Trecento', *Rivista storica italiana*, 85 (1973), pp. 22ff.

[131] See D. Herlihy, *Medieval and Renaissance Pistoia* (New Haven-London, 1967), pp. 226ff.

tenacious yet flexible continuity of the *signore*'s rule, supported by a clientèle without scruples, converged with a durable and active social structure, rooted in a protected centre, to result in unlimited political expansion.

And so the Visconti inherited the broad range of political intervention formerly characteristic of the powers that operated in Milan in the pre-communal period, a range of interest subsequently clear in the commune's anti-imperial wars, when it led the Lombard Leagues, and in the loyalty to the della Torre of their clientèles in Lodi, Bergamo, Como and Novara. At the same time they resumed the experiment of grouping together systematically all the communal cities spread to the south and north of the middle stretch of the Po; Oberto Pelavicino had attempted this earlier, when he put his military ability at the service of parties and dominant groups in each city and then raised that service into a political pre-eminence, which had been formally recognized through the conferral of prolonged terms as podestà, general captaincies, and lordships by various civic 'councils'. The Visconti took more than seventy years to build these various tendencies into a single stable political framework. In particular, around the middle of the fourteenth century (in the time of Archbishop Giovanni Visconti), they made new use of the office of archbishop. When the Visconti lordship was first established in Milan, this office had given Otto Visconti the means of acting through the church, the economy and personal clients in order to unite the clientèles of the family and of the party of the nobles, while in the pre-communal period, at the time of Archbishop Aribert, the archbishop had represented Milan at the highest level in developing the city's political action in Lombardy.

But in relation to the political power of Milan and the Visconti, the archiepiscopal power in the mid-fourteenth century was now no longer the heart of an urban hegemony, as it had been in the eleventh century, or of the hegemony of a party and a family, as it had been for twenty years in the thirteenth century. It was, rather, one instrument among many, and an instrument which, besides, had been extorted from the Roman church by the arrogant conduct of the family in Lombardy, in a pause in the struggle which the Avignon papacy waged almost uninterruptedly against the uncheckable growth of the Visconti political organization. Giovanni Visconti had been a cardinal of the anti-pope created in Rome in 1328 against the Roman pope residing at Avignon, at the desire of Louis of Bavaria; Giovanni had been his cardinal and apostolic legate in Lombardy with the role of administrator of the Ambrosian church. It was the necessities of the struggle with Louis that brought the Avignon Curia to unbend towards the Visconti, to the extent of creating Giovanni first bishop of Novara and then archbishop of Milan, two Lombard cities close to the family. And the archbishop, when he was head of the family and officially lord of Milan, pursued territorial expansion so unscrupulously that in 1350 he bought Bologna for 170,000 florins from the Pepoli, lords of the city, even though for decades the papacy had been claiming Bologna in the name of donations and 'restitutions' made by the Frankish and German kings over the course of the centuries. In buying the city he promised the Pepoli that the Visconti would pay the expenses of lifting the excommunication that the pope would certainly place on the Pepoli for the sale they had made.[132] In the event the archbishop too was excommunicated, but none the less Pope Clement VI brought himself to recognize him as lord of Bologna for twelve years as vicar of the Roman church, with a promise from the archbishop to pay 100,000 florins to the Avignon Curia in addition to the 12,000 florins which the Visconti had undertaken to pay the Curia annually when they replaced the Pepoli as lords of the city. Nor did this sum include the huge gifts which, according to Matteo Villani, the archbishop had had distributed in the papal court and the court of France to obtain his goal.[133]

Milan's financial strength was the secret behind both the happy outcome of the manoeuvres carried out by the Visconti in the Bologna episode and the great Visconti territorial construction in general. This strength was well used politically, through a system of links between taxes, the farming out of revenues, banking operations giving advances and loans, and treasury services supported by the bankers.[134] It was suitably complemented by a wide network of solidarity in all the city communes where the signoria belonged to the Visconti and had been entrusted to their vicars. This strength in finance and in their clientèle permitted the skilful employment of mercenary militias which completely replaced the civic armies.

It was without doubt a great and multi-tentacled tyranny, concealed by the splendours of palaces and gardens, by the early enticements offered to literary figures (Petrarch, for example), and sustained by the prestige it acquired from the 'peace' it imposed on noble *consorterie* and on factions, city by city, wherever it penetrated. The first signs of this tyranny were shrewdly recognized in 1317 by the *missi* sent by the Avignon Curia to Lombardy to impose truces directed towards a Guelf

[132] A. Sorbelli, *La signoria di Giovanni Visconti a Bologna e le sue relazioni con la Toscana* (Bologna, 1901), pp. 26ff, 56ff.

[133] Villani, *Cronica*, I, III, c. 2 (vol. 2, p. 8).

[134] F. Cognasso, *I Visconti* (Milan, 1966), pp. 212ff.

reorganization of Italy.[135] When, approaching from the western Alps, they drew near to Milan, they clearly perceived the great fear that Matteo Visconti spread around him. Matteo was affable towards the papal *missi* but gave no answers without consulting his advisers, and, to illustrate conditions in Lombardy, caused the representatives of those friendly cities which he then 'dominated' in various ways – Milan and Pavia, Tortona and Alessandria, Novara, Piacenza – to speak; they spoke at length, sometimes confusedly, one after the other, and 'pleaded in defence' of 'lord Matteo' that 'he was a lover and restorer of peace', and that there was no need for papal truces in the cities ruled by him. But the *missi* also secretly questioned the clergy and the friends of the Roman church; discontent was great, particularly because of the many exactions and the many 'cruel' mercenaries in the service of Matteo and the other 'tyrants' of Lombardy. And yet when they sent this information to Avignon the *missi* reported that according to the opinion of very many clerics, lay-people and monks, Lombardy (*patria Lombardiae*) would never know peace until it had 'its own king and natural lord, not of a barbaric nation, a king whose descendants would naturally continue the kingdom'.[136]

In short, this meant a king who would live among the 'Lombards', and not descend from Germany from time to time involuntarily bringing disorder rather than peace; a moderating dynasty that would free them from the 'unbearable yoke of tyranny' and would guarantee 'peace and justice'. The papal *missi* obviously did not think that the dynasty of Matteo, the tyrant, could aspire to such a royal task! But Petrarch himself was to write to Luchino Visconti, son of Matteo and brother of Archbishop Giovanni, as to a man of supreme greatness who lacked nothing to make him a king except the royal title.[137] Northern Italy was tending towards a state structure through tyranny, and that structure, in some of its regional aspects, was to preserve the stamp of tyranny.

Although it is quite clear that Visconti rule was directed towards the creation of a vast territorial and institutional organic body, it would be quite inaccurate to think of it in terms of a state structure in the

[135] *Vatikanische Akten zur deutschen Geschichte in der Zeit Kaiser Ludwigs des Bayern*, ed. S. Reizler (Innsbruck, 1891), pp. 22ff.
[136] *Vatikanische Akten*, p. 37. See G. Tabacco, 'Un presunto disegno domenicano-angioino per l'unificazione politica dell'Italia', *Rivista storica italiana*, 61 (1949), pp. 492ff, 524ff.
[137] F. Petrarch, *Le Familiari*, I. VII, ep. 15, ed. V. Rossi (Florence, 1934), vol. 2, p. 131.

fourteenth century. It was not only that their rule lacked coherent, stable and well-defined boundaries, expanding as it was in all directions: it reached Genoa in the mid-fourteenth century but in the form of a precarious signoria, penetrated Tuscany without success, and found its way at the end of the century as far as Perugia but briefly and without any territorial continuity. It is more important to note that even the most solid territorial block, in the heart of the Po plain, was anything but a uniform political body. Here it is particularly worth noting that Visconti rule – at least until the time of Gian Galeazzo and the imperial creation of the duchy in 1395, and even later – essentially took the form of a grouping of cities under the same lord. And the duchy itself, as a legal entity created from above, was certainly not the stimulus for systematic reorganization of the territory, even though the definition of the duchy's area was careful to reflect the position already reached by the Visconti,[138] and even though the legal inclusion of Visconti territorial strength among the feudal principalities of the Empire in its turn certainly helped suggest a more systematic use of feudal institutions by the dukes to organize the signorial forces.[139] In reality the imperial diplomas concerning the duchy, just like the earlier ones of the vicariate, themselves bear witness in certain of their formulations that the Visconti power appeared to itself and to the world to be essentially a co-ordination of cities. While historiographical tradition has gone too far in conceiving the history of Italy in almost purely urban terms, there is no doubt that in its political aspect, at least from the twelfth to the fourteenth centuries, imperial Italy centred for the most part on the hegemony of the cities. And the dynasty and *consorteria* of the Visconti, a 'kindred' so oddly resilient despite its harsh internal disagreements, rested primarily for the whole of the fourteenth century on the forces of Milan, and on the possibility of linking them with the forces of the other cities, inserting them not only into communal institutions, through adroit legal fictions, but also into the living fabric of the socially prominent groups living in those cities. Luchino Visconti, the *signore* celebrated by Petrarch for his severe justice, 'glorified Milan by the offices given principally to the Milanesi in the cities', according to the chronicler and notary Pietro Azario, originally from Novara, who served the Visconti in Milan and elsewhere.[140] In this judgement and in

138 See Ercole, *Dal comune al principato*, p. 294 note 1, p. 301 note 1.

139 G. Chittolini, 'Infeudazioni e politica feudale nel ducato visconteo-sforzesco', *Quaderni storici*, 19 (1972), pp. 85ff.

140 *Petri Azari liber gestorum in Lombardia*, ed. F. Cognasso (Muratori, *Rerum Italicarum Scriptores*, new ed., vol. 16.4 (Bologna, 1939)), p. 46. See the preface by Cognasso, pp. xviiff.

his own activity Azario provides evidence of the double tie which the Visconti domination established between Milan and the other Lombard cities, by distributing Milanese everywhere in positions of responsibility and by summoning loyal elements from every city. These were ties between urban elements, however. The tradition of autonomy of the various cities re-emerged, having been depressed but not extinguished, as was clearly evident when Gian Galeazzo died in 1402.

We have stressed the urban aspect of both the centre and the usual component parts of this dominion; such a structure could signify greater strength in the operation of the highly heterogeneous Visconti organization, but also resulted in a more fragile unity. However it must be added at once that the urban aspect did not completely account for the network of interests which had formed around the Visconti, except in the sense that the many powerful families linked with the Visconti, and endowed with strong patrimonies and seigneurial bases in the various contadi, normally found that their own respective cities provided the place to co-ordinate their own means and interests and to put them into action. This was so much the case that gaps in the area of Visconti control appeared more often wherever the seigneurial families and ecclesiastical lordships continued to have a predominantly rural character. But fundamentally it was enough for the Visconti to keep a hold by force on their urban strongpoints, with their respective networks of jurisdiction and the conventions that bound them to most of the lesser centres of power in the contado, in order to control the Lombard territory.

Naturally the problem of a more systematic organization of the territory presented itself. That is, it was necessary to bring to completion, zone by zone, the process of communal rule over the contado, a task that should not be underestimated when one considers that the enormous majority of the population was still rural. Historical research is now discovering that the gaps within the Visconti territory, within its broad and transient geographical boundaries, were numerous.[141] The old concept elaborated in the city communes, of the natural supremacy of each urban centre with an episcopal tradition over the territory which corresponded to its diocese, or to its early medieval county, suffered from too many exceptions through the political penetration of some cities into the contadi of others, and had too doctrinaire and generic a character, for it to be a sufficient foundation for the uniform

---

[141] Chittolini, 'Infeudazioni', pp. 59ff. See also Chittolini, 'La crisi delle libertà comunali', pp. 105ff; 'Signorie rurali e feudi alla fine del medioevo, 1: Il luogo di Mercato, il comune di Parma e i marchesi Pallavicini di Pellegrino', *Nuova rivista storica*, 57 (1973).

subordination of castles, towns and villages to the Visconti as lords of the cities. In this respect it is still usual to speak sometimes of 'feudal' survivals and revivals, with all the inaccuracies and ambiguities of such language. If, by 'feudal', one means (using a vocabulary not justified by the sources) any complex of autonomous seigneurial powers, then it is certainly permissible to say that extensive survivals and developments of this kind were involved, although it should be pointed out that they included not only fairly humble seigneurial dynasties but quite often ecclesiastical lordships, tenacious in preserving the powers of command and jurisdiction connected with the presence of landed patrimonies; and they also included areas ruled by smaller communal towns, anxious to maintain their own political district in order to escape at least in part the fiscal and administrative supremacy of the city. If, however, in speaking of 'feudalism' we are thinking of the legal relationships that were expressed by the investiture of powers exercised as fiefs by a vassal, this is obviously an error, since in many cases such a form of legitimization of local powers by the city government, the Visconti signoria or the Empire, was lacking (that is, in every case where such powers were held in free 'allod' according to the purest medieval tradition). This error also prevents us from understanding the so-called process of 're-feudalization', which, on the contrary, was not infrequently nothing more than a process of initial 'feudalization', taking place slowly and with many delays in the heart of the Visconti dominion often even after the legal creation of the Visconti 'duchy' and through the whole of the fifteenth century.[142] Using feudal law, this process aimed to place the lesser seigneurial powers within a uniform structure; it was in harmony with the experience of earlier centuries (referred to above in considering the territorial co-ordinations of the twelfth century onwards), which had been particularly intense in the peripheral regions of northern Italy, due to the great military dynasties of western Lombardy (present-day Piedmont) and the northern Apennines, the ecclesiastical principalities of Trent and the patriarch of Aquileia, and to the communes themselves, such as the powerful republics of Vercelli and Asti.

This does not mean that in those areas where the Visconti in the fourteenth century still did not have recourse to feudal institutions, the autonomies that persisted within the geographical limits subject to Visconti hegemony did not recognize their supremacy at a formal level. Occasionally they did refuse to recognize it, and then they stressed a direct tie with the imperial authority, requesting from the emperor feudal investitures or generic confirmation of their rights. But the

[142] Chittolini, 'Infeudazioni', pp. 85ff, 'Signorie rurali', pp. 14, 47ff.

territorial supremacy of the Visconti was normally accepted even by the lords, ecclesiastical or lay, who avoided a feudal bond with the Visconti or with Visconti cities and so maintained intact the title (whether acquired through purchase, donation or ancient custom) by virtue of which they exercised local powers in allod; these lords received from the Visconti formal acts which recognized and confirmed their own jurisdictions and immunities. There was a whole interplay of forms that expressed the compromise between a political desire for unification and the still effective existence of the traditional autonomies. This compromise tended to stabilize the different situations within a diversified hierarchical system, and left an ever-decreasing space for the weaker nuclei of power; hence, side by side with the gradual retreat of the citizenry from the active exercise of power, the rural populations gradually lost any possibility of political movement.

The major example of the Visconti permits us to understand the composite and still somewhat summary nature of the regional states which appeared in outline in the fourteenth and fifteenth centuries. There is no doubt that the Visconti rule sought unlimited expansion in Italy, and had some real chances of constructing a coherent 'kingdom' to replace the now little more than theoretical 'Italian kingdom' in German hands, and this has always attracted the interest of literary scholars and researchers who concentrate on the strength of nations and their power. But what counted at the time, for the populations of Italy, was the structure that power was taking on, the power that took the form of a multiple system of restrictions in city after city and contado after contado. This structure might be directed regionally by the Visconti, or by the Scaligeri, whose power at one point radiated outwards from Verona, or by the Italian offshoots of the alpine power of the Savoy, as was still the case in a considerable part of present-day Piedmont at the end of the fourteenth century, and this question could not be unimportant for individual cities, but the process that established the system centring on a princely court remained substantially the same. Alternatively, the system centred on increasingly stable and restricted city oligarchies, as in Tuscany or on the margins of the region of the Veneto, where the Venetian oligarchy was beginning to penetrate in order to defend the lagoon and its own commerce from the dangers of the lordships of both the Veneto and Lombardy.

There was in fact a large area, between the Italian kingdom and the kingdom of the South, which was taking on a shape of its own; the Papal State was being born. This was indeed an exceptional structure, because of the systematic way in which it was being realized in the thirteenth and fourteenth centuries, within a territorial boundary which was roughly suggested by the 'donations' of the Early Middle Ages but which had for some time lacked any coherence. It was born not through the radiation outwards of the forces of an important urban centre or of a well-rooted military clientèle, but rather through the willpower of a Curia. The Papal Curia possessed a tenacious memory and was able to develop new generalized models of government and inject them into the vigorous world of urban and seigneurial autonomies; within that world it was increasingly active diplomatically and militarily, issuing interdicts and excommunications, hiring mercenary companies, and legislating. It was assisted by highly-skilled and experienced ecclesiastics, and sought out financial resources across Christendom with increasingly efficient techniques.

The territory claimed was still that defined in the eighth century by the two formerly Byzantine blocks of the Ravennate exarchate and the Roman duchy, with the link created between them by the Pentapolis and the territory of Perugia and with some extension, provided for from the eighth century, into formerly Lombard territory so as to include a large part of the old duchy of Spoleto. Up to the twelfth century, despite certain formal 'restitutions' to the pope, the presence of the Italian kings and emperors was widely felt in this territorial complex, particularly in its northern regions, even if in many cases it was only in the form of a hegemony over multiple local nuclei of power, to which, as we have seen, the royal power was normally reduced in all imperial Italy. But during the pontificate of Innocent III (1198–1216), during the crisis of the Empire in Italy and of the Staufer dynasty in Germany, the Roman church on the one hand succeeded in obtaining definitive imperial renunciations, and on the other hand began to extend and intensify its particular influence in the various regions of its theoretical territories, obtaining official recognition of that influence from several communal cities (for example Perugia[143]) while granting bulls of 'protection'. In addition it began to create provinces, entrusted to rectors, and to claim, buy or receive in donation lands and centres of differing sizes that the rectors governed by sending out bailiffs, vicars, castellans and podestà. This expansion was made easier by the intensity of the rivalry and conflicts between the local powers, and was carried out in the most diverse forms and with all the gradations possible in the exercise of rights of political and jurisdictional superiority. The rectors also, from time to time, convened 'parliaments' for individual areas or provinces, which reached relatively uniform decisions, above all fiscal and military in

---

[143] D. Segolini, 'Bartolo da Sassoferrato e la civitas Perusina', in *Bartolo da Sassoferrato. Studi e documenti per il VI centenario*, pp. 71ff.

nature,[144] convocations which were in practice not always easy, given the frequent state of rebellion or of belligerence between themselves of the organizations represented in the parliaments.

From this there emerged in the thirteenth and fourteenth centuries a unique situation, which was in some ways transitional between the political interplay of imperial Italy, which was no longer restrained in any way, and the order of the Angevin kingdom, which, though often disturbed, was still functioning as the normal political framework. In this situation it was possible for the commune of Rome itself, which had appeared in the twelfth century, to conduct over the middle of the thirteenth century its own policy of expansion, through military means as well, in the territory around the city; its leader was the Bolognese Brancaleone degli Andalò, a senator in the regime of the *popolo* which had arisen through conflict with the Roman barons. These latter were as powerful within and outside the city (and in the College of Cardinals) as were the 'magnates' of other Italian cities, and indeed more so. That same commune, a century later, found an even more prestigious spokesman in a cultivated and inspired member of the *popolo*, Cola di Rienzo. Alternately supported and abandoned by his own militia, at one moment he was committed to resolving problems of urban administration and political establishment within the territory, and at the next he boldly faced the boundless problems of Italy and the world. In this situation a restless commune such as Perugia could link itself with the Guelf cities of Tuscany and display its own Guelfism against the Ghibellines of central Italy, supporting in its own particular way the military and political operations of the popes and their legates in order to form its own little empire, until finally in its turn it found its own autonomy directly threatened by the progress of the Papal State and, despairing of other assistance, it turned at last to none other than the Visconti. In the Romagna, a tangled web developed between the *consorterie* rooted to their patrimonies in the contado and the evolving cities, which calls to mind the bold signorial experiments of Ezzelino da Romano and Oberto Pelavicino, but here, thanks to the lesser economic strength of many Romagnol cities compared to those of Lombardy, this tangle was to last for some time. But despite this structure, which was still more diversified, changeable and violent than that of the theoretically imperial part of Italy, cardinal legates, provincial rectors and lesser papal functionaries carried out their duties, and parliaments

---

[144] G. Ermini, *I parlamenti dello stato della chiesa dalle origini al periodi albornoziano* (Bologna, 1930), 'Caratteri della sovranità temporale dei papi nei secoli XIII e XIV', *Zeitschrift der Savigny-Stiftung für Rechtsgeschichte*, 58 (1938), Kan. Abt. pp. 315ff.

met. A condottiere cardinal, Egidio di Albornoz, developed earlier legislation and then promulgated, in 1357, the Egidian Constitutions, which were to remain the foundation of the Papal State up to the Napoleonic period;[145] he acted as if a Papal State did indeed already exist, as if certain, by an act of faith, that in the end the institutional network superimposed on the chaotic political forces would triumph.

In fact it did triumph, although slowly, just as the 'state' structure with a broad territorial base triumphed almost everywhere, creating new problems for the inhabitants' daily lives, for the construction of social hierarchies, for economic activity and the development of culture at all levels. The Angevin kingdom was no longer an exception in the peninsula at the end of the fourteenth century. However much they were still shifting in terms of defining regions, the state structures of imperial Italy were settling down amongst themselves and alongside the area of papal rule. Meanwhile Sicily was about to be subjected to a coherent regime by the kings of Aragon. Sardinia had been the object of initiatives by mercantile and seigneurial Pisan families and had experienced very diffuse forms of local government of the communal type, largely under the growing control in the thirteenth and early fourteenth centuries of rectors and podestà, captains and castellans sent from Pisa. From the first half of the fourteenth century onwards it underwent conquest by the Aragonese, and was being organized through a network of Aragonese functionaries, interwoven with numerous enfeoffments of towns and villages to faithful subjects of the king of Aragon, while surviving urban autonomies became ever more limited; this was in part analogous to experiences characteristic of all the southern part of Italy in the last centuries.[146] Corsica on the contrary remained, with the elimination of the Pisans, in the hands of the commune of Genoa, which gradually tamed the lords of the mountains and supported and controlled the movements of the population against local lords; however, when faced with collusion between the island's

[145] F. Filippini, *Il cardinale Egidio Albornoz* (Bologna, 1933), pp. 141ff; E. Dupré-Theseider, *Roma dal comune di popolo alla signoria pontifica (1252–1377)* (Bologna, 1952); A. Vasina, *I Romagnoli fra autonomie cittadine e accentramento papale nell'età di Dante* (Florence, 1964); Segolini, 'Bartolo di Sassoferrato'; J. Larner, *Signorie di Romagna* (Bologna, 1972).

[146] See A. Boscolo, *Medioevo aragonese* (Padua, 1958), pp. 143ff, and the foreword by the same author to the volume *Il feudalesimo in Sardegna* (Cagliari, 1967). For the period preceding the Aragonese conquest, see F. Artizzu, *Rendite pisane nel giudicato di Cagliari agli inizi del secolo XIV* (Padua 1957 and 1958, extracts from the *Archivio storico sardo*, 25); M. Tangheroni, *Gli Alliata, Una famiglia pisana nel medioevo* (Padua, 1969), pp. 38ff.

nobility and the Aragonese court, it assigned the island in 1378 (following methods also used for some other Genoese colonial dominions in the East) to the initiative and exploitation of a 'maona', an association of capitalists.[147] This is further proof, although with not very happy results in this particular case, of the weight acquired by financial forces in determining or attempting military reconquests and political rearrangements.

It would appear, then, that after more than half a millennium of political dispersion, one region after another saw the formation of a restrictive and unified apparatus, a structure susceptible to endemic crises in its working but intimately rooted in the stable hierarchy of social hegemonies which suffered and sustained it, and that the masses and the aristocracy could express no opinions or wishes other than the official ones. Several signs would lead one to think so: the progressive exaltation of the ruler or of some rigid oligarchy, the interplay of interests, tightly bound to each other but increasingly silent, around the closed spectacle of a small court or around the hidden operations of the bureaucracy, the abundant rhetoric of literary figures and artists in celebration of power, a culture in many aspects concerned with uncontroversial themes. But in this half-millennium too much had taken place outside any model, too much experimentation in every direction, from *villae novae* to banks, from knightly rituals to the most spontaneous and prophetic expressions of religious piety, from the multiplication of 'consuls', *anziani* and 'captains of the *popolo*' to the investment of recent capital in new rural lordships and in ennobling 'fiefs'; it was not possible that the triumph of a 'pacifying' repression could completely wipe out either the memory and the pressures of such contradictory experiments, which had been translated into numerous institutional impulses and cultural developments, or the constant circulation of these experiences across Italy and between Italy and the rest of Europe. Was power elevated into an almost divine halo around the ruler? This was possible only to a limited extent, in comparison with the practices of antiquity, after power, shattered and disintegrated, had for centuries been given and sold in fragments and had been created in new nuclei in imitation of those same fragments or as a new invention by landed lords, merchants and notaries, by armed *consorterie* and by *villani*. The extreme elevation of power was no longer possible, just as it was no longer possible to restore the *villani* to their old servile condition, even though a rich symbolism of power survived at the royal and imperial level throughout all the Latin–Germanic Middle Ages. To estimate correctly the mythology and

[147] See Volpe, *Storia della Corsica*, pp. 20ff.

liturgy of power, one must compare it with that of antiquity and of the East, with the model, far more sumptuous and encumbering, that was offered to the West by the *basileus* of Byzantium. Besides, this mythology refers to the highest forms of rule, precisely those forms which in Italy were most obviously without effective content; the devaluation suffered by the most important official authorities is, in a way, reflected also on the symbols which surrounded them. As a result the symbols used by tyrants turned princes, which were intended to create an unsurmountable distance between themselves and their subjects, were also devalued. There were no longer any unsurmountable distances. The Middle Ages, the period which to many still represents the triumph of fertile and image-laden myths and symbols, had demythologized power.

APPENDIX: THE INSTITUTIONAL SYNTHESIS OF BISHOP AND CITY IN ITALY, AND THE SUCCEEDING COMMUNAL *RES PUBLICA*

With respect to the text printed above, the essay published here represents a further reflection on the transition of the Italian cities from the episcopal regime to communal institutions, a problem which is traditionally central to Italian medieval historical research, as is clear from the historiographical introduction to the present volume. This essay began as a talk given at the Istituto Storico Italo-Germanico in Trento, in the context of a seminar series on the 'Temporal powers of bishops in Italy and in Germany' (13-18 September 1976), whose proceedings have been published. I thank the Istituto for agreeing to its publication.

The theme dealt with here concerns the relations between bishops and communes, not as institutions opposed to each other on the basis of a conceptual distinction between religious authority and political power, but rather insofar as the bishop, who possessed (even if only by virtue of his religious prestige) a responsibility and political role which had a purely secular character, was faced with the emergence of another political organism produced by the city. The interest of this durable traditional theme lies today in the possibility of reviving it in the light of systematic and comparative research into the socio-cultural developments illustrated by the transformations of the political structure of the individual cities. Here we intend to consider only the core of the problem, an interweaving of institutions which is laden with ambiguity. Think of it! A religious authority based on the city and supplied with its own means of spiritual coercion and operation but accustomed, precisely because of its particular effectiveness, to practise a coercion which was also violent in nature (and so in complete contrast with the character of its own coercive force), in order to provide public protection by supporting or replacing the kingdom – this authority is now faced with an organism emerging from urban society and destined in its turn, with its own autonomous capacity for coercion, to work as a *res publica* towards those same ends of complementing and replacing the kingdom. Thus the problem is primarily one of the substitution of the kingdom by the ecclesiastical and civic organisms which coexist in the city.

To tell the truth, the perspective in which these substitutions are usually placed is much less that of a simultaneous presence than that of a chronological succession. There was indeed an effective succession, from the substitutive power exercised by the bishop to that assumed by the commune. But in order to understand the significance of this change it is in fact advisable to pay attention to the aspect of simultaneity, and to stress the length of the transitional phase by seeking its first roots in the structures of urban society. Here we must not anticipate the appearance of the commune by supposing that, in the city dominated or in some way controlled by the bishop, organisms such as the *concio* or the *concilium seniorum* were working in collaboration with each other in the same way as the assemblies and councils recorded for the communal period. There are well-known interpretations which tend in that direction, and which have been pursued to their most extreme consequences in the case of Verona.[1] But the analysis of the sources around Rather of Verona which has been repeatedly put forward by Cavallari, with this aim, cannot easily be accepted. His bravely executed attempt has been useful precisely because it has shown the impossibility of finding strong textual support for this thesis; Cavallari himself has not glossed over the risk of deducing the presence of definite pre-communal organisms from expressions set in very vague contexts in Rather's writings.[2] But the problem is not that of identifying institutionalized

[1] V. Cavallari, *Raterio e Verona* (Verona, 1967), pp. 82ff, 100–1.

[2] *Ibid.*, p. 83. As evidence of the inadequacy of the indications cited in support of this thesis, one should consider that in the *Praeloquia* of Rather the expression *consilium seniorum* appears in a generic context, among the warnings to the *adolescentes*: 'In consilio seniorum cum sederis, manum ori adhibe, intentus ausculta, sedulus disce, ut percipiens senum sententias colligas sollicite quod in maiori serves aetate aliquando' (Migne, *Patrologia Latina* CXXXVI, col. 210). Similarly for the term *concio*, used at the beginning of the *Praeloquia* in a warning to all Christians: 'Vis esse Christianus, bonus

sub-divisions within a pre-communal citizenry, functioning with minimal juridical delimitation and stability, but rather that of understanding the actual collectivity of the city as an autonomous entity in the making, which had already, for some time, been tending as a whole towards its own particular institutional shape.

In fact we have no right, on the basis of our own limited experience, to deny that traditional modes of coexistence were able to realize collective desires outside regulated bodies. One should think of the interplay of initiatives of leading citizens, distributed in groups with a spontaneous economic and social solidarity and in small fluid hierarchies, stratified according to the importance gradually acquired by individuals and by families. In smaller settlements this can be documented. An example is Lazise on Lake Garda, where in 1077 some 'pauperes homines piscatores' ('poor fishermen'; in reality individuals of some local importance, since among them are named an archpriest and a 'nobilis diaconus') took the initiative of seeking from Henry IV at Verona the concession of a generous privilege to 'illis reliquisque hominibus omnibus in ipso loco habitantibus', and the list of the twenty or so 'piscatores' who went to Verona begins with members of a single kin group, presumably more eminent than the others, an 'Ubertus et alius Ubertus et eorum fratres'.[3] Here we can grasp the spontaneous nature of a selection process which allowed the local collectivity to express its wishes through a more restricted group of individuals. For the urban collectivity a similarly selective social mechanism was undoubtedly more difficult, but even so it was still possible, on the basis of the varying importance and general reputation which *milites* and *negotiatores* acquired in the city.

In short, the inhabitants of the urban space already constituted, in the pre-communal period, a body which socially was far from formless even though it was not yet articulated into juridical sub-divisions; it was capable of operating on the level of the great institutions of the kingdom and the episcopate – episodically or intermittently, certainly, but with an element of coherence that tended to take on an institutional character. That was clearly the case from the tenth century onwards; one thinks of the well-known diplomas promulgated by Berengar II and Adalbert in

Christianus de multis Christianis, de populo, de coetu, de concione, de plebe, de circumforaneis, de agrestibus? Esto laborator non solum iustus, sed et assiduus, tuis contentus, nullum fraudans, neminem laedens, neminem vituperans, non aliquem calumnians' (*ibid.*, col. 149).

[3] *MGH, Diplomata regum et imperatorum Germaniae*, vol. 6, p. 375 n. 287, a. 1077. See Tabacco, *I liberi del re*, p. 153.

favour of the Genoese and by Otto III in favour of the Cremonesi.[4] Indeed the events in Cremona, when the urban collectivity had to act without the knowledge of the bishop and saw their own initiative fail through the latter's intervention, lead one to revise the (by now) standard judgement of the role that the episcopal regime historically exercised in orienting the city towards the communal regime. The need for commercial freedoms, already obvious since the Carolingian period when the Cremonesi fitted out their own boats for traffic on the Po,[5] together with the need for free enjoyment of pastures and woodland, drove the citizens, 'omnes cives Cremonenses liberos, divites ac pauperes', to place themselves in a direct relationship with the kingdom: they obtained a privilege from Otto in 996 which conceded, among other things 'quicquid ad rem publicam pertinere noscitur' from the mouth of the Adda to the port of Vulpariolo. This concession of goods and income, since it also virtually legitimated the operation of a port, would (if the privilege had not been revoked in the same year) have steered the urban collectivity towards organizing some control by a nucleus of its own forces, following the example of the ecclesiastical bodies.[6]

In the case of Cremona the episcopal power thus constituted an impediment to the appearance of the autonomous city at the institutional level; this city was clearly ripe for self-government, but was constrained to tolerate the episcopal administration of fiscal duties, and an alliance between kingdom and episcopate. Hence, after the revocation of the Ottonian diploma and the explicit recognition of episcopal rights along the banks of the Po that was imposed on specific groups of leading citizens,[7] there resulted a further, prolonged, *conspiratio* and *coniuratio* of

---

[4] Schiaparelli, *I diplomi di Ugo e di Lotario, di Berengario II e di Adalberto*, pp. 325ff n. 11 (diploma for the Genoese of 18 July 958); *MGH Diplomata regum et imperatorum Germaniae*, vol. 2.2, pp. 606–7, n. 198 (diploma for the Cremonesi of 22 May 996) (see Uhlirz, *Die Regesten des Kaiserreiches unter Otto III*, p. 620, n. 1173, in Böhmer, *Regesta imperii*, vol. 2.3). The discussion of L. von Heinemann, *Zur Entstehung der Stadtverfassung in Italien* (Leipzig, 1896), pp. 15ff, 27ff, 41ff, concerning the *boni homines* of the southern cities, is still of importance.

[5] Manaresi, *I placiti del 'regnum Italiae'*, vol. 1 (Rome, 1955), p. 195 n. 56 a. 851 or 852. See L. Schiaparelli, *I diplomi italiani di Lodovico III e di Rodolfo II* (Rome, 1910), p. 110 n. 5, 27 September 924.

[6] *MGH, Diplomata regum et imperatorum Germaniae*, vol. 2.2, p. 606 n. 198.

[7] *MGH, Diplomata regum et imperatorum Germaniae*, vol. 6, pp. 635–6, n. 222 (3 August 996, imperial revocation) (see Uhlirz, *Die Regesten des Kaiserreiches unter Otto III*, p. 635 n. 1205). Groups of leading citizens recognized the

the *cives*, and an effective rebellion that was drawn out over decades and saw, at the time of Conrad II, the bishop driven out, his fortifications destroyed, the old city ruined and extensive new construction begun.[8] The intensity and duration of the revolutionary movement, associated with such major building activity, presupposes groups endowed with strong capacities for organization. It is worth stressing that both Conrad II and Henry III enjoined the people of Cremona to attend the *placitum* ‹ of the bishop, to guarantee its judicial operation. Conrad II ordered the citizens: 'homicidas et latrones qui infra civitatem sunt, de quibus episcopus legem et iustitiam facere vult, per rectam fidem ante presentiam eius conducatis et eos legaliter iudicare episcopum adiuvetis'.[9] The bishop, in the city, was thus no longer in a position to exercise his *districtus* in the most delicate of public functions, criminal justice. The political and military initiative obviously rested with the *cives*, who detained prisoners[10] and paralysed the temporal jurisdiction of the bishop by not permitting him any 'potestatem extra portam sue domus',[11] and so the need for their active assistance in the functioning of justice was recognized even by the imperial power. In his turn Henry III, addressing the people of the diocese and the city through his chancellor and *nuntius*, enjoined them all to come together at the *placitum* 'comuniter' each time that it was summoned by the bishop, and to submit to his judicial coercion ('per eum, sicut rectum et iustum est, vos constringatis'), giving him unanimous assistance against whomever rejected subordination: 'omnes adiutorium iam dicto episcopo unanimiter prestetis contra eum qui diabolica suasione ad eius placitum venire seu per eum distringere noluerit'.[12] Thus the autonomous action

episcopal rights in placiti of October 998; Manaresi, *I placiti del 'regnum Italiae'*, vol. 2.1 (Rom, 1957), pp. 397ff (n. 243), 400ff (n. 244).

[8] *MGH, Diplomata regum et imperatorum Germaniae* vol. 4, p. 347 n. 251 (diploma of Conrad II, presumably of 1037) (see H. Appelt, *Die Regesten des Kaiserreiches unter Konrad II* (Graz, 1951), p. 128 n. 262 in Böhmer, *Regesta imperii*, vol. 3.1). See the welcome discussion of Dilcher, *Die Entstehung der lombardischen Stadtkommune*, pp. 107–8, on the juridical importance given to the *coniuratio* by its duration.

[9] *MGH, Diplomata regum et imperatorum Germaniae* vol. 4, p. 349 n. 253 (diploma of Conrad II, presumably of 1037) (see H. Appelt, *Die Regesten*, p. 129 n. 264).

[10] 'Osbertum neque illius pares contra voluntatem vestri senioris nullo modo teneatis' (*ibid.*). See *Codex diplomaticus Cremonae*, ed. L. Astegiano, vol. 2 (Turin, 1898), p. 271.

[11] *MGH, Diplomata regum et imperatorum Germaniae*, vol. 4, p. 347, n. 251.

[12] *Ibid.*, vol. 5, pp. 524–5, n. 382.

of the city persisted and was also reflected in the contado, placing the temporal jurisdiction of the bishop in crisis everywhere.

The injunction of the chancellor and *nuntius* of Henry III was in fact addressed to a composite group: 'omnibus militibus, vavassoribus omnique populo in episcopatu cremonensi seu in comitatu habitantibus, nec non civibus tam maioribus quam minoribus'. The way that the *milites* are explicitly placed within the territorial framework of the diocese, although it certainly does not exclude the presence of *milites* among the *cives maiores*,[13] shows that the bishop had his own military apparatus which encompassed the various areas of the episcopal church's temporal presence and which took on a particular form with respect to the urban collectivity; but the parallel which is set out between *milites* and *cives* also show that the centuries-long urban tradition of resistance to episcopal exploitation had by now managed to draw in the military apparatus as well. The latter had the character of a body of vassals, with all the problems of internal discipline which had been characteristic of the *militia* in Italy as a whole for some decades.[14] This had already been apparent at Cremona in 1007 when Henry II, in order to protect the goods of the church from depredations which were most frequent in the periods when the episcopal See was vacant, took under his *mundeburdium* the bishop with his clerics and *famuli*, and decreed as punishment of the transgressor, if he was a 'miles ipsius ecclesie', a fine and the loss of the benefice held 'ex parte ipsius ecclesie', while if the transgressor was 'civis aut suburbanus' he would lose all his property.[15] One may argue from this that, at least during periods of episcopal vacancy, to which Henry II's diploma particularly refers, the goods and income of the church and the individuals belonging to it such as clerics and *famuli* were at the mercy of the initiative of and connivance between *milites* and *cives*, a factor which was favoured by the probable recruitment of the *milites* among the *cives* as well. It is certain that by this or other paths the nucleus of vassals was involved in the actions of the *cives*; as a result Henry III was brought to extend his own injunctions to the *militia* present in the contado and to the population of the contado which was under

[13] See *Codex diplomaticus Cremonae*, vol. 2, p. 254; U. Gualazzini, *Dalle prime affermazioni del 'populus' di Cremona agli Statuti della 'societas populi' del 1229* (Milan, 1937), p. 9 (extract from *Archivio storico lombardo*, 1937).

[14] M. Handloike, *Die lombardischen Städte unter der Herrschaft der Bischöfe und die Entstehung der Communen* (Berlin, 1883), pp. 105ff; H. Keller, 'Die Entstehung der italienischen Stadtkommunen als Problem der Sozialgeschichte', *Frühmittelalterliche Studien*, 10 (1976) pp. 184ff.

[15] *MGH, Diplomata regum et imperatorum Germaniae*, vol. 3, p. 203 n. 172.

its hegemony, and thus he denounced a developing process which was undermining the episcopal lordship and orienting the territory as a whole towards acceptance of the *civitas* as a centre of co-ordination.[16]

In Cremona, then, we can see a competition from the ninth to the eleventh century, between a temporal apparatus of the bishop, administered by the clerics, *famuli* and *ministeriales*[17] and by vassals, and an economically lively urban collectivity, which was controlled by the episcopal apparatus but was capable of resistance and autonomous affirmation around groups of leading citizens, and of open rebellion and military action, and which finally placed in crisis the armed support of the episcopal apparatus, thus taking the first step towards replacing it in the city by the communal organization. But the events of Cremona, which we have chosen as particularly striking evidence for a political–military capacity oriented towards institutional development, whose potential was checked by the ecclesiastical presence, have an outcome during the transition to the communal period which is at first surprising. Indeed it is difficult *not* to be surprised that at the end of the eleventh century, when the political action of the Cremonesi was now freely taking place outside any traditional conflict with the bishopric and in a positively European context, the city in defining its own legal status sought to shelter behind the bishop. One may compare the information given by the chronicles on the alliance between Cremona and other *civitates* of Lombardy, Milan, Lodi and Piacenza against Henry IV in 1093[18] with the act of enfeoffment made by Countess Matilda to the church and city of Cremona in 1098 which concerns the 'insula Fulcherii', the important territory of Crema.[19] The alliance of 1093, where the cities were protagonists in the political development of the Patarine movement, is evidence for the breadth of autonomy they had achieved at the practical level. And yet the act of enfeoffment of the 'insula Fulcherii', five years later, shows that at Cremona the awareness of the city's institutional autonomy is as uncertain as ever. The tone of the document is extremely significant in several respects. The countess invests 'nomine beneficii' three 'homines Cremone' who are acting 'a parte sancte Marie Cremonensis ecclesie seu ad comunum ipsius

[16] I believe that from this perspective one can overcome the doubts raised in Violante, 'Aspetti della politica italiana di Enrico III', *Rivista storica italiana*, 64 (1952), pp. 309ff, over whether the document is genuine.

[17] *MGH, Diplomata regum et imperatorum Germaniae*, vol. 4, p. 347 n. 251.

[18] G. Meyer von Knonau, *Jahrbücher des deutschen Reiches unter Heinrich IV und Heinrich V* (Leipzig, 1903), p. 395 note 6.

[19] *Codex diplomaticus Cremonae*, vol. 1 (Turin, 1895), p. 91 n. 203.

Cremone civitatis'[20] – that is, they represent simultaneously the episcopal church and the interests of the city, which is conceived as holding the common patrimony of the citizens. But who was to render the *servitium* corresponding to the concession of the *beneficium*? The episcopal See was vacant at that point,[21] and the document specifies 'quod capitanei ipsius ecclesie debent servire ad infrascriptam Matildem comitissam, donec episcopus venerit infra ipsum episcopatum scilicet Cremonensis ecclesie', and the bishop, when he arrived, 'cum suis capitaneis seu aliorum ceterorum militum [*sic*] bene serviat'. Thus the *servitium* was to be rendered by the military apparatus of the bishop, even before the bishop arrived. But the document foresees the possibility that the *capitanei* might refuse; in that case, 'si capitanei ipsius civitatis servire noluerint, ceteri homines ipsius civitatis serviant per prenominatum beneficium', and the benefice, as the end of the *dispositio* specifically notes, must be understood as possessed in perpetuity by the episcopal church and the *comunum* of the city.

Here two observations need to be made. The *capitanei* are referred to within a brief space as both *capitanei ecclesie* and *capitanei civitatis*; they provide an organized framework for the *ceteri milites* of the bishop and also appear among the 'ceteri homines ipsius civitatis'. They form the tangible link between the firmly established ecclesiastical institution, seen as a temporal organization, and the institution of the city as an entity endowed with its own will and means of operation, which was still at an early stage of development although it had been incubating for two centuries.[22] One might say that the document proclaims the institutional symbiosis between episcopal church and city, and that the *capitanei*, present in both, express this symbiosis. But, and this is our second observation, the *capitanei* appear as a group which is in its turn operating with its own purpose and thus is capable of paralysing the military apparatus of the bishop, the necessary instrument of his temporal activity, and of simultaneously depriving the city itself of its

[20] On the uncertain significance of the term *comunum* in this document, see O. Banti, '"Civitas" e "comune" nelle fonti italiane dei secoli XI e XII', *Critica storica*, 9 (1972), pp. 9ff of the extract.

[21] Schwartz, *Die Besetzung der Bistümer Reichsitaliens*, p. 114.

[22] G. Dilcher, 'Bischof und Stadtverfassung in Oberitalien', *Zeitschrift der Savigny-Stiftung für Rechtsgeschichte*, 81 (1964), p. 259, states clearly the position of the Lombard bishops, at the end of the eleventh century, faced with cities with increased populations and strength; 'Doch treten sie noch einmal gleichsam als juristischer Schild, vor die Comune, die in diesen Jahren zwar vorhanden, zu einer festen Rechtsinstitution aber immer noch nicht ausgereift ist.'

normal military structures, forcing it to render the *servitium* owing the countess through other elements of the citizenry. The institutional symbiosis was therefore not centred only on the *capitanei*. The latter could defect without that symbiosis being endangered, because the *ceteri homines* of the city then intervened to take the place of the bishop's military apparatus to render a service which, one should note, was in the first place formally owed by the bishop. The urban collectivity seems to act in a subordinate role with respect to the episcopal church; the symbiosis is not between two institutions placed at the same level, but between an institution accepted *ab immemorabili* by the kingdom, and therefore by Countess Matilda, and an entity which was internally divided into groups whose mutual ties were difficult, and which was still struggling to define itself juridically, and therefore relied on the official importance of the bishopric. It relied on it formally to such a point that it proclaimed the will of the church even when the bishop was absent and when his temporal apparatus did not give a guarantee on his behalf. But it is equally clear that in this symbiosis the formal prevalence of the bishop is countered by the prevalence of the will of the city, as a totality of its population, certainly represented by the initiative of the leading citizens but chiefly by those citizens who, unlike the *capitanei*, were not at the same time included in the specific apparatus of the bishop. The true partner in the dialogue with Countess Matilda was Cremona, which, with the consent of the countess, involved the church in the legal agreement and committed its bishop in advance for the moment when he arrived.

So, if even at the opening of the communal period, when the political will of the episcopate showed itself weakened, a restless city such as Cremona still refrained from developing all the institutional potential which was inherent in its urban reality, in order to remain within the framework of ecclesiastical tradition despite the violent conflicts of the past, it then becomes clear in what sense the church, at Cremona and elsewhere, could form an obstacle to the autonomous institutional development of the city. Whether in conflict or in collaboration, the episcopal apparatus had imposed itself on the urban collectivity, through its massive presence in the heart or at the margins of the city and through its strong tie with the kingdom; when faced with the weakness, crisis and dissolution of the public order in the eleventh century, it had assumed the responsibility for civic discipline and the sole representation of the interests of the city without any intermediary. Confronted with the problem of relations between the kingdom, the supreme public jurisdiction and the cities, by now poorly protected by royal representatives, the bishop had offered the easiest solution, rendering other more difficult and uncertain solutions superfluous. The city's first movements towards a true autonomy had been re-absorbed, spontaneously or forcibly, by the episcopal authority, and when, despite everything, these tendencies began to develop further they not uncommonly remained concealed or veiled, as has been seen for Cremona, behind the convenient cloak of the ecclesiastical institution. It is worth noting specifically that they remained hidden in the official documents not because the writers of these documents had an abstract and out-of-date vision of the urban reality, but because this reality was truly expressed in partnership with the episcopal reality. The forms in which the city, the church and the *capitanei* are presented in the Cremonese document of 1098 should not be judged either as the spontaneous and crude product of whomever dictated it, or as the effect of a doctrinaire position. Certainly they can be called, as De Vergottini said in a valuable analysis of similar texts, a *fictio iuris*,[23] but it should be made clear that the legal fiction of such documents was not one that left reality out of consideration, but rather a construction that aimed to interpret with juridical accuracy the real forms of behaviour of the urban collectivity in some of its decisions; these forms did not affect transactions only superficially but set them within a cultural environment, and not infrequently a material environment as well, which was able to remove the risks associated with their provisional character. Examples are furnished by the court cases which took place in the episcopal palace even when the urban collectivity operated in its own name: in a document of 1118 we read how the *populus* of Cremona, in order to enfeoff the castle of Soncino to the *milites* of the same castle, 'elegit in curia eiusdem episcopii septem viros urbis Cremone et precepit eis quatinus investirent, populi vice, eos milites per feudum de curia Soncini', and how subsequently the seven chosen individuals invested the *milites* 'in eadem curia episcopii et in presentia eiusdem populi Cremone'.[24] In the bishop's palace the election of the delegates of the people and the investiture of the *milites* took on a clearer official significance, through being linked with the tradition of the city which had for centuries been under the hegemony of the episcopal church.

The position of the Italian urban commune vis-à-vis the temporal functions of the episcopal church thus, in its first institutional uncertainties, referred back to the traditions of the city, which was never completely identified with the episcopal church no matter what its religious patriotism, but which none the less coexisted with it very

[23] De Vergottini, 'Origine e sviluppo storico della comitatinanza', pp. 386, 390, 393, 401.
[24] *Codex diplomaticus Cremonae*, vol. 1, p. 100 n. 36.

intimately, taking on a privileged relationship with the bishop. The latter had a well-defined legal position, and posssessed diverse means of action directed towards formally established ends, in a relationship with the kingdom which was as strong as it was ambiguous;[25] at the same time he was able, by associating in a more or less authoritarian fashion with the *cives* and making use of his solid institutional position, to take on the further role of representing the urban collectivity within a framework of new ambiguities. The time has now come to evaluate this second role in all its complexity. As the events at Cremona have suggested when considered over their full course, the bishop's role was that of a stimulus which directed the crises of public power into autonomous institutional developments of a more explicitly civic character. But this observation should not allow us to forget that the episcopal government of the city, in the very act by which it resolved through itself the impulses of the *cives* towards autonomy, made itself the instrument of a less adventurous realization of particular tendencies of urban society in the context of the kingdom. The ecclesiastical cloak, in short, operated in two ways: it maintained the citizens within the limits of a local subordination to the old institutional context, but in its relations with those same citizens it brought into being a new political nucleus.

The bishop in the Italian city, when he compensated for the deficiencies of the kingdom, could not present himself purely as an ecclesiastical lord invested with powers of royal origin. Casual but precise evidence for this is found in the oldest official records of his new powers. One may take as an example one of the most significant diplomas conceded to the bishops by Berengar I, which was granted in 904 to the episcopal church of Bergamo, a diploma whose contents are above suspicion since we have the original copy. The recipient was the bishop, but this was because city towers and walls should be rebuilt 'labore et studio prefati episcopi suorumque concivium et ibi confugientium'.[26] *Potestas* and *defensio* over the towers, walls and gates of the city were conferred on the bishop,[27] but the rebuilding had to take place 'ubique predictus episcopus et concives necessarium duxerint'.[28]

[25] G. Tabacco, 'L'ambiguità delle istituzioni nell'Europa costruita dai Franchi', *Rivista storica italiana*, 87 (1975), pp. 405ff, 430ff.
[26] Schiaparelli, *I diplomi di Berengario I*, p. 137 n. 47. See C. G. Mor, 'Topografia giuridica', in *Topografia urbana e vita cittadina nell'alto medioevo in Occidente* (XXI Settimana di studio del Centro italiano di studi sull' alto medioevo, Spoleto, 1974), p. 333; G. Rossetti, 'Formazione e caratteri delle signorie di castello e dei poteri territoriali dei vescovi sulle città nella "Langobardia" del secolo X', *Aevum*, 48 (1974), p. 5 of the extract.
[27] Schiaparelli, *I diplomi di Berengario I*, p. 138.   [28] *Ibid.*, p. 137.

One should note the emphasis with which the bishop is described as a member of the civic collectivity and operating together with his *concives*;[29] he was certainly also operating jointly with the *confugientes*, those who fled to the city for the protection of its walls, but according to a plan which is conceived as specifically that of the bishop and his *concives*. The logic of the concession would suggest, then, that it should be addressed to the collectivity of the citizens, however organized, if it were not that the bishop was present within it as the formal head of an ecclesiastical body which had its religious centre and its capital in the city. Hence a solution was reached which had a deeply ambiguous significance, matching the need to put the royal concession into immediate operation; the head of the civic collectivity is identified with the head of the church, and as a consequence, an institutional vision of the city is renounced in favour of the ecclesiastical institution. This is reflected in the whole formal construction of the diploma, which opens with a prologue drawn from the usual privileges of religious bodies and culminates in the cession to the episcopal church of Bergamo of the public power in the city, 'districta vero ipsius civitatis omnia, quae ad rei publice pertinent potestam, sub eiusdem ecclesiae tuitionis defensione predestinamus permanere, eo videlicet ordine, ut pontifex iam dictae ecclesiae, qui pro tempore ipsi prefueri, supradicta omnia ad ius et dominium ipsius ecclesiae habeat, teneat, possideat, disponat, vindicet atque iudicet'.

This broad formulation, however, deserves careful consideration. It arises from a *contaminatio*. The attribution of public control of the city to the bishop, presented by the redactor of the document as the assignation of the *districta civitatis* to the *tuitio* of the church, is contaminated by the formula ('eo videlicet ordine...') used a few months earlier in the donation of a royal *curtis* to the same episcopal church of Bergamo.[30] The formula, in both diplomas, closes by specifying that the bishop will hold, respectively, the *curtis* and the *districta* 'prout omnes alias res que a pontificibus eiusdem ecclesie priscis temporibus fuerunt possesse ac vindicate', a clause which fits well with the cession of a *curtis* but is somewhat forced in its application to the *districta*. This power is incorporated into the proprietorial sphere of the bishopric to signify the political autonomy of the bishop with respect to the state,[31] responsibility for a public office is contaminated by the idea of dominion and exploitation, and as a result the formulae of immunity

[29] See Dilcher, *Die Entstehung der lombardischen Stadtkommune*, p. 53 and p. 81 (for the precedent of 895).
[30] Schiaparelli, *I diplomi di Berengario I*, p. 127 n. 43.
[31] See Tabacco, 'L'allodialità', pp. 588ff, 602ff.

put the city on a parallel with ecclesiastical land.[32] This was the seigneurial direction in which the transfer of the city to the episcopal power took place. But the overall structure of the diploma, with its orientation towards allodial property, cannot obscure the tension between differing concepts of authority which induced the redactor to stress the idea of *concives*.

The redaction of this diploma, with its internal difficulties in treating the situation systematically, in fact reflects reality, as is suggested by another diploma of Berengar concerning the destruction of buildings situated in the city of Pavia, carried out by the Pavians when a Hungarian attack was imminent. The diploma reads that 'propter munitionem ipsius civitatis a civibus et domus destructe fuerint et murus civitatis edificatus sit'.[33] It is possible that at Pavia too, even though it was the capital of the kingdom, destruction and construction took place under the direction of the bishops,[34] pre-eminent among the *cives* and supplied with the moral authority and apparatus of power necessary to co-ordinate such a complex activity. It remains true that the redactor makes direct reference only to the urban collectivity, which is directly engaged in the building activity; *it* is the protagonist, whatever the body, ecclesiastical or possibly even public, around which it operated.

From what has been said up to now it seems clear that the temporal power of the bishop underwent profound complications wherever it was organically extended over the city in Italy. In the very act of influencing the urban collectivity, the institutional link of the bishop with the *cives* reflected back on to the nature of the episcopal power. This has not always been perceived, not even by historians who recognized the particular conditions in the most active Italian cities. Some clarification is therefore appropriate. Karl Hegel gave due importance to the 'Selbstgefühl' of the hegemonic groups emerging in the cities from the Early Middle Ages onwards.[35] Referring to the example of Strasbourg but attributing to it the value of a paradigm for post-Carolingian Europe, he declared that in the cities in which episcopal lordship was fully realized (and thus in his opinion not in Italy), this lordship gave the

[32] Schiaparelli, *I diplomi di Berengario I*, pp. 138–9: 'et nullus comes seu vicecomes vel publice partis iudex et gastaldio vel alia quaelibet persona infra sepe nominatum urbem sive in monasteriis, xenodochiis vel ecclesiis baptismalibus aut cardinalibus seu oraculis vel cunctis possessionibus, quas sepe dicta ecclesia habere dinoscitur...ad causas iudiciario more audiendas conventum facere vel freda exigere...presumat'.

[33] Schiaparelli, *I diplomi di Berengario I*, p. 263 n. 100 (1 September 915). See Mor, *L'età feudale*, vol. 2, pp. 79, 102, note 58.

[34] Hoff, *Pavia*, pp. 130ff.   [35] Hegel, *Geschichte*, vol. 2, p. 88.

collectivity of the inhabitants a juridical unity not in the sense of liberty, but rather in the sense of unfreedom, that is, in the form of an attenuated manorial law; full civil liberty was guaranteed in Italy by the struggle with the bishops, not by episcopal authority.[36] One should not confuse Hegel's extreme position (which is not a chance formulation, since he restated it in his interpretation of the disputes in Milan in the tenth and eleventh centuries[37]) with the interpretation which we have given of episcopal initiatives in Cremona and Bergamo. The important thing is to recognize the difference between, on the one hand, the obstacles that the episcopacy presented by its very existence to a collectivity potentially organized for self-government, and, on the other hand, a plan (for which there is no documentary proof) to reduce the *cives* to the condition of residents on ecclesiastical lands. But when Hegel considers this plan to have failed, he shows that he has understood, though in a confused way, the differences between the power pursued by the bishop over the citizens and the development of immunities on landed property. We have stressed above, in the case of Bergamo, parallels between the city and the ecclesiastical lands in formulae of immunity, but, at the same time, the insistent references to *concives*. The power of the bishop over the citizens could not change them into a property, except in the sense that that power was attributed to the episcopal church with the same characteristics of inalienability and autonomy which marked out the ecclesiastical patrimony as *res sacra*. In its transfer from the *res publica* to the *res ecclesiae* that power maintained the characteristics of a relationship with men who were fully free, and whose individual freedom of action was not uncommonly guaranteed by the possession of goods in allod, those 'omnes cives...liberi, divites ac pauperes' whom we have met in the case of Cremona.

This argument has recently been expressed by Gerhard Dilcher, when he stresses the juridically public ('öffentlich–rechtlich') character that the power of the bishop took on in its organic extension over the city as a replacement for the kingdom.[38] The language of Dilcher deserves particular emphasis since for some decades there has been widespread embarrassment among German medievalists over using the concept of public authority to indicate the exercise of political force, even at the highest levels, in the central centuries of the Middle Ages; they have preferred the less compromising concept of 'Herrschaft', referring back

[36] *Ibid.*, pp. 85–6.
[37] *Ibid.*, pp. 99–100.
[38] Dilcher, *Die Entstehung der lombardischen Stadtkommune*, p. 54.

to an elementary and Germanic tradition of power.[39] In reality Dilcher too employs the expression 'Stadtherrschaft', but only in order to indicate the seigneurial aspect of the urban power of the bishop, as represented by the royal diplomas which transfer to the episcopal church *dominium* over fiscal property and extend it to the territorial powers of command and jurisdiction.[40] The other aspect of episcopal power in the city is the public one, in the sense indicated above of a function exercised over an organic collectivity of free men.[41]

Indeed Dilcher goes further. He translates his conception of the bishop as civic public authority into that of the bishop as a functionary of the king, and introduces into the complex figure of this functionary and lord a limitation which derives from the rights of the citizens, rights understood as characteristic of a community, a 'Genossenschaft'.[42] Here particularly one may observe the application to the Lombard cities of the model which has been used since the last century to evoke the events of the German world. Dilcher presents as generically and typically medieval that which Gierke, in describing the interplay of relations between 'Herrschaft' and 'Genossenschaft', interpreted as 'Neigung des deutschen Rechtes, die Gegensätze zu verbinden'.[43] But Gierke employed this model at all social levels and for all juridical situations, even to explain the relationships between landed lord and peasant collectivities (including simply collectivities of *conservi*) within the framework of a *curtis*.[44] A model with such a general social character cannot be of much help in understanding the Italian cities – on the contrary it may lead us astray from judging correctly the 'public' character which Dilcher attributed to the urban authority of the bishop; this character was imposed (as one should specify, when faced with Dilcher's claims) not by the formal assumption of the role of king's representative but rather by the behaviour of the citizens, who were equals of the bishop in personal liberty, capable of sharing political responsibility, and barely tolerant of any power which was conceived in terms of exploitation rather than functional to the service of collective interests.

---

[39] See the criticisms of K. Koreschell, *Haus und Herrschaft im frühen deutschen Recht* (Göttingen, 1968), pp. 17ff.

[40] Dilcher, *Die Entstehung der lombardischen Stadtkommune*, p. 66.

[41] *Ibid.*, p. 65: 'Die Einwohner bleiben weiterhim *liberi herimanni, homines liberi, ingenui, homines iuris publici*; der freiheitliche Kern der Stadt bleibt erhalten.'

[42] *Ibid.*, p. 66.

[43] O. von Gierke, *Das deutsche Genossenschaftsrecht*, vol. 1 (reproduced Darmstadt, 1954), p. XIII ex.

[44] Gierke, *Das deutsche Genossenschaft*, vol. 1, pp. 162ff.

This is the new political nucleus, brought into being by the bishop in his bond with the *cives*, in forms which changed the traditional synthesis of the episcopate with its patrimonial power and illustrated a different symbiosis, in which the cultural outlook of the city, as the centre of interests of free men, drove the episcopal church to find spontaneously in its own cultural tradition the idea of a government exercised in the service of free men and in collaboration with them.[45] As for the kingdom, it offered explicit or tacit recognition and its protection to the nuclei of power centred on the churches, whatever character they were assuming, and intervened at long intervals in their operation, whether ecclesiastical or temporal, patrimonial or 'public', in order to maintain the efficacy of the network of its heterogeneous clientèle; it functioned as a territorially supreme power without being concerned as to whether its specifically public function was rigorously coherent.[46] The persistent tie with the kingdom was therefore not sufficient to define the urban power of the bishop in any particular direction. Certainly it was not a juridically feudal relationship,[47] because, as is well known, only after the Concordat of Worms was the temporal power of the church inclined to take on a feudal form, modifying its original allodial nature;[48] but it was even less the relationship of a normal delegation of public functions to an agent of the king, because the bishop formally acted on behalf of his church, in whose dominion – if we interpret literally the diplomas which have come down to us – the public functions had been included as part of its patrimony. The king could certainly control them, but only because he was the guardian of ecclesiastical institutions and of the properties and power belonging to such institutions, and because in theory he could control everything, as supreme guarantor of peace in the

---

45   Tabacco, 'Ordinamento pubblico e sviluppo signorile nei secoli centrali del medioevo', *Bullettino dell'Istituto storico italiano per il medioevo*, 79 (1968), pp. 44–5. The *imitatio comitis*, which I pointed out there as 'obvious in bishops and abbots between the tenth and eleventh centuries', is also present in seigneurial dominations, ecclesiastical and lay, founded on local landed power, but it was most fully developed in the episcopal cities, where it was not seriously influenced by the idea of proprietary power.

46   See H. Krause, 'Königtum und Rechtsordnung in der Zeit der sächsischen und salischen Herrscher', *Zeitschrift der Savigny-Stiftung für Rechtsgeschichte*, 82 (1965), p. 94 ('Das Privileg als Mittel der Regierung').

47   Dilcher, *Die Entstehung der lombardischen Stadtkommune*, p. 65: 'Der Bischof wird nie zum Feudalherrn über die Stadt.'

48   P. Classen, 'Das Wormser Konkordat in der deutschen Verfassungs-geschichte', in *Investiturstreit und Reichsverfassung* (Vorträge und Forschungen XVII, Sigmarigen, 1973), pp. 422ff (see J. Fried, 'Der Regalienbegriff im 11. und 12. Jahrhundert', *Deutsches Archiv*, 29 (1973), pp. 523ff).

kingdom, passing beyond any distinction between ecclesiastical, public or private.[49]

This was still the relationship between the kingdom and the episcopal city when, in the eleventh and twelfth centuries, civic organizations were forming and functioning with increasing stability, according to norms of their own which were separate from the apparatus of the bishop. A particular problem then appeared more clearly, that of the symbiosis between urban institutions which was tolerated, recognized or encouraged by the kingdom, and the language used by the sources suggests, as well as the new difficulties and contradictions, some important tendencies towards unexpected concepts. Perhaps the most significant example is that provided by the Milanese chronicle of Landulf Junior, where the notion of the kingdom as a *res publica* which cannot be confused with ecclesiastical institutions emerges from the background in the context of the movement towards autonomy displayed by the civic organizations.

First we should consider the well-known assembly of 1117, in which the two tribunals described by Landulf Junior express the distinction between the powers exercised by the archbishop's curia and those exercised by the consulate. The *consules urbis*, as they are called in this context, are at the same time described as consuls of the archbishop, in the same context and also in a passage which makes a further reference to the same period: *consules eius, consules sui*.[50] This is surprising in the light of Milan's autonomy of action at the beginning of the twelfth century: so much so that some historians, unwisely disregarding the constant significance of the term *consules* in the chronicles, have tried to interpret the consuls of the archbishop in the generic sense of councillors, distinguishing them from the consuls of the city.[51] In reality, the institutional uncertainty of the Milanese consulate between attribution to the city and attribution to the archbishop finds a counterpart elsewhere: in the documents from Asti, for example, which Gian Giacomo Fissore has recently analysed from the point of view of their diplomatic. In these documents the image of the commune of Asti is still that of an integral part of a whole which culminates in the bishop.[52] This

---

[49] On the double image of kingship from the Carolingian period onwards and on complications of a patrimonial character, which were also influenced by the example of the church, see Tabacco, 'L'ambiguità'.

[50] *Landulphi Iunioris historia Mediolanensis*, c. 44 and 48 (vol. 5.3, pp. 28 and 31).

[51] Barni, 'Milano verso l'egemonia', p. 320.

[52] G. G. Fissore, *Autonomia notarile e organizzazione cancelleresca nel comune di Asti* (Spoleto, 1977).

uncertainty finds another counterpart in what we have observed in the Cremona document of 1098, where the *capitanei ecclesie* are simultaneously described as *capitanei civitatis*. But the need, clear in Landulf Junior and in keeping with his position in the Milanese church,[53] to set the consulate as a magistracy within the episcopal administrative framework of the city, coexists with the different need, present in the same chronicler and in keeping with his legal culture and with the role he exercised as 'epistolarum dictator' for the consuls,[54] to define the public character in the nascent commune, by distinguishing it from the ecclesiastical institution and setting it in relation to the kingdom – that is, in relation to the old *res publica* within whose perspective the new *res publica* sought a more rational position.

Two places in the chronicle are illuminating in this respect when compared with each other. Where he gives an account of the trial by fire of the priest Liprand in 1103 at Milan, Landulf details the acquisition of the necessary firewood as follows: 'Tunc Grosulani (the archbishop) et rei publicae ministri quercina ligna, ad flamam et ad calorem aptissima, triginta solidis denariorum emerunt.'[55] Who are these *ministri* of the archbishop and of the *res publica*? Certainly not agents of Henry IV or Henry V, who were then busy in Germany. They were officials serving the bishopric and the nascent commune, who met a need which was urgently felt by the population, a need to define the much disputed position of Grossolano as archbishop. But in what sense can the local officials be called, in the language of Landulf, *ministri rei publicae*, borrowing the expression from the usage which traditionally referred it to royal officials? Here one may make a valid comparison with another passage, where Landulf promises to given an exact account of events concerning public and religious life: 'Quia sincere adhuc cupio scribere ea que in ecclesia et in regno, per pontifices et abates et sacerdotes et levitas, per consulos et cives, et allios ecclesie et regni ministros, semnata et operata sunt, non tantum ad augmentum sed etiam ad detrimentum religionis et directe consuetudinis.'[56] One can only stress the coherence with which he contrasts first the *ecclesia* and the *regnum*, then the priests and other ecclesiastics on one hand and the consuls with the citizens on

---

[53] For Landulf Junior, 'always alert to any convergence and encounter between the church and the political organism of his Milan', see Zerbi, 'La Chiesa Ambrosiana di fronte alla Chiesa Romana dal 1120 al 1135', *Studi medievali*, ser. III, 4 (1963), pp. 161, 170ff, 177.

[54] *Landulphi Iunioris historia Mediolanensis*, c. 23 (vol. 5.3, p. 15), see p. ix.

[55] *Ibid.*, p. 11. See A. Bosisio, *Origini del comune di Milano* (Messina-Milan, 1933), p. 175 note 49.

[56] *Landulphi Iunioris historia Mediolanensis* c. 35 (vol. 5.3, p. 22).

the other, with the generic dual addition of the remaining ministers of the church and ministers of the kingdom, and the final addition of religion and correct custom, by virtue of the gains and damages which the events caused to one or the other. *Religio* and *consuetudo* are certainly not concepts which are mutually exclusive, but one obviously corresponds to the *ecclesia* and its *ministri*, while the other stretches to include what is entrusted to the consuls and their colleagues. To make this clearer it should be pointed out that in the episode just recalled, of the two tribunals raised before the assembly of 1117 (an episode that Landulf recounts later than the passage we are now examining), the prelates who surround the archbishop are balanced by the consuls, the 'viri legum et morum periti',[57] who are expert in public legislation and in correct custom, just as the *ecclesiarum prelati* are expert in *religio*. The insistent parallel in the passage we are now examining thus unequivocally places the consuls among the *regni ministri* with the significance of *ministri rei publicae*. In making themselves distinct from the ecclesiastical apparatus, the communal magistracies and the *civitas* as a unitary organism (we should not forget that the *cives* are placed together with the consuls in opposition to the clergy and prelates) spontaneously set themselves within the framework of the *regnum*, which is understood in the specific sense of the old *res publica*. Earlier we stressed that it was not a relationship of normal delegation of office from ruler to bishop which preserved an uncorrupted public nature in the Italian cities which were subject to an episcopal regime up to the threshold of the communal period; rather, it was their own social structure, to which ecclesiastical power spontaneously adapted itself. Now we may add that it is possible, on the contrary, that it was the cities, in Italy, which contributed to revive the specifically public notion of the kingdom, which in the tenth and eleventh centuries had become an almost formless hegemonic power and which was much more often the protector of episcopal, canonical and monastic lands than a force committed to guarantee the functioning of a rationally distributed political power.

It is important to be quite clear about this. If the Italian city in the transition to the communal period could offer such a contribution, this occurred because the kingdom, despite its deformations, still took the form in legal culture of a single and true *res publica*. The kingdom existed in the framework of ambiguities already present in the Carolingian period, when its symbiosis with the episcopate took definite shape – a symbiosis destined to be translated later, in the context of seigneurial developments, into a composite pattern of institutions. But within this

[57] *Ibid.*, p. 27.

pattern, faced with patrimonial interpretations of an increasingly dispersed public power, the urban environment was marked out by its own clear territorial features, by an animated and complex population grouping, and by a culture in which, thanks to the intensity of social relations, the 'legum et morum periti' were not marginal. Even when caught up in the framework of ecclesiastical power, this environment could fulfil its own particular role, instigating the clarification of institutions which was already at the heart of the great debate that had then arisen between *regnum* and *sacerdotium*. Indeed we should not forget the years in which Landulf Junior lived, during which the maturation of the commune at the heart of a particular tradition of civic life coincided with the intellectual clarification imposed by the movement for ecclesiastical reform. The most generous of the diplomas conceded by Henry IV to the Italian cities, that promulgated for Pisa in 1081 (it was drawn up outside the royal chancery,[58] and was thus a product of the city itself which was so highly privileged), corresponds to one of the fiercest moments of Henry's struggle against Gregory VII and Countess Matilda. This struggle inspired among others the *Liber ad Gebehardum* of Manegold of Lautenbach, where the foundation of the prince's power is seen as the power of justice, which has been negotiated with the people: 'At vero si quando pactum, quo eligitur, infringit, ad ea disturbanda et confundenda, que corrigere constitutus, eruperit, iuste rationis consideratione populum subiectionis debito absolvit.'[59] In this cultural movement the ecclesiastical claim that the kingdom was restricted to its civic role converged with the agreements negotiated by the king with the more energetic citizen bodies; one thinks of the commitment which

[58] *MGH, Diplomata regum et imperatorum Germaniae*, vol. 6, pp. 442–3, n. 336.
[59] *MGH, Libelli di lite*, vol. 1, pp. 391–2. The well-known passage of Manegold has sometimes been compared too decidedly to modern contractualist doctrines, as is stressed by P. De Leo, 'Ricerche sul "Liber ad Gebehardum" di Manegoldo di Lautenbach', *Rivista di storia e letteratura religiosa*, 10 (1974), p. 115, but the ecclesiological aspect present in thought such as this removes nothing from its civic significance: 'Quid igitur mirum, si haec disciplina sub christiana religione custoditur, dum antiqui Romani, etate videlicet illustrium virorum Collatini et Bruti, Tarquinii regis superbiam non ferentes...ne quisquam imperii diuturnitate insolesceret, annua sibi imperia per binos exinde consules crearent? Aliud est regnare, aliud in regno tyrannidem exercere' (*Libello de lite*, vol. 1, p. 365). The discovery of the centrality that the ecclesiological debate had in the eleventh century tends today to make us less sensitive towards certain real novelties which emerged in that debate and in the thought of Gregory VII himself. See Tabacco, 'Autorità pontificia e impero', in *Le istituzioni ecclesiastiche della 'societas christiana' dei secoli XI–XII: papato, cardinalato ed episcopato, Atti della V Settimana internazionale di studio della Mendola*, (Milan, 1974), pp. 142ff; see pp. 126, 129.

Henry gave not to send to Tuscany a marquis unpopular with the Pisans, the latter being represented by twelve men elected in the civic assembly duly convened 'sonantibus campanis'.[60] It is not surprising, then, that the nascent commune, even in episcopal cities, decided to depict itself as the local version of public activity in a framework that coincided with the kingdom.

The problem was to restructure the Italian kingdom, to recover its specific function through setting up direct ties with the *cives*, to humble those dynasties, such as the Canossa, that were competitors with the kingdom, or to reduce the urban power of the bishops and make it increasingly marginal, as at Milan. But how was a type of co-ordination to be invented in which civic forces could find the kingdom's justice to be the rational framework for their own development? Here the ecclesiastical example, and the monarchical orientation taken on by the reforming papacy, was misleading, as was the legal culture dominated by the texts transmitted from the Roman Empire. The problem showed itself to be too difficult for a peaceful solution, and the whole Staufer period suffered as a result. The city, as it gradually completed its emancipation from the dynastic powers and from the temporal powers of the bishops, thus became increasingly consciously an autonomous *res publica*, even in opposition to the kingdom; it set itself up as a political institution parallel to the territorial principalities, in a perspective which would annihilate royal authority as a functioning power. But we prevent ourselves from understanding this process if we leave out the first communal phase; here the city, when it was taking up the position of a *res publica*,[61] was not yet describing itself as a sort of city state operating within the inert framework of the kingdom, but rather established its own existence as a local aspect, operating through local forces, of a public order which rationally culminated in the kingdom.[62] This kingdom was set up to gaurd the *consuetudines* and *libertates* which

---

[60] *MGH, Diplomata regum et imperatorum Germaniae*, vol. 6, p. 443.

[61] See O. Banti, 'Per la storia della cancelleria del comune di Pisa nei secoli XII e XIII', *Bullettino dell'istituto storico italiano per il medio evo*, 73 (1962), pp. 142–3.

[62] G. Tabacco, 'La costituzione del regno italico al tempo di Federico Barbarossa', in *Popolo e Stato in Italia nell'età di Federico Barbarossa* (XXXIII Congresso storico subalpino, Turin 1970) pp. 106ff, draws attention, as a parallel with Italian usage, to the letter of a cleric of the diocese of Rheims at the beginning of the twelfth century in which the expression 'nostra res publica' is contrasted with the notion of *patria* and the diocese is referred to as part of a greater *res publica*, the kingdom of France (see A. Wilmart, 'Deux lettres concernant Raoul le Vert, l'ami de saint Bruno', *Revue bénédictine*, 51 (1939), p. 273).

distinguished each of the constituent cities and their individual territories, and was conceived as the ecclesiastical order, drawn gradually with growing rigidity into the papal monarchy, became progressively less able to represent civic liberties. The relationships of *comitatinantia*, so shrewdly studied by De Vergottini as an expression of the political supremacy of the urban commune over the old comital territory, underwent a theoretical elaboration which served from the twelfth century onwards as an expedient to justify the territorial conquests of the cities,[63] but which at its origin certainly answered a spontaneous mental attitude of the *cives* who saw the urban space as centre of a circumscription of the kingdom, which was to be reconstituted. The exact territorial limits of the old circumscription were on the whole forgotten, and so very frequently recourse had to be made at the practical level to references to the diocese; 'the bonds of the diocese,' stresses De Vergottini, 'much more than the civil ones, aided the communal city in its territorial expansion'.[64] Yet he himself adds: 'but it is natural that this should be conceived as expansion into the county, because the county represented the civil territorial unit'. Now that was 'natural' only insofar as one admits that the Italian cities at the beginning of the communal period were aware of being civic population centres which were consubstantial with the kingdom, and which were partners with it in the process of differentiation from the ecclesiastical order that was under way. Therefore the episcopal church was indeed utilized, as a firmly recognized institution, in many episodes of the political systemization and territorial expansion of the early commune, but at the same time it was gradually deprived of authority in the exercise of political power and jurisdiction, in favour of citizen bodies which could be conceptually incorporated into the kingdom understood as a pure *res publica*.

In this phase, when it was being progressively forced to the margins of political life in the city, episcopal enjoyment of its remaining incomes and rights of public origin took the opposite path to that which it had followed in the first penetration of ecclesiastical patrimonial power into the urban area. It lost any civic significance, and shrank to an appendage of the administration of economic property, as the port of Vulpariolo had been, for example, for the Cremonese church from the Carolingian period onwards. Certainly this impoverishment did not take place everywhere at the same speed, just as the episcopal hegemony over the cities had been built up with differing rhythms, forms and intensities.

[63] De Vergottini, 'Origine e sviluppo storico della comitatinanza', pp. 415ff, 428ff.
[64] *Ibid.*, pp. 412–13.

We have followed the most typically Italian lines of development, those of the cities which were destined to become protagonists in the arduous metamorphosis of the Italian kingdom (to use the language of Muratori[65]) into a plurality of autonomous political centres tending towards a state structure, protagonists in a revolution of the political order which, leaving aside specific individual histories, involved even the manner of conceiving of power, and represented it according to the needs of a society in development. But it is well known that not all the episcopal cities of Italy had such an intense life.

Volpe, for example, emphasizes the 'delay' at Massa and Volterra in the construction of the episcopal political structure and in its dissolution;[66] at the beginning of the thirteenth century the temporal presence of the episcopate in the city still had a strong political importance. One may add that in such cases the delay, obviously connected with slower urban development, also altered the significance of the episcopal power-structure. The latter did not grow as a juxtaposition of the urban power of the bishop and a rural power of a more purely ecclesiastical and patrimonial orientation, but reached maturity as a political structure which arose solely from this latter, seigneurial, basis; with effort, it acquired a greater civic role as the episcopal landholdings gradually developed their own potential for hegemony over an organized territory with its own coherence, in a fashion similar to that followed by some alpine and transalpine ecclesiastical principalities. The city where the bishop lived, tightly entangled in the power of the church, did not, then, give any appreciable or original support to the bishop's government, nor did it experience the phase where the commune, set in opposition to the prelate, could represent a culture that tended to interpret the city as instrument for restructuring the kingdom within more rationally conceived territorial limits. At the disintegration of ecclesiastical control, however, these cities invariably set themselves to replace the kingdom completely, imitating the greater cities and struggling to compete with them.

The precocious or delayed political decay of the bishopric naturally did not signify the end of the temporal power of the bishops in the city, but the bishop lost his particular institutional character, and was reduced to a tool of the social groups which struggled to conquer, limit, or replace the commune. The traditional convergence from the beginning

[65] See Tabacco, 'Muratori medievista', *Rivista storica italiana*, 85 (1973), pp. 204ff.
[66] Volpe, *Toscana medievale*, pp. 15ff, 59ff, 149ff.

of the Middle Ages between social hegemonies, political ambitions, aɪ
the occupation of episcopal Sees, with the aim of exploiting ecclesiastic
wealth and influence, is indeed obviously different from the organizatic
of public power carried out by the churches, even where they were
partnership with the action of family and social groupings. Even tl
image of the bishop engaged in the urban political struggle deteriorate
from the time of Archbishop Aribert to that of Otto Visconti (if v
limit ourselves to the important example of Milan). Both these prelat
represented the interests of the city intermingled with the interests of ɛ
aristocracy. But Aribert set these interests around the See of S. Ambros
using the episcopal curia to give expression to a civil government whic
was perceived as an energetic extension of the bishop's activity, whi
Archbishop Otto set his political actions within a family structur
which he directed so that it took on an institutional shape of its own ɪ
the government of the city. And it is a fact worthy of greater attentio
that between these two experiments there took place the ecclesiastic;
reform movement and the efforts to elaborate a communal *res publicɛ*
That means that the political strength of the Italian cities, which nevє
ceased to involve the church even after the intellectual and practicɛ
clarification of the difference between the two official organizations c
power, eventually turned the episcopate into a political instrumen
outside any institutional synthesis, in even more burdensome anɪ
obvious ways, despite the advances of the papal monarchy. Indeed thi
instrumentalization was often connected with the growing demands o
the papacy, up to the cynical bargaining of Giovanni Visconti, bishoɪ
and archbishop, with the Avignon court, which, in Novara and Milan
in the final crisis of the Lombard communal order, reached levels o
boldness which can hardly be surpassed.

⋆ The publisher wishes to acknowledge the help of Dr C. J. Wickham of the
University of Birmingham in preparing the typescript for publication.

SELECT BIBLIOGRAPHY

G. L. Barni, 'Milano verso l'egemonia', in *Storia di Milano*, vol. 3 (Milan, 1954).

H. Baron, *The Crisis of the Early Italian Renaissance*, vol. 2 (Princeton, 1955).

M. B. Becker, *Florence in Transition* (Baltimore, 1967–8).

K. J. Beloch, *Bevölkerungsgeschichte Italiens*, vol. 2 (Berlin, 1940).

O. Bertolini, *Roma di fronte a Bisanzio e ai Longobardi*, vol. 9 of *Storia di Roma*, (Bologna, 1941).

E. Besta and G. L. Barni, *Liber consuetudinum Mediolani anni MCCXVI* (Milan, 1949).

G. P. Bognetti, 'Terrore e securezza sotto re nostrani e sotto re stranieri', in *Storia di Milano*, vol. 2 (Milan, 1954).

S. Borsari, 'L'amministrazione del tema di Sicilia', *Rivista storica italiana*, 66 (1954).
    Il monachesimo bizantino nella Sicilia e nell'Italia meridionale prenormanne (Naples, 1963).

A. Bozzola, 'Un capitano di guerra e signore subalpino: Guglielmo VII di Monferrato (1254–1292)', *Miscellanea di storia italiana*, ser. III, 19 (1920).

P. Brancoli Busdraghi, *La formazione storica del feudo lombardo come diritto reale* (Milan, 1965).

G. A. Brucker, *Florentine Politics and Society (1343–78)* (Princeton, 1962).

C. Brühl, *Fodrum, gistum, servitium regis* (Cologne-Graz, 1968).

G. Buzzi, 'Ricerche per la storia di Ravenna e di Roma dall' 850 al 1118', *Archivio della Società romana di storia patria*, 38 (1915).

R. Caggese, *Roberto d'Angiò e i suoi tempi*, vol. I (Florence, 1922).

C. Cahen, *Le Régime féodal de l'Italie normande* (Paris, 1940).

F. Calasso, *La legislazione statutaria dell'Italia meridionale*, vol. I (Bologna, 1929).

P. Cammarosano, 'Il territorio della Berardenga nei secoli XI–XIII', *Studi medievali*, ser. III, 10.2 (1969).

E. Caspar, *Geschichte des Papsttums* (Tübingen, 1930–3).

Der Papsttum unter fränkischer Herrschaft (Darmstadt, 1965).

F. Chalandon, *Histoire de la domination normande en Italie et en Sicile*, vol. 2 (New York, 1960).

A. Chastagnol, *La Préfecture urbaine à Rome sous le Bas-Empitre* (Paris, 1960).

Les Fastes de la préfecture de Rome au Bas-Empire (Paris, 1962).

G. Chittolini, 'La crisi delle libertà comunali e le origini dello stato territoriale', *Rivista storica italiana*, 82 (1970).

F. Cognasso, *Storia di Torino* (Milan, 1959).

E. Conti, *La formazione della struttura agraria moderna nel contado fiorentino* (Rome, 1965–6).

E. Cristiani, *Nobiltà e popolo nel comune di Pisa* (Naples, 1962).

B. Croce, *Storia della storiografia italiana nel secolo decimonono* (Bari, 1930).

R. Davidsohn, *Forschungen zur Geschichte von Florenz* (Berlin, 1896–1908).

Storia di Firenze (Florence, 1956–65).

J. Déer, *Papsttum und Normannen* (Cologne-Vienna, 1972).

Deliberazioni del Maggior Consiglio di Venezia ed. R. Cessi, vol. 1 (Bologna, 1950).

F. De Martino, *Storia della costituzione romana* (Naples, 1960–7).

G. De Vergottino, 'Origine e sviluppo storico della comitatinanza', *Studi senesi*, 43 (1929).

'Problemi di storia della costituzione comunale', *Rivista storica italiana*, 59 (1942).

Arti e popolo nella prima metà del secolo XIII (Milan, 1943).

Il diritto publico italiano nei secoli XII-XV, vol. 2 (Milan, 1959).

C. Diehl, *Etudes sur l'administration byzantine dans l'exarchat de Ravenne (568–751)* (Paris, 1888).

G. Dilcher, *Die Entstehung der lombardischen Stadtkommune* (Aalen, 1967).

G. Duby, *L'economia rurale nell'Europe medievale*, vol. 1, 2nd ed. (Bari, 1970).

E. Dupré-Theseider, 'Vescovi e città nell'Italia precomunale', in *Vescovi e diocesi in Italia nel medioevo, Atti del II Convegno di storia della Chiesa in Italia* (Padua, 1964).

E. Eickhoff, *Seekrieg und Seepolitik zwischen Islam und Abendland* (Berlin, 1966).

W. Ensslin, *Theoderich der Grosse* (Munich, 1947).

'Zur Verwaltung Siziliens vom Ende des weströmischen Reiches bis zum Beginn der Themenverfassung', *Atti dell' VIII Congresso internazionale di studi bizantini*, vol. 1 (Rome, 1953).

F. Ercole, *Dal comune al principato* (Florence, 1929).

V. von Falkenhausen, *Untersuchungen über die byzantinische Herrschaft in Süditalien vom 9. bis ins 11. Jahrhundert* (Wiesbaden, 1967).

G. Fasoli, 'Ricerche sulla legislazione antimagnitizia nei comuni dell'alta e media Italia', *Rivista di storia del diritto italiano*, 12 (1939).

E. Fiumi, 'Fioritura e decadenza dell'economia fiorentina, II: Demografia e movimento urbanistico', *Archivio storico italiano*, 116 (1958).

G. Franceschini, 'La vita sociale e politica nel duecento', in *Storia di Milano*, vol. 4 (Milan, 1954).

J. Gaudemet, *L'Eglise dans l'empire romain* (Paris, 1958).

P. Goubert, *Byzance avant l'Islam*, vol. 2 (Paris, 1965).

R. Grosse, *Römische Militärgeschichte von Gallienus bis zum Beginn der byzantinischen Themenverfassung* (Berlin, 1920).

A. Guillou, 'Grecs d'Italie du Sud et de Sicile au moyen-âge: les moines', *Mélanges d'archéologie et d'histoire*, 75 (1963).

Régionalisme et indépendance dans l'empire byzantin au VIIe siècle. L'example de l'Exarchat et de la Pentapole d'Italie (Rome, 1969).

L. M. Hartmann, *Untersuchungen zur Geschichte der byzantinischen Verwaltung in Italien* (Leipzig, 1889).

Geschichte Italiens im Mittelalter, vol. 1, 2nd ed. (Gotha, 1923), vol. 2 (Leipzig, 1900–3).

A. Haverkamp, *Herrschaftsformen der Frühstaufer in Reichsitalien* (Stuttgart, 1970–1).

E. Hlawitschka, *Franken, Alemannen, Bayern und Burgunder in Oberitalien* (Freiburg im Breisgau, 1960).

H. Kretschmayr, *Geschichte von Venedig* (Aalen, 1964).

Landulphi Iunioris historia Mediolanensis, in Muratori, *Rerum Italicarum Scriptores*, vol. 5.3, new ed. (Bologna, 1934).

Landulphi Senioris historia Mediolanensis, in Muratori, *Rerum Italicarum Scriptores*, vol. 4.2, new ed. (Bologna, 1942).

P. S. Leicht, *Operai, artigiani, agricoltori in Italia dal secolo VI al XVI* (Milan, 1946).

'Il feudo in Italia nell'età carolingia', in *I problemi della civiltà carolingia* (Spoleto, 1954).

G. Luzzatto, *Studi di storia economica veneziana* (Padua, 1954).

C. Manaresi, *Gli atti del comune di Milano fino all'anno MCCXVI* (Milan, 1919).

I placiti del 'regnum Italiae' (Rome, 1955–60).

A. Marongiu, 'Il regime bipartitico nel trattato sui guelfi e i ghibellini', in *Bartolo da Sassoferrato. Studi e documenti per il VI centenario* (Milan, 1962).

G. Martini, *Siena da Montaperti alla caduta dei Nove* (Siena, 1961).

G. Masi, 'La struttura sociale delle fazioni politiche fiorentine ai tempi di Dante', *Giornale dantesco*, 31 (1930).

M. Merores, *Gaeta im frühen Mittelalter* (Gotha, 1911).

'Der Venezianische Adel', *Vierteljahrschrift für Sozial- und Wirtschaftsgeschichte*, 19 (1926).

H. Mitteis, *Lehnrecht und Staatsgewalt* (Weimar, 1958).

G. M. Monti, 'La dottrina anti-imperiale degli Angioini di Napoli', in *Studi di storia e diritto in onore di Arrigo Solmi*, vol. 2 (Milan, 1941).

C. G. Mor, *L'età feudale* (Milan, 1952–3).

'Aspetti della vita costituzionale veneziana fino alla fine del x secolo', in *Le origini di Venezia* (Florence, 1964).

'Dalla caduta dell'impero al comune', in *Verona e il suo territorio*, vol. 2 (Verona, 1964).

G. Morello, 'Dal "custos castri Plocasci" alla consorteria signorile di Piossasco e Scalenghe', *Bollettino storico–bibliografico subalpino*, 71 (1973).

H. Müller, *Topographische und genealogische Untersuchungen zur Geschichte des Herzogtums Spoleto und der Sabina von 800 bis 1100* (Greifswald, 1930).

A. I. Njeussychin, *Die Entstehung der abhañgigen Bauernschaft als Klasse der frühfeudalen Gesellschaft in Westeuropa* (Berlin, 1961).

N. Ottokar, *Il comune di Firenze alla fine del dugento* (Turin, 1962).

U. Pasqui, *Documenti per la storia della città di Arezzo nel medioevo*, vols. 2–3 (Florence, 1916–37), vol. 4 (Arezzo, 1904).

R. Poupardin, *Les Institutions politiques et administratives des principautés lombardes de l'Italie méridionale* (Paris, 1907).

R. Ripanti, 'Dominio fondiario e poteri bannali del capitolo di Casale Monferrato nell'età comunale', *Bollettino storico–bibliografico subalpino*, 68 (1970).

G. Romano, A. Solmi, *Le dominazioni barbariche in Italia (395–880)* (Milan, 1940).

R. Romeo, *Il comune rurale di Origgio nel secolo XIII* (Assisi 1970).

L. Ruggini, *Economia e società nell' 'Italia annonaria'* (Milan, 1961).

L. Salvatorelli, 'La politica interna di Perugia in un poemetto volgare della metà del Trecento', *Bollettino della Deputazione di storia patria per l'Umbria*, 50 (1953).

G. Salvemini, *Magnati e popolani in Firenze dal 1280 al 1295* (Turin, 1960).

L. Schiaparelli, *Codice diplomatico longobardo* (Rome, 1929–33).

L. Schmidt, *Geschichte der deutschen Stämme bis zum Ausgang der Völkerwanderung. Die Ostgermanen* (Munich, 1941).

G. Schwartz, *Die Besetzung der Bistümer Reichsitaliens unter den sächsischen und salischen Kaisern* (Leipzig-Berlin, 1913).

H. Schwarzmaier, *Lucca und das Reich bis zum Ende des 11. Jahrhunderts* (Tübingen, 1972).

E. Sestan, 'La composizione etnica della società in rapporto allo svolgimento della civiltà in Italia nel secolo VII', in *Caratteri del secolo VII in Occidente* (Spoleto, 1958).

A. Simonini, *Autocefalia ed esarcato in Italia* (Ravenna, 1969).

B. Stahl, *Adel und Volk im Florentiner Dugento* (Cologne-Graz, 1965).

E. Stein, *Histoire du Bas-Empire* (Bruges, 1949–59).

K. F. Stroheker, *Der senatorische Adel im spätantiken Gallien* (Tübingen, 1948).

G. Tabacco, *La casa di Francia nell'azione politica di papa Giovanni XXII* (Rome, 1953).

I liberi del re nell'Italia carolingia e postcarolingia (Spoleto, 1966).

'Dai possessori dell'età carolingia agli esercitali dell'età longobarda', *Studi medievali*, ser. III, 10.1 (1969).

'L'allodialità del potere nel medioevo', *Studi medievali*, ser. III, 11.2 (1970).

'L'ambiguità delle istituzioni nell'Europa costruita dai Franchi', *Rivista storica italiana*, 87 (1975).

P. Toubert, *Les Structures du Latium médiéval. Le Latium méridional et la Sabine du IXe siècle à la fin du XIIe siècle*, 2 vols. (Rome, 1973).

P. Torelli, *Un comune cittadino in territorio ad economia agricola* (Mantua, 1930–52).

P. Vaccari, *La territorialità come base dell'ordinamento giuridico del contado nell'Italia medioevale* (Milan, 1963).

G. Villani, *Cronica* (Florence, 1823).

C. Violante, *La società milanese nell'età precomunale*, 2nd ed. (Bari, 1974).

G. Volpe, *Toscana medievale* (Florence, 1964).

Studi sulle istituzioni comunali a Pisa, 2nd ed. (Florence, 1970).

J. Werner, 'Die Langobarden in Pannonien', *Abhandlungen der Bayerischen Akademie der Wissenschaften, Phil.-hist. Klasse 55a* (Munich, 1962).

M. A. Wes, *Das Ende des Kaisertums im Westen des Römischen Reiches* ('s Gravenhage, 1967).

Index

350